AUGMENTED REALITY – SOME EMERGING APPLICATION AREAS

Edited by **Andrew Yeh Ching Nee**

Augmented Reality – Some Emerging Application Areas
Edited by Andrew Yeh Ching Nee

Published by InTech
Janeza Trdine 9, 51000 Rijeka, Croatia

Publishing Process Manager Romana Vukelic

Technical Editor Teodora Smiljanic

Cover Designer InTech Design Team

Additional hard copies can be obtained from orders@intechopen.com

Augmented Reality – Some Emerging Application Areas,
Edited by Andrew Yeh Ching Nee
p. cm.
ISBN 978-953-307-422-1

For EU product safety concerns:
IN TECH d.o.o., Prolaz Marije Krucifikse Kozulić 3, 51000 Rijeka, Croatia,
info@intechopen.com or visit our website at intechopen.com.

Meet the editor

Professor A.Y.C. Nee has been a professor in the Department of Mechanical Engineering since 1989. He received his PhD and Doctor of Engineering from Manchester and UMIST respectively. His research interest is in CAD of tool, die, fixture and process planning, and augmented reality applications in manufacturing. In 1990, he was elected as a fellow of CIRP (International Academy for Production Engineering) and SME (Society of Manufacturing Engineers). Currently, he is the President of CIRP (2011-2012). He serves as chief editor of Springer, World Scientific, and the Scrivener-Wiley book series on manufacturing technologies. He is also the Asian editor of IJAMT and IJMTM and has worked on editorial boards of some 20 international journals. He has published over 450 refereed journal and conference papers and has been an editor and author of 10 books.

Contents

Preface XI

Part 1 Outdoor and Mobile AR Applications 1

Chapter 1 **Mixed Reality on a Virtual Globe 3**
Zhuming Ai and Mark A. Livingston

Chapter 2 **An Augmented Reality (AR) CAD System at Construction Sites 15**
Jesús Gimeno, Pedro Morillo, Sergio Casas and Marcos Fernández

Chapter 3 **The Cloud-Mobile Convergence Paradigm for Augmented Reality 33**
Xun Luo

Chapter 4 **Augmented Reality for Restoration/Reconstruction of Artefacts with Artistic or Historical Value 59**
Giovanni Saggio and Davide Borra

Part 2 AR in Biological, Medical and Human Modeling and Applications 87

Chapter 5 **Augmented Reality Talking Heads as a Support for Speech Perception and Production 89**
Olov Engwall

Chapter 6 **Mobile Mixed Reality System for Architectural and Construction Site Visualization 115**
Charles Woodward and Mika Hakkarainen

Chapter 7 **NeuAR – A Review of the VR/AR Applications in the Neuroscience Domain 131**
Pedro Gamito, Jorge Oliveira, Diogo Morais, Pedro Rosa and Tomaz Saraiva

Chapter 8 **Augmented Reality Assisted Upper Limb Rehabilitation Following Stroke 155**
Kimberlee Jordan and Marcus King

Chapter 9 **Post-Biological Agency in Real-Time Mixed Reality Data Transfer 175**
Julian Stadon

Chapter 10 **Intraoperative Visual Guidance and Control Interface for Augmented Reality Robotic Surgery 191**
Rong Wen, Chee-Kong Chui and Kah-Bin Lim

Part 3 Novel AR Applications in Daily Living and Learning 209

Chapter 11 **Augmented Reality Platform for Collaborative E-Maintenance Systems 211**
Samir Benbelkacem, Nadia Zenati-Henda, Fayçal Zerarga, Abdelkader Bellarbi, Mahmoud Belhocine, Salim Malek and Mohamed Tadjine

Chapter 12 **The Design and Implementation of On-Line Multi-User Augmented Reality Integrated System 227**
Hsiao-shen Wang and Chih-Wei Chiu

Chapter 13 **Physical Variable Analysis Involved in Head-Up Display Systems Applied to Automobiles 243**
J. Alejandro Betancur

Preface

Augmented Reality (AR) technologies and tools have found numerous applications since their appearance two decades ago. At present, applications can be found in the gaming world, the movie industry, advertising, interior design, fashion, education and learning, medical and surgical operations, product design and manufacturing, construction and archeological restoration, and countless other areas. AR is a natural development from virtual reality (VR), which was developed several decades before AR. In terms of application, AR complements VR in many ways. Due to the advantages of a user being able to see both the real and virtual objects simultaneously, AR has the upper hand, though it is not completely free from human factors and other restrictions. AR also doesn't consume as much time and effort in many applications because it's not required to construct the entire virtual scene, which can be tedious and time-consuming.

In this book, several new and emerging application areas of AR are presented. It is divided into three sections. The first section contains applications in outdoor and mobile AR, such as construction, restoration, security, and surveillance. The second section deals with AR in medical, biological, and human bodies. The third and final section contains a number of new and useful applications in daily living and learning.

Section 1 – Outdoor and Mobile AR Applications (Chapters 1-4)

In Chapter 1, Ai and Livingston described a mixed reality (MR) based system for security monitoring, and large area intelligence gathering or global monitoring, where geo-registered information is integrated with live video streams. The authors called this Collaborative AR because the 3D models, aerial photos from Google Earth, and video streams are combined to form one MR environment in real time.

In Chapter 2, Gimeno et al. presented an AR CAD system at construction sites. Mobile computing has been suggested as a feasible platform for the development of AR applications for construction sites. Their system manages three different sources of information: viz., background images, AutoCAD DXF as 2D design plans and as-built images. By merging these data, a new augmented CAD (AR-CAD) data model is defined, allowing building plans to be annotated with real images from the current state of the building work.

In Chapter 3, Luo presented a new computing paradigm called Cloud-Mobile Convergence (CMC) for implementing a mobile AR system. The design principle of CMC is introduced and several sample scenarios were applied to illustrate the paradigm developed. Scalable gesture interaction for large display systems has been demonstrated. The CMC approach has good potential to be used in a wide range of mobile AR systems.

In Chapter 4, Saggio and Borra used AR tools for the realization of virtual reconstruction/restoration of historical structures with artistic or historical values, heritage, cultural artifacts, etc., before starting such a project. The role played by AR is highlighted, among other various techniques and applications, such as auto-stereoscopy, different input devices, human-computer interaction, etc. New methods and materials for future work in reducing time, effort, and cost are also mentioned.

Section 2 – AR in Biological, Medical and Human Modeling and Applications (Chapters 5-10)

In Chapter 5, Engwall constructed a computer-animated face of a speaker, the talking head, to produce the same articulatory movements as the speaker. This development has good potential for supporting speech perception and production. The developed speech perception support is less susceptible to automatic speech recognition errors, and is more efficient in displaying the recognized text strings. The AR talking head display also allows a human or virtual instructor to guide the learner to change the articulation for achieving the correct pronunciation.

In Chapter 6, Woodward and Hakkarainen reported the application of AR in the architecture, engineering, and construction sector using mobile technology. The chapter presents an overall review of their software system, its background, current state, and future plans. The lightweight mobile phone is used to implement the system. Field test results are tested and presented.

In Chapter 7, NeuAR, an AR application in the neurosciences area, was reported by Gamito et al. This chapter first describes the application of virtual reality (VR) in treating mental disorders, such as phobias like acrophobia, agoraphobia, schizophrenia, and rehabilitation of post-traumatic stress disorder, traumatic brain injury, etc. The authors then mentioned that AR presents additional advantages over VR since the patients can see their own hands and arms in AR while in VR, avatars to simulate patients' bodies need to be built, but they are never realistic in most cases.

In Chapter 8, AR-assisted therapy for upper limb rehabilitation is reported by Jordan and King. AR provides a composite view of the real and virtual and hence has significant advantages over VR for neurorehabilitation. Many physical issues giving rise to a stroke-induced impoverished environment can be solved or circumvented using augmented environments. The system they developed has the potential to provide a calibrated range of exercises to suit the physical and cognitive abilities of a patient.

In Chapter 9, Stadon addresses social and cultural impacts of mixed reality systems, using traditional explanation of humans integrating themselves as individuals in a greater social context. The chapter then discusses the "deterritorialisation" of the human body through its dispersion into multiple reality manifestations in relation to mixed reality data transfer, which can be both biological and physical, e.g. bio-imaging, motion tracking, bio-microscopy, etc. The so-called "hypersurfacing" system is discussed, and this could result in a media convergence, creating the collective intelligence which exists in a global society of knowledge transfer.

In Chapter 10, Wen et al. developed an AR interface for robot-assisted surgery. AR technology is used as a therapeutic intervention combining the virtual augmented physical model with locally detected real-time medical information such as geometric variance and respiration rate. The interface is coupled with the augmented physical model, the surgeon's operation, and robotic implementation through vision-based tracking and hand gesture recognition. The interface provides a powerful integrated medical AR platform linking all other medical devices and equipment in the operating theatre.

Section 3 – Novel AR Applications in Daily Living and Learning (Chapters 11-13)

In Chapter 11, an AR platform for collaborative e-maintenance system is described by Benbelkacem et al. Their study comprises of the establishment of a distributed platform for collaboration between technicians and remote experts using AR techniques. A collaboration strategy based on Service Oriented Architecture (SOA) is proposed. Maintenance procedures are transferred from the remote expert to the work site in real time, creating a visual space shared by the technician and the remote expert.

In Chapter 12, Wang and Chiu described the use of AR technology for effective use in education to enhance the students for more productive learning. The Multi-user augmented reality integrated system (OMARIS) was developed to offer instructional material, providing personal AR learning and collaborative AR learning systems to be more flexible with use and reuse of AR materials.

In Chapter 13, Betancur presented a Head-Up Display (HUD) system in projecting the dashboard information onto the windshield of an automobile. This chapter focuses on the approach of the functional design requirements of the HUD in current automobiles. The automobile's display information, such as driving speed, engine rotation speed, music system, etc. can be displayed onto the windshield, thus easing the driver from the need of looking down at the dashboard, while at the same time watching the road condition. This system provides an improved virtual user interface, and could eliminate any potential distraction from the driver.

This book presents a snapshot of some of the useful and emerging applications of AR technologies, while hundreds of other applications have been reported elsewhere.

With the rapid advent of tools and algorithms contributed by thousands of scientists and technologists worldwide, AR is expected to shape the world that we live in, by connecting every person and object in an unprecedented way since the development of IT. We truly look forward to an augmented world, body and life, to come in time.

Special thanks are due to Associate Professor S. K. Ong for making valuable discussions and suggestions during the editing of the book. This is much appreciated by the Editor Professor A. Y. C. Nee.

November, 2011

A.Y.C. Nee
National University of Singapore

Part 1

Outdoor and Mobile AR Applications

1

Mixed Reality on a Virtual Globe

Zhuming Ai and Mark A. Livingston
3D Virtual and Mixed Environments
Information Management and Decision Architectures,
Naval Research Laboratory
Washington
USA

1. Introduction

Augmented reality (AR) and mixed reality (MR) are being used in urban leader tactical response, awareness and visualization applications (Livingston et al., 2006; *Urban Leader Tactical Response, Awareness & Visualization (ULTRA-Vis)*, n.d.). Fixed-position surveillance cameras, mobile cameras, and other image sensors are widely used in security monitoring and command and control for special operations. Video images from video see-through AR display and optical tracking devices may also be fed to command and control centers. The ability to let the command and control center have a view of what is happening on the ground in real time is very important for situation awareness. Decisions need to be made quickly based on a large amount of information from multiple image sensors from different locations and angles. Usually video streams are displayed on separate screens. Each image is a 2D projection of the 3D world from a particular position at a particular angle with a certain field of view. The users must understand the relationship among the images, and recreate a 3D scene in their minds. It is a frustrating process, especially when it is a unfamiliar area, as may be the case for tactical operations.

AR is, in general, a first-person experience. It is the combination of real world and computer-generated data from the user's perspective. For instance, an AR user might wear translucent goggles; through these, he can see the real world as well as computer-generated images projected on top of that world (Azuma, 1997). In some AR applications, such as the battle field situation awareness AR application and other mobile outdoor AR applications (Höllerer et al., 1999; Piekarski & Thomas, 2003), it is useful to let a command and control center monitor the situation from a third-person perspective.

Our objective is to integrate geometric information, georegistered image information, and other georeferenced information into one mixed environment that reveals the geometric relationship among them. The system can be used for security monitoring, or by a command and control center to direct a field operation in an area where multiple operators are engaging in a collaborative mission, such as a SWAT team operation, border patrol, security monitoring, etc. It can also be used for large area intelligence gathering or global monitoring. For outdoor MR applications, geographic information systems (GIS) or virtual globe systems can be used as platforms for such a purpose.

2. Related work

On the reality-virtuality continuum (Milgram et al., 1995), our work is close to augmented virtuality, where the real world images are dynamically integrated into the virtual world in real time (Milgram & Kishino, 1994). This project works together closely with our AR situation awareness application, so it will be referred as a MR based application in this paper.

Although projecting real time images on top of 3D models has been widely practiced (Hagbi et al., 2008), and there are some attempts on augmenting live video streams for remote participation (Wittkämper et al., 2007) and remote videoconferencing (Regenbrecht et al., 2003), no work on integrating georegistered information on a virtual globe for MR applications has been found.

Google Earth has been explored for AR/MR related applications to give "remote viewing" of geo-spatial information (Fröhlich et al., 2006) and urban planning (Phan & Choo, 2010). Keyhole Markup Language (KML) files used in Google Earth have been used for defining the augmented object and its placement (Honkamaa, 2007). Different interaction techniques are designed and evaluated for navigating Google Earth (Dubois et al., 2007).

The benefit of the third-person perspective in AR was discussed in (Salamin et al., 2006). They found that the third-person perspective is usually preferred for displacement actions and interaction with moving objects. It is mainly due to the larger field of view provided by the position of the camera for this perspective. We believe that our AR applications can also benefit from their findings.

There are some studies of AR from the third-person view in gaming. To avoid the use of expensive, delicate head-mounted displays, a dice game in a third-person AR was developed (Colvin et al., 2003). The user-tests found that players have no problem adapting to the third-person screen. The third-person view was also used as an interactive tool in a mobile AR application to allow users to view the contents from points of view that would normally be difficult or impossible to achieve (Bane & Hollerer, 2004).

AR technology has been used together with GIS and virtual globe systems (Hugues et al., 2011). A GIS system has been used to work with AR techniques to visualize landscape (Ghadirian & Bishop, 2008). A handheld AR system has been developed for underground infrastructure visualization (Schall et al., 2009). A mobile phone AR system tried to get content from Google Earth (Henrysson & Andel, 2007).

The novelty of our approach lies in overlaying georegistered information, such as real time images, icons, and 3D models, on top of Google Earth. This not only allows a viewer to view it from the camera's position, but also a third person perspective. When information from multiple sources are integrated, it provides a useful tool for command and control centers.

3. Methods

Our approach is to partially recreate and update the live 3D scene of the area of interest by integrating information with spatial georegistration and time registration from different sources on a virtual globe in real time that can be viewed from any perspective. This information includes video images (fixed or mobile surveillance cameras, traffic control cameras, and other video cameras that are accessible on the network), photos from high altitude sensors (satellite and unmanned aerial vehicle), tracked objects (personal and vehicle agents and tracked targets), and 3D models of the monitored area.

GIS or virtual globe systems are used as platforms for such a purpose. The freely available virtual globe application, Google Earth, is very suitable for such an application, and was used in our preliminary study to demonstrate the concept.

The target application for this study is an AR situation awareness application for military or public security uses such as battlefield situation awareness or security monitoring. An AR application that allows multiple users wearing a backpack-based AR system or viewing a vehicle mounted AR system to perform different tasks collaboratively has been developed(Livingston et al., 2006). Fixed position surveillance cameras are also included in the system. In these collaborative missions each user's client sends his/her own location to other users as well as to the command and control center. In addition to the position of the users, networked cameras on each user's system can stream videos back to the command and control center.

The ability to let the command and control center have a view of what is happening on the ground in real time is very important. This is usually done by overlaying the position markers on a map and displaying videos on separate screens. In this study position markers and videos are integrated in one view. This can be done within the AR application, but freely available virtual globe applications, such as Google Earth, are also very suitable for such a need if live AR information can be overlaid on the globe. It also has the advantage of having satellite or aerial photos available at any time. When the avatars and video images are projected on a virtual globe, it will give command and control operators a detailed view not only of the geometric structure but also the live image of what is happening.

3.1 Georegistration

In order to integrate the video images on the virtual globe, they first need to be georegistered so that they can be projected at the right place. The position, orientation, and field of view of all the image sensors are needed.

For mobile cameras, such as vehicle mounted or head mounted cameras, the position and orientation of the camera are tracked by GPS and inertial devices. For a fixed-position surveillance camera, the position is fixed and can be surveyed with a surveying tool. A calibration process was developed to correct the errors.

The field of view and orientation of the cameras may be determined (up to a scale factor) by a variety of camera calibration methods from the literature (Hartley & Zisserman, 2004). For a pan-tilt-zoom camera, all the needed parameters are determined from the readings of the camera after initial calibration. The calibration of the orientation and the field of view is done manually by overlaying the video image on the aerial photo images on Google Earth.

3.2 Projection

In general there are two kind of georegistered objects that need to be displayed on the virtual globe. One is objects with 3D position information, such as icons representing the position of users or objects. The other is 2D image information.

To overlay iconic georegistered information on Google Earth is relatively simple. The AR system distributes each user's location to all other users. This information is converted from the local coordinate system to the globe longitude, latitude, and elevation. Then an icon can be placed on Google Earth at this location. This icon can be updated at a predefined interval, so that the movement of all the objects can be displayed.

Overlaying the 2D live video images on the virtual globe is complex. The images need to be projected on the ground, as well as on all the other objects, such as buildings. From a strict viewpoint these projections couldn't be performed if not all of the 3D information were known along the projection paths. However, it is accurate enough in practice to just project the images on the ground and the large objects such as buildings. Many studies have been done to create urban models based on image sequences (Beardsley et al., 1996; Jurisch & Mountain, 2008; Tanikawa et al., 2002). It is a non-trivial task to obtain these attributes in the general case of an arbitrary location in the world. Automated systems (Pollefeys, 2005; Teller, 1999) are active research topics, and semi-automated methods have been demonstrated at both large and small scales (Julier et al., 2001; Lee et al., 2002; Piekarski & Thomas, 2003). Since it is difficult to recreate 3D models in real time with few images, the images on known 3D models are projected instead at least in the early stages of the study.

To display the images on Google Earth correctly, the projected texture maps on the ground and the buildings are created. This requires the projected images and location and orientation of the texture maps. An OpenSceneGraph (*OpenSceneGraph*, n.d.) based rendering program is used to create the texture maps in the frame-buffer. This is done by treating the video image as a rectangle with texture. The rectangle's position and orientation are calculated from the camera's position and orientation. When viewing from the camera position and using proper viewing and projection transformations, the needed texture maps can be created by rendering the scene to the frame-buffer.

The projection planes are the ground plane and the building walls. This geometric information comes from a database created for the target zone. Although Google Earth has 3D buildings in many areas, including our target zone, this information is not available for Google Earth users and thus cannot be used for our calculations. Besides, the accuracy of Google Earth 3D buildings various from places to places. Our measurements show that our database is much more accurate in this area.

To create the texture map of the wall, an asymmetric perspective viewing volume is needed. The viewing direction is perpendicular to the wall so when the video image is projected on the wall, the texture map can be created. The viewing volume is a frustum of a pyramid which is formed with the camera position as the apex, and the wall (a rectangle) as the base.

When projecting on the ground, the area of interest is first divided into grids of proper size. When each rectangular region of the grid is used instead of the wall, the same projection method for the wall described above can be used to render the texture map in the frame-buffer.

The position and size of the rectangular region are changing when the camera moves or rotates. the resolution of the texture map is kept roughly the same as the video image regardless of the size of the region, so that the details of the video image can be maintained while the memory requirement is kept at a minimum. To calculate the region of the projection on the ground, a transformation matrix is needed to project the corners of the video image to the ground:

$$M = P \times T \times R$$

where R and T are the rotation and translation matrices that transform the camera to the right position and orientation, and P is the projection matrix, which is

$$P = \begin{bmatrix} d & 0 & 0 & 0 \\ 0 & d & 0 & 0 \\ 0 & 0 & -d & 0 \\ 0 & 0 & 1 & 0 \end{bmatrix}$$

where d is the distance between the camera and the projection plane (the ground).

While the camera is moving, it is possible to keep the previous textures and only update the parts where new images are available. In this way, a large region will be eventually updated when the camera pans over the area.

The zooming factor of the video camera can be converted to the field of view. Together with the position and orientation of the camera that are tracked by GPS, inertial devices, and pan-tilt readings from the camera, we can calculate where to put the video images. The position and size of the image can be arbitrary as long as it is along the camera viewing direction, with the right orientation and a proportional size.

3.3 Rendering

The rendering of the texture is done with our AR/MR rendering engine which is based on OpenSceneGraph. A two-pass rendering process is performed to remove part of the views blocked by the buildings.

In the first pass, all of the 3D objects in our database are disabled and only the camera image rectangle is in the scene. The rendered image is grabbed from the frame-buffer. Thus a projected image of the video is obtained. In the second pass the camera image rectangle is removed from the scene. The grabbed image in the first pass is used as a texture map and applied on the projection plane (the ground or the walls). All the 3D objects in the database (mainly buildings) are rendered as solid surfaces with a predefined color so that the part on the projection plane that is blocked is covered. The resulting image is read from the frame-buffer and used as texture map in Google Earth. A post-processing stage changes the blocked area to transparent so that the satellite/aerial photos on Google Earth are still visible.

3.4 Google Earth interface

Google Earth uses KML to overlay placemarks, images, etc. on the virtual globe. 3D models can be built in Collada format and displayed on Google Earth. A Google Earth interface module for our MR system has been developed. This module is an hyper-text transfer protocol (HTTP) server that sends icons and image data to Google Earth. A small KML file is loaded into Google Earth that sends update requests to the server at a certain interval, and updates the received icons and images on Google Earth.

4. Results

An information integration prototype module with the Battlefield Augmented Reality System (BARS) (Livingston et al., 2004) has been implemented. This module is an HTTP server implemented in C++ that sends icons and image data to Google Earth. The methods are tested in a typical urban environment. One user roams the area while another object is a fixed pan-tilt-zoom network surveillance camera (AXIS 213 PTZ Network Camera) mounted on top of the roof on a building by a parking lot. This simulates a forward observation post in military applications or surveillance camera in security applications. The command and control center is located at a remote location running the MR application and Google Earth. Both the server module and Google Earth are running on a Windows XP machine with dual 3.06 GHz Intel Xeon CPU, 2 GB RAM, and a NVIDIA Quadro4 900XGL graphics card.

Fig. 1. Video image of the parking lot and part of a building from a surveillance video camera on the roof top.

The testing area is a parking lot and some buildings nearby. Figure 1 is the video image from the roof top pan-tilt-zoom camera when it is pointing to the parking lot. One of the parking lot corners with a building is in the camera view. Another AR user is on the ground of the parking lot, the image captured by this user in shown in Figure 2 which shows part of the building.

Google Earth can display 3D buildings in this area. When the 3D building feature in Google Earth is enabled, the final result is shown in Figure 4. The images are projected on the buildings as well as on the ground and overlaid on Google Earth, together with the icon of an AR user (right in the image) and the icon representing the camera on the roof of the building (far left in the image). The parking lot part is projected on the ground and the building part

Fig. 2. Image from a AR user on the ground.

Fig. 3. Image of the target zone on Google Earth.

Fig. 4. Recreated 3D scene viewed with 3D buildings on Google Earth. The two field operator's icons and the video image are overlaid on Google Earth.

(the windows, the door, and part of the walls) is projected on vertical polygons representing the walls of the building. The model of the building is from the database used in our AR/MR system. When the texture was created, the part that is not covered by the video image is transparent so it blended into the aerial image well. The part of the view blocked by the building is removed from the projected image on the ground.

Google Earth supports 3D interaction; the user can navigate in 3D. This gives the user the ability to move the viewpoint to any position. Figure 4 is from Google Earth viewed from an angle instead of looking straight down. This third-person view is very suitable in command and control applications. The projected images are updated at a 0.5 second interval, so viewers can see what is happening live on the ground. It needs to point out that the 3D building information in Google Earth is not very accurate in this area (especially the height of the buildings), but is a good reference for our study.

The result shows the value of this study which integrates information from multiple sources into one mixed environment. From the source images (Figure 1 and Figure 2), it is difficult to see how they are related. By integrating images, icons, and 3D model as shown in Figure 4, it is very easy for the command and control center to monitor what is happening live on the ground. In this particular position, the AR user on the ground and the simulated forward observation post on the roof top can not see each other. The method can be integrated into our existing AR applications so that each on-site user will be able to see live images from other users' video cameras or fixed surveillance cameras. This will extend the X-ray viewing feature of AR systems by adding information not only from computer generated graphics but also live images from other users in the field.

5. Discussion

The projection errors on the building in Figure 4 are pretty obvious. There are several sources of errors involved. One is the accuracy of the models of the buildings. More serious problems come from camera tracking, calibration, and lens distortion. The lens distortion are not calibrated in this study due to limited time, which is probably one of the major causes of error. This will be done in the near future.

Camera position, orientation, and field of view calibration is another issue. In our study, the roof top camera position is fixed and surveyed with a surveying tool, it is assumed that it is accurate enough and is not considered in the calibration. The orientation and field of view were calibrated by overlaying the video image on the aerial photo images on Google Earth. The moving AR user on the ground is tracked by GPS and inertial devices which can be inaccurate. However in a feature-based tracking system such as simultaneous localization and mapping (SLAM) (Durrant-Whyte & Bailey, 2006), the video sensors can be used to feed Google Earth and accuracy should be pretty good as long as the tracking feature is working.

The prerequisite of projecting the images on the wall or other 3D objects is that a database of the models of all the objects is created so that the projection planes can be determined. The availability of the models of such big fixed objects like buildings are in general not a problem. However there is no single method exist that can reliably and accurately create all the models. Moving objects such as cars or persons will cause blocked parts that can not be removed using the methods that are used in this study. Research has been done to detect moving objects based on video images (Carmona et al., 2008). While in theory it is possible to project the video image on these moving objects, it is not really necessary in our applications.

Google Earth has 3D buildings in many areas; this information may be available for Google Earth users and thus could be used for the calculations. The accuracy of Google Earth 3D buildings varies from place to place; a more accurate model may be needed to get desired results. Techniques as simple as manual surveying or as complex as reconstruction from Light Detection and Ranging (LIDAR) sensing may be used to generate such a model. Many studies have been done to create urban models based on image sequences (Beardsley et al., 1996; Jurisch & Mountain, 2008; Tanikawa et al., 2002). It is a non-trivial task to obtain these attributes in the general case of an arbitrary location in the world. Automated systems are an active research topic (Pollefeys, 2005; Teller, 1999), and semi-automated methods have been demonstrated at both large and small scales (Julier et al., 2001).

6. Future work

This is a preliminary implementation of the concept. Continuing this on-going effort, the method will be improved in a few aspects. This includes registration improvement between our exiting models and the Google Earth images as well as the calibration issues noted above. The zooming feature of the camera has not been used yet, which will require establishing a relation between the zooming factor and the field of view, another aspect of camera calibration. Other future work includes user studies related to effectiveness and efficiency of the system in terms of collaboration.

Currently when the texture map is updated, the old texture is discarded, it is possible to keep the previous textures and only update the parts where new images are available. In this way, a large region will be eventually updated when the camera pans over a larger area.

There are a few aspects contributing to the error of the system that should be addressed in the future. This will be done in the near future.

7. Conclusion

In this preliminary study, the methods of integrating georegistered information on a virtual globe is investigated. The application can be used for a command and control center to monitor the field operation where multiple AR users are engaging in a collaborative mission. Google Earth is used to demonstrate the methods. The system integrates georegistered icons, live video streams from field operators or surveillance cameras, 3D models, and satellite or aerial photos into one MR environment. The study shows how the projection of images is calibrated and properly projected onto an approximate world model in real time.

8. References

Azuma, R. T. (1997). A Survey of Augmented Reality, *Presence* 6: 355–385.
URL: *http://citeseerx.ist.psu.edu/viewdoc/summary?doi=10.1.1.30.4999*

Bane, R. & Hollerer, T. (2004). Interactive Tools for Virtual X-Ray Vision in Mobile Augmented Reality, *ismar* 00: 231–239.
URL: *http://dx.doi.org/10.1109/ISMAR.2004.36*

Beardsley, P. A., Torr, P. H. S. & Zisserman, A. (1996). 3D Model Acquisition from Extended Image Sequences, *ECCV (2)*, pp. 683–695.
URL: *http://citeseerx.ist.psu.edu/viewdoc/summary?doi=10.1.1.29.4494*

Carmona, E. J., Cantos, J. M. & Mira, J. (2008). A new video segmentation method of moving objects based on blob-level knowledge, *Pattern Recogn. Lett.* 29(3): 272–285.
URL: *http://dx.doi.org/10.1016/j.patrec.2007.10.007*

Colvin, R., Hung, T., Jimison, D., Johnson, B., Myers, E. & Blaine, T. (2003). A dice game in third person augmented reality, *Augmented Reality Toolkit Workshop, 2003. IEEE International*, pp. 3–4.
URL: *http://dx.doi.org/10.1109/ART.2003.1320416*

Dubois, E., Truillet, P. & Bach, C. (2007). Evaluating Advanced Interaction Techniques for Navigating Google Earth, *Proceedings of the 21st BCS HCI Group Conference*, Vol. 2.

Durrant-Whyte, H. & Bailey, T. (2006). Simultaneous localization and mapping: part I, *IEEE Robotics & Automation Magazine* 13(2): 99–110.
URL: *http://dx.doi.org/10.1109/MRA.2006.1638022*

Fröhlich, P., Simon, R., Baillie, L. & Anegg, H. (2006). Comparing conceptual designs for mobile access to geo-spatial information, *MobileHCI '06: Proceedings of the 8th conference on Human-computer interaction with mobile devices and services*, ACM, New York, NY, USA, pp. 109–112.
URL: *http://dx.doi.org/10.1145/1152215.1152238*

Ghadirian, P. & Bishop, I. D. (2008). Integration of augmented reality and GIS: A new approach to realistic landscape visualisation, *Landscape and Urban Planning* 86(3-4): 226–232.
URL: *http://dx.doi.org/10.1016/j.landurbplan.2008.03.004*

Hagbi, N., Bergig, O., El-Sana, J., Kedem, K. & Billinghurst, M. (2008). In-place Augmented Reality, *Mixed and Augmented Reality, 2008. ISMAR 2008. 7th IEEE/ACM International Symposium on*, pp. 135–138.
URL: *http://dx.doi.org/10.1109/ISMAR.2008.4637339*

Hartley, R. & Zisserman, A. (2004). *Multiple View Geometry in Computer Vision*, 2 edn, Cambridge University Press.
URL: *http://www.amazon.com/exec/obidos/redirect?tag=citeulike07-20&path=ASIN/0521540518*

Henrysson, A. & Andel, M. (2007). Augmented Earth: Towards Ubiquitous AR Messaging, *Artificial Reality and Telexistence, 17th International Conference on*, pp. 197–204.
URL: *http://dx.doi.org/10.1109/ICAT.2007.48*

Höllerer, T., Feiner, S., Terauchi, T., Rashid, G. & Hallaway, D. (1999). Exploring MARS: Developing Indoor and Outdoor User Interfaces to a Mobile Augmented Reality System, *Computers and Graphics* 23(6): 779–785.

Honkamaa (2007). Interactive outdoor mobile augmentation using markerless tracking and GPS, *In Proc. Virtual Reality International Conference (VRIC)* .
URL: *http://virtual.vtt.fi/multimedia/publications/aronsite-vric2007.pdf*

Hugues, O., Cieutat, J.-M. & Guitton, P. (2011). GIS and Augmented Reality : State ofthe Art and Issues, *in* B. Furht (ed.), *Handbook of Augmented Reality*, chapter 1, pp. 1–23.
URL: *http://hal.archives-ouvertes.fr/hal-00595205/*

Julier, S., Baillot, Y., Lanzagorta, M., Rosenblum, L. & Brown, D. (2001). Urban Terrain Modeling for Augmented Reality Applications, *in* M. Abdelguerfi (ed.), *3D Synthetic Environments Reconstruction*, Kluwer Academic Publishers, Dordrecht, pp. 119–136.

Jurisch, A. & Mountain, D. (2008). Evaluating the Viability of Pictometry Imagery for Creating Models of the Built Environment., *in* O. Gervasi, B. Murgante, A. Laganà, D. Taniar, Y. Mun & M. L. Gavrilova (eds), *Lecture Notes in Computer Science*, Vol. 5072, Springer, pp. 663–677.
URL: *http://dblp.uni-trier.de/db/conf/iccsa/iccsa2008-1.html#JurischM08*

Lee, J., Hirota, G. & State, A. (2002). Modeling Real Objects Using Video See-Through Augmented Reality, *Presence: Teleoperators & Virtual Environments* 11(2): 144–157.

Livingston, M. A., Edward, Julier, S. J., Baillot, Y., Brown, D. G., Rosenblum, L. J., Gabbard, J. L., Höllerer, T. H. & Hix, D. (2004). Evaluating System Capabilities and User Performance in the Battlefield Augmented Reality System, *Performance Metrics for Intelligent Systems Workshop*, Gaithersburg, MD.

Livingston, M. A., Julier, S. J. & Brown, D. (2006). Situation Awareness for Teams of Dismounted Warfighters and Unmanned Vehicles, *Enhanced and Synthetic Vision Conference, SPIE Defense and Security Symposium*.

Milgram, P. & Kishino, F. (1994). A Taxonomy of Mixed Reality Visual Displays, *IEICE Transactions on Information Systems* E77-D(12).
URL: *http://vered.rose.utoronto.ca/people/paul_dir/IEICE94/ieice.html*

Milgram, P., Takemura, H., Utsumi, A. & Kishino, F. (1995). Augmented Reality: A Class of Displays on the Reality-Virtuality Continuum, *Proceedings of the SPIE Conference on Telemanipulator and Telepresence Technologies*, Vol. 2351 of *Proceedings of SPIE*, Boston, Massachusetts, USA, pp. 282–292.

OpenSceneGraph (n.d.). `http://www.openscenegraph.org/projects/osg`.

Phan, V. T. & Choo, S. Y. (2010). A Combination of Augmented Reality and Google Earth's facilities for urban planning in idea stage, *International Journal of Computer Applications* 4(3): 26–34.

Piekarski, W. & Thomas, B. H. (2003). Interactive Augmented Reality Techniques for Construction at a Distance of 3D Geometry, *7th Int'l Workshop on Immersive Projection Technology / 9th Eurographics Workshop on Virtual Environments*, Zurich, Switzerland.

Pollefeys, M. (2005). *3-D Modeling from Images*, Springer-Verlag New York, Inc., Secaucus, NJ, USA.

Regenbrecht, H., Ott, C., Wagner, M., Lum, T., Kohler, P., Wilke, W. & Mueller, E. (2003). An augmented virtuality approach to 3D videoconferencing, *Mixed and Augmented Reality, 2003. Proceedings. The Second IEEE and ACM International Symposium on*, pp. 290–291.
URL: *http://dx.doi.org/10.1109/ISMAR.2003.1240725*

Salamin, P., Thalmann, D. & Vexo, F. (2006). The benefits of third-person perspective in virtual and augmented reality?, *VRST '06: Proceedings of the ACM symposium on Virtual reality software and technology*, ACM, New York, NY, USA, pp. 27–30.
URL: *http://dx.doi.org/10.1145/1180495.1180502*

Schall, G., Mendez, E., Kruijff, E., Veas, E., Junghanns, S., Reitinger, B. & Schmalstieg, D. (2009). Handheld Augmented Reality for underground infrastructure visualization, *Personal Ubiquitous Comput.* 13(4): 281–291.
URL: *http://dx.doi.org/10.1007/s00779-008-0204-5*

Tanikawa, T., Hirota, K. & Hirose, M. (2002). A Study for Image-Based Integrated Virtual Environment, *ISMAR '02: Proceedings of the 1st International Symposium on Mixed and Augmented Reality*, IEEE Computer Society, Washington, DC, USA, p. 225.

Teller, S. (1999). Automated Urban Model Acquisition: Project Rationale and Status, *Bulletin de la SFPT* (153): 56–63.
URL: *http://citeseer.ist.psu.edu/111110.html*

Urban Leader Tactical Response, Awareness & Visualization (ULTRA-Vis) (n.d.). http://www.darpa.mil/ipto/Programs/uvis/uvis.asp.

Wittkämper, M., Lindt, I., Broll, W., Ohlenburg, J., Herling, J. & Ghellal, S. (2007). Exploring augmented live video streams for remote participation, *CHI '07 extended abstracts on Human factors in computing systems*, ACM, New York, NY, USA, pp. 1881–1886.
URL: *http://dx.doi.org/10.1145/1240866.1240915*

2

An Augmented Reality (AR) CAD System at Construction Sites

Jesús Gimeno, Pedro Morillo, Sergio Casas and Marcos Fernández
Universidad de Valencia
Spain

1. Introduction

Augmented Reality (AR) technologies allow computer-generated content to be superimposed over a live camera view of the real world. Although AR is still a very promising technology, currently only a few commercial applications for industrial purposes exploit the potential of adding contextual content to real scenarios. Most of AR applications are oriented to fields such as education or entertainment, where the requirements in terms of repeatability, fault tolerance, reliability and safety are low. Different visualization devices, tracking methods and interaction techniques are described in the literature, establishing a classification between Indoor and Outdoor AR systems. On the one hand, the most common AR developments correspond to Indoor AR systems where environment conditions can be easily controlled. In these systems, AR applications have been oriented traditionally to the visualization of 3D models using markers. On the other hand, outdoor AR developments must face additional difficulties such as the variation on lighting conditions, moving or new objects within the scene, large scale tracking, etc… which hinder the development of new systems in real scenarios.

Although AR technologies could be used as a visual aid to guide current processes in building construction as well as inspection tasks in the execution of construction projects, the special features involving construction site environments must be taken into account. Construction environments can be considered as specially difficult outdoor AR scenarios for several reasons: structures change frequently, additional structures (scaffolding or cranes) cover several visual elements during the simulation, every technological part (sensors, wearable computers, hand held devices) can be easily broken, etc. For this reason, although the capability of AR technologies in construction site environments is a hot-topic research, very few developments have been presented in this area beyond of laboratory studies or ad-hoc prototypes.

In this work, key aspects of AR in construction sites are faced and a construction AR aided inspecting system is proposed and tested. Real world would appear in the background with the construction plans superimposed, allowing users not only to inspect all the visible elements of a given building, but also to guarantee that these elements are built in the correct place and orientation. Besides merging computer-generated information from CAD (Computer Aided Design) plans and real images of the building process, the proposed system allows users to add annotation, comment or errors as the building process is completed. Since this information is saved in DXF (Drawing Exchange Format) format, a new layer can be added to the original CAD plans including the accomplished modifications. Therefore, users can import original CAD plans to be visualized on real environments, to perform the required modifications using actual image from the current states of the construction site and, finally, to save the final results in the original CAD file. The aim of this new way of working is not to replace the usual CAD applications, but to add a new, more intuitive, faster and reliable stage, in the testing, assessment and modification of plans for construction and reconstruction projects.

2. Background

The term Augmented Reality (AR) is often used to define computer graphic procedures where the real-world view is superimposed by computer-generated objects in real-time (Azuma, 1997). Unlike Virtual Reality, where the user is provided with a completely natural experience in a realistic simulated world, the goal of Augmented Reality is to realistically enhance the user's view of the real-world with visual information provided by virtual objects. AR systems are currently used in numerous applications such as medical, maintenance, scientific visualization, maintenance, cultural heritage and military applications (Cawood & Fiala, 2008).

Besides these contexts, outdoor construction is considered as a suitable application area for AR developments (Thomas et al., 2000), (Klinker et al., 2001; Piekarski & Thomas, 2003; Honkamaa et al., 2007; Izkara et al., 2007; Hunter, 2009; Dunston & Shin, 2009; Hakkarainen et al., 2009). In fact, the development of a construction project includes an important number of three-dimensional activities. Professional traits and work behaviours are all oriented towards the design, understanding, visualization and development of 3D procedures. Workers are used to graphical descriptions such as 2D/3D maps or designs. Moreover, most of this information is already represented and communicated in a graphical form. Therefore, new graphical user interfaces like Augmented Reality could be introduced very naturally into current work practices.

Most of AR applications specifically developed for the construction industry are oriented to outdoor construction processes (Thomas et al., 2000; Klinker et al., 2001; Honkamaa et al., 2007). Initially, the aim of these AR systems was to provide the users with a sense of space and realism about the size and dimensions of the construction tasks developed in outdoor environments (Thomas et al., 2000). Moreover, new approaches based on augmented video sequences, and live video streams of large outdoor scenarios with detailed models of prestigious new architectures (such as TV towers and bridges) were presented (Klinker et al., 2001). Currently, the last developments of AR applications oriented to construction processes not only avoid the use of external markers within the real scene, but also integrate sensors such as GPS devices, rate gyroscopes, digital compasses and tilt orientation elements of the viewer's location (Honkamaa et al., 2007).

Although the marketplace offers several toolkits for the development of AR applications, some of them have been specially oriented towards the necessities of applications in the construction sector (Thomas et al., 2000; Piekarski & Thomas, 2003). In much the same way, the design of TINMITH2 (Piekarski & Thomas, 2003) is based on a highly modular architecture where the software system is split into various modules that communicate with each other using the connection oriented TCP/IP protocol. Otherwise, the architecture proposed in a similar approach (Piekarski & Thomas, 2003) is optimised to develop mobile AR and other interactive 3D applications on portable platforms with limited resources. This architecture is implemented in C++ with an object-oriented data flow design and manages an object store based on the Unix file system model.

Mobile computing could offer a suitable hardware platform for the development of AR applications to be executed in construction sites (Piekarski & Thomas, 2003; Honkamaa et al., 2007; Izkara et al., 2007; Hakkarainen et al., 2009). These contributions address a number of problems affecting mobile AR and similar environments related to performance and portability constraints of the equipments (Piekarski & Thomas, 2003). In much the same way, an AR mobile application developed for architectural purposes (Honkamaa et al., 2007) includes a feature tracking for estimating camera motion as the user turns the mobile device and examines the augmented scene. Another approach integrates an RFID reader, a headset and a wristband to be used by workers in order to improve their safety at work place in construction sites (Izkara et al., 2007). A recent work presents an AR system which places the models in geographical coordinates, as well as managing data intensive building information models (BIM) on thin mobile clients (Hakkarainen et al., 2009).

Along with the developments of mobile computing, the technologies based on Augmented Reality exploit a promising field for wearable computers oriented to construction sector (Piekarski & Thomas, 2003; Hunter, 2009). Since the main idea behind wearable computing is the augmentation of human capabilities by wearing devices, these technologies allow construction workers to facilitate critical tasks such as determining the proper excavation for buildings (Dunston & Shin, 2009), visualising conceptual designs in-situ (Piekarski & Thomas, 2003), making modifications on site, and representing construction and engineering data on real-time (Hunter, 2009). In addition to these purposes oriented to the construction sector, the setting out process has been denoted as a challenge when AR technologies are applied to the construction sector (Dunston & Shin, 2009). This process guarantees that components are built in the right position and to the correct level from the location information provided by design plans. Although these technologies could (with a proper visualization device) be used by construction technicians to identify the positions of reference points easily and mark them on the site by simply observing the rendered virtual reference points, from our knowledge all the current approaches are under development and not in commercial use at the present time.

3. AR-CAD, augmenting the traditional CAD

The aim of this work is to introduce AR guidance technologies into the daily tasks performed in construction sites, in order to create a construction control system. For that purpose, instead of creating a new AR system including complex and fragile visualization systems and 3D models, a well-known CAD package (AutoCAD®) and other 2D/3D design tools that export files to a DXF format, have been selected as a base to develop an AR tool that adds new features to the existing ones that CAD users are familiar with. As a result, the common tools for 2D data design such as measuring, annotation, selection, etc. are augmented with tools that allow visualizing these actions over the real image obtained from the current state of the construction site. As a quick walk-through of the construction site, the users can measure the distance between two existing pillars or even the area delimited by a new concreting area and, therefore, check if the obtained results coincide with the expected data included within the original design plans. In case the user finds differences between the original and the obtained measurements, then some quick notes, draws or pictures denoting these differences can be on the augmented view of the construction site. Therefore, some of the inspection tasks in construction sites can be performed using a computer remotely in the same way that 2D plans are used on-site in the construction zones.

This system manage three different sources of information: background images, AutoCAD DXF as 2D design plans and as-built images. As a result of the merging of these types of data, a new augmented CAD (denoted as AR-CAD) data model is defined, where the common building plans are augmented with both annotation and real images from the current state of the building work. Moreover, the new augmented CAD information can be visualized over the images obtained from the building work. By means of managing this new type of CAD information, both the coherence among 2D design plans and the execution of the construction projects can be easily controlled. Thus, a new link between the traditional CAD information and the on-site tasks in construction works is defined.

Following the same approach and objectives, the next sections describes some software modules oriented to transform classical CAD tools and operations into new versions able to work with real images from the current state of the construction site.

3.1 Scene navigation in AR-CAD

The user can navigate through the augmented construction plans in the same way as he would do it in a conventional 2D CAD plan, by moving the user's view and performing zoom in/out actions. Moreover, a new user's action, denoted as "orbitation", enables the user to move the augmented view around a focus point. In this new mode, the system controls a Pan-Tilt-Zoom (PTZ) camera aiming towards the same focus point of the augmented view, so all the elements around the real camera can be inspected in detail. Figure 1 shows how the PTZ camera, described in Section 4.3, follows the movement indicated by the user and therefore different zones (belonging to the same construction site) can be controlled using a single device. The operation of the PTZ camera is transparent to the user, since the camera movements are calculated automatically depending on the user's action within the augmented view of AR-CAD.

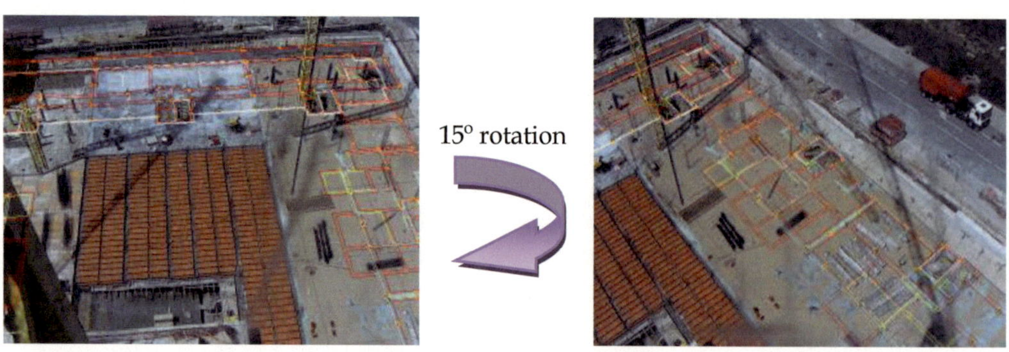

Fig. 1. AR-CAD scene rotation when using the PTZ camera.

3.2 Dynamical image interaction for AR-CAD

In order to help users in the interaction process of the augmented image in AR-CAD, a magnet-based feature has been developed. This user's action is well-known in some CAD programs such as AutoCAD® or SolidWorks® and snaps the cursor into the correct location more accurately than common mechanism of selection based on grids or grips. In case of AR-CAD, the magnet option make common operations on augmented views -such as scene calibration, note addition, measurement, etc- easier for the user. Following the same approach, an augmented magnet has been developed, so that the user can select lines in the real image in the same way that it would be performed in the 2D design plans, as shown in Figure 2. As a result, when the user tries to measure a distance between two points within the augmented image, the mouse is automatically snapped into the nearest outline instead of expecting a manual positioning of points by the user. In this sense, the user's experience is significantly improved since the users of AR-CAD work with a new but familiar tool because of its similarities to the most common operations in CAD applications. The right picture of Figure 2 shows the results of this feature, which is especially useful when a significant zoom-in operation is performed and the user has to select lines on a blurred image. In addition, a more precise measure can be obtained because the new snap position is calculated using the straight line detected instead a single pixel coordinate, so sub-pixel precision can be obtained.

Fig. 2. AR-CAD line selection. A red line shows the line computed from the blue border pixels detected near the mouse. A white cross and a black pointer show the final pointer position (left). The result of the line selection process for a low resolution augmented image (right).

4. System description

The proposed setting out system for construction sites consists of a hardware platform and an Augmented Reality application. Since one of the main goals of the system is the development of a more affordable alternative than conventional equipment for surveying purposes in construction sites, the hardware platform has been developed using commercial off-the-shelf (COTS) components.

This type of developments is oriented to reduce expenses and to shorten the development time, while maintaining the quality of the final product. Moreover, the AR application has been designed following a component-based model to enable a continuous increase of functionality and portability.

4.1 Hardware description

The hardware device of the proposed system includes a high performance PTZ network camera, a reliable 3G-WiFi router and an AC voltage stabilizer in a 15-inch watertight box. This box is made of fiberglass and is located at the top of the main crane obtaining a high resolution top view of the overall construction site. Figure 3 shows an image of the final aspect of development as well as the final location of the hardware device when the experiment tests, described in Section 5, were completed.

In order to fulfil the high performance PTZ network camera requirements, a Toshiba IKWB-21A model was selected (see Figure 3). This IP camera includes a 1280x960 resolution CCD camera with a 15x optical zoom lens. In addition, this camera operates as a stand-alone unit with a built-in web server where the AR application connects and obtains top-view images of the construction site in real time.

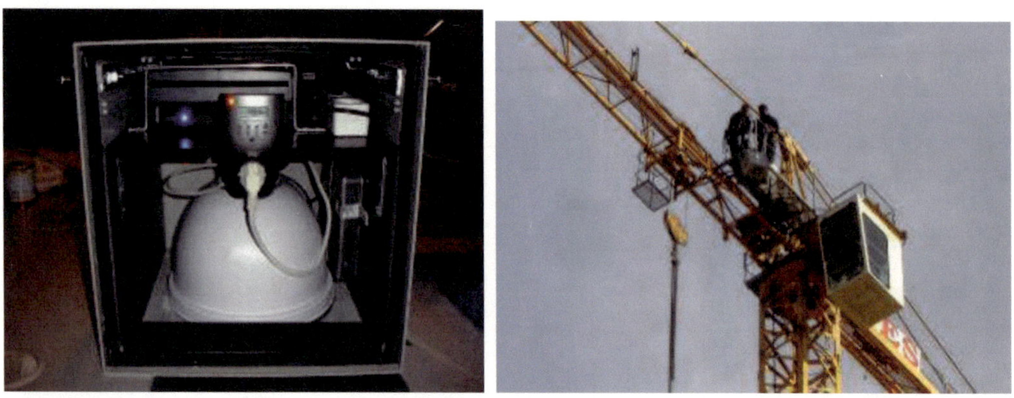

Fig. 3. PTZ camera (left); installation of the camera on a crane (right).

4.2 Software description

The design of the software application for the proposed system has a software architecture following an "event-driven object-oriented" model. These software designs describe synchronous event-driven architectures composed of a set of components (modules), which are based on a classic object-oriented approach. The modules exchange custom messages that model internal actions or external events captured in real-time. In the case of the proposed application, the software system is composed of 8 independent and interrelated subcomponents, which work concurrently in a real-time manner. Figure 4 shows the diagram view of the architecture that relies on a centralized approach around an AR engine. The kernel of the proposed system, denoted as SICURA Engine, is responsible for launching the application, controlling the user interface, and keeping the coherence among the rest of the modules. The three Data I/O modules manage all the information: construction plans, as-built photos and external camera images, so all this data can be loaded and saved.

Finally, three functionality modules -"Image analyzer", "Measure & annotation" and "Background calibration"- implement the system functionalities. All these modules are detailed in the next sections.

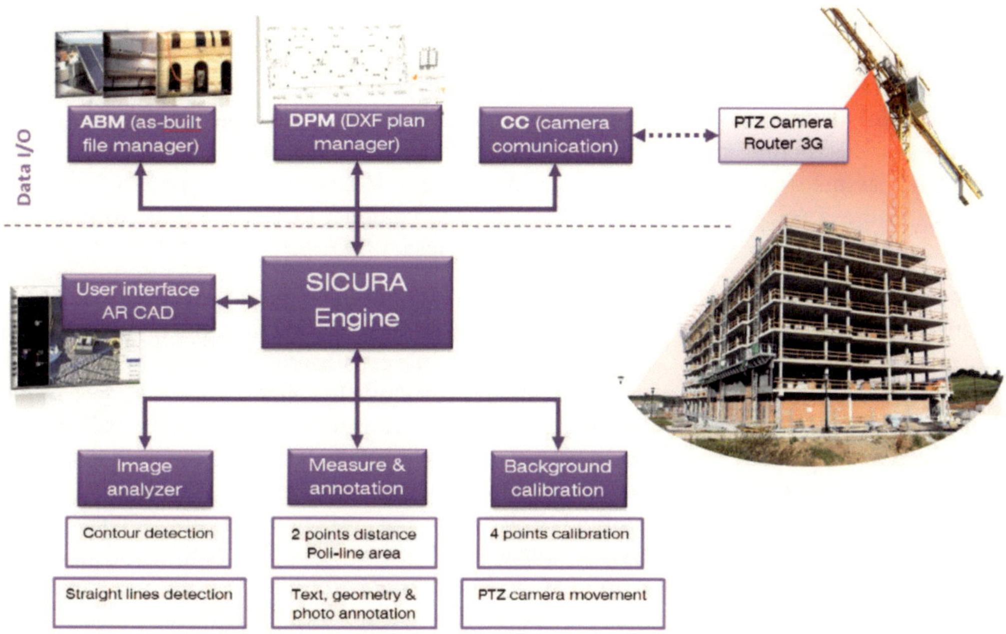

Fig. 4. SICURA software system architecture.

4.3 Data Input/Output modules

The software architecture designed for the proposed system includes three input-output data modules denoted as *AS-Built Manager (ABM)*, *DXF-Plan Manager (DPM)* and *Camera Communication (CC)*. The ABM module manages the AS-Built images, obtained from relevant areas of the construction site, and inserts additional information into the images using the EXIF fields. The EXIF format was created by the Japan Electronic Industry Development Association and is referenced as the preferred image format for digital cameras in ISO 12234-1 (Gulbins & Steinmueller, 2010). Basically, this format defines a header, which is stored into an "application segment" of a JPEG file, or as privately defined tags in a TIFF file. As a result, the resulting JPEG or TIFF images keep a standard format readable by applications that are ignorant of EXIF information. In the proposed system, the EXIF fields save information related to the exact point of the construction site where the picture was taken, additional comments, relevant elements included within the picture, etc. The DPM module opens, reads and writes the 2D design plans of the construction site exported in DXF format. Moreover, this module accesses to the different layers, which are commonly included in the plans. These layers are defined by the architects or draftsmen and allow to organize information about the setting out, structure, pipelines, etc. The properties, comments and measurements related to each layer are also accessible and modifiable by the DPM module. Finally, the CC module provides the communication with the IP-camera, receives images from it and produces basic commands to modify the orientation, zoom and image resolution of the camera. This module makes the camera communication transparent to the rest of the system, so different IP cameras could be used simply modifying the CC module.

4.4 The user's interface in AR-CAD

The user's interface module integrates the graphical user interface (commonly denoted as GUI module) defining a single point of communication to the user within the entire application. This module controls the 2D design plan user's view, the configuration dialogs and shows as many augmented views of the construction zone as the user defines. The pictures used as background images within the augmented views can be selected as real-time video images, static images and compound images.

The option corresponding to the real-time video images seems the most appropriate choice because they make the most of the features of the PTZ camera located at the top of the main crane of the construction site. Otherwise, the static image is useful in scenarios where it is not possible to properly locate a camera in the top of a crane to cover the main surface of the construction site. In those cases, aerial pictures taken from helicopters, helium balloons or specialized small planes can be used as input to the module for defining the background of the augmented view of the scene. Finally, the compound images are a special type of background, which is generated automatically from the images of the augmented views, regardless if they were real-time video images or static images. The compound image is located under the 2D design plan and can be hidden depending of the user's preferences. Section 5 shows some examples of different scenarios and types of background images.

The GUI module of the proposed AR system has been developed under Microsoft Windows Xp/Vista/7 operative systems as a .NET Windows Forms application in C++ using Microsoft Visual Studio 2010. All the windows handled by the application are dockable windows so the workspace is completely configurable. This dock feature is very useful due to the important amount of augmented views that a user can create for the same construction site. Figure 5 shows different views of the user's interface of the system.

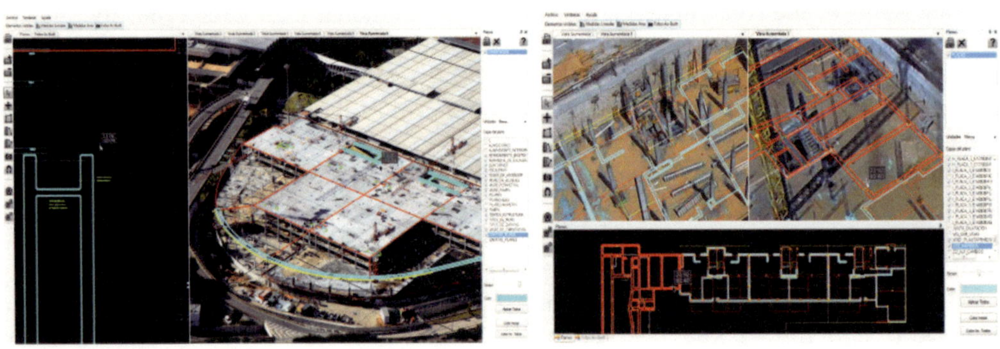

Fig. 5. Distintas vistas del interfaz de usuario.

In order to properly represent and to visualize the augmented view of the construction site, OpenSceneGraph has been selected as a high performance graphics library (Burns &

Osfield, 2004). OpenSceneGraph is an OpenGL-based high performance 3D graphics toolkit for visual simulation, games, virtual reality, scientific visualization, and modeling. Basically, this toolkit is a scene graph-based open source graphics library, which provides all the functions required for representing three-dimensional models in virtual environments. Besides the common features included in OpenSceneGraph, the library has been extended (with a so-called NodeKit) by means of an own development incorporating not only AR features, but also configurable graphic windows oriented to AR content. This interface allows users to show, to hide and to modify layers included in the original DXF design plans, to visualize and to edit measurements and annotations. Moreover, the interface can be used to adjust common image parameters, such as brightness, contrast and saturation, for each one of the background images of the augmented views, separately. This feature allows to represent images in black and white or gray scale in order to bring out the color images of the design plans, when they are superimposed to real images from the camera in the augmented views. Since this feature generates a computational intensive operation when the real-time video image is selected as background of the augmented views, a shader has been defined to perform this operation into the GPU.

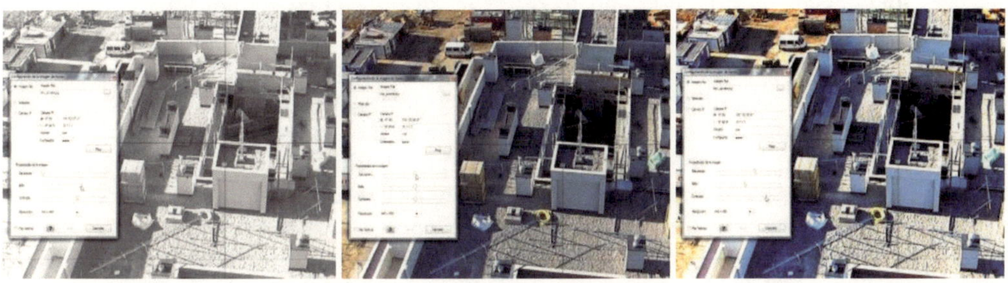

Fig. 6. Examples of the modification of brightness, contrast and saturation of the background images in the augmented views.

One of the main problems concerning to the development of the interface was that OpenGL (a low level graphics interface supporting OpenSceneGraph) cannot properly render irregular 4-vertex textured polygons. The left and center images of Figure 7 show the deformation effect of the texturing process performed by with OpenGL for a regular (left)

Fig. 7. 4-vertex regular textured polygon (left); OpenGL problem on 4-vertex irregular textured polygon (center); 4-vertex irregular textured polygon using our correction shader.

and irregular polygon (center). In order to solve this OpenGL visualization problem, a two-step software correction has been developed. In the first step, a correspondence matrix between the irregular polygon and the square texture is calculated, obtaining a 3x3 homography matrix. Next, in a second step, a *fragment shader* computes the proper texture coordinates for each pixel of the irregular polygon, using the pixel coordinates and the homography matrix. Figure 7 shows the differences between the original texture on a regular polygon (left), the distortion effect on an irregular polygon (center) and the result of the developed two-step solution.

4.5 Image analyzer

The Image Analyzer module (IA) analyzes the image in order to obtain supporting data as input for the magnet-based feature for lines in the augmented view. This module examines the static images (or even the real-time video image), extracts contours, finds the nearest contour points from the cursor and calculates the corresponding straight line (when possible), all these in real time. Since there are several moving objects in a construction site environment, as well as objects not related to the construction process of the building, a lot of unnecessary information is computed if the whole process is performed for each new image. In order not to evaluate unnecessary information and to result in an interactive system for the users, this operation should be performed as quickly as possible, so the tasks related to the interaction process with lines have been divided into two decoupled steps. In the first step, the contour points are identified each time the background image changes (Fig. 8 left). Next, in a second step, the closest contour points to the current position of the cursor are obtained, and, finally (starting with these points) the straight line is computed. This second step is only executed when the user moves the mouse cursor and therefore a significant computation time is saved decoupling this process. In this sense and for the purposes of the magnet tool, it is only necessary to obtain the straight line among the closest zone to the place where the user is working on. Figure 8 (left) shows the total obtained contour points in a 1440x920 pixels image and the straight line (right) obtained from the current cursor position. The blue pixels in the right picture of Figure 8 correspond to the selected contour points and the red pixels of this figure define the obtained line. In addition, a white cursor has been included to show the initial position of the cursors for the IA module and the black cursor indicates the position of this element obtained by the two-step process.

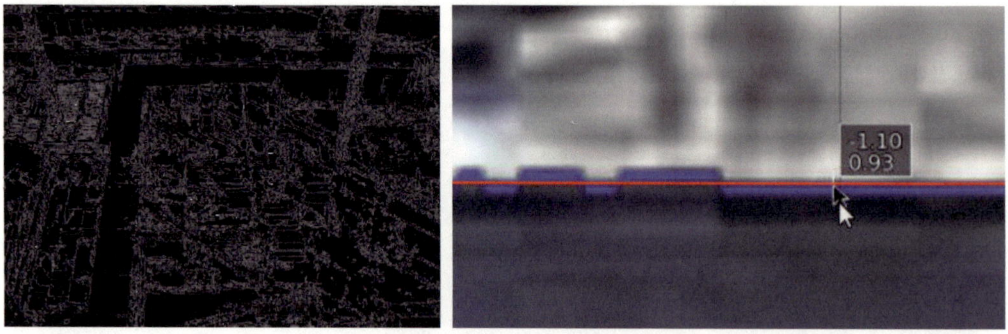

Fig. 8. Contour mask extracted from the background image (left); straight line computed (red line) and pixels selected (blue) from the initial white cursor position to obtain the final black cursor position (right).

4.6 Measure & annotation tools

The proposed system includes a module oriented to directly add measurements and annotations to the original 2D design plans. In this sense, this module allows the user to quantify and to draw the deviations of the execution of the construction project, as well as to save them with the original plans in a unified manner. The development loop is closed by means of this module since the original 2D design plans are made by a commercial CAD application. Then, these plans are completed with measurements and geometry showing the reality of the execution of the construction project and, finally, the last version of these updated plans is generated following the same format in which they were initially created. The aim of this module is not to replace the drawing and design features of current CAD commercial application (such as Autocad®, Intellicad®, MicroStation®, etc.), but to include a reduced set of tools in a AR development to edit directly and efficiently construction plans.

The measurement functions include two different options denoted as lineal or area estimations. The option for lineal measurements obtains an estimation of the distance between two points, while the option for area estimations infers the area surface in a polyline. In both cases, the user uses the mouse to select the different points on the 2D original map, or in the augmented view, and the result of the measurement appears on the selected zone.

For the case of the annotations, three types of tagging elements, denoted as text marks, geometric marks and AS-BUILT images have been developed. The text annotations consist of a reduced text describing a situation or a problem detected. The central image of the Figure 9 shows an example how these annotations are placed together with a 2D reference indicating the beginning of the position of the text mark within the plan. The geometric annotations follow the same procedure that was developed for the area measurements in polylines since the objective of this module is not to replace a CAD commercial application, but to include some common drawing and labeling features. The last type of annotation corresponds to the AS-BUILT images and assigns pictures, showing the current state of the construction site, to the place where they were taken. Usually, these pictures are managed by the construction site manager who has to organize and classify them into several criteria as well as creating the construction site delivery document, denoted also as CSDD. The developed system not only lets users to organize, categorize and classify the AS-BUILT

Fig. 9. Lineal and area measure (left); text and geometric annotations (center); as-built photo annotation (right).

images, but also allows these images to be inserted into exact points within the 2D original plans and the augmented views of the construction site. The right image of Figure 9 shows an example of the result of these features. This annotation method is especially useful for the construction site manager in the last stages of the construction process, where it is necessary to control and review the task performed by outsourced work-teams such as carpenters, electricians, etc.

4.7 Background calibration

This module computes the correspondence between the background image of the augmented views and the computer-generated information. This correspondence is a key aspect of the system because all the geometrical information (including measures) is computed using this correspondence. The accuracy of the system proposed depends directly on the precision of the calibration performed for each augmented view. Due to the importance of the calibration process, an easy-to-use calibration tool has been developed. Using this tool the user defines the points of correspondence between the real background images and the 2D design plans. This action can be performed using the magnet-based feature for lines and its augmented version if a higher degree of accuracy is desirable. When this correspondence has been established, the system obtains the position and orientation of the camera, which collected the image. The user can modify the calibration points and watch the result in real time, so it is possible to improve the initial estimation only moving each point to its correct place. This process needs to know the intrinsic parameters of the camera, in terms of camera geometry, in order to complete the calibration successfully.

Moreover, this module obtains de proper movements from controlling the PTZ camera according to the CAD augmented view when the orbital mode is selected. In this sense, the corresponding values for the pan, tilt and zoom parameters that the system needs to point the camera at any given position are obtained from the initial calibration of the augmented view. In the cases where the desired point to monitor is physically unreachable because of the camera placement, the system locates the camera pointing at the closest zone to the desired point, always within the eye camera field-of-view. Using this correspondence, the orbital mode is automatically restricted to the feasible zoom and camera operations that can be performed by the system camera.

5. Experiments and results

Different experiments have been conducted in actual construction sites in order to evaluate the system performance of the proposed approach. This section shows the description and the obtained results in the three more representative cases corresponding to the construction of a building of apartments, the enlargement of a parking area and the tasks for the rehabilitation of an old building.

5.1 A low-height construction site building

The first performed evaluation corresponds to the use of the system in the monitoring processes for the construction of a seven-floor building for apartments. The size of the construction size is roughly 6840 (95x72) square meters. In this experiment, a Toshiba IKWBA-21A camera, described in Section 4.1, has been used. This camera was located at top of a tower crane of 50 meters high. Using this configuration, it was impossible to obtain a high resolution top view of the overall construction site in a single snapshot of the camera. To improve this situation, an augmented view of the system was configured including three different views of the same construction site. Figure 10 shows the configuration of the three different views of the scene as well as the obtained results.

In this first experiment, the construction site manager used the system to verify the setting out of pillars in the building. This process has to be completed in order to guarantee that the pillars belonging to the building are constructed in the right position and level from the location information provided by the 2D design plans. Although the construction of pillars should be a very accurately tasks, some errors can occur because bad interpretations of the plans, or even because of non-commented last-moment modifications performed by the topographers. These mistakes are especially dangerous if they are not detected in the early stages of the construction site process, since sometimes they cannot be solved and involve modifying the original design plans.

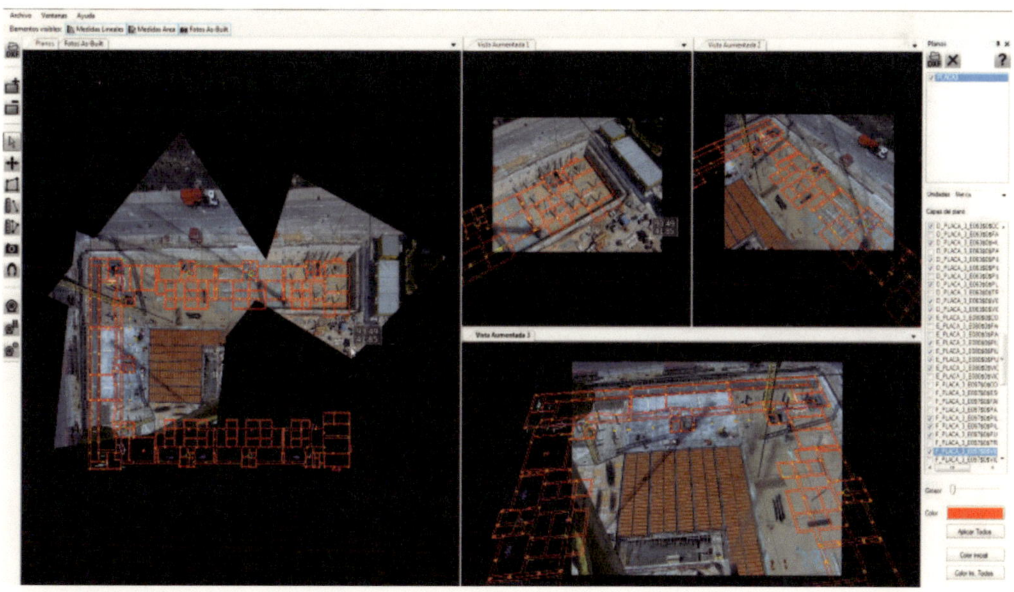

Fig. 10. Example of the use of the system in a construction site for a 7-floor building; three augmented views(right) and composed background mixed with 2D plan (left).

The construction site manager (an expert AutoCAD © user) learnt easily the main features and operations of the system, following a two-hour tutorial, and worked with the system for a period of 3 months, until the end of the setting out tasks in the construction site. For this period of time, the main problems were caused by the unexpected low performance of the wireless connection to the system camera, caused by the radio magnetic interferences generated by the surveillance equipment of a very near military building. As a result of the use of the system, the manager showed a high level of satisfaction and emphasized the ease of the system to check the setting out tasks at a glance, when testing pillars, elevator holes, stairs, etc. Moreover, the resulting accuracy of these verifications was enough to measure the length and width of pillars remotely because of the optical zoom provided by the PTZ camera.

5.2 Construction and enlargement of a parking area

In this experiment, the system was evaluated to monitor the construction and enlargement of a three-floor parking lot with an area of 19.800 (165x120) square meters. Because not only by the large surface of the construction site, but also by the low height of the installed tower cranes, the system worked with aerial images obtained by an air company specialized in this type of services. Figure 11 shows an example of the use of the system using this type of pictures, which were obtained every two weeks providing a complete evolution of execution of the construction project. Since aerial pictures are not usually taken with conventional digital cameras, it was necessary to calculate the intrinsic parameters of the camera along with the distortions at a predefined number of measured points of focus and zoom. In order to complete this tuning process, a set of different 50 pictures corresponding to a calibration pattern for this professional camera was provided by the air company.

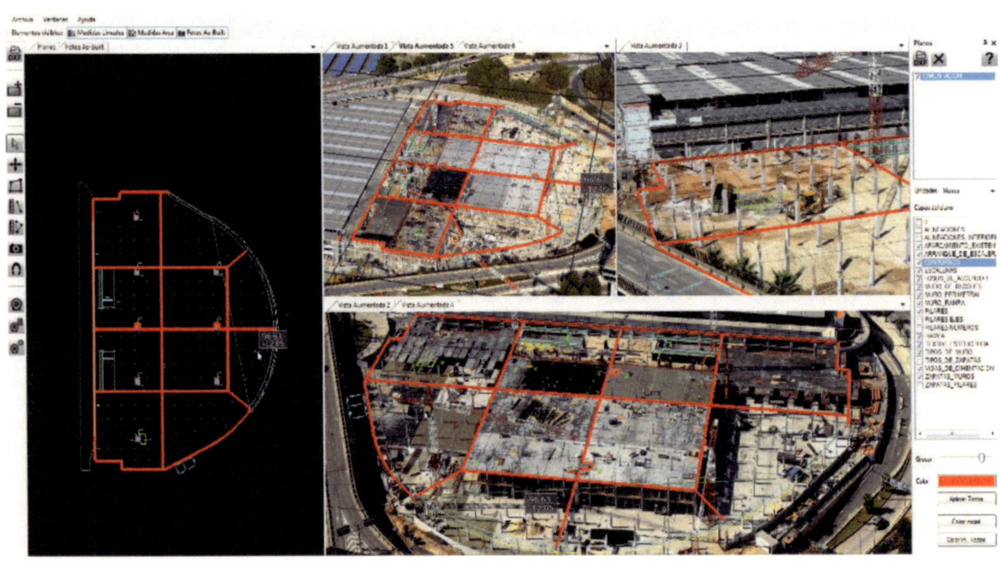

Fig. 11. Image of the system in the construction of a parking area using aerial images as background for the augmented views.

As in the previous experiment, the construction site manager was trained in a one-day course and evaluated the performance of the system, which was used for eleven months. In this case, the most profitable feature by the manager was the measurement of irregular areas. This measurement is significantly important in the development of the daily tasks in a construction site environment, since it sets the amount of money to be paid to outsourcers (concrete company, companies providing metallic framework, etc…) as they complete their tasks. In most cases, the measurements of areas (which are finished by the subcontractors) are obtained from either the initial 2D design plans, or a topographic service. Both solutions, or could be erroneous, because the differences between the scheduled and the executed tasks, or even are difficult to perform in all the cases since. Concretely, some completed elements in a construction work cannot be measured by a topographic service, because the occlusions problems in a classical construction process.

5.3 Restoration of a building (Nou de Octubre)

The last presented experiment corresponds to the use of SICURA for the restoration tasks of an old building converted into an office building with communal services. The three-floor building covers an area of roughly 4.340 (70x62) square meters. In this project a Sony DSCF828, 8MP compact digital camera, was used as input device for the images inserted into the background of the augmented views.

One of the main features of the building restoration projects is the important amount of work related to the review, estimation and updating of the 2D original plans with the restoration actions to be performed. The restoration actions assign information about material, task description, estimated time, etc. to different points of the 2D original plans. These actions require several visits to the construction site to review measurement, estimations and tasks to be performed.

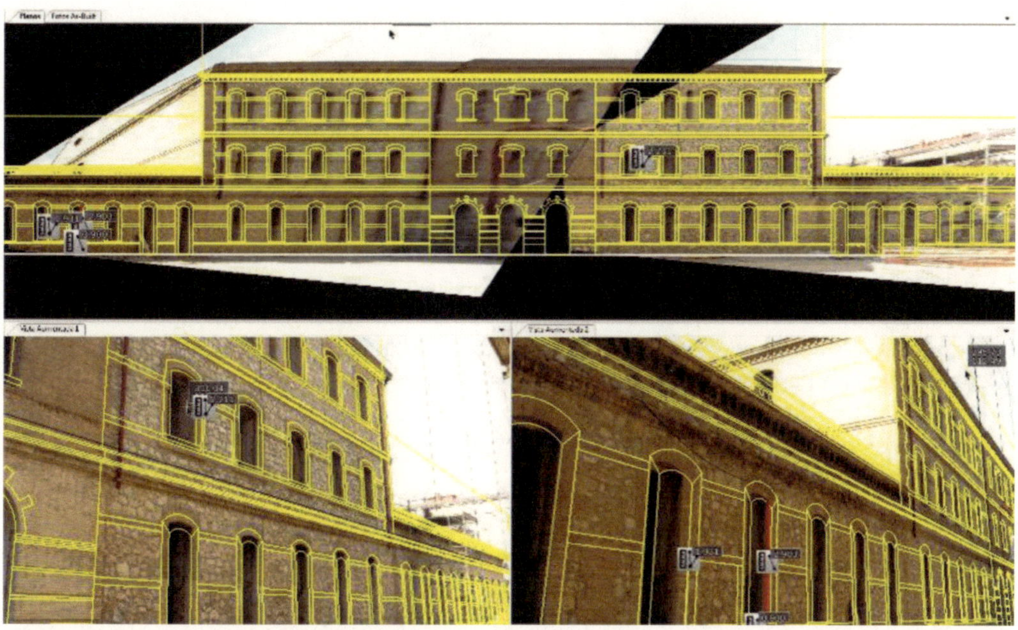

Fig. 12. Example of the restoration process using compound images.

In this case, the system was evaluated by two restoration building technicians, who use the system in the restoration tasks corresponding to the building facades. As in the previous experiments, the users were considered as experts AutoCAD© and passed a one-day training season. After an evaluation of two-month of duration, the users stressed the speed of the annotation operations since they were performed on actual pictures of the building under restoration.

In this sense, SICURA was also considered as valuable new way of inspection and planning for construction purposes. The reasons of these considerations are not only the time and costs savings in the measurement of facades, but also the speed in the annotation taks for the cataloguing processes. Figures 12 and 13 show some results of the use of SICURA for restoration purposes in an actual building restoration project. As a result, the restoration technicians could update and add measurements and restoration tasks to be performed regardless the topography department of the construction company. Moreover, all the new or updated measurement and annotations were exported into an AutoCAD© format to generate the final restoration project for the building.

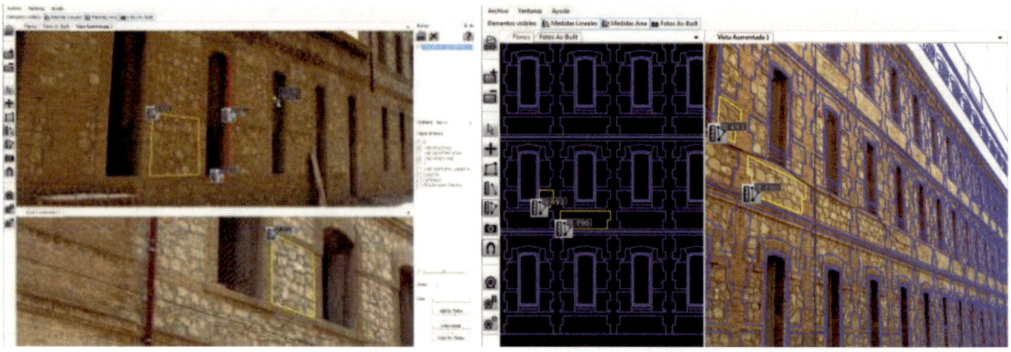

Fig. 13. Snapshots of the system in the restoration process of an old building. Area and lineal measurements over the real image (left); plane and measures superimposed the real image (right).

6. Conclusions

In this paper, we have proposed a new system based on Augmented Reality technologies for the area of building construction. The system is devised to the improvement in the building control process performed by the construction responsible in building areas. The system has been designed and created with current CAD tools (widespread used in this area) in mind, in order to minimize the learning curve for the final users and to guarantee a good level of acceptance of the new functionalities included in our system.

With the SICURA system we have been able to merge three different information sources into the building control process: AS-BUILT photographs, CAD planes and background images from different sources. The SICURA system becomes, thus, an enhanced CAD system, that we call AR CAD. The system is able to combine in a coherent an accurate way these different sources offering an interesting framework for the indicated supervision task.

To show the potentialities of the system three different scenarios of use have been tested. The selection of the scenarios has been based on different types of building area, building heights and the kind of construction tasks required in each case. In all of them, the system worked properly, with only a few issues in the wireless camera connection, due to frequency inhibitors placed in a close building.

After the tests, interviews were performed with the supervisors of each building area. All users showed a good degree of acceptance of the system. We think that this is because of two main reasons: on the one hand, the appearance of the software with the same look and feel and the same interaction present in current CAD systems, so they feel quite familiarized with the use of the system. On the other hand, the extra functionalities included in the system where very appreciated because with non-extra 3D models or physics models they were able to compare real images with CAD designs in an accurate way, being able to even make measurements and quite precise estimations of deviations from initial designs without even being physically in the building area.

However there are still some minor issues to improve in order to make easier the actual introduction of this system in the daily control of the building process. In this way, the main drawback that users found using the system was the calibration method. Although all the users understood why this process was necessary, the most of the users suggested a more automatic calibration process, instead of placing the control points, which can be sometimes confusing. So, these are the kind of considerations we are using to drive our work to obtain a more usable system.

7. Acknowledgment

This investigation was partially founded by DRAGADOS and the Spanish Government. All the tests of the systems and photographs correspond to DRAGADOS real constructions works.

8. References

Azuma, R. (1997). Survey of Augmented Reality. *Presence: Teleoperators and Virtual Environments*, Vol. 6, No. 4, pp. 355-385

Cawood, S. & Fiala, M. (2008). *Augmented Reality: A Practical Guide*, Pragmatic Bookshelf, ISBN 978-1934356036

Dunston, P. & Shin, D.H. (2009). Key Areas And Issues For Augmented Reality Applications On Construction Sites, In: *Mixed Reality in Architecture, Design and Construction*, X. Wang and M.A. Schnabel (Ed.), pp. 157-170, Springer Verlag, ISBN: 978-1-4020-9088-2_7

Gulbins, J. & Steinmueller, U. (2010). *The Digital Photograpy Workflow Handbook*, Rocky Nook, ISBN 978-1-933952-71-0

Hakkarainen, M., Woodward, C. & Rainio, K. (2009). Software Architecture for Mobile Mixed Reality and 4D BIM Interaction, *Proceedings of the 25th CIB W78 Conference*, Istanbul, Turkey, October 2009

Honkamaa, P., Siltanen, S., Jappinen, J., Woodward, C. & Korkalo, O. (2007). B.H. Interactive Outdoor Mobile Augmentation Using Markerless Tracking and GPS, *Proceedings of the Virtual Reality International Conference (VRIC)*, Laval, France, April 2007

Hunter, B. (2009). Augmented Reality Visualisation Facilitating The Architectural Process , In: *Mixed Reality in Architecture, Design and Construction*, X. Wang and M.A. Schnabel (Ed.), pp. 105-118, Springer Verlag, ISBN: 978-1-4020-9088-2_7

Izkara, J.L., Perez, J., Basogain, X. & Borro, D. (2007). Mobile Augmented Reality, an Advanced Tool for the Construction Sector, *Proceedings of the 24th CIB W78 Conference*, Maribor, Slovakia, June 2007

Klinker, G., Stricker, D. & Reiners, D. (2001). Augmented Reality for Exterior Construction Applications, In: *Augmented Reality and Wearable Computers,* W. Barfield and T. Caudell (Ed.), pp. 397-427, Lawrence Erlbaum Press

Muskett, J. (1995). *Site Surveying,* Blackwell Science Ltd, ISBN 0-632-03848-9, Berlin, Germany

Piekarski, W. & Thomas, B.H. (2003). An Object-oriented Software Architecture for 3D Mixed Reality Applications, *Proceedings of the 2nd IEEE-ACM International Symposium on Mixed and Augmente Reality (ISMAR),* Tokio, Japan, October 2003

Thomas, B.H., Piekarski, W. & Gunther, B. (2000). Using Augmented Reality to Visualize Architecture Designs in an Outdoor Environment. *International Journal of Design Computing,* Vol. 2

Burns, D. & Osfield, R. (2004). Open Scene Graph A: Introduction, B: Examples and Applications, *Proceedings of the IEEE Virtual Reality Conference (VR),* ISBN 0-7803-8415-6, Chicago, US, March 2004

3

The Cloud-Mobile Convergence Paradigm for Augmented Reality

Xun Luo
Office of the Chief Scientist, Qualcomm Inc.
USA

1. Introduction

Mobile computing for massive users has gained enormous progresses in the last few years. Among the main propelling forces for this momentum are the performance improvements of mobile application processors, increasing of storage and sensing capabilities, as well as breakthroughs in manufacturing technologies for high-quality mobile displays. Along with such progresses, the way people perceive mobile devices evolved over time as well, maybe best reflected by the changing names. During the 1990s, the mobile devices were called cellular phones and PDAs (personal digital assistants), to differentiate between the then-major functionalities of voice communication and handheld computing. Later the word "smart phone" was more popularly used, attesting the convergence between communication and computing elements. Nowadays, new technical jargons such as tablets, pads, and smart books are often used to refer to mobile devices. Behind the hype of this name changing game is the simple fact that personal computing is rapidly shifting towards being mobile.

There are large number of applications and services designed and optimized for mobile computing. Within the herd Augmented Reality (AR) stands out and attracts considerable attention. AR is the technology that superimposes computer generated graphics over real-life live video feeds, using registration as the magic glue to blend the two seamlessly together. The origin of the term "Augmented Reality" can be traced back to 1990, although applications featuring some of the basic characteristics had been in place as early as the 1960s. On the other hand, mobile AR systems which are of practical use are relatively new and did not emerge until recently. The reason is that such systems put high requirements on the hosting device's software and hardware configurations.

To better understand the challenges, let's take a look at Figure 1 which illustrates the components of a conceptual mobile AR system. In this system, sensor (including both the camera sensor and others) inputs are used to estimate the six degree-of-freedom pose of the on-device camera. The sensor inputs are also used by a user interaction module which implements functionality of gesture control. An I/O module reads graphics models from a database and provides them to a rendering module. The latter combines rendered graphics with live video. As the orchestrated output of all the modules, the interactive and augmented scene is presented to the end user.

Now we examine what are the necessities to make the illustrated system capable of providing smooth user experiences. First of all, the system needs to have *interactivity*, which translates

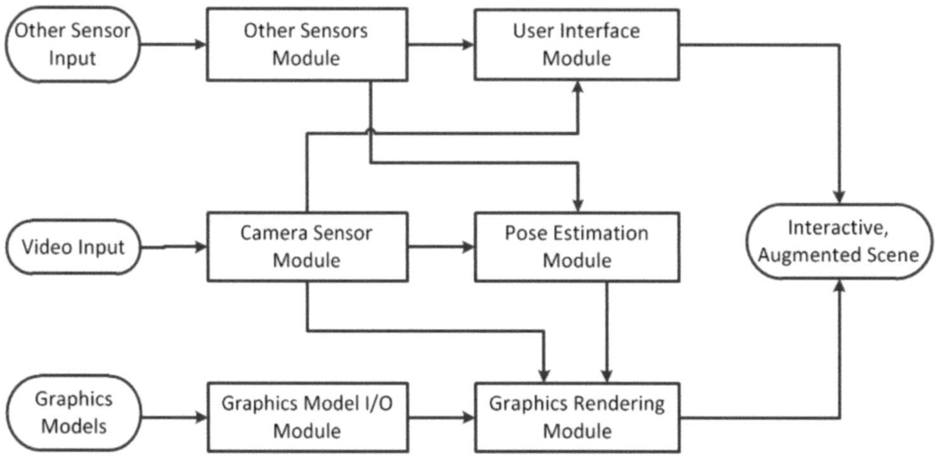

Fig. 1. The components of a typical mobile AR system.

to frame rates above a minimum number, usually 30 frames per second. *Fidelity* is another requirement, which means resolution of the final combined frames should achieve beyond a decent level such as VGA (640 by 480 pixels), with sufficient graphical details. A further requirement is *scalability*, indicating that there shall not be stringent restrictions on the quantity of graphics models, nor the size of each individual ones. Last but not least, users desire *robustness*, that is, even under noisy and complex environment conditions the pose estimation module should still function with satisfactory detection rate and accuracy. Not surprisingly, meeting these requirements calls for fast video processing, high I/O bandwidth and efficient algorithm computation. These have been equipped more or less by modern mobile devices, but not yet enough. The obstacles are multi-folds:

- Architecture difference – It is often the case that mobile application processors are designed to have different architectures from high-end servers and even low-end PCs. The rationale for such differences is mostly for power efficiency. At the price of this design choice is the performance discrepancy introduced by architecture difference.
- Hardware capability – It is not completely uncommon for mobile devices to share the same or similar architectures with their stationed counterparts. However, even under this situation, significant capability gap may still exist between them. Take multi-core architecture for example: the number of cores in a mobile multi-core processor is usually much fewer than that of a desktop multi-core processor. Programable GPU architecture is another example: most mobile GPUs implement only a subset of the functionalities of the desktop products.
- System availability – Because mobile devices do not have the luxury of unlimited power, energy conservation is a must-have for them. This impacts the system availability accordingly. For instance, we cannot assume a smart phone in the field to run an intensive computer vision task overnight without being plugged with external power supply. Albeit the same operation could be conducted by a desktop PC with the same processor clock frequency without difficulty.

Up to now, the approaches to tackle these constraints have been mainly focused on designing algorithms as "lean and mean" as possible on the mobile devices. From this point of view, the endeavors of making AR to work on mobile devices are very similar to those of making AR to work on PCs a decade ago. But unlike PCs by then, mobile devices nowadays often find themselves surrounded by abundantly available cloud-based resources. In addition to that, it is even often the case that correspondent AR components have been implemented on these cloud peers more efficiently already. In this chapter we attempt to look at the problem from a new and different perspective, i.e. closely integrate the computing resources on the mobile device as well as in its cloud environment. We propose a novel alternative paradigm, named Cloud-Mobile Convergence (CMC). Both the high-level design principle and low-level proof-of-concept implementations of CMC are presented.

The rest of this chapter is organized as follows. In section 2 a review of traditional techniques to solve "performance vs. resource" problem in AR is briefly given. Section 3 describes key concepts and high-level design principles of CMC. Following that, several sample scenarios are presented in section 4. Section 5 conducts a deeper dive by studying in detail a proof-of-concept application, which applies CMC paradigm to accelerate computer vision-based human-computer interaction. We conclude the chapter in section 6 with discussions.

2. Existing optimization measures for mobile AR

As illustrated in Figure 1, AR systems can use multiple sources of sensor inputs for camera pose estimation and interaction. In practice, the camera sensor is mostly used. For simplicity reasons, from now on if not specifically mentioned, the AR systems we discuss only include vision-based ones. In such systems, vision-based processing tasks consists of *recognition* and *tracking*.

Recognition is the task to find one or multiple pre-defined objects in the video scene. The objects are first summarized – off-line or on-line – into digital presentation of features, and then matched with the features extracted from the video scene. If there are matches found, the corresponding objects are recognized. There have been a large number of feature detection and description methods proposed and developed in recent decades. Representative ones among them include Harris Corners (Harris & Stephens, 1988), Shi and Tomasi (Shi & Tomasi, 1994), SIFT (Lowe, 2004), SURF (Bay et al., 2006), FERNS (Ozuysal et al., 2007), and FAST (Rosten & Drummond, 2003; 2005). Tracking is the task to keep track of the recognized objects in video scene, and estimate camera pose continuously. In contrast to recognition task, tracking task is free (or largely liberated) from the obligations of feature detection, description and matching. This advantage makes it relatively faster to perform.

Although often underlooked, video acquisition itself is by no means a cheap operation. Quite a few pre-processing steps need to be done before the video is supplied to recognition and tracking tasks with satisfying quality: exposure control, focusing tuning, color adjustment etc. State-of-art camera sensors try best to automate these steps, at the price of pre-processing time that could be of the magnitude of tens of mini-seconds. The time taken by video acquisition further tightens tracking and detection budgets.

One of the research directions undertaken is to make use of hardware elements that are more efficient for computer vision algorithms processing than general-purpose CPUs. For instance, with the rapid growing of programmable GPU capabilities, researchers have explored the feasibility of porting some of the fundamental computer vision algorithms used by AR to

GPU and showcased proven performance gains. Wu developed a software library for the SIFT feature detector and descriptor (Wu, 2007). Terriberry et al. focused their efforts on SURF (Terriberry et al., 2008) and provided a working prototype. But the gains provided by following this direction were not as large as AR system designers and users had expected. On one hand, parallelism potentials of many computer vision algorithms are intrinsically limited, leaving a constrained space to fully utilize the GPU capability. On the other hand, heavy communications cost introduced by data transfer between the CPU and GPU, or among multiple GPU cores further handicapped the benefits introduced by the usage of parallel computing. It is worth noting that the numbers in (Wu, 2007) and (Terriberry et al., 2008) were based on the more favorable experimental results of using desktop GPU processors. The benchmark values on mobile GPUs would obviously be even worse.

Another viable path is to reduce the complexity of the AR tasks. Not surprisingly, this has been more or less used by most mobile AR developers. There have been several popular practices:

1. Image resolution reduction. This is intuitive to understand with a simple example: the number of pixels contained in a QVGA (320 by 240) resolution video frame is only a quarter of those in a VGA (640 by 480) resolution counterpart. Although processing complexity is not strictly linearly correlated with number of pixels, the reduction of pixels normally brings down required CPU cycles considerably. Many mobile AR systems down-sample camera frames with a gaussian kernel to archive the goal of pixel reduction.
2. Parametric tuning for computer vision algorithms. For example, the original SIFT (Lowe, 2004) implementation used a 128-dimension feature descriptor. Some variant implementation, such as (Wagner et al., 2009) used data dimension less than that to lower processing time and memory usage. Similar measures had been taken by some systems by restricting the number of feature points to detect and match.
3. Utilization of assumptions and heuristics. In a specific AR application, some useful assumptions and heuristics can be made use of to make the computer vision tasks easier. Quite a few mobile AR systems in the literature assumed that there should be no drastic camera displacements across adjacent frames. By asserting this, the burden of extensive area processing for tracking is eased. In the gesture recognition system described in (Kolsch et al., 2004), users are required to put the hand within a certain sub-region of the camera view in order to start the system. Consequently the detection cost was much lower than a full frame search. Similar requirements were also imposed by some real-time text translation applications on mobile devices (Fragoso et al., 2011).

Strictly speaking, the practices listed above should not be regarded as optimization measures. The reason is that they are not able to realize repeatable results of tackling the problem at original complexity: Down-sampling VGA resolution frames to QVGA might improve the frame rate, but it is more likely to decrease the detection rate and tracking continuity; Tuning feature descriptor dimension brings down both memory usage and detection accuracy; Assumptions and heuristics work "most of the time" and fail in corner cases, which are sometimes not rare at all to spot. Use of such techniques should be carefully thought of and conducted.

Yet another approach is to optimize the AR processing pipeline. Because there are multiple computer vision tasks in a mobile AR system, processing of them could be optimized by using concurrent programming techniques such as multi-threading. In a typical acquisition-recognition-tracking pipeline, each downstream stage of the pipeline can start as a separate thread and synchronize with the upper stream counterparts in parallel. When the camera imager thread acquires a new frame and delivers it to recognition thread, it starts the next frame acquisition right away instead of waiting for the latter to complete. Recognition thread works in a similar relationship with the tracking thread. In general, this mechanism can be applied for any intermediate processing stages in the pipeline: In the Envisor (DiVerdi et al., 2008) system, an inertial sensor interpolation thread and a vision-based calibration thread complemented each other for tracking and map construction. In the HandyAR (Lee & Hollerer, 2007) system, separation was made for a foreground recognition thread using low-cost features and a background calibration thread using expensive features.

Limitation of the pipeline optimization approach is that even under the most idealistic situation, total processing time of the pipeline is still capped by the duration of the most time-consuming stage. The work of (Wagner et al., 2009) proposed a solution which partially alleviated this problem. The solution amortized the most expensive processing task, i.e. target detection into multiple consecutive frames. By using this technique, it achieved the relatively best performance among peers at the time of publication (multiple target recognition and tracking in real-time on mobile phones). The caveat was that the number of frames involved for task amortization could not be too large otherwise the system could be subject to stability issues.

3. The Cloud-Mobile Convergence paradigm

In section 2 we briefly reviewed the existing performance optimization measures for mobile AR. It can be seen that none of them could solve the performance issue with full satisfaction. These measures differ largely from each other, but share one thing in common: they rely only on the mobile device itself to overcome its intrinsic shortcoming of constrained resources.

In this section, we think "outside of the device" and present a novel paradigm called Cloud-Mobile Convergence (CMC). CMC is based on the observation that present day mobile devices are surrounded by abundantly available cloud resources, and access to these resources has never been as convenient before. The fundamental difference between CMC and other state-of-art solutions is that CMC considers performance improvement factors external of the mobile device, in conjunction with those on the device itself.

Under the CMC paradigm, when a mobile AR system is designed at high level, the resources pool available to it is not considered to merely reside locally. Instead, all the resources are regarded as being possible to present either internally or externally of the device. The only differentiations among the resources are the benefits they bring and the costs to use them, rather than whether they reside on the mobile device or in the cloud. This is the "convergence" essence of the paradigm.

The CMC paradigm considers computing for mobile AR tasks an optimization problem with the optional requirement of satisfying multiple constraints. If we denote $R_1, R_2, ..., R_N$ as the N available resources, $B(R_i)$ to be the benefits brought by resource i, $C(R_i)$ to be the cost of using resource i, $T_1, T_2, ..., T_M$ to be the M constraints to be satisfied, then the problem of optimizing a mobile AR system can be abstracted as:

$$
\begin{aligned}
& maximize \sum_{i=1}^{N} B(R_i) \\
& s.t. \\
& T_1, T_2, ..., T_M \\
& optionally, \\
& minimize \sum_{i=1}^{N} C(R_i)
\end{aligned}
\tag{1}
$$

Now that the abstraction is in place, it is time to look at how to apply the CMC paradigm to a specific mobile AR system. In a real world application, each of the variables in Equation 1 is mapped to an application-specific factor. Let's use one hypothetical system as example. This system employs two resources in the recognition stage: a worker thread R_1 that matches features extracted from the video scene to the local database, and another worker thread R_2 which performs the same matching task but against a video library stored in a data center. In this scenario two sets of definitions can be used to model benefits and costs, leading to two different resource convergence strategies adopted by the system. In one set of definition, $B(R_i)$ is the total number of objects available in R_i, and $C(R_i)$ is the average recognition time for each object in the video scene. This set of definition is obviously favorable to cloud resource R_2, because R_2 is able to provide more object candidates and perform faster object recognition using data center processor farms. In another set of definition, $B(R_i)$ is the number of objects accessible in unit time in R_i, and $C(R_i)$ is the average access latency. In contrast to the first set of definition, this one favors local resource R_1, because of the higher I/O throughput and lower access latency provided by R_1. Under both sets of definitions, constraint T can be defined as a threshold of unit time power consumption, i.e. T regulates the battery draining rate.

The above example clearly manifests the power of CMC paradigm: the generalized description is concise, yet the parameterized interpretation is flexible. Because of these advantages, CMC is an effective meta-method and philosophy that has the potential to be used widely for mobile AR system design and implementation.

4. Sample scenarios for CMC paradigm

In this section we showcase three different sample scenarios where CMC paradigm could be beneficial. Each of the scenarios sets up an unique environmental mix of on-device and cloud resources. It is worth noting that the classification criteria of these scenarios resemble those used for mobile networking characterization. The subtle difference here is that they are modeled by computing and not communications contexts. In all three scenarios, we define the benefit of a resource $B(R)$ to be its processing power, and the cost $C(R)$ to be its access latency.

4.1 Enterprise

It is common that in an enterprise environment, mobile device users have access to high quality-of-service infrastructure of Wi-Fi network, as well as powerful backend servers. Such servers could be maintained by the IT department of the enterprise itself, or leased from server farm providers such as the Amazon Elastic Computing Cloud[1]. In this scenario, $B(R)$ is high and $C(R)$ is low for the cloud resources. It is thus possible to fully offload some of the computing intensive tasks, like recognition and tracking to the cloud resources, and render the processed result on mobile device, making the latter a thin client (e.g. (Taylor & Pasquale, 2010)).

4.2 Hotspot

In some public locations, limited computing service might be provided by the venue management. For example, at a metropolitan airport, in addition to the complementary Wi-Fi service, computer nodes attached to the Wi-Fi access points could be offering users with their processing capacities complementarily or at a nominal charge. In some literatures, such enhanced network access points are called "Access Point 2.0". The characteristics of this scenario is that $B(R)$ has a moderate value, but $C(R)$ is also considerable. With the presence of "Access Point 2.0", the preferred approach is to rely on the on-device resources to perform tasks that require low latency, in the mean time utilize the cloud resources to perform tasks that are not sensitive to latency. For example, tracking could be conducted on-device, while recognition could be accomplished in the cloud. Because the latter is either conducted at application starting time or as a background task, latency introduced by using cloud-based resources is less detrimental.

4.3 At home

In the home environment, each family member could own one or more mobile devices. Additionally, these devices are capable of communicating with each other through ad-hoc or home Wi-Fi network, or other short range radios such as Bluetooth®. The resources provided by each mobile devices to others can be regarded as in the cloud from the other parties' point of view. In this scenario, $B(R)$ is low and $C(R)$ is high for the cloud resources, making them less popular than in the previous two scenarios. Cloud resources thus cannot play primary roles in computing, but only serve as auxiliary assistants. Possible usage of the CMC paradigm include assigning some of the off-line tasks in AR to cloud resources. Such kind of tasks include object database construction, feature updating in the database, and so on.

5. A proof-of-concept application

In this section we analyze an application in-depth to further study the CMC paradigm. This application employs vision-based techniques for natural human-computer interaction with the mobile device. As a result, it is subject to expensive computation of processing camera frames and track the hand in real-time, which exceeds the capability of the mobile device itself. We show that by using a computer cluster which is in the mobile device's proximity, the system performance can be speeded up and achieve significantly better usability. Abstract of this work was originally published in (Luo & Kenyon, 2009). This section is an extended version of the original publication.

[1] http://aws.amazon.com/ec2/

Fig. 2. A user interacts with a display wall with gestures, performing 2D window resizing and moving tasks. Video frames are captured by a single camera on the tripod but processed by multiple nodes of the cluster driving the display wall.

5.1 Background of the application

The last decade witnessed an increasing need for multi-million pixel resolution displays, propelled by applications such as scientific visualization, viewing satellite/aerial imagery, teleconferencing and a plethora of others. A successfully implemented solution to address this need is to construct display systems that consist of multiple screen tiles driven by a computer cluster. In such systems, each node in the computer cluster powers one or more of the display tiles. Building on this hardware configuration, the synergy among the cluster nodes ensures that pixel rendering across all the tiles are coordinated to provide the user with a large "single" screen experience. Cluster-driven large displays can be a projection-based wall(Mechdyne, 2008), flat panel-based wall (Jeong et al., 2006; Sandin et al., 2005; Sandstrom et al., 2003) or flat panel-based tabletop (Krumbholz et al., 2005). Two detailed reviews of recent progress on large displays can be found in (Wallace et al., 2005) and (Ni et al., 2006).

Vision-based gesture interaction methods have focused on the most dexterous part of the human body – the hand – so as to provide an intuitive means for human computer interaction (HCI). For a large number of applications that use large displays, these approaches can be especially advantageous compared to instrument-based counterparts under certain circumstances. For instance, interacting from-afar the screens will provide more freedom for the user to do arms-reach tasks. Similarly, during a tele-collaborative session, remote speaker's gestures can be automatically mapped to proper computer operation commands (e.g. playing forward or backward presentation slides), in this way the users' actions become intuitive and they need not resort to any additional devices. That said, gesture-based methods face a number of the performance challenges because of the requirements for low latency and high throughput needed for video processing. High latency causes lengthy response time and jeopardizes the user interactivity. On the other hand, low throughput forces the system to monitor a limited field of view, which in turn constrains the user's movement space.

A promising way to address the performance challenge is using scalable computing techniques to accelerate vision-based gesture interactions. This is based on the observation that large displays boast not only display size, but also computing power. The number of computer nodes in a cluster-driven large display system is usually considerable. In the mean time, the CPU performance of each node is growing exponentially with Moore's Law. For example, Varrier (Sandin et al., 2005), a 35-tile system uses an 18-node cluster. While Hyperwall (Sandstrom et al., 2003), a 49-tile system uses a 49-node cluster. In this section we describe the scalable computing techniques for vision-based gesture interaction that utilize the computing power inherent in cluster-driven displays. The processing of captured video frames from a single camera is parallelized by multiple nodes of the cluster. Consequently, we are able to achieve a lower processing latency and a higher processing throughput. When the user's hand is in the field of view of the camera, performance of predefined gestures is interpreted into interaction commands for the large display system. Figure 2 shows a prototypical vision-based gesture interface in use by a display wall, with the help of the proposed methods. Our work has three major contributions: first, it analyzes the task partitioning strategies for frame image scanning, a key task in both hand detection and gesture identification. By examining in detail the advantages and disadvantages of two strategies: by-region and by-scale, a hybrid strategy is developed by combining both of them. Furthermore, a novel data structure, named the scanning tree, is devised for computing nodes management. A load balancing algorithm for workload distribution across scanning tree nodes is also presented. Last but not least, implementation has been accomplished to incorporate the scalable computing techniques into a vision-based gesture interface for a ultra-high-resolution tiled display wall. Evaluation results show the effectiveness of our proposed techniques.

The rest of this section is organized as follows. Section 5.2 reviews related work in the existing literature. The by-region and by-scale task partitioning strategies are discussed in section 5.3. Based on the discussions, our final hybrid approach is presented. Section 5.4 describes the scanning tree data structure, together with the load balancing algorithm. Integration work of the prototypical vision-based gesture interface with the display wall is described in section 5.7. Section 5.8 illustrates the evaluation results which validate the effectiveness of the proposed techniques. At last, section 5.9 concludes the section.

5.2 Similar systems

Gesture-based HCI has been an active research topic for decades (Crowley et al., 2000; Kage et al., 1999). Due to hardware limitations, early systems used tethered mechanical or electromagnetic sensors to monitor hand gestures. For example, the MIT Media Room (Bolt, 1980) used an electromagnetical tracking sensor embedded in the wrist cuff to track spatial translation of the user's hand. The tracked gestures acted as an auxiliary control to move objects displayed on a projection screen. The CHARADE system (Baudel & Beaudouin-lafon, 1993) improved gesture detection by having the user wear a data glove. Finger segments positions reported by the glove are interpreted as gestures and then mapped to commands to control computerized objects. With the advances of camera hardware and CPU processing power, vision-based systems began to emerge for interaction with display systems. The early systems used simple features and could recognize a limited number of gestures. Freeman et al (Freeman & Weissman, 1995) used a video camera to detect hand movement. In their system only one hand gesture, i.e. the open hand facing the camera could be identified. By waving the hand from side to side, the user was able to remotely control the sound volume of a television. Segen et al (Segen & Kumar, 1998; 2000) constructed a two-camera system to extract the fingertips of a hand from video, applied reverse kinematics to derive an articulated hand model, and subsequently used the derived hand posture for gesture-commands interpretation. Their system was fast (60Hz) because only the fingertips needed to be tracked. However it was also prone to low accuracy since reverse kinematics compute multiple hand postures for the the same fingertip configuration, which leaded to ambiguous gesture interpretations. A comprehensive survey of these systems can be found in (Joseph J. LaViola, 1999).

Besides the images of the hand itself, projected hand shadows could also be utilized for the recognition of certain gestures. The Barehands system (Ringel, 2001) used infrared LED arrays to illuminate a translucent touch screen from the rear. When the user's hand touched the screen a camera (with infrared filter) captured the hand's shadow and translated it into gesture commands. Image processing for Barehand was not computationally intensive, averaged 13.37 ms per frame. However, the needs for a touch-screen and high-intensity infrared illumination limited its use for large displays needing interaction from-afar.

HandVu (Kolsch et al., 2004) is a vision-based gesture HCI developed by Kolsh et al. It allows real-time capturing and processing of VGA-quality video frames, from a HMD-mounted camera. HandVu is capable of working under different illumination conditions as well as with various image backgrounds. Not surprisingly, such advantages are gained at the price of computation-intensive image processing on multiple features: shape, color, optical flow, and motion constraints. HandVu employs MPI(Message Passing Interface)-based parallel processing for off-line model training but not for online video processing. To optimize online processing performance, it takes several trade-offs in the implementation. For example, hand presence is only detected in a sub-region of the camera's field of view to initiate the interaction. In the mean time, when running under asynchronous mode where response time is guaranteed, unprocessed frames are discarded when timed out in a wait queue.

Researchers at the University of Toronto investigated interaction with large displays with pen-based (Cao & Balakrishnan, 2003) and gesture-based techniques (Malik et al., 2006). The work presented in (Malik et al., 2006) was a vision-based bimanual interaction system, which used two 320×240 cameras to track the user's fingers on a touch pad of black background. The system mapped a rich set of gestural input on the touch pad to interaction commands for a large display. Although detailed performance data was not available from the paper, the authors discussed that frame processing time prevented the deployment of higher resolution cameras. As a consequence, some users' object-manipulation experiences were undermined.

It can be learned from (Kolsch et al., 2004) and (Malik et al., 2006) that the performance of a single computer has already been one of the bottlenecks deterring the deployment of computation-intensive image processing methods for vision-based gesture interaction systems. Our scalable techniques are designed to address this challenge. The proposed solution partitions the processing workload of each captured video frame across multiple cluster nodes. Through such approach, it effectively improves the system performance.

Our solution complements other research work in the literature that uses computer cluster to speed up image processing. In the RPV (Real-time Parallel Vision) programming environment (Arita et al., 2000), three low level cluster computing functionalities, namely data transfer, synchronization and error recovery are taken care of by the environment, and the user can use these functionalities directly instead of implement his/her own. An extension work called RPV-II (Arita & ichiro Taniguchi, 2001) introduces stream data transfer to RPV, thus the transmission latency is reduced. However, both RPV and RPV-II are only programming environments and put the responsibility on their users to design parallel algorithms for a specific computer vision application. A similar middleware is FlowVR (Allard & Raffin, 2006), which provides a data-flow model to encapsulate computation and I/O tasks for parallel image processing. Most recently, the GrImage platform (Allard et al., 2007) proposes a complete scalable vision architecture for real-time 3D modeling but not gesture interaction, which is the question to be addressed by this paper.

5.3 Design of task partitioning strategy

Vision-based gesture interaction can be modeled as a pipeline process that consists of four stages: detection, tracking, identification and interpretation. These stages can be disjointly sequential with each other or have overlaps depending on the specific system. Generally the pipeline runs as follows. First, *detection* senses the presence of the hand in the camera's field of view. *Tracking* is then conducted to monitor the hand position and report its spatial coordinates. Any user gesture that has matches an entry in the predefined gesture vocabulary is recognized by *identification*. As a final step, identified gestures are mapped to interaction commands through *interpretation*.

It would be impractical to devise a universal solution for all vision-based gesture HCI systems due to the large variety of implementations. To strike a balance between specificity and generality, we examine the group of systems that use template matching during the detection and identification stages. Such systems count for a considerable portion of the state-of-art vision-based gesture HCIs. In them each incoming frame from the camera is scanned to find possible matches with defined templates. If a match is found during the detection stage, the hand is regarded to be in the camera's field-of-view. Similarly, matches found during the identification stage are recognized as gestures performed by the user. From this point of view both the detection and identification stages can be abstracted to the same task of image scanning. The difference is that they might use distinct template databases. Section 5.3.1 elaborates on the image scanning task.

5.3.1 Analysis of the image scanning task

In the image scanning task, each sub-window of the frame image of the templates' size are compared with templates stored in the vocabulary database. If the similarity between the sub-window image and a template image satisfies a certain threshold, a template match is reported. To enumerate all sub-windows of the frame image, the task scans along X and Y dimensions in small steps until the whole image has been examined.

The size of the template remains constant once defined, but the size of the hand appearing in a frame image could vary dynamically with viewing depth. To address this, it is necessary for the image scanning task to do comparisons at multiple scales. Either the template or the captured image can be scaled for this purpose. Which one is scaled does not affect the overall computation complexity. Algorithm 1, which assumes that the captured frame image is scaled to multiple levels, illustrates an abstracted image scanning task.

Algorithm 1 shows that the image scanning task fulfills a group of comparisons between sub-windows of the captured frame image and the template. Because size of the template

Algorithm 1 An abstracted image scanning task

Input:
frame image: F.
template: T.
scanning translation steps: X_{step}, Y_{step}.
scanning start/stop scales: S_{start}, S_{stop}.
scanning scale step: S_{step}.

Output:
set of template matches: M.

1: $M \leftarrow \Phi$
2: $S \leftarrow S_{start}$
3: **while** $S < S_{stop}$ **do**
4: Scale F at S
5: $X \leftarrow 0$
6: $Y \leftarrow 0$
7: $W \leftarrow$ width of F at scale S
8: $H \leftarrow$ height of F at scale S
9: **while** $X < W$ **do**
10: **while** $Y < H$ **do**
11: Compare sub-window of F starting at (X, Y) with T
12: **if** there is a match **then**
13: Add the match into M
14: **end if**
15: $Y \leftarrow Y + Y_{step}$
16: **end while**
17: $X \leftarrow X + X_{step}$
18: **end while**
19: $S \leftarrow S + S_{step}$
20: **end whilereturn** M

is an invariant, processing load of each comparison (line 11 in Algorithm 1) is a constant. If this group of comparisons could be distributed evenly over multiple computing nodes, the image scanning task would be gracefully parallelized. In the next sections the two partitioning strategy candidates, by-region and by-scale, are discussed. The by-region strategy divides a frame image into multiple sub-regions, and assigns the processing of each sub-region to a computing node. The by-scale strategy assigns the processing of the whole frame image to computing nodes, but each of these nodes only handles certain scale levels.

5.3.2 The by-region choice

Figure 3 illustrates the principle of the by-region task partitioning strategy. Blocks of identical color indicate that they are processed by the same cluster node. With this strategy, a given cluster node is always assigned to process a fixed portion of the whole frame image, and processes this portion at all scales levels. For example, assuming that the frame image is captured at 640×480 resolution, and node A is assigned to process a sub-region with the corner coordinates to be [0, 0, 320, 240] (coordinates are in the form of

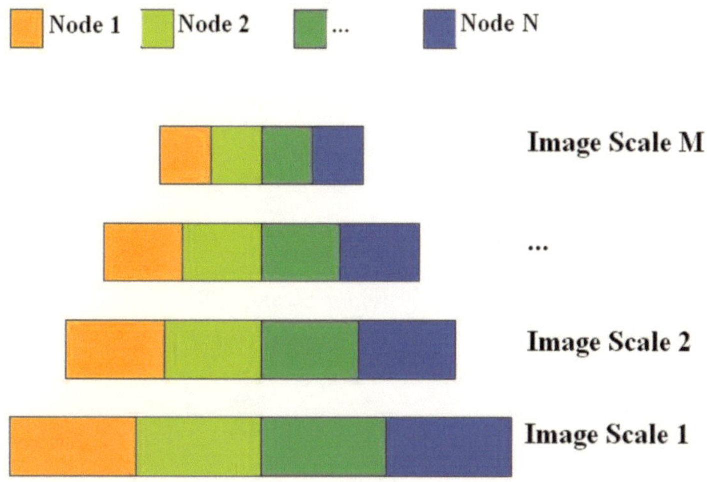

Fig. 3. Illustration of the by-region task partitioning strategy.

$[X_{left}, X_{right}, Y_{top}, Y_{bottom}]$) for the scanning scale of 1. When the scanning scale becomes 0.5, the frame image is reduced to 320×240, and the sub-region to which node A is assigned changes accordingly to $[0, 0, 160, 120]$.

One advantage of the by-region strategy is straightforward load balancing: as long as the sub-regions assigned to different cluster nodes are of same size, workload distribution will be theoretically even. However, this strategy is subject to the drawback of high processing overhead. To illustrate this, consider the situation where the hand appears in the image area that crosses two sub-regions. If the two sub-regions are disjoint, the appearance of the hand will be missed by the image scanning task, causing reduced detection and identification rates. Thus it is necessary for the sub-regions to overlap with each other to make sure that sub-region borders are properly taken care of. The size of the overlapped area is solely determined by the size of the template. In Equation 2, the quantitative measure $R_{overhead}$ is defined as the overhead ratio. $R_{overhead}$ is calculated as the ratio between the size of the sub-region that a cluster node actually has to process versus the sub-region size that is assigned to it[2]. Table 1 shows how the overhead ratio values grow at several representative scanning scales.

$$R_{overhead} = \frac{(W_{subregion} \times S + W_{template})(H_{subregion} \times S + H_{template})}{(W_{subregion} \times S) \times (H_{subregion} \times S)} \tag{2}$$

5.3.3 The by-scale choice

Figure 4 illustrates the principle of the by-scale task partitioning strategy. The same legends for Figure 3 are used here. With this strategy, all cluster nodes are assigned to process the whole frame image, but each with a different range of scanning scales. For instance, for an

[2] For simplicity reasons, boundary conditions are not discussed for all equations and algorithms listed in this section.

Scanning Scale	Overhead Ratio
0.2	211%
0.3	170%
0.4	151%
0.5	140%
0.6	133%
0.7	128%
0.8	124%
0.9	121%
1	119%

Table 1. Overhead Ratio vs. Scales for By-region Strategy
($W_{subregion} = 320, H_{subregion} = 240, W_{template} = 25, H_{template} = 25$)

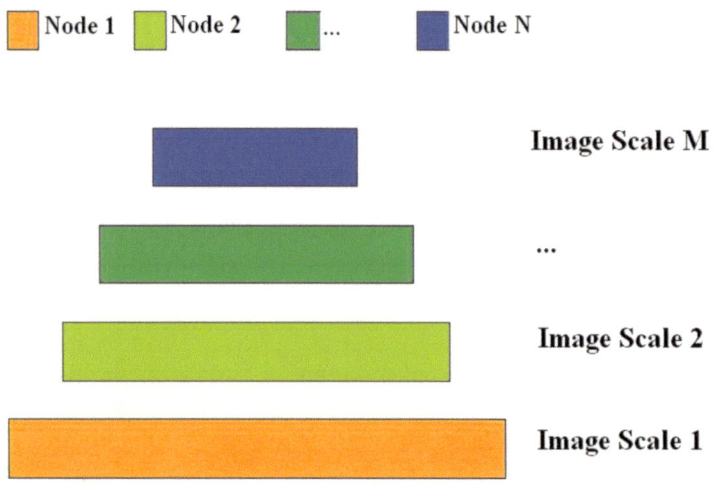

Fig. 4. Illustration of the by-scale task partitioning strategy.

image frame of 640 × 480 resolution, node A is assigned to process the scale levels within the range of 1-0.8. Node B is assigned to process the scale levels within the range of 0.7-0.5, and so on. The advantage of the by-scale strategy is that no processing overhead is introduced by sub-region overlapping, because each cluster node processes the whole image frame. However, there are unbalanced workloads at each image scale. When the image scanning task is performed at high scales, there are more sub-windows to compare. Consequently, the number of template comparisons is large. Similarly this number is small when the image scanning task is performed at a low scale. Because each template comparison takes the same amount of processing time, cluster nodes with different assigned scale ranges will have different workloads. Equation 3 presents the number of template comparisons needed at a given scanning scale S. With this equation, Table 2 shows that the number of comparisons needed increases at roughly the second order of the scanning scale. It is clear in the table that the highest number of comparisons (at scale 1.0) can be a magnitude higher than the lowest value (at scale 0.2).

Scanning Scale	Number of Comparisons
0.2	1219
0.3	3312
0.4	6430
0.5	10571
0.6	15736
0.7	21926
0.8	29138
0.9	37376
1	46638

Table 2. Number of Template Comparisons vs. Scales for By-scale Strategy ($W_{frame} = 640, H_{frame} = 480, W_{template} = 25, H_{template} = 25, X_{step} = 3, Y_{step} = 2$)

$$N_{comparison} = \frac{(W_{frame} \times S - W_{template})}{X_{step}} \times \frac{(H_{frame} \times S - H_{template})}{Y_{step}} \quad (3)$$

5.3.4 The final hybrid approach

Based on the previous discussions, it can be asserted that using either by-region or by-scale strategy alone will not be sufficient to achieve effective partitioning for the image scanning task. The by-region strategy creates high overhead for each single cluster node, and lowers the overall performance of parallel processing. On the other hand, the by-scale strategy overly engages the cluster nodes which scan at large scale levels, at the same time underly utilizes the cluster nodes which scan at small scale levels. The result is that parallel processing performance as a whole is affected.

We propose a hybrid approach that uses both by-region and by-scale task partitioning. The basic idea is to take advantage of the better load balancing inherent in by-region strategy, and lower the computation overhead, as much as possible, by exploiting the characteristics of by-scale strategy. More specifically, this approach works as follows:

- The captured image frame is distributed to all cluster nodes at the same level. Each cluster node is assigned to process the whole frame image at a single scale level, or within a certain scale level range.
- Scanning tasks at small scale levels, which are less computationally demanding, are grouped and assigned to a single cluster node. In this way the light workloads are aggregated to avoid under-utilized cluster nodes.
- A cluster node which has been assigned to scan at a large scale level further partitions its workload using the by-region strategy, and assigns the processing of sub-regions to next level cluster nodes.
- If the workload of scanning at a scale level is comparable to either aggregated small scanning scale levels or partitioned large scanning scales, it is assigned to a single cluster node.
- The partitioning process is repeated recursively until an optimized overall system performance is achieved.

Implementing this hybrid approach requires two additional components. The first component is a data structure that is capable of managing the cluster nodes involved in the image scanning task with a layered architecture, because the hybrid approach partitions workload at multiple levels. Therefore, a data structure called a scanning tree is designed to handle this need. The second is a load balancing algorithm based on the scanning tree data structure. This algorithm is responsible for fine tuning three configuration tasks in the hybrid approach: workload grouping for scanning at small scale levels, workload partitioning for scanning at large scale levels, and the determination of scale levels that need neither grouping nor further partitioning. Section 5.5 introduces the scanning tree and Section 5.6 the load balancing algorithm.

5.4 Node management and load balancing

Designing of the hybrid task partitioning strategy lays out the foundation for a concrete implementation. One part of the implementation is the formation of the underlying system, i.e. management of the cluster nodes. The other part of the implementation is the synergistic scheme, of which the the load balancing algorithm is a main component.

5.5 The scanning tree

In our solution the scanning tree data structure is designed to manage the cluster nodes for the image scanning task. Figure 5 gives a graphical presentation of this data structure. The scanning tree can have one or more levels. Every node of the tree represents a cluster node and is indexed with a unique key, which is the node's IP address. Each edge of the scanning tree maps to a dulplex network link between the two connected nodes.

A node of the scanning tree has two data attributes: scan_region and scale_range. The scan_region attribute is a quadruple $[X_{left}, X_{right}, Y_{top}, Y_{bottom}]$ that specifies the unscaled sub-region coordinates to be scanned in the frame image. The scale_range attribute is a triple $[S_{start}, S_{step}, S_{stop}]$ that denotes the start, step and stop of scanning scales performed by the node on its scan_region. To make these descriptions more intuitive, two examples are given below, assuming that the frame image is of resolution 640×480:

- Node A has the index "10.0.8.120" and the data attributes {scan_region: [0, 0, 640, 480], scale_range [1.0, 0, 1.0]}. This is a cluster node with an IP address 10.0.8.120 which scans the whole frame image, at the single scale value of 1.0.
- Node B has the index "10.0.8.121" and the data attributes {scan_region: [0, 0, 320, 240], scale_range [0.5, 0.1, 0.8]}. This is a cluster node with an IP address 10.0.8.121 which scans the upper left quarter portion of the frame image, at four scales 0.5, 0.6, 0.7 and 0.8.

Each node of the scanning tree does three jobs: distributing the frame image to its children (with the leaf nodes being exceptions); scanning the specified sub-region at the specified scale_range; and reporting to its parent (with the head node being an exception) any template matches found by the subtree headed by itself. Under this mechanism, starting from the head node, a frame image is passed to all the nodes of the scanning tree in a top-down fashion. In a reverse flow fashion, template match results are gathered in a bottom-up manner and eventually converge at the head node.

The workload of a scanning tree node is determined by its data attributes. These data attributes can be manually planned based on the principles described in section 5.3.4, or constructed by an automated process as described in the next section.

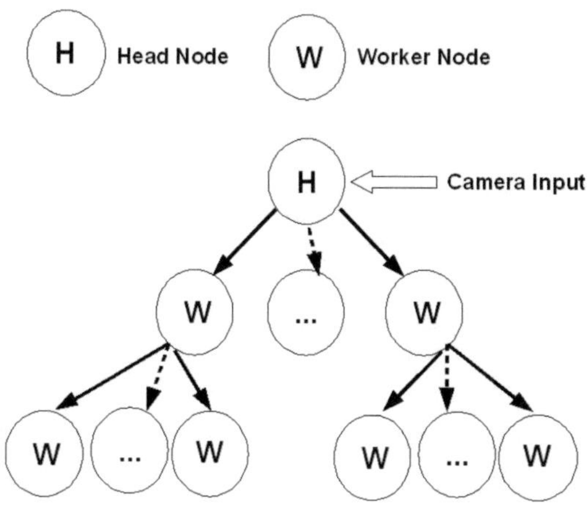

Fig. 5. The scanning tree.

5.6 Load balancing algorithm

Algorithm 2 automates the planning work for:

- **Construction of the scanning tree:** given a desired speedup P_{desire}, this algorithm constructs a scanning tree T_{scan}, the number of nodes in the scanning tree N_{nodes}, and an estimated best-effort speedup P_{est} to match P_{desire}.
- **Load balancing across the scanning tree nodes:** this algorithm distributes workload across scanning tree nodes as evenly as possible, using the hybrid task partitioning strategy.
- **Estimation of the communication costs:** this algorithm outputs the estimations for two communication costs: the cost at the head node C_{head} and the cost across the scanning tree $C_{overall}$. The unit of these costs is number of frame image copies transmitted.

Following the pseudo-code for Algorithm 2 below, the algorithm works as follows. It first calculates the number of template comparisons at each of the scanning scale values, and sums these numbers to get the total number of template comparisons needed for the image scanning task (lines 8-13). The template comparison numbers are then normalized as percentages of the totalled number. Besides the percentages array, an integral percentages array is also constructed, for each scanning scale value(lines 15-19). The classification of low, middle and high scanning scales is based on the desired speedup. According to the value of desired speedup, line 21 finds the value below which are treated as low scanning scales. Subsequently, line 22 finds the value beyond which are treated as high scanning scales. The values in-between fall into the category of middle scan scales. Once is classification is completed, the rest of the algorithm handles the processing for each class of scan scales respectively. All scanning scales in the low class are grouped to form a scan scale range. The first scanning scale in the middle class is handled by the head node. And the rest of each middle scanning scales is handled by a single node. For the processing of high scan scales, the by-region strategy is first applied and the algorithm is used recursively to construct a sub-tree for each high scanning scale (lines 34-36). Upon the creation of each tree node its workload is defined, through the scan_region and scale_range attributes. When the algorithm finishes, the image scanning task has been partitioned to nodes across the constructed scanning tree.

Algorithm 2 Scanning tree construction and load balancing

Input:
desired speedup: P_{desire}.
width and height of the image frame: W_{frame}, H_{frame}.
width and height of the template: $W_{template}$, $H_{template}$.
scanning translation steps: X_{step}, Y_{step}.
scanning start/stop scales: S_{start}, S_{stop}.
scanning scale step: S_{step}.

Output:
scanning tree: T_{scan}.
number of nodes in the scanning tree: N_{nodes}.
estimated speedup: P_{est}.
estimated communication cost at head node: C_{head}.
estimated communication cost across scanning tree: $C_{overall}$.

$T_{scan} \leftarrow \phi$
$N_{nodes} \leftarrow 0$
$P_{est} \leftarrow 0$
$C_{head} \leftarrow 0$
$C_{overall} \leftarrow 0$

Populate *Array_Scales* with scale values from S_{start} to S_{stop} at interval S_{step}, record the size of *Array_Scales* as *Len*
Zeros $Array\_N_{comparison}$ of size *Len*
$N_{total} \leftarrow 0$
for (i = 1 to *Len*) **do**
    Calculate $Array\_N_{comparison}[i]$ using Equation 3, with the parameters $Array\_Scales[i]$, W_{frame}, H_{frame}, $W_{template}$, $H_{template}$, X_{step}, Y_{step}
    $N_{total} \leftarrow N_{total} + Array\_N_{comparison}[i]$
end for

Zeros *Array_Pecentage, Array_Grouped_Pecentage* of size *Len*
for (i = 1 to *Len*) **do**
    $Array\_Pecentage[i] = Array\_N_{comparison}[i] / N_{total}$
    $Array\_Grouped\_Pecentage[i] = \Sigma(Array\_Pecentage[1:i])$
end for

5.7 Display wall integration

A gesture interface is implemented using the OpenCV computer vision library, with KLT feature-based template comparison. The implementation uses parallel frame image. A baseline implementation that does not use the scalable computing techniques is also implemented for evaluation purposes. The gesture interface is then integrated with an

Algorithm 2 Scanning tree construction and load balancing (continued)

Find the highest index I_{group} that satisfies $Array\_Grouped\_Pecentage[I_{group}] \leq 1/P$
Find the lowest index I_{split} that satisfies $Array\_Pecentage[I_{split}] \geq$ to $1/P$

Create $Node_{head}$ with scan region to be $[0,0,W_{frame},H_{frame}]$ and scanning scale value of $Array\_Scales[I_{group}+1]$
Add $Node_{head}$ to T_{scan} as head node

for ($i_{middle} = (I_{group}+2)$ to $(I_{split}-1)$) **do**
    Create a node $Node_{middle}$ with scan region to be $[0,0,W_{frame},H_{frame}]$ and scanning scale value of $Array\_Scales[i_{middle}]$. Add $Node_{middle}$ to T_{scan} as a child of the head node
end for

Create a node $Node_{group}$ with scan region to be $[0,0,W_{frame},H_{frame}]$ and scanning range of $[Array\_Scales[1], S_{step}, Array\_Scales[I_{group}]]$, add $Node_{group}$ to T_{scan} as a child of the head node
$P_{est} \leftarrow 1/Array\_Grouped\_Pecentage[I_{group}]$

for ($i_{split} = I_{split}$ to Len) **do**
    Use the by-region strategy to partition the processing at $Array\_Scales[i_{split}]$ into a sub-tree, add this subtree as a child to the head node of T_{scan}
end for

$N_{nodes} \leftarrow$ total number of nodes in T_{scan}
$C_{head} \leftarrow$ number of children of the head node in T_{scan}
$C_{overall} \leftarrow$ total number of edges in T_{scan}
    return $T_{scan}, N_{nodes}, P_{est}, C_{head}, C_{overall}$

ultra-high-resolution tiled display wall. The wall has 55 LCD screen tiles, and is driven by a 32-node cluster. Each node in the cluster has a 64bit architecture with two 2GHz AMD processors and 4GB RAM. Nodes are interconnected with gigabit network interfaces. An open source high performance graphics streaming middleware SAGE (Jeong et al., 2006) is used by the display wall for frame rendering and UI management.

Hardware integration is performed as follows. The head node of the computer cluster is connected to a Dragonfly camera (Pointgrey Research Inc). The Dragonfly captures frame image at 640×480 resolution, 30 Hz rate and 8-bit gray scale. All nodes in the computer cluster participate visualization, coordinated by SAGE. A subset of them are used for the gesture interface under the management of a scanning tree. Regardless of the number of nodes in the scanning tree, it always uses the cluster head node as its head node. Communications among the scanning tree nodes are handled by the open source library QUANTA (He et al., 2003).

On the software integration side, the gesture interface runs as a standalone application, independent of the SAGE middleware. Interprocess communication using socket connection is setup between the gesture interface and SAGE. Whenever a user gesture is identified, the interface sends an interaction command to SAGE. SAGE then performs corresponding 2D window manipulation operations based on the interaction command. With this collaboration

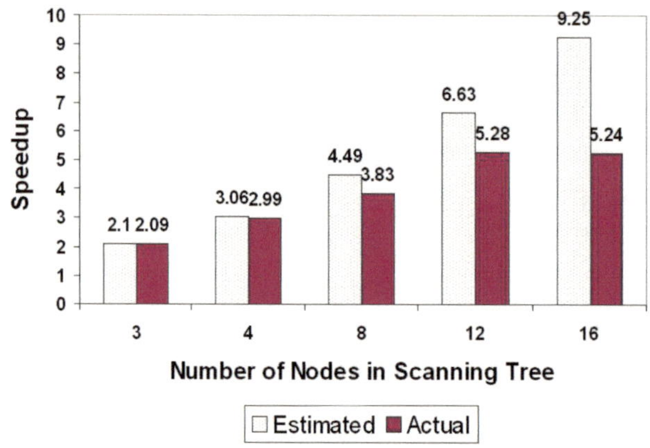

Fig. 6. Estimated vs. Actual Speedup Values.

the user can move, resize and close application windows displayed on the wall using free-hand gestures, as shown in Figure 2.

5.8 Evaluation results

A set of experiments are conducted with the gesture interface to evaluate the scalable computing techniques. These experiments measure three groups of metrics: speedup values under different scanning tree configurations, workload balance across nodes in the scanning tree, as well as performance impacts to the graphics streaming.

5.8.1 Speedup

Using the desired speedup values of 2.0, 3.0, 4.0, 6.0 and 9.0, algorithm 2 constructs five scanning trees. The node numbers in these trees are 3, 4, 8, 12 and 16 respectively. The estimated speedup values are 2.1, 3.06, 4.49, 6.63 and 9.25.

The times taken for frame image scanning during the detection and identification stages are profiled in the gesture interface. Same profiling are performed in the baseline implementation. Speedup values are obtained by calculating the ratio of averaged baseline processing times for image scanning over the counterpart in parallelized processing. Figure 6 shows the actual speedup values measured for the five scanning tree configurations described above. The measured speedup values are very close to the estimations for the 3-, 4- and 8-node scanning trees (difference is within 20%). For 12- and 16-node scanning trees the discrepancies are relatively large. This is mainly due to the increased communication cost during parallel processing. Communication costs are not taken into account in Algorithm 2. This fact leads to estimation errors.

5.8.2 Load balancing

Figure 7 illustrates the workload distribution estimated by the load balancing algorithm and the actual measured numbers, over a an 8-node scanning tree. Note the difference in units used by the top and bottom plots of figure 7. The estimated numbers are represented as the percentages of processing amount at all nodes against the processing amount of baseline

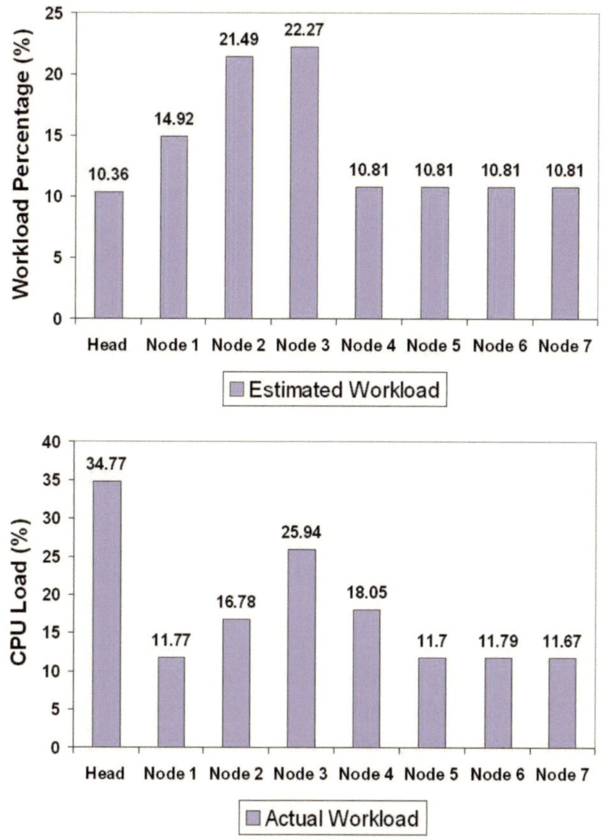

Fig. 7. Estimated and actual workload distributions across a 8-node scanning tree. Note that the units used by top and bottom plots are different.

implementation. In the mean time, the actual workload values are measured as average CPU load recorded at each of the nodes. Although the numbers in the top and bottom plots are not directly comparable, it can be seen that the actual workload distribution roughly follows the estimated outcome, with the exception at the head node. The larger readings at the head node is because that CPU load is measured as a whole for the gesture interface. Besides the work of image scanning, the head node is also in charge of video capturing, whose CPU usage is not easily separated when doing application-level profiling.

5.8.3 Performance impacts

Because the gesture interface shares the same computing resources with the SAGE middleware, its impact on the graphics streaming performance of SAGE is of interest. This experiment is conducted by running the OpenGL "Atlantis" application over SAGE, with the application window covering 20 display tiles. The profiling tools that come with SAGE is used to measure its display bandwidth and display frame rate. The display bandwidth reflects SAGE data throughput, which is calculated as the product of number of frames streamed in unit time and the data size of each frame. The display frame rate indicates the update rate

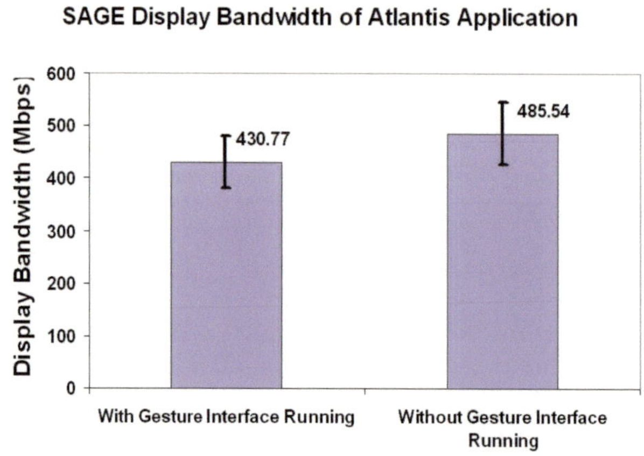

Fig. 8. Display bandwidths of the SAGE middleware, with and without the gesture interface running.

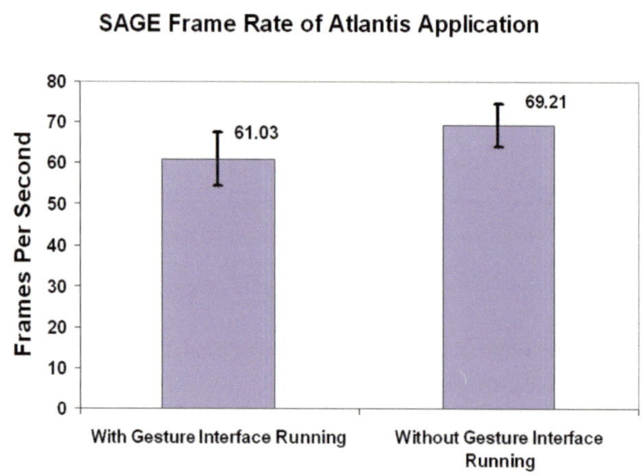

Fig. 9. Frame Rates of the SAGE middleware, with and without the gesture interface running.

SAGE could maintain across the display wall. Two conditions are tested, i.e. with and without the gesture interface running. For the "with gesture interface running" condition, a 12-node scanning tree is used for parallel processing. The nodes of the scanning tree belong to a subset of the nodes that drive the 20 LCD tiles where "Atlantis" is displayed.

Figure 8 shows the side-by-side comparison results of SAGE display bandwidth under two conditions. Without gesture interface in place, the display bandwidth is $485.54 \pm 59.74 Mbps$. While with gesture interface running, the display bandwidth is $430.77 \pm 49.84 Mbps$. Display bandwidth drops by 11% when the gesture interface is active. Similar results on display frame rates can be seen in figure 9. Without the gesture interface active the frame rate is 69.21 ± 5.26. With gesture interface active, frame rate becomes 61.03 ± 6.44. The frame rate decrease is about 12%. Considering the gain of a five-fold speedup for gesture detection and recognition, the performance impacts to graphics streaming are relatively insignificant.

5.9 Results discussion

This section explores the techniques to utilize the computing power of cluster-driven large displays to alleviate the performance needs for vision-based gesture interaction. It makes three contributions: 1) an analysis of the task partitioning choices, which leads to the proposition of a hybrid strategy, 2) the scanning tree data structure together with the load balancing algorithm, and 3) implementation and evaluation of the integration with a real system. Experimental results show that the proposed techniques are effective and exhibits promising speedup, estimation accuracy and performance impact metrics. To our best knowledge, this section is the first to address scalable gesture interaction for large display systems.

The solution presented can be applied to a broader range of computer vision interfaces beyond gesture-based systems, such as silhouette tracking. Being at the application-level, it is also feasible to be stacked on programming environment-level parallelization techniques and achieve further performance gains.

Presently communication factors, such as latency, overhead and bandwidth are not explicitly addressed in system modeling. As can be seen in section 5.8, this limitation can cause considerable estimation inaccuracy when data distribution is intensive. One extension could be the addition of several communication parameters in the LogP model (Culler et al., 1993) into the solution design. We leave it as a future work.

6. Conclusions and discussions

In this chapter we presented our work to enhance mobile AR system performance with a novel computing paradigm, named Cloud-Mobile Convergence (CMC). The design principle and philosophy of CMC is introduced, and several sample scenarios to put this paradigm into practical use are discussed. We also described in detail a real life application which adopts CMC paradigm. As a meta computing method, CMC exhibits potentials to be used in a wide range of mobile AR systems.

It should be pointed out that the research of using CMC for AR applications is still in its growing age. Solutions to some interesting problems remain largely unexplored. One of these problems is how to discover the cloud-based resources and configure the collaboration relationship between the mobile device and its cloud environment in an automated fashion. Up to now we always assumed that the mobile device had obtained information about its environment before conducting computation using CMC paradigm. We also assumed that the cloud-based resources were ready to be utilized as soon as requested by the mobile device. Both assumptions were simplified and might not be true under real world circumstances. For this, some well-established discovery and auto-configuration protocols, software implementations and standards may be integrated into a CMC application. Examples of such protocols, implementations and standards include Apple Inc's Bonjour (Apple, 2005), UPnP Forum's UPnP (UPnP, 2011), and Qualcomm Inc's AllJoyn (Qualcomm, 2011), to name just a few.

Another problem is inter-operability across heterogenous systems. When mobile device is collaborating with its cloud environment, they need to work out a solution to address possible heterogeneities at the levels of operating system, application programming interface, data format, and many others. To deal with the OS and API discrepancies, inter-process communication methods such as RPC (Remote Procedure Call) may be useful. While data format differences need to be solved by techniques like interpretation middleware and application gateway. The importance of unification and standardization has been realized by the community, but to be able to get some real progresses there are still long roads to go.

In a broader sense, CMC paradigm belongs to the field of collaboration computing, and people had split views on collaborative computing. User experience had long been a controversial topic in the debates. Proponents argued that the performance gains collaborative computing brought to the table helped to achieve better user satisfaction. While the opponents believed that the discontinuity in service quality actually hampered user experience and so that collaborative computing would not be preferred by the mass users. With all these opinions said, there haven't been decisive and convincing evidences for either side found in the literature. To concretely evaluate the users' preference of CMC paradigm, extensive user study and human factors experiments should be conducted. We leave this as a potential future direction of the follow-up work.

Optimization using hybrid approaches, involving the CMC paradigm and methods discussed in section 2 would also be an interesting direction to explore. What if we reduce the computing problem complexity on the mobile device to get coarse tracking results, and refine it with the reminder of the computing task done outside of the device? What if we unify the parameter tuning both internal and external of the device, and make the cloud-based resources scheduling part of the parameter tuning process? Such hybrid approaches might very likely open new avenues to the performance improvement challenges. We will keep polishing the CMC paradigm to reflect the new findings and improvements.

7. References

Allard, J., Ménier, C., Raffin, B., Boyer, E. & Faure, F. (2007). Grimage: Markerless 3d interactions, *Proceedings of ACM SIGGRAPH 07*, San Diego, USA. Emerging Technology.

Allard, J. & Raffin, B. (2006). Distributed physical based simulations for large vr applications, *IEEE Virtual Reality Conference*, Alexandria, USA.

Apple (2005). Bonjour, http://www.apple.com/support/bonjour/, last accessed June 2011.

Arita, D., Hamada, Y., Yonemoto, S. & ichiro Taniguchi, R. (2000). Rpv: A programming environment for real-time parallel vision - specification and programming methodology, *IPDPS '00: Proceedings of the 15 IPDPS 2000 Workshops on Parallel and Distributed Processing*, Springer-Verlag, London, UK, pp. 218–225.

Arita, D. & ichiro Taniguchi, R. (2001). Rpv-ii: A stream-based real-time parallel vision system and its application to real-time volume reconstruction, *ICVS '01: Proceedings of the Second International Workshop on Computer Vision Systems*, Springer-Verlag, London, UK, pp. 174–189.

Baudel, T. & Beaudouin-lafon, M. (1993). Charade: Remote control of objects using free-hand gestures, *Communications of the ACM* 36: 28–35.

Bay, H., Tuytelaars, T. & Gool, L. V. (2006). Surf: Speeded up robust features, *In ECCV*, pp. 404–417.

Bolt, R. A. (1980). Put-that-there: Voice and gesture at the graphics interface, *SIGGRAPH '80: Proceedings of the 7th annual conference on Computer graphics and interactive techniques*, ACM, New York, NY, USA, pp. 262–270.

Cao, X. & Balakrishnan, R. (2003). Visionwand: interaction techniques for large displays using a passive wand tracked in 3d, *UIST '03: Proceedings of the 16th annual ACM symposium on User interface software and technology*, ACM, New York, NY, USA, pp. 173–182.

Crowley, J. L., Coutaz, J. & Berard, F. (2000). Perceptual user interfaces: things that see, *ACM Communications* 43(3): 54–58.

Culler, D., Karp, R., Patterson, D., Sahay, A., Schauser, K. E., Santos, E., Subramonian, R. & von Eicken, T. (1993). Logp: towards a realistic model of parallel computation, *SIGPLAN Not.* 28(7): 1–12.

DiVerdi, S., Wither, J. & Hollerei, T. (2008). Envisor: Online environment map construction for mixed reality, *Virtual Reality Conference, 2008. VR '08. IEEE*, pp. 19 –26.

Fragoso, V., Gauglitz, S., Zamora, S., Kleban, J. & Turk, M. (2011). Translatar: A mobile augmented reality translator, *IEEE Workshop on Applications of Computer Vision (WACV'11)*, Kona, Hawaii.

Freeman, W. T. & Weissman, C. D. (1995). Television control by hand gestures, *International Workshop on Automatic Face and Gesture Recognition*, pp. 179–183.

Harris, C. & Stephens, M. (1988). A combined corner and edge detector, *Proceedings of the 4th Alvey Vision Conference*, pp. 147–151.

He, E., Alimohideen, J., Eliason, J., Krishnaprasad, N. K., Leigh, J., Yu, O. & DeFanti, T. A. (2003). Quanta: a toolkit for high performance data delivery over photonic networks, *Future Generation Computer Systems* 19(6): 919–933.

Jeong, B., Renambot, L., Jagodic, R., Singh, R., Aguilera, J., Johnson, A. & Leigh, J. (2006). High-performance dynamic graphics streaming for scalable adaptive graphics environment, *Supercomputing '06*, IEEE Computer Society, Los Alamitos, CA, USA, pp. 24–32.

Joseph J. LaViola, J. (1999). A survey of hand posture and gesture recognition techniques and technology, *Technical report*, Providence, RI, USA.

Kage, H., Tanaka, K., Kyuma, K., Weissman, C. D., Freeman, W. T., Freeman, W. T., Beardsley, P. A. & Beardsley, P. A. (1999). Computer vision for computer interaction, *ACM SIGGRAPH Computer Graphics* 33: 65–68.

Kolsch, M., Turk, M., HÃllerer, T. & Chainey, J. (2004). Vision-based interfaces for mobility, *In Intl. Conference on Mobile and Ubiquitous Systems (MobiQuitous)*.

Krumbholz, C., Leigh, J., Johnson, A., Renambot, L. & Kooima, R. (2005). Lambda table: High resolution tiled display table for interacting with large visualizations, *Proceedings of Workshop for Advanced Collaborative Environments (WACE) 2005*.

Lee, T. & Hollerer, T. (2007). Handy ar: Markerless inspection of augmented reality objects using fingertip tracking, *Proceedings of the 2007 11th IEEE International Symposium on Wearable Computers*, IEEE Computer Society, Washington, DC, USA, pp. 1–8.
URL: *http://dl.acm.org/citation.cfm?id=1524303.1524850*

Lowe, D. G. (2004). Distinctive image features from scale-invariant keypoints, *Int. J. Comput. Vision* 60: 91–110.

Luo, X. & Kenyon, R. (2009). Scalable vision-based gesture interaction for cluster-driven high resolution display systems, *Virtual Reality Conference, 2009. VR 2009. IEEE*, pp. 231 –232.

Malik, S., Ranjan, A. & Balakrishnan, R. (2006). Interacting with large displays from a distance with vision-tracked multi-finger gestural input, *SIGGRAPH '06: ACM SIGGRAPH 2006 Sketches*, ACM, New York, NY, USA, p. 5.

Mechdyne (2008). Powerwall, http://www.mechdyne.com/, last accessed September 2008.

Ni, T., Schmidt, G., Staadt, O., Livingston, M., Ball, R. & May, R. (2006). A survey of large high-resolution display technologies, techniques, and applications, *Proceedings of IEEE Virtual Reality 2006*, pp. 223–236.

Ozuysal, M., Fua, P. & Lepetit, V. (2007). Fast keypoint recognition in ten lines of code, *Computer Vision and Pattern Recognition, 2007. CVPR '07. IEEE Conference on*, pp. 1 –8.

Qualcomm (2011). Alljoyn, https://www.alljoyn.org/, last accessed June 2011.

Ringel, M. (2001). Barehands: implement-free interaction with a wall-mounted display, *ACM CHI*, Press, pp. 367–368.

Rosten, E. & Drummond, T. (2003). Rapid rendering of apparent contours of implicit surfaces for realtime tracking, *British Machine Vision Conference*, pp. 719–728.

Rosten, E. & Drummond, T. (2005). Fusing points and lines for high performance tracking., *IEEE International Conference on Computer Vision*, Vol. 2, pp. 1508–1511.

Sandin, D. J., Margolis, T., Ge, J., Girado, J., Peterka, T. & DeFanti, T. A. (2005). The varrier autostereoscopic virtual reality display, *SIGGRAPH '05: ACM SIGGRAPH 2005 Papers*, ACM, New York, NY, USA, pp. 894–903.

Sandstrom, T. A., Henze, C. & Levit, C. (2003). The hyperwall, *CMV '03: Proceedings of the conference on Coordinated and Multiple Views In Exploratory Visualization*, IEEE Computer Society, Washington, DC, USA, p. 124.

Segen, J. & Kumar, S. (1998). Gesture vr: vision-based 3d hand interace for spatial interaction, *MULTIMEDIA '98: Proceedings of the sixth ACM international conference on Multimedia*, ACM, New York, NY, USA, pp. 455–464.

Segen, J. & Kumar, S. (2000). Look ma, no mouse!, *ACM Communications* 43(7): 102–109.

Shi, J. & Tomasi, C. (1994). Good features to track, *1994 IEEE Conference on Computer Vision and Pattern Recognition (CVPR'94)*, pp. 593 – 600.

Taylor, C. & Pasquale, J. (2010). Towards a Proximal Resource-based Architecture to Support Augmented Reality Applications, *Proceedings of the Workshop on Cloud-Mobile Convergence for Virtual Reality (CMCVR)*, Waltham, MA.

Terriberry, T. B., French, L. M. & Helmsen, J. (2008). Gpu accelerating speeded-up robust features.

UPnP (2011). Upnp, http://www.upnp.org/, last accessed June 2011.

Wagner, D., Schmalstieg, D. & Bischof, H. (2009). Multiple target detection and tracking with guaranteed framerates on mobile phones, *ISMAR*, pp. 57–64.

Wallace, G., Anshus, O. J., Bi, P., Chen, H., Chen, Y., Clark, D., Cook, P., Finkelstein, A., Funkhouser, T., Gupta, A., Hibbs, M., Li, K., Liu, Z., Samanta, R., Sukthankar, R. & Troyanskaya, O. (2005). Tools and applications for large-scale display walls, *IEEE Computer Graphics and Applications* 25(4): 24–33.

Wu, C. (2007). SiftGPU: A GPU implementation of scale invariant feature transform (SIFT), `http://cs.unc.edu/~ccwu/siftgpu`.

4

Augmented Reality for Restoration/Reconstruction of Artefacts with Artistic or Historical Value

Giovanni Saggio[1] and Davide Borra[2]
[1]*University of Rome "Tor Vergata"*
[2]*No Real, Virtuality & New Media Applications*
Italy

1. Introduction

The artistic or historical value of a structure, such as a monument, a mosaic, a painting or, generally speaking, an artefact, arises from the novelty and the development it represents in a certain field and in a certain time of the human activity. The more faithfully the structure preserves its original status, the greater its artistic and historical value is. For this reason it is fundamental to preserve its original condition, maintaining it as genuine as possible over the time. Nevertheless the preservation of a structure cannot be always possible (for traumatic events as wars can occur), or has not always been realized, simply for negligence, incompetence, or even guilty unwillingness. So, unfortunately, nowadays the status of a not irrelevant number of such structures can range from bad to even catastrophic.

In such a frame the current technology furnishes a fundamental help for reconstruction/ restoration purposes, so to bring back a structure to its original historical value and condition. Among the modern facilities, new possibilities arise from the Augmented Reality (AR) tools, which combine the Virtual Reality (VR) settings with real physical materials and instruments.

The idea is to realize a virtual reconstruction/restoration before materially acting on the structure itself. In this way main advantages are obtained among which: the manpower and machine power are utilized only in the last phase of the reconstruction; potential damages/abrasions of some parts of the structure are avoided during the cataloguing phase; it is possible to precisely define the forms and dimensions of the eventually missing pieces, etc. Actually the virtual reconstruction/restoration can be even improved taking advantages of the AR, which furnish lots of added informative parameters, which can be even fundamental under specific circumstances. So we want here detail the AR application to restore and reconstruct the structures with artistic and/or historical value.

2. Reality vs. Virtuality

With the *Virtuality-Reality Continuum* is intended a scale ranging from a complete real world to a complete virtual world, passing through intermediate positions (Fig. 1, Milgram &

Kishino, 1994). So we can refer to *Reality* or *Real Environment* (*RE*), *Augmented Reality* (*AR*), *Augmented Virtuality* (*AV*), *Virtual Environment* (*VE*) or *Virtuality* or *Virtual Reality* (*VR*). Intuitively the *RE* is defined as the world how is perceived by our senses, and the *VE* defines totally constructed or reconstructed scenario with computers. The intermediate values of the scale are generally referred as *Mixed Reality* (*MR*), which can be made with different "percentages" of reality vs. virtuality.

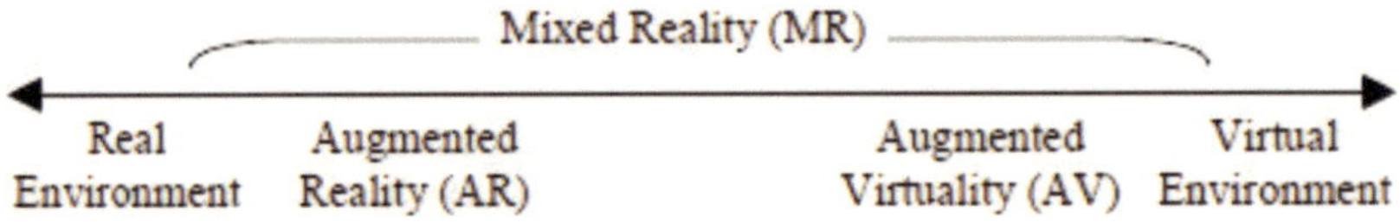

Fig. 1. Virtuality-Reality Continuum.

So, *AV* refers to scenarios where the virtual part is predominant, but where the physical parts (real objects, real subjects) are integrated too, with the possibility for them to dynamically interact with the virtual world (preferably in real-time), so the scenarios to be considered as "immersive" as, for instance, a "Cave Automatic Virtual Environment" can be (Cruz-Neira et al., 1992).

On the other hand, the term *AR* refers to scenarios where the real part is predominant, for which artificial information about the environment and its objects are overlaid on the real world, thanks to a medium such as a computer, a smart phone, or a simply TV screen, so additional information directly related to what we are seeing are easily obtained (see Fig. 2 as an example).

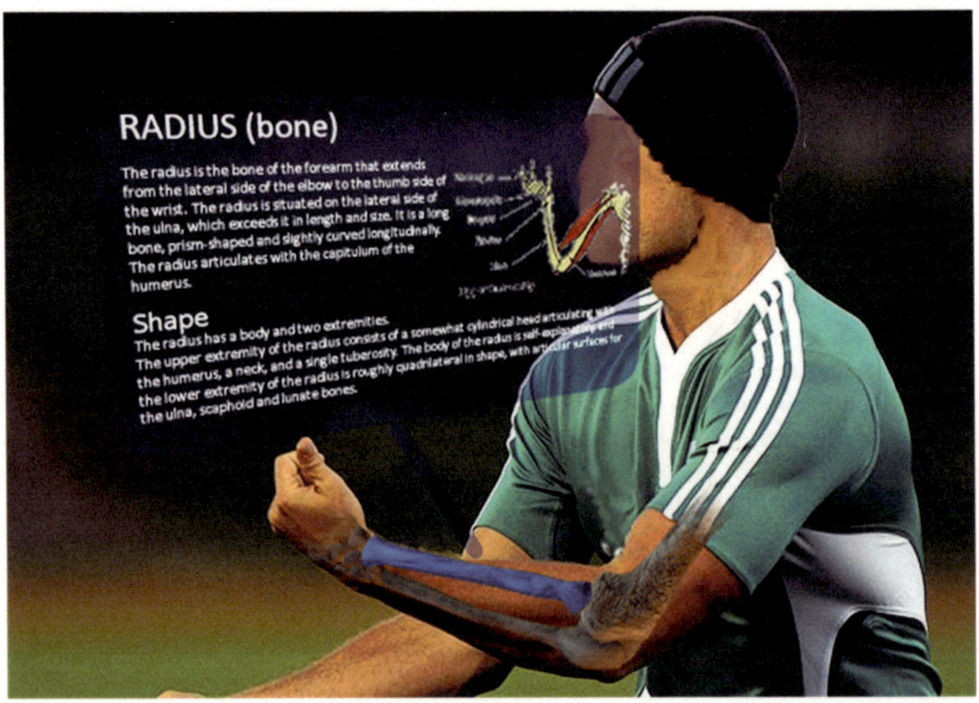

Fig. 2. Virtual information overlaid on a real image.

2.1 The reconstruction/restoration cycle

Generally speaking the *VR* can be "self consistent", in a sense that some virtual scenario remain within its boundaries and utilized as such, let's think about some playstation's games for instance. On the contrary, when we deal with restoration and/or reconstruction of architectural heritages or historical artefacts, it is commonly adopted a criteria for which the Virtuality-Reality Continuum is crossed (see Fig. 3). This happens in the sense that we start from the real status of matters (RE step), perform the analysis of the current status (*AR* step), run a virtual restoration/reconstruction of artefacts and materials (*AV* step) and produce a complete virtual representation of reconstructed scenario (*VE* step). All of these steps are finalized to accurately describe, analyze and indicate the exact passages to be executed in reality to obtain the best possible operational results.

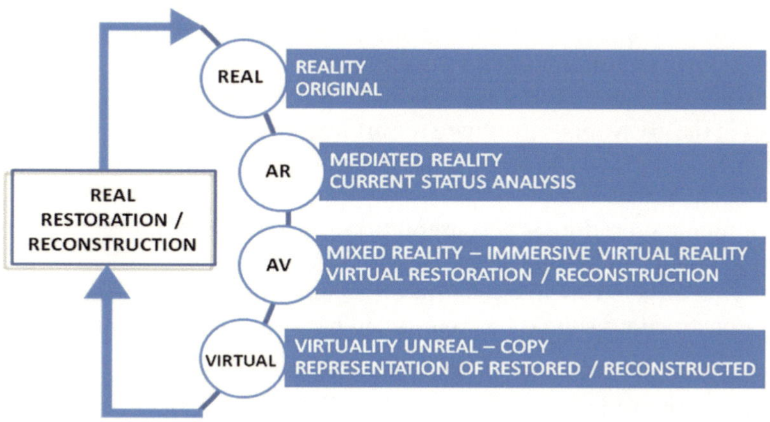

Fig. 3. V-R Continuum, and the flow diagram for architectural heritages reconstruction/restoration.

At first glance, the concept to operate in reality passing through the virtuality seems to be not so practical. After all we change our domain (the reality) for another one (the virtuality) but with the final aim to return to the starting one (the reality). Conversely to cross the Virtuality-Reality Continuum offers some advantages discussed in a while.

We can report a similar occurrence in the electronic field, for which the circuital analysis, necessary in the *time* domain, is realized in the *frequency* domain and then returning to the *time* as an independent variable. This way of proceeding is applied because of its advantages (less time consuming procedures, algorithms with minor complexity, filters which can be more easily implemented).

The idea to exploit the potentialities of the VR and AR domains in archaeology is not new. Examples come from "Geist" (Ursula et al., 2001) and "Archeoguide" projects (Vassilios et al., 2001; Vlahakis et al., 2002). The first allows the users to see the history of the places while walking in the city, and was tested in the Heidelberg castle. The second wants to create a system to behave like an electronic guide during the tours made by the visitors in cultural sites, and was used in the archaeological site of Olympia in Greece. After these early examples, many other projects come in the latest years, as the one that regards a virtual exploration of underwater archaeological sites (Haydar et al., 2010).

But we want here point out that the AR can be successfully used for restoration and/or reconstruction purposes, so can play an *active role*, rather than be utilized for mere tutorial reasons, so to be confined in a *passive part*. To this aim, it is really useful to start from the mere real side of the problem, to cross the Virtuality-Reality Continuum, passing through *AR* and *AV*, till the mere virtual side, and to come back to the origin, as already stressed. This is for several reasons:

- restoration and/or reconstruction time can be reduced;
- the costs for restoration and/or reconstruction can be reduced: manpower and machinery are utilized only at the real final step, so even the energy consumption is saved;
- some potential breakages or risk of destruction of the archeological, often fragile but valuable, artifacts to be restored and/or reconstructed can be avoided;
- some potential abrasions/changes in colors of the artifacts can be avoided;
- it is possible to establish forms and dimensions of the parts which are eventually incomplete so to rebuilt the artifact in an exact manner;
- it is possible to assemble the artifacts without damage its remains and even cause damages in the excavation site where the artifact was found;
- it is possible to preview the possibilities of assembling more easily, reducing errors and the time spent in those tasks;
- the 3D scanning procedure is also useful to create a database, for cataloging reasons, for tourism promotion aims, for comparison studies, etc.;
- in cases where the structural stability of a monument is not in danger, nonintrusive visual reconstructions should be preferred to physical reconstruction;

and so on.

VR played an *active role* in a project concerning the recovery of some artifacts that were buried in the Museum of the Terra Cotta Warriors and Horses, Lin Tong, Xi'an, China (Zheng & Li, 1999). Another example comes from a project to assemble a monument, like the Parthenon at the Acropolis of Athens (Georgios et al., 2001), for which one of the motivation to utilize the VR was the size and height of the blocks and the distance between one block and a possible match, so VR helps the archaeologists in reconstructing monuments or artifacts avoiding the manual test of verifying if a fragment match with another.

Archaeologists can spend even several weeks drawing plans and maps, taking notes and pictures of the archaeological findings. But VR offers systems to create a 3D reconstruction by simply take several pictures by which it is possible to get a 3D model of the artifacts (Pollefeys et al., 2003).

Among all the possibilities, we want here to point out that VR and, especially, AR can furnish a further meaningful help if joined with Human-Computer Interaction (HMI) possibilities. To do so, we will further detail new acquisition systems capable to measure human movements and translating them into actions, useful for the user to virtually interact with an AR scenario where archaeological artifacts are visualized (see paragraphs 4.3 and 4.4).

2.2 The models

In addition to the previous flow diagram regarding the restoration cycle (Fig. 3), it makes sense to define also the evolving situation of the artefacts to be restored during that cycle. So we can distinguish: *original*, *state*, *restoration*, and *reconstruction* models.

The *original* model concerns the parts of the monument, mosaic, painting, ancient structures,.. or, generally speaking, artefacts, which survive intact today without being subjected to tampering, just as they were in the past.

The *state* model just regards the current situation of the artefacts, with its *original* model but after being integrated with "addictions".

The *restoration* model consists of the *original* model with manual interventions of addictions of what has been destroyed over time, so to bring back the artefacts to their native status.

The *reconstruction* model is defined when we are not limited to "simply" manual intervention of "addictions", because of so little remains that even an *original* model is difficult to define. So the interventions are quite addressed to built something almost from beginning, taking account only of really "skinny" original parts of the artefact.

So, *restoration* model can be visualized for the *Colosseum* (also known as *Coliseum*) originally the *Flavian Amphitheatre* in the centre of the city of Rome (Italy), while *reconstruction* model is for the Jewish Second Temple practically destroyed by the Roman legions under Titus.

The *restoration* and *reconstruction* models can be realized by means of mixed reality in the V-R continuum.

3. AR applications

We know pretty well that the AR term refers to the fact that a viewer observes a view of the real world upon which is superimposed computer generated graphics. But the viewer can have a direct view of the real world, or can experience a mediated observation of the reality via video coupling or, finally, can experience an observation of post-processing real images. We will refer to this latter case. Being not completely virtual and not fully real, AR has quite extreme requirements to be suitably adopted. But its great potentiality makes AR both an interesting and challenging subject from scientific and business perspectives.

At one side we have the reality, or its digital representation (which we understand as real data), and at the other we have a system of representation of such a form of informative multimedia database (the digital information). The connection between these two worlds is the geo-referentiation, understood in a broad sense, that is the need to place the information coherently upon the data element, in the three-dimensional space.

The information can be represented in various shapes: a written text, floating windows with images, graphics, videos or other multimedia item, or rendering of the 3D virtual reconstruction, mono or stereoscopic, generated in a real time by trough a virtual model.

The contributions can come from specific files "*ad hoc*" prepared, structured database, search engines or blog generated by users. The databases can be off-line or on-line. The AR applications can restrict the user in exploring the informative setting by using the eyes movement (directly or through a device) or in offering different interactions, some of which we later detail according to our experiences, that allow to choose among the informative set available.

The geo-referencing can be accomplished by GPS detectors (outdoor), position/motion tracking systems (indoor), until the simplest recognising shaping system based on graphic markers framed by a webcam (AR desktop).

Although AR is usually used to identify a strongly oriented images technology, its general sense is the benchmark also for the description of the audio or tactile/haptic AR experiences.

The virtual audio panorama generation, the geo-places audio notice and the virtual strengthening of the tact, have to be included in the general AR discipline; these aspects play an important and innovative role for the CH improvement. Therefore, the overall added value of this technology is the contextualization of real data and virtual information, and that value increases because of two main factors: the real-time interaction and the multi-dimensionality.

With real-time interaction, we can understand both the need to have a visual rendering at 25fps, to ensure a good visual exploration of the real/virtual space and also the ability to make queries and actions in the informative database so that determine changes in a status of the system (human in the loop).

For example, if an architect could choose the maximum and minimum values of a static deformation's map of a facade of a historic building under restoration (derived from a real-time simulation), and if the results of this query will be visible superimposed on this facade, certainly would be a better understanding of the variables to control to make decisions.

Within this frame, the multi-dimensionality furnish an improvement, leading to the possibility to use images in stereoscopy (or stereophony/holophony, the third dimension anyway) and to scroll the information displayed along the time (the fourth dimension). In paragraph 4.2 we will furnish some new elements that we experienced in our labs.

These technological extensions become strategic in every operative field dealing with the space and matter like architecture, cultural heritage, engineering, design etc. In fact, thanks to the stereoscopic vision, is possible to create an effective spatial representation of the deepness that is fundamental in an AR application that allow to wander in the ruins of an archaeological site visualising the 3D reconstruction hypothesis upon the real volumes, as already highlighted in this article with the "Archeoguide" project.

If we could choose among a series of virtual *anastylosis* from different historical periods, we would obtain the best representation of a time machine available in a very natural way.

This type of experience allow to come in contact with the information linked to a place, architecture, ruin or object in a way completely different than in the past, thanks to the possibility to explore the real-virtual space in a real scale (immersion) and in a high level of *embodiment* that is produced, i.e. in being in the space, actively, offering the moving body to the cognitive process (in fact "embodied" or "embodiment" is the concepts that identify the body and immersion in a subject's perceptual and experiential information).

It's the paradigm of the *enaction*, or *enactive*, i.e. the *knowledge, enactive interfaces, enactive didactic*, which are terms coined by Bruner and later by H. Maturana and F. Varela to identify interactive processes put in place between the subject and significance of the subject in which the action is fundamental to the process of learning (Maturana & Varela 1980; Varela et al., 1991; Bruner, 1996). *Enaction* can be proposed as a theoretical model to understand the way of development of knowledge starting from the perceptual-motion interaction with the environment. This neuro-physiological approach is based on the idea that the cognitive activity is embodied, that not separable from the corporeal perception and that it can come out only in a well defined context through the direct action of the user with the context and with the other users. Interactivity, immersion, embodiment and enactivity are the key words of the new VR paradigm that, in the case of AR, shows all its power.

3.1 Criticalness

The represented technology is not immune by criticalness anyway:

- the need to have power of calculation and the speed of data transmission, to grant effective performances in the interaction;
- the need to have a rendering software able to get high level of photorealism in real-time;
- the need to create virtual light, audio and haptic condition as close as possible to the reality, all calculated in real-time. The trend is to measure the lighting condition through the construction of a HDRI map (Hight Dynamic Range Images on the "use of" in computer graphics, that visit the site of their greatest contemporary), by means of web-cam images, immediately applied to the virtual set;
- the need to increase the effectiveness of the tracking, in different environmental conditions;
- the adoption of video, audio and haptic hardware that can be worn easily even by people with a physical or cognitive limitations;
- the need to propose usable interfaces when the state of application changes (language, detail of the elaboration, historic period, etc..)

It is certainly not an exhaustive list, but he wants to be significant analysis of the importance of the current state of the art, when you design an application of AR.

3.2 Evolution of the AR techniques in the computer graphic

Apart from the well known computer graphic techniques that get into the AR family, like the bi-dimensional superimposing, the green/blue screen used in the cinema (augmented reality), the television virtual set (augmented virtuality) or the sophisticated technologies used by James Cameron for the known "Avatar" (mixed reality), we will try to offer a point of view about the AR used in a general purposes or in the specific VCH (Virtual Cultural Heritage) field (meaning the discipline that studies and proposes the application of digital technologies of virtual cultural experience understood in the broad sense, including photos, architectural walktrough, video anastylosis, virtual interactive objects, 3D websites, mobile applications, virtual reality and, of course, mixed reality), detailing:

1. AR desktop marker-based
2. AR desktop marker-less
3. AR freehand marker-less
4. AR by mobile
5. AR by projection
6. Collaborative AR
7. Stereo & Auto-Stereoscopic AR
8. Physics AR
9. Robotic AR

3.2.1 AR desktop marker-based

It's the best known AR application as it is the predecessor of the following evolutions. It, basically, is based upon the space trends tracking of a graphical marker, usually a geometric black&white symbol called "confidence marker" on which you can hook in real time a bi/three-dimensional input. The trace is possible using common web-cam with a simple shape recognition software by color contrast. The marker can be printed on a rigid support to allow an easily handling, but some more flexible supports are already available.

The most common application published so far allow the user to explore a 3D model object, experiencing 360 degree vision, as he holds in his hand (see Fig. 4). The model can be static, animated or interactive. The application can have many markers associated to different objects displayed one by one or all at the same time.

In the VCH area, the best known applications have been realized flanking the archaeological piece showed in the case side by side both to the marker (printed on the catalogue, on the invitation card or on special rigid support) and to the multimedia totem that hosts the AR application. In this way the user can simulate the extraction of the object from the case and see it from every point of view. He can also use many markers at the same time to compare the archaeological evolution of a building in the time.

The NoReal.it company we are dealing with, showed many experiences during some scientific exhibit like the "XXI Rassegna del Cinema Archeologico di Rovereto" (TN-Italy) and "Archeovirtual stand" into the "Borsa Mediterranea del Turismo Archeologico di Paestum" (SA - Italy).

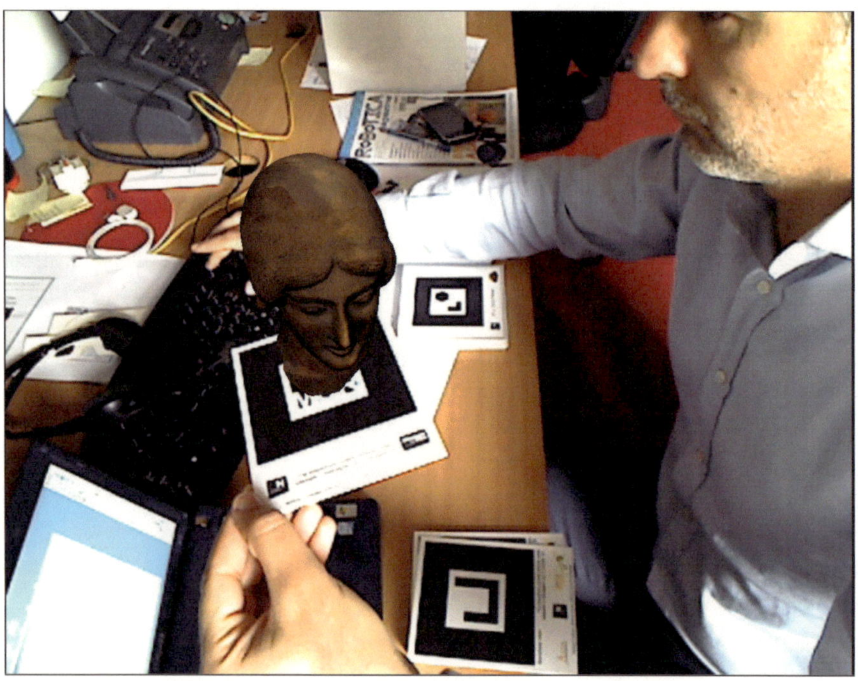

Fig. 4. An example of marker-based AR desktop session with a simplified 3D model of an ancient woman's head. The model was created using data derived from 3D laser scanner.

The technology is useful to solve a very important problem of the new archaeological museums: the will to carry on the emotion even after the visit has finished. Thanks to the AR marker-based, the user can connect to the museum's website, switch on the web-cam, print the graphic markers and start the interaction with the AR applications, realizing a very effective home edutainment session and customer loyalty in the action of the latest techniques museum marketing require. Some examples come from the Paul Getty Museum in Los Angeles or cited in the "Augmented reality Encyclopaedia".

Another advantage of the AR marker-based is the possibility to highlight it, in a clear way, the contributions in AR, printing the graphic symbol everywhere. This freedom is very useful in technical paper, interactive catalogues, virtual pop-up books, interactive books, that link the traditional information to the new one. "ARSights" is a software that allow to associate 3D Sketch-Up model to an AR marker so that you can visualize almost all the Google Earth buildings, working with a big worldwide CH database.

3.2.2 AR desktop marker-less

You can realize AR applications even without a geometric marker through a process that recognize graphically a generic image or a portion of it, after which the tracking system will be able to recognize identity and orientation. In this way, a newspaper page, or part of it, will become the marker and the AR contribution will be able to integrate the virtual content directly in the graphic context of the paper, without resorting to a specific symbol.

From another side, you need to make people understand that that page has been created to receive an AR contribution, as it is not in the symbol. You use the same interaction as in the marker-based applications, with one or multiple AR objects linked to one or different part of the printed image. There are many applications for the VCH: see, for example, the "AR-Museum" realized in 2007 by a small Norwegian company (bought a year later by Metaio), where you can visualize virtual characters interacting with the real furniture into the real space of the museum room.

Fig. 5. A frame of the AR-Museum application that superimpose a character animation to the real museum's rooms. The characters, in real scale, offer an immediate sense of presence.

3.2.3 AR freehand marker-less

We can include in the "AR freehand marker-less" category:

- applications that trace position, orientation and direction of the user look, using tracking systems and various movement sensors, associated to a gesture recognition software;
- applications that recognize the spatial orientation of the visual device.

The main difference, within the previous two categories, is the user role: in the first case the user interacts with his own body, in the second he activates a bound visualizing device spatially traced. In both cases the application control experiences through natural interactive system are becoming very common thanks to Microsoft "Kinetc" or the "Wavi Xtion" by PrimeSense with Asus3D, or even the Nintendo "Wii-mote" and the Sony "PlayStation Move", that still require a pointing device.

But the most extraordinary applications, even in the VCH, are the ones where the user can walk in an archaeological site, visualizing the reconstruction hypothesis superimposed to the real ruins. The first experience is from an European project called "Archeoguide" (http://archeoguide.intranet.gr), where a rudimentary system made of a laptop and stereoscopic viewer allowed to alternate the real vision to the virtual one. Recently, an Italian company named "Altair4" realized a 3D reconstruction of the "Tempio di Marte Ultore", temple in the "Foro di Augusto" in Rome, although the hardware is still cumbersome and the need to have a real time calculation remains fundamental.

A third field of application could be to calculate the structural integrity of architectural building with a sort of wearable AR device that permit a x-ray view from the inside of the object around. This kind of application has been presented at the IEEE VR 2009 by Avery et al. (2009) (IEEE VR is the event devoted to Virtual Reality, organized by the IEEE Computer Society, a professional organization, founded in the mid-twentieth century, with the aim of enhancing the advancement of new technologies).

3.2.4 AR by mobile

The latest frontier of the AR technology involves the personal mobile devices, like the mobile phones. Using the GPS, the gyroscope and the standard web-cam hosted in the mobile devices, you can create the optimal conditions for the geo-reference of the information, comparing them with the maps and the satellite orthophotos available by the most common geo-browser (Google Maps, Microsoft Bing, etc).

The possibility to be connected, from every place in the world, permits to choose the type of information to superimpose. In the last five years the first testing were born for Apple mobile devices (iPhone, iPad, iPod), Android, and Windows CE devices. The applications today available tend to exploit the Google Map geo-referencing to suggest informative tags located in the real space, following the mobile camera. You can see, for example, "NearestWiki" for iPhone or "Wikitude" for iPhone, Android and Symbian OS, but many other application are coming out. A particular application VCH is "Tuscany+" that publishes AR informative tags in AR, specific for a virtual tour in the the tuscanies cities with various types of 2D and 3D contributes.

During "Siggraph 2008", the IGD Fraunhofer with ZGDV, presented their first version of "InstantReality", a framework for VR and AR that used historical and archaeological images as a markers to apply the 3D model of the reconstruction hypothesis. Another example of VCH AR application, made for the interactive didactics, has been carried out in Austria (see www.youtube.com/watch?v=denVteXjHlc).

3.2.5 AR by projection

The 3D video-mapping techniques has to be included in the AR applications. It is known because of its application to the entertainment, to the facade of historical and recent buildings, but also used to augmented the physical prototypes used the same way as three-dimensional displays.

The geo-referencing is not subjected by a tracking technique, as in the previous cases, but through the perfect superimpose setting of the lighting projection on the building's wall with the virtual projection on the same wall, virtually duplicated. The video is not planar but is distorted, in compliance with the 3D volumes of the wall. The "degree of freedom" of the visitor is total, but in some case the projection could be of a lower quality cause of the unique direction of the lighting beam.

Today we don't know many 3D video-mapping applications for the edutainment, but many entertainment experiences can be reported. 3D video-mapping can be used to expose different hypothesis solution of a facade building in different historical ages or to simulate a virtual restoration, as it is for the original color simulation of the famous "Ara Pacis" in Rome (Fig. 6).

Fig. 6. A frame of the Ara Pacis work. On the main facade of the monument, a high-definition projection presents the hypothesis of ancient colors.

3.2.6 Collaborative AR

The "Second Life" explosion, during the 2008-2009 years, bring the light on the meta-verses like 3D collaborative on-line engines, with many usable capabilities and a high level of production of new 3D interactive contents and the avatar customization. The aesthetic results, and the character animation, obtained a very high technical level.

Other useful aspects of the generic MMORG (*Massively Multiplayer Online Role-Playing Game*, a type of computer role-playing game within a virtual world) allow to develop and gather together big content-making communities and content generators, in particular script generators that extend the applicative possibilities and the usable devices. "Second Life" and "Open Sim", for instance, have been used by T. Lang & B. Macintyre, two Researchers of Georgia Institute of Technology in Atlanta and of Ludwig-Maximilians Universitat in Monaco, as a rendering engine able to publish avatar and objects in AR (see http://arsecondlife.gvu.gatech.edu). This approach makes the AR experience not only interactive, but also shareable by the users and pursuant to the 2.0 protocol. We can stand that it's the first home low cost tele-presence experience.

Fig. 7. The SL avatar in AR, in real scale, and controlled by a brain interface.

An effective use of the system was obtained in the movie "Machinima Futurista" by J. Vandagriff, who reinvent the Italian movie "Vita Futurista" in AR. Other recent experiment by D. Carnovale, link Second Life, the AR and a Brain Control Interface to interact at home with his own avatar, in real scale, with anything but his own thoughts (Fig. 7).

We don't know yet a specific use in the VCH area, but we surely think about an avatar in AR school experiences, a museum guide, an experimental archaeology co-worker, a cultural entertainer for kids, a reproduction of ancient characters and so on.

3.2.7 Stereo & auto-stereoscopic AR

The Stereoscopic/Auto-Stereoscopic visualization is used in VCH as an improving instrument in the spatial exploration of objects and environments, both addressed to the entertainment and the experimental research, and it draw on the industrial research, applied since 10 years, that consider the AR stereoscopic use as fundamental.

The ASTOR project has been presented at Siggraph 2004, by some Royal Institute of Technology of Stockholm-Sweden (Olwal et al., 2005) teaching fellows, but thanks to the new auto-stereoscopic devices, we will increase it's possibilities in the near future. Currently, the only suite that include Stereoscopy and Auto-Stereoscopy in the marker-based/free AR applications is Linceo VR by Seac02, that manage the real-time binoculars rendering using a prismatic lens up the ordinary monitors.

Mobile devices like "Nintendo3D" and the "LG Optimus 3D" will positively influence the use for a museum interactive didactics, both indoor and outdoor experiences.

3.2.8 Physics AR

Recently, AR techniques have be applied to the interactive simulation processes, pursuant to the user actions or reactions as happens, for instance, with simulation of the physical behaviour of objects (as the DNA ellipses can be). The AR physical apparatus simulation can be used in the VCH to visualise tissues, elastic elements, ancient earthquake or tsunami, fleeing crowd, and so on.

3.2.9 Robotic AR

Robotics and AR, so far, match together for some experiments to put a web-cam on different drone and then create AR session with and without markers. There are examples of such experiments which realized esacopter and land vehicle. "AR Drone" is the first UAV (Unmanned Aerial Vehicle) Wi-Fi controlled through iPhone or iPad that transmit in real time images of the flights and augmented information (see www.parrot.com). "Liceo VR" that include SDK to control the Wowee Rovio. With "Lego Mindstorm NXT Robot" and the "Flex HR" software, you can build robotic domestic experiences.

There are new ways for an AR virtual visit, from high level point of view, dangerous for a real visit or underwater. The greatest difficulties are the limited Wi-Fi connection, the public securities laws (because of flying objects), the flight autonomy and/or robot movement.

Fig. 8. A frame of a AR Drone in action. On the iPhone screen you can see the camera frames, in real time, with superimposed information. Currently it is used as a game device. In a future we will use for VCH aerial explorations.

3.3 Commercial software and open-source

We can list the most popular AR software currently in use. The commercial company are the German Metaio (Munich, San Francisco), the Italian SEAC02 (Turin), the French Inglobe technologies (Ceccano, FR), the American Total Immersion (Los Angeles, Paris, London, Hong Kong). Every software house proposes different solutions in term of rendering performances, 3D editing tools, format import from external 3d modelling software, type and quantity of control devices, etc. The commercial offer is based on different user licence. Some open/free suite are available with different GNU licences, and the most known is "ARToolKit", usable in its original format or Flash-included ("FLARToolKit") or with the more user friendly interface by "FLARManager". But more and more other solution are coming.

The VCH natural mission is the spatial exploration, seen as an open environment (the ground, the archaeological site, the ancient city), as a close environment (the museum or a building), and as a simple object (the ruin, the ancient object). The user can live this experience in the real time, perceiving himself as a unit ad exploiting all his/her senses and the movement to complete and improve the comprehension of the formal meaning he/she's surrounded by. The mobile technologies allow to acquire information consistent to the spatial position, while the information technologies make the 3D virtual stereoscopic rendering reconstruction very realistic. The VCH will pass through MR technologies, intended as an informative cloud that involve, complete and deepen the knowledge and as possibility to share virtual visit with people online.

4. New materials and methods

For the aim of the restoration/reconstruction of structures with artistic or historical values, architectural heritages, cultural artefacts and archaeological materials, three steps have been fundamentals since now: *acquiring* the real images, *representing* the real (or even virtualized) images, *superimposing* the virtual information on the real images represented keeping the virtual scene in sync with reality. But with the enhanced latest technologies, each of these steps can find interesting improvements, and a even a fourth step can be implemented. We refer to the possibility that the images can be acquired and represented with auto-stereoscopic technologies, that an user can see his/her gestures mapped on the represented images, and that these gestures can be used to virtually interact with the real or modelled objects. So after a brief description of the standard techniques of image acquisition (paragraph 4.1), we will discuss, on the basis of our experiences, on the new auto-stereoscopy possibilities (paragraph 4.2), on the new low-cost systems to record human gestures (paragraph 4.3) and to convert them into actions useful to modify the represented scenario (paragraph 4.4), for an immersive human-machine interaction.

4.1 3D Image acquisition

Nowadays the possibility to obtain 3D data images of object appearance and to convert them into useful data, comes mainly from manual measuring (Stojakovic and Tepavcevica, 2009), stereo-photogrammetry surveying, 3D laser-scanner apparatuses, or an mixture of them (Mancera-Taboada et al., 2010).

The stereo-photogrammetry allows the determination of the geometric properties of objects from photographic images. Image-based measurements have been carried out especially for huge architectural heritages (Jun et al., 2008) and with application of spatial information technology (Feng et al., 2008) for instance by means of balloon images assisted with terrestrial laser scanning (Tsingas et al., 2008) or ad-hoc payload model helicopter (Scaioni et al., 2009) or, so called, Unmanned Aerial Vehicles or UAVs (van Blyenburg, 1999), capable to allow a high resolution image acquisition.

With the laser-scanner can be obtained the spatial coordination of the surface points of the objects under investigation (Mancera-Taboada et al., 2010, Costantino et al., 2010) as, for example, we did for the pieces of an ancient column of the archeological site of Pompeii (see Fig. 9). Anyway, according to our experience, the data acquired with laser-scanner are not so useful when it is necessary to share them on the web, since the huge amount of data generated, especially for large objects with many parts to be detailed. In addition, laser-scanning measurements can often be characterized by errors of different nature, so analytical model must be applied to estimate the differential terms necessary to compute the object's curvature measures. So statistical analyses are generally adopted to overcome the problem (Crosilla et al., 2009).

(a)

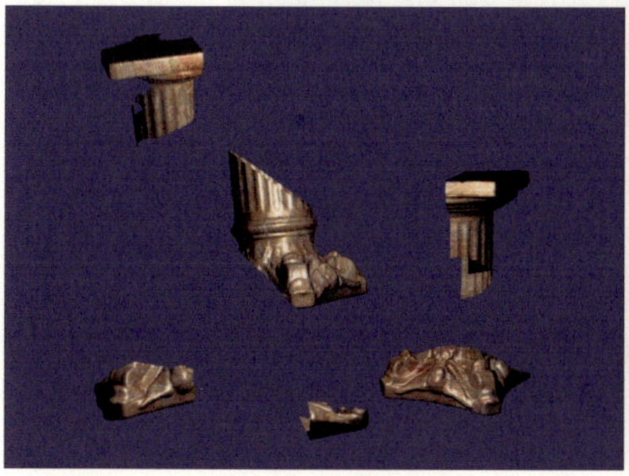

(b)

(c)

Fig. 9. (a) A picture from Pompeii archeological site (Italy) with parts of an ancient column on the right, (b) pieces of a laser scanned column, (c) the column after the virtual reconstruction.

In any case, the 3D data images can be useful adopted both for VR than for AR. In fact, in the first case data are used to build virtual environments, more or less detailed and even linked to a cartographic model (Arriaga & Lozano, 2009), in the second occurrence data are used to superimpose useful information (dimensions, distances, virtual "ghost" representation of hidden parts,...) over the real scene, beyond mere presentation purposes towards being a tool for analytical work. The superimposed information must be deducted from analysis of the building materials, structural engineering criteria and architectural aspects.

The latest technological possibilities allow online image acquisition for auto-stereoscopic effects. These present the fundamental advantage that 3D vision can be realized without the need for the user to don special glasses as currently done. In particular we refer to a system we have adopted and improved, detailed in the following paragraph.

4.2 Auto-stereoscopy

The "feeling as sensation of present" in a AR scene is a fundamental requirement. The movements, the virtual interaction with the represented environment and the use of some interfaces are possible only if the user "feels the space" and understands where all the virtual objects are located. But the level of immersion in the AR highly depends on the display devices used. Strictly regarding the criteria of the representation, the general approach of the scenario visualization helps to understand the dynamic behaviour of a system better as well as faster. But the real boost in the representation comes, in the latest years, from a 3D approach which offers help in communication and discussion of decisions with non-experts too. The creation of a 3D visual information or the representation of a "illusion" of depth in a real or virtual image is generally referred as Stereoscopy. A strategy to obtain this is through eyeglasses, worn by the viewer, utilized to combine separate images from two offset sources or to filter offset images from a single source separated to each eye. But the eyeglass based systems can suffer from uncomfortable eyewear, control wires, cross-talk levels up to 10% (Bos, 1993), image flickering and reduction in brightness. On the other end, AutoStereoscopy is the technique to display stereoscopic images without the use of special headgear or glasses on the part of the viewer. Viewing freedom can be enhanced: presenting a large number of views so that, as the observer moves, a different pair of the views is seen for each new position; tracking the position of the observer and update the display optics so that the observer is maintained in the AutoStereoscopic condition (Woodgate et al., 1998). Since AutoStereoscopic displays require no viewing aids seem to be a more natural long-term route to 3D display products, even if can present loss of image (typically caused by inadequate display bandwidth) and cross-talk between image channels (due to scattering and aberrations of the optical system. In any case we want here to focus on the AutoStereoscopy for realizing what we believe to be, at the moment, the more interesting 3D representations for AR.

Current AutoStereoscopic systems are based on different technologies which include lenticular lens (array of magnifying lenses), parallax barrier (alternating points of view), volumetric (via the emission, scattering, or relaying of illumination from well-defined regions in space), electro-holographic (a holographic optical images are projected for the two eyes and reflected by a convex mirror on a screen), and light field displays (consisting of two layered parallax barriers).

Our efforts are currently devoted respect to four main aspects: user comfort, amount of data to process, image realism, deal both with real objects or graphical models. In such a view, our collaboration involves the Alioscopy company (www.alioscopy.com) regarding their 3D AutoStereoscopy visualization system which, despite non completely satisfy all the requirements, remain one of the most affordable systems, in terms of cost and time efforts. The 3D monitor is based on the standard Full HD LCD and its feature back 8 points of view is called "multiscope". Each pixel of the panel combines three sub-pixel colour (red, green and blue) and the arrays of lenticular lenses cast different images onto each eye, since magnify different point of view for each eye viewed from slightly different angles (see Fig. 10).

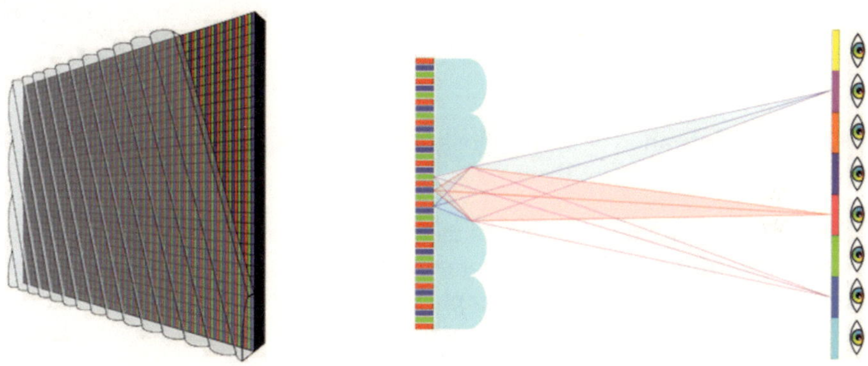

(a) (b)

Fig. 10. (a) LCD panel with lenticular lenses, (b) Eight points of view of the same scene from eight cameras.

This results in a state of the art visual stereo effect rendered with typical 3D software such as 3ds Max, Maya, Lightwave, and XSI. The display uses 8 interleaved images to produce the AutoStereoscopic 3D effect with multiple viewpoints. We realized 3D images and videos, adopting two different approaches for graphical and real model. The graphical model is easily managed thanks to the 3D Studio Max Alioscopy plug-in, which is not usable for real images, and for which it is necessary a set of multi-cameras to recover 8 view-points.

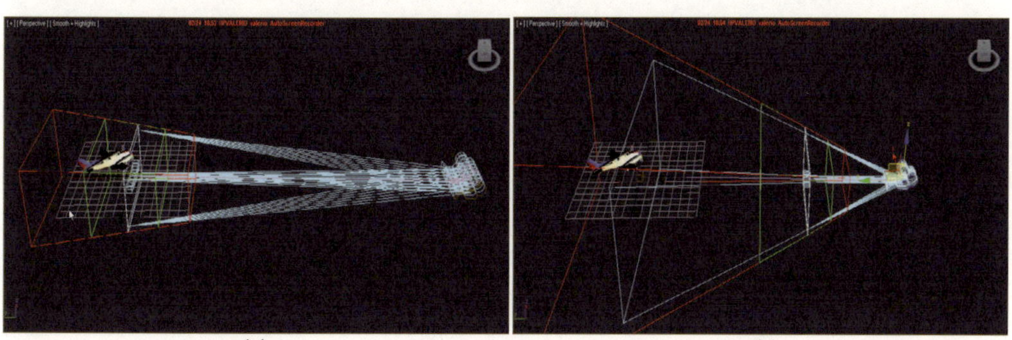

(a) (b)

Fig. 11. The eight cameras with (a) more or (b) less spacing between them, focusing the object at different distances

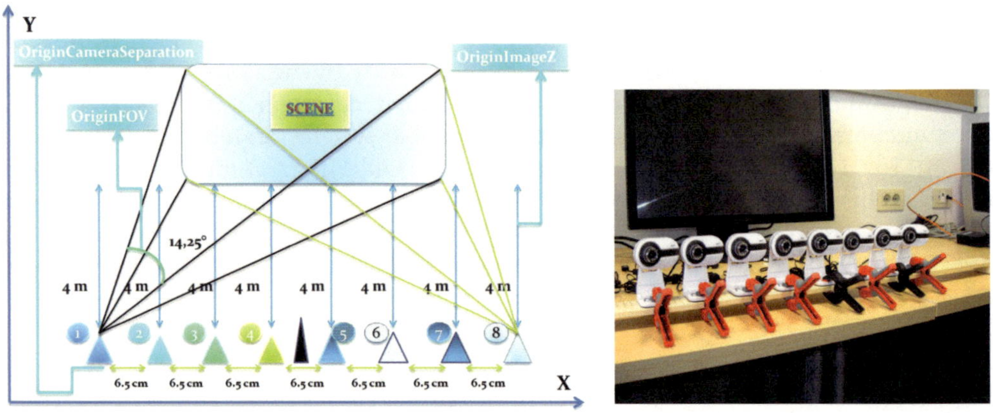

(a) (b)

Fig. 12. (a) schematization of the positions of the cameras among them and from the scene, (b) the layout we adopted for them

The virtual or real captured images are then mixed, by means of OpenGL tools, in groups of eight to realize AutoStereoscopic 3D scenes. We paid special attention in positioning the cameras to obtain a correct motion capture of a model or a real image, in particular the cameras must have the same distance apart (6.5 cm is the optimal distance) and each camera must "see" the same scene but from a different angle.

Fig. 13 reports screen capture of three realized videos. The images show blur effects when reproduced in a non AutoStereoscopic way. In particular, the image in Fig. 13c reproduces eight numbers (from 1 to 8), and the user see only one number at time depending on his/her angular position with respect the monitor.

(a) (b) (c)

Fig. 13. Some of realized images for 3D full HD LCD monitors based on lenticular lenses. (c) image represents 8 numbers seeing on at time by the user depending from his/her angle of view.

The great advantage of the AutoStereoscopic systems consists of an "immersive" experience of the user, with unmatched 3D pop-out and depth effects on video screens, and this without the uncomfortable eyewear of any kind of glasses. On the other end, an important amount of data must be processed for every frame since it is formed by eight images at the same time. Current personal computers are, in any case, capable to deal with these amount of data since the powerful graphic cards available today.

4.3 Input devices

The human-machine interaction has historically been realized by means of conventional input devices, namely keyboard, mouse, touch screen panel, graphic tablet, trackball, pen-based input in 2D environment, and three dimensional mouse, joystick, joypad in 3D space. But new advanced user interfaces can be much more user friendly, can ensure higher user mobility and allow new possibilities of interaction. The new input devices for advanced interactions take advantage from the possibility of measuring human static postures and body motions, translating them into actions in an AR scenario. But there are so many different human static and dynamic posture measurement systems that a classification can be helpful. For this, a suggestion comes from one of our work (Saggio & Sbernini, 2011), completing a previous proposal (Wang, 2005), which refers of a schematization, based on position of the sensors and the sources (see Fig. 14). Specifically:

- *Outside-In Systems*: the sensors are somewhere in the world, the sources are attached to the body.
- *Inside-Out Systems*: the sensors are positioned on the body, the sources are somewhere else in the world.
- *Inside-In Systems*: the sensors and sources are on the user's body.
- *Outside-Out Systems*: both sensors and sources are not (directly) placed on the user's body

The *Outside-In Systems* typically involve optical techniques with markers, which are the sources, strategically placed on the wearer's body parts which are to be tracked. Cameras, which are the sensors, capture the wearer's movement, and the motion of those markers can be tracked and analyzed. An example of application can be found in the "Lord of the Rings" movie productions to track movements for the CGI "Gollum" character. This kind of system is widespread adopted (Gavrila, 1999) since it is probably the oldest and perfected ones, but the accuracy and robustness of the AR overlay process can be greatly influenced by the quality of the calibration obtained between camera and camera-mounted tracking markers (Bianchi et al., 2005).

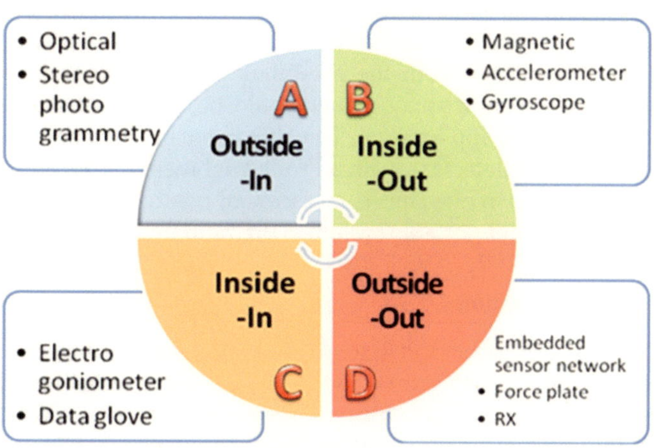

Fig. 14. Classifications of systems for measuring postures and kinematics of the human body.

The *Inside-Out Systems* deal with sensors attached to the body while sources are located somewhere else in the world. Examples are the systems based on accelerometers (Fiorentino et al., 2011; Mostarac et al., 2011; Silva et al., 2011), MEMS (Bifulco et al., 2011), ensemble of inertial sensors such as accelerometers, gyroscopes and magnetometers (Benedetti, Manca et al., 2011), RFID, or IMUs which we applied to successfully measure movements of the human trunk (Saggio & Sbernini, 2011). Within this frame, same research groups and commercial companies have developed sensorized garments for all the parts of the body, over the past 10-15 years, obtaining interesting results (Giorgino et al., 2009; Lorussi, Tognetti et al., 2005; Post et al., 2000).

The *Inside-In Systems* are particularly used to track body part movements and/or relative movements between specific parts of the body, having no knowledge of the 3D world the user is in. Such systems are for sensors and sources which are for the most part realized within the same device and are placed directly on the body segment to be measured or even sewed inside the user's garment. The design and implementation of sensors that are minimally obtrusive, have low-power consumption, and that can be attached to the body or can be part of clothes, with the employ of wireless technology, allows to obtain data over an extended period of time and without significant discomfort. Examples of the *Inside-In Systems* come from application of strain gauges for stress measurements (Ming et al., 2009), conductive ink based materials (Koehly et al., 2006) by which it is possible to realize bend / touch / force / pressure sensors, piezoelectric materials or PEDOT:PSS basic elements for realizing bend sensors (Latessa et al., 2008) and so on.

The *Outside-Out Systems* consider both sensors and sources not directly placed on the user's body but in the surrounding world. Let's consider, for instance, the new Wireless Embedded Sensor Networks which consist of sensors embedded in object such as an armchair. The sensors detect the human postures and, on the basis of the recorded measures, furnish information to modify the shape of the armchair to best fit the user body (even taking into account the environment changes). Another application is the tracking of the hand's motions utilized as a pointing device in a 3D environment (Colombo et al., 2003).

In a next future it is probable that the winning rule will be played by a technology which will take advantages from mixed systems, i.e. including only the most relevant advantages of *Outside-In* and/or *Inside-Out* and/or *Inside-In* and/or *Outside-Out Systems*. In this sense an interesting application comes from the Fraunhofer IPMS, where the researchers have developed a bidirectional micro-display, which could be used in Head-Mounted Displays (HMD) for gaze triggered AR applications. The chips contain both an active OLED matrix and therein integrated photo-detectors, with a Front brightness higher than 1500 cd/m^2. The combination of both matrixes in one chip is an essential possibility for system integrators to design smaller, lightweight and portable systems with both functionalities.

4.4 Human-computer interaction

As stated at the beginning of paragraph 4, we want here to point out on the utilization of the measurements of the human postures and kinematics in order to convert them into actions useful to somehow virtually interact with represented real or virtual scenario. We are representing here the concept of Human-Computer Interaction (HCI), with functionality and usability as its major issues (Te'eni et al., 2007). In literature there are several examples of HMI (Karray et al., 2008).

In the latest year our research group realized systems capable to measure human postures and movements and to convert them into actions or commands for pc based applications. This can be intended an example of Human Computer Interaction (HCI) which, more specifically, can be defined as the study, the planning and the design of the interaction between users and computers. We designed and realized different systems which can be framed into both the *Inside-Out* and *Inside-In ones*. An example comes from our "data glove", named *Hiteg glove* since our acronym (*Health Involved Technical Engineering Group*). The glove is capable to measure all the degree of freedom of the human hand, and the recorded movements can be then simply represented on a screen (Fig. 15a) or adopted to virtually interact, manipulate, handle object on a VR/AR scenario (Fig. 15b).

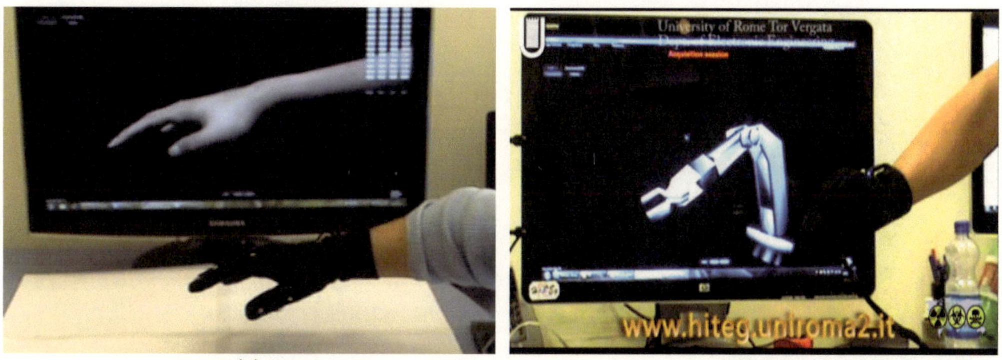

(a) (b)

Fig. 15. Hiteg Data Glove measures human hand movements (a) simple reproduced on a computer screen or (b) utilized to handle a virtual robotic arm.

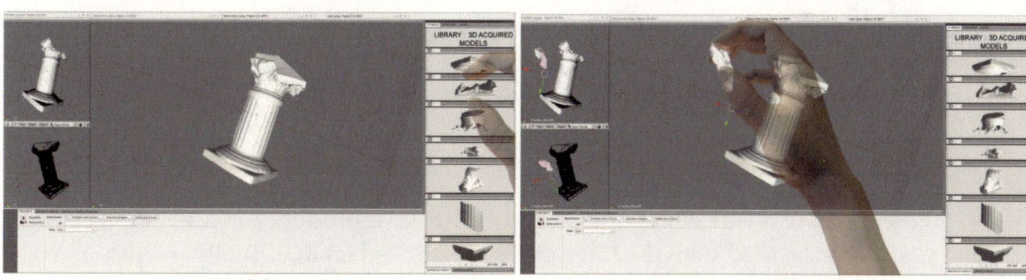

(a) (b)

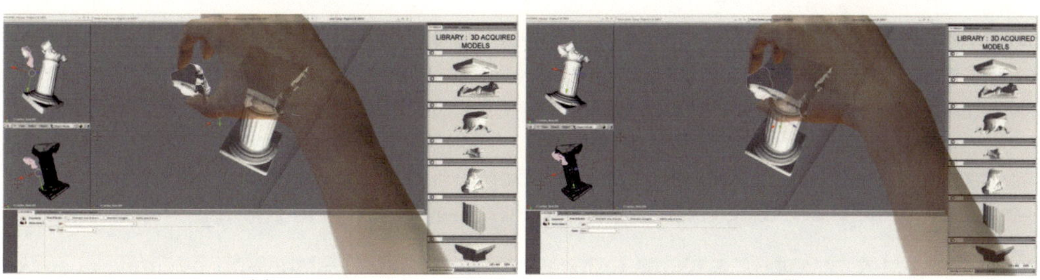

(c) (d)

Fig. 16. The restoration/reconstruction of an ancient column. From (a) to (d) the passages to integrate a last piece

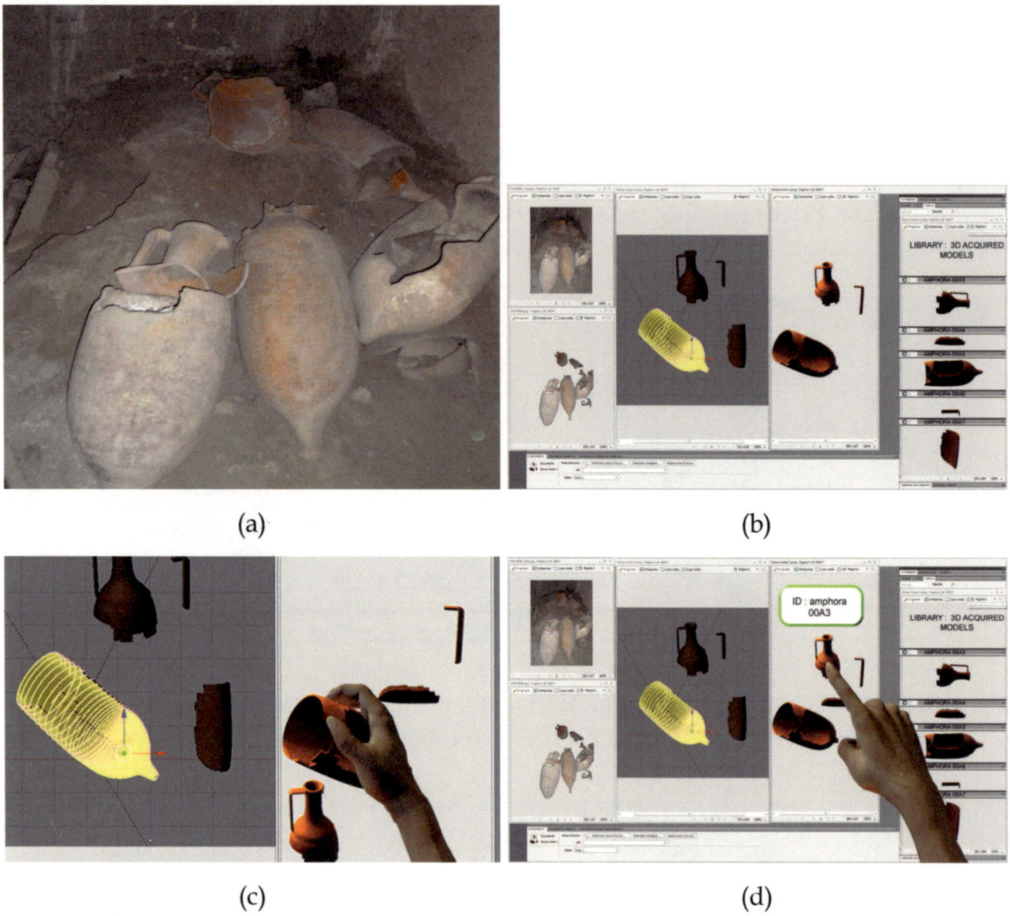

Fig. 17. (a) the pieces of an ancient amphora are (b) virtual reproduced in a VR scenario and the hand gestures measured with the hiteg glove are utilized (c) to virtually interact or (d) to retrieve additional information of the selected piece

On the basis of the *Hiteg glove* and of a home-made software, we realized a project for the virtual restoration/reconstruction of historical artifacts. It starts from acquiring the spatial coordinates of each part of the artifact to be restored/reconstructed by means of laser scanner facilities. Each of these pieces are then virtually represented in a VR scenario, and the user can manipulate them to virtually represent the possibilities of a restoration/ econstruction steps detailing each single maneuver (see Fig. 16 and Fig. 17).

We developed noninvasive systems to measure human trunk static and dynamic postures too. The results are illustrated in Fig. 18a,b where sensors are applied to a home-made dummy, capable to perform the real trunk movements of a person, and the measured positions are replicated by an avatar on a computer screen.

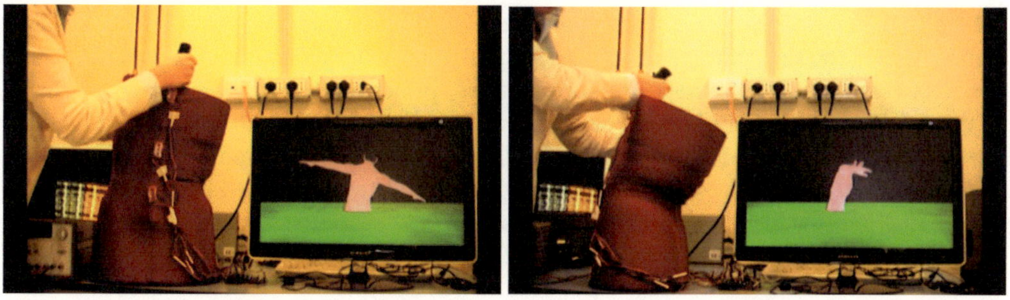

(a) (b)

Fig. 18. (a) Lateral and (b) front measured trunk movements are replicated on a pc screen.

Thanks to the measured movements, one can see him-herself directly immersed into an AR scenario, and his/her gestures can virtually manipulate the virtual represented objects. But the mixed reality can be even addressed to more sophisticated possibilities. In fact, adopting systems which furnish feedback to the user, it is possible to make the action of virtually touch a real object seen in a pc screen, but having the sensation of the touch as being real. So, the usual one-way communication between man and computer, can now become a bidirectional information transfer providing a user-interface return channel (see Fig. 19).

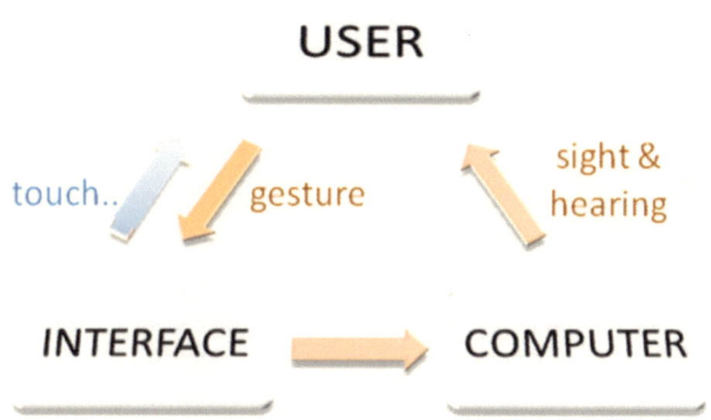

Fig. 19. Exchange information between user and computer

We can have sensations to the skin and muscles through touch, weight and relative rigidity of non existing objects. Generally speaking we can treat of *force* or *haptic* feedbacks, properties which can be integrated into VR and AR scenario. The *force* feedback consists in equipment to furnish the physical sensation of resistance, to trigger kinetic stimuli in the user, while the *haptic* consists in apparatus that interfaces with the user through the sense of touch (for its calibration, registration, and synchronization problems see Harders et al., 2009). In particular the so called *affective haptic* involves the study and design of devices and systems that can elicit, enhance, or influence emotional state of a human just by means of sense of touch. Four basic haptic (tactile) channels governing our emotions can be distinguished: *physiological changes* (e.g., heart beat rate, body temperature, etc.), *physical stimulation* (e.g., tickling), *social touch* (e.g., hug, handshake), *emotional haptic design* (e.g., shape of device, material, texture) (Wikipedia,

2011). In our context frame we refer only on the *physical stimulation* part, since it is the less emotional but the only that makes sense for our purposes. Within it the *tactile sensation* is the most relevant and includes pressure, texture, puncture, thermal properties, softness, wetness, friction-induced phenomena such as slip, adhesion, and micro failures, as well as local features of objects such as shape, edges, embossing and recessed features (Hayward et al., 2004). But also vibro-tactile sensations, in the sense of the perception of oscillating objects in contact with the skin can be relevant for HCI aspects. A possibility to simulate the grasping of virtual objects can be realized by means of small pneumatic pistons in a hand worn solution, which make it possible to achieve a low weight and hence portable device (an example is the force-feedback glove from the HMI Laboratory at the Rutgers University, Burdea et al., 1992)

5. Conclusion

Stands the importance of restoration and/or reconstruction of structures with artistic or historical values, architectural heritages, cultural artefacts and archaeological materials, this chapter discussed about the meaning and importance of AR applications within this frame. So, after a brief overview, we focused on the *restoration cycle*, underlining the Reality and Virtuality cross relations and how them support AR scenarios. An entire paragraph was devoted to AR applications, its criticalness, developments, and related software. Particular attention was paid for new materials and methods to discover (more or less) future possibilities which can considerably improve restoration/reconstruction processes of artefacts, in terms of time, efforts and cost reductions.

6. References

Arriaga & Lozano (2009), "Space throughout time - Application of 3D virtual reconstruction and light projection techniques in the analysis and reconstruction of cultural heritage," *Proceedings of the 3rd ISPRS Int. Workshop 3D-ARCH 2009, 3D Virtual Reconstruction and Visualization of Complex Architectures*, Trento, Italy, Feb. 2009

Avery B., Sandor C., & Thomas B.H., (2009). *IEEE VR* 2009, Available from www.youtube.com/watch?v=BTPBNggldTw&feature=related

Bianchi G., Wengert C., Harders M., Cattin P. & Szekely G., (2005) "Camera-Marker Alignment Framework and Comparison with Hand-Eye Calibration for Augmented Reality Applcations," In *ISMAR*, 2005

Bifulco P., Cesarelli M., Fratini A., Ruffo M., Pasquariello G. & Gargiluo G., (2011) "A wearable device for recording of biopotentials and body movements," *Proceedings IEEE Int. Symposium on Medical Measurements and Applications,* Bari, Italy, May 2011

Benedetti M.G., Manca M., Sicari M., Ferraresi G., Casadio G., Buganè F. & Leardini A. (2011) "Gait measures in patients with and without afo for equinus varus/drop foot," *Proceedings of IEEE International Symposium on Medical Measurements and Applications,* Bari, Italy, May 2011

Bos P.J. (1993) Liquid-crystal shutter systems for time multiplexed stereoscopic displays, in: D.F. McAllister (Ed.), *Stereo Computer Graphics and Other true 3D Technologies*, Princeton University Press, Princeton, pp. 90-118.

Bruner J., (1996) "Toward a theory of instruction," Harvard University Press: Cambridge, MA, 1996

Burdea, G.C., Zhuang, J.A., Rosko, E., Silver, D. & Langrama, N. (1992), "A portable dextrous master with force feedback", *Presence: Teleoperators and Virtual Environments*, vol. 1, pp. 18-28

Colombo C., Del Bimbo A. & Valli A., (2003) Visual Capture and Understanding of Hand Pointing Actions in a 3-D Environment, *IEEE Transactions on Systems, Man, and Cybernetics – part B: Cybernetics*, vol. 33, no. 4, august 2003

Costantino D., Angelini M.G. & Caprino G., (2010) Laser Scanner Survey Of An Archaeological Site: Scala Di Furno (Lecce, Italy), *International Archives of Photogrammetry, Remote Sensing and Spatial Information Sciences*, Vol. XXXVIII, Part 5 Commission V Symposium, Newcastle upon Tyne, UK., 2010

Crosilla F., Visintini D. & Sepic F., (2009) Automatic Modeling of Laser Point Clouds by Statistical Analysis of Surface Curvature Values, *Proceedings of the 3rd ISPRS International Workshop 3D-ARCH 2009, 3D Virtual Reconstruction and Visualization of Complex Architectures*, Trento, Italy

Cruz-Neira C., Sandin D.J., DeFanti T.A., Kenyon R.V. & Hart J.C., (1992) "The CAVE: Audio Visual Experience Automatic Virtual Environment," *Communications of the ACM*, vol. 35(6), 1992, pp. 64-72. DOI:10.1145/129888.129892

Feng M., Ze L., Wensheng Z., Jianxi H. & Qiang L., (2008) The research and application of spatial information technology in cultural heritage conservation - case study on Grand Canal of China, The International Archives of the Photogrammetry, *Remote Sensing and Spatial Information Sciences*, Vol. XXXVII-B5. Beijing 2008, pp. 999-1005

Fiorentino M., Uva A.E. & Foglia M.M., (2011) "Wearable rumble device for active asymmetry measurement and corrections in lower limb mobility," *Proceedings of IEEE Int. Symposium on Medical Measurements and Applications*, Bari, Italy, May 2011

Gavrila D.M., (1999) "The visual analysis of human movement: a survey", *Computer Vision and Image Understanding*, 73(1), pp 82-98, 1999

Georgios P., Evaggelia-Aggeliki K &, Theoharis T., (2001) "Virtual Archaeologist: Assembling the Past," *IEEE Comput. Graph. Appl.*, vol. 21, pp. 53-59, 2001

Giorgino T., Tormene P., Maggioni G., Capozzi D., Quaglini S &, Pistarini C., (2009) "Assessment of sensorized garments as a flexible support to self-administered post-stroke physical rehabilitation" *Eur. J. Phys. Rehabil. Med.* 2009;45:75-84

Harders M, Bianchi G., Knoerlein B. & Székely G., "Calibration, Registration, and Synchronization for High Precision Augmented Reality Haptics," *IEEE Transactions on Visualization and Computer Graphics*, vol. 15 no. 1, Jan/Feb 2009, pp. 138-149

Haydar M., Roussel D., Maidi M., Otmane S. & Mallem M., (2010) "Virtual and augmented reality for cultural computing and heritage: a case study of virtual exploration of underwater archaeological sites," *Virtual Reality*, DOI 10.1007/s10055-010-0176-4

Hayward V, Astley O.R., Cruz-Hernandez M., Grant D. & Robles-De-La-Torre G., (2004) "Haptic interfaces and devices," *Sensor Review*, vol. 24, no. 1, 2004, pp. 16–29

Karray F., Alemzadeh M., Saleh J.A. & Arab M.N. (2008) "Human-Computer Interaction: Overview on State of the Art," *International Journal on Smart Sensing and Intelligent Systems*, vol. 1, no. 1, march 2008, pp. 137-159

Koehly R., Curtil D. & Wanderley M.M., (2006) "Paper FSRs and Latex/Fabric Traction Sensors: Methods for the Development of Home-Made Touch Sensors," *Proceedings of the 2006 International Conference on New Interfaces for Musical Expression (NIME06)*, Paris, France, 2006

Jun C., Yousong Z., Anping L., Shuping J. & Hongwei Z., (2008) Image-Based Measurement of The Ming Great Wall, *The International Archives of the Photogrammetry, Remote Sensing and Spatial Information Sciences*, Vol. XXXVII-B5. Beijing 2008, pp. 969-973

Latessa G., Brunetti F., Reale A., Saggio G. & Di Carlo A., (2008) "Electrochemical synthesis and characterization of flexible PEDOT:PSS based sensors" *Sensors and Actuators B: Chemical* (2008), doi:10.1016/j.snb.2009.03.063

Lorussi F., Tognetti A., Tescioni M., Zupone G., Bartalesi R. & De Rossi D. (2005) "Electroactive Fabrics for Distributed, Confortable and Interactive Systems" in *Techn. and Informatics* vol.117, Personalized Health Management Systems, Ed. Chris D. Nugent et al., IOS Press, 2005

Mancera-Taboada J., Rodríguez-Gonzálvez P., González-Aguilera D., Muñoz-Nieto Á., Gómez-Lahoz J., Herrero-Pascual J. & Picón-Cabrera I., (2010) On the use of laser scanner and photogrammetry for the global digitization of the medieval walls of Avila, In: Paparoditis N., Pierrot-Deseilligny M., Mallet C., Tournaire O. (Eds), *IAPRS*, Vol. XXXVIII, Part 3A – Saint-Mandé, France, September 1-3, 2010

Maturana H. & Varela F., (1985) "Autopoiesis and Cognition: the Realization of the Living," I ed. 1980, tr.it. *Autopoiesi e cognizione. La realizzazione del vivente*, Editore Marsilio, Venezia, Italy, 1985

Milgram P. & Kishino F., (1994) A Taxonomy of Mixed Reality Visual Displays, *IEICE Transactions on Information Systems*, vol. E77-D, no.12, December 1994

Ming D., Liu X., Dai Y &, Wan B., (2009) "Indirect biomechanics measurement on shoulder joint moments of walker-assisted gait", *Proc. of IEEE Int. Conf. on Virtual Environments, Human-Computer Interfaces, and Measurement Systems*, Hong Kong, China, May 11-13, 2009

Mostarac P., Malaric R., Jurčević M., Hegeduš H., Lay-Ekuakille A. & Vergallo P., (2011) "System for monitoring and fall detection of patients using mobile 3-axis accelerometers sensors," *Proceedings of IEEE International Symposium on Medical Measurements and Applications*, Bari, Italy, May 2011

Olwal, A., Lindfors, C., Gustafsson, J., Kjellberg, T. & Mattson, L., (2005) "ASTOR: An Autostereoscopic Optical See-through Augmented Reality System," *ISMAR 2005 Proceedings of IEEE and ACM International Symposium on Mixed and Augmented Reality*, Vienna, Austria, Oct 5-8, 2005

Pollefeys M., Van Gool L., Vergauwen M., Cornelis K., Verbiest F. & Tops J., (2003) "3D recording for archaeological fieldwork," *Computer Graphics and Applications*, IEEE, vol. 23, pp. 20-27, 2003

Post E. R., Orth , Russo P. R. & Gershenfeld N., "E-broidery: design and fabrication of textile-based computing," *IBM Systems Journal* Vol. 39 Issue 3-4, July 2000

Saggio G., Bocchetti S., Pinto C. A., Orengo G. & Giannini F., (2009) A novel application method for wearable bend sensors, ISABEL2009, *Proceedings of 2nd International Symposium on Applied Sciences in Biomedical and Communication Technologies.* Bratislava, Slovak Republic, November 24-27, 2009, pp. 1–3

Saggio G., Bocchetti S., Pinto C.A. & Orengo G., (2010), Wireless Data Glove System developed for HMI, *ISABEL2010, Proceedings of 3rd International Symposium on Applied Sciences in Biomedical and Communication Technologies,* Rome, Italy, November 7-10, 2010

Saggio G. & Sbernini L., (2011) New scenarios in human trunk posture measurements for clinical applications, *IEEE Int. Symposium on Medical Measurements and Applications,* 30-31 May 2011, Bari, Italy

Scaioni M., Barazzetti L., Brumana R., Cuca B., Fassi F. & Prandi F., (2009), RC-Heli and Structure & Motion techniques for the 3-D reconstruction of a Milan Dome spire, Proceedings of *the 3rd ISPRS International Workshop 3D-ARCH 2009, 3D Virtual Reconstruction and Visualization of Complex Architectures,* Trento, Italy, Feb. 2009

Silva H., Lourenco A., Tomas R., Lee V. & Going S., (2011) "Accelerometry-based Study of Body Vibration Dampening During Whole-Body Vibration Training," *Proceedings of IEEE International Symposium on Medical Measurements and Applications,* Bari, Italy, May 2011

Stojakovic V. & Tepavcevica B., (2009) Optimal Methodes For 3d Modeling Of Devastated Arhitectural Objects, Proceedings of *the 3rd ISPRS International Workshop 3D-ARCH 2009, 3D Virtual Reconstruction and Visualization of Complex Architectures,* Trento, Italy, 25-28 February 2009

Te'eni D., Carey J. & Zhang P., (2007) "Human Computer Interaction: Developing Effective Organizational Information Systems," John Wiley & Sons, Hoboken, 2007.

Tsingas V., Liapakis C., Xylia V., Mavromati D., Moulou D., Grammatikopoulos L. & Stentoumis C., (2008) 3D modelling of the acropolis of Athens using balloon images and terrestrial laser scanning, The *Int. Archives of the Photogrammetry, Remote Sensing and Spatial Information Sciences.* vol. XXXVII-B5. Beijing 2008, pp. 1101-1105

Ursula K., Volker C., Ulrike S., Dieter G., Kerstin S., Isabel R. & Rainer M., (2001) "Meeting the spirit of history," *Proceedings of the 2001 conference on Virtual reality, archeology, and cultural heritage,* Glyfada, Greece: ACM, 2001

Varela F.J., Thompson E. & Rosch E., (1991) "The embodied mind: Cognitive science and human experience," MIT Press: Cambridge, MA, 1991

Vassilios V., John K., Manolis T., Michael G., Luis A., Didier S., Tim G., Ioannis T. C., Renzo C. & Nikos I., "Archeoguide: first results of an augmented reality, mobile computing system in cultural heritage sites," *Proceedings of the 2001 conference on Virtual reality, archeology, and cultural heritage,* Glyfada, Greece: ACM, 2001

Vlahakis V., Ioannidis M., Karigiannis J., Tsotros M., Gounaris M., Stricker D., Gleue T., Daehne P. & Almeida L., "Archeoguide: an AR guide for archaeological sites," *Computer Graphics and Applications,* IEEE, vol. 22, pp. 52-60, 2002

Wang Y., (2005) Human movement tracking using a wearable wireless sensor network. Master Thesis. Iowa State University. Ames, Iowa

Woodgate G.J., Ezra D., Harrold J., Holliman N.S., Jones G.R. & Moseley R.R. (1998) "Autostereoscopic 3D display systems with observer tracking," *Signal Processing: Image Communication* 14 (1998) 131-145

Zheng J. Y. & Li Z.Z, (1999) "Virtual recovery of excavated relics," *Computer Graphics and Applications*, IEEE, vol. 19, pp. 6-11, 1999

Part 2

AR in Biological, Medical and Human Modeling and Applications

5

Augmented Reality Talking Heads as a Support for Speech Perception and Production

Olov Engwall
Centre for Speech Technology, School of Computer Science and Communication, KTH (Royal Institute of Technology), Stockholm Sweden

1. Introduction

Visual face gestures, such as lip, head and eyebrow movements, are important in all human speech communication as a support to the acoustic signal. This is true even if the speaker's face is computer-animated. The visual information about the phonemes, i.e. speech sounds, results in better speech perception (Benoît et al., 1994; Massaro, 1998) and the benefit is all the greater if the acoustic signal is degraded by noise (Benoît & LeGoff, 1998; Sumby & Pollack, 1954) or a hearing-impairment (Agelfors et al., 1998; Summerfield, 1979).

Many phonemes are however impossible to identify by only seeing the speaker's face, because they are visually identical to other phonemes. Examples are sounds that only differ in voicing, such as [b] *vs.* [p], or sounds for which the difference in the articulation is too far back in the mouth to be seen from the outside, such as [k] *vs.* [ŋ] or [h]. A good speech reader can determine to which viseme, i.e. which group of visually identical phonemes, a speech sound belongs to, but must guess within this group. A growing community of hearing-impaired persons with residual hearing therefore relies on cued speech (Cornett & Daisey, 1992) to identify the phoneme within each viseme group. With cued speech, the speaker conveys additional phonetic information with hand sign gestures. The hand sign gestures are however arbitrary and must be learned by both the speaker and the listener. Cued speech can furthermore only be used when the speaker and listener see each other.

An alternative to cued speech would therefore be that the differences between the phonemes are directly visible in an augmented reality display of the speaker's face. The basic idea is the following: Speech recognition is performed on the speaker's utterances, resulting in a continuous transcription of phonemes. These phonemes are used in real time as input to a computer-animated talking head, to generate an animation in which the talking head produces the same articulatory movements as the speaker just did. By delaying the acoustic signal from the speaker slightly (about 200 ms), the original speech can be presented together with the computer animation, thus giving the listener the possibility to use audiovisual information for the speech perception. An automatic lip reading support of this type already exists, in the SYNFACE extension (Beskow et al., 2004) to the internet telephony application Skype. Using the same technology, but adding augmented reality, the speech perception support can be extended to display not only facial movements, but face and tongue movements together, in displays similar to the ones shown in Fig. 1. This type of speech perception support is less vulnerable to automatic speech recognition errors and is therefore preferred over displaying the recognized text string.

Similarly, second language learners and children with speech disorders may have difficulties understanding how a particular sound is articulated or what the difference compared to another phoneme is. Both these groups may be helped by an augmented reality display showing and describing tongue positions and movements. The AR talking head display allows a human or virtual teacher to instruct the learner on how to change the articulation in order to reach the correct pronunciation.

For both types of applications, augmented reality is created by removing parts of the facial skin or making it transparent, in order to provide additional information on how the speech sounds are produced. In this chapter, we are solely dealing with computer-animated talking heads, rather than the face of a real speaker, but we nevertheless consider this as a good example of augmented reality, rather than virtual reality, for two reasons: Firstly, the displayed articulatory movements are, to the largest extent possible, real speech movements, and hence relate to the actual reality, rather than to a virtual, and possibly different, one. Secondly, the listener's perception of reality (the sounds produced) is enhanced using an augmented display showing another layer of speech production. In addition, many of the findings and discussions presented in this chapter would also be also relevant if the augmented reality information about tongue movements was displayed on a real speaker's cheek.

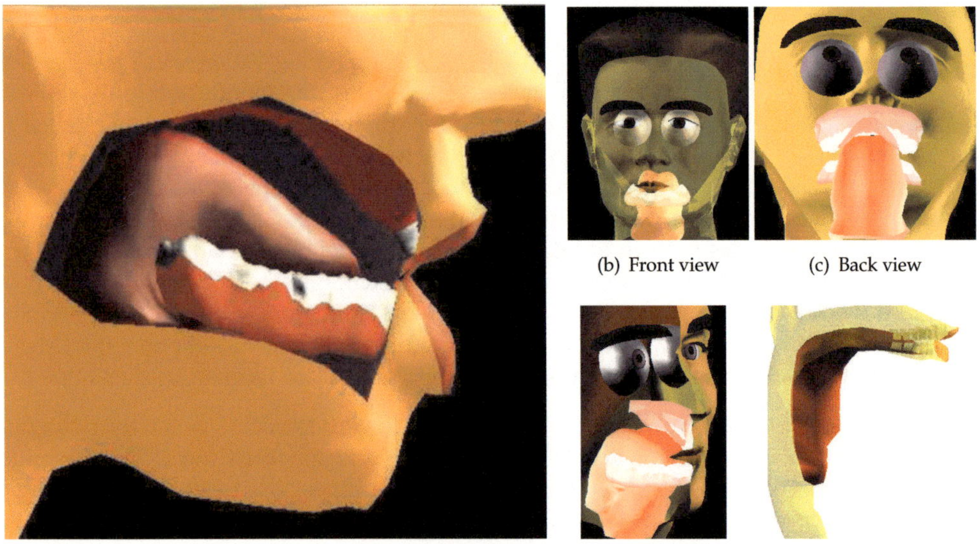

(a) Side view (b) Front view (c) Back view (d) Half head view (e) Vocal tract view

Fig. 1. Illustration of different alternatives to create the augmented reality display. (a) Skin made transparent in order to show the movements of the articulators. Display used for the experiments described in Section 3.2. (b) Front view with transparent skin, similar to one option in Massaro & Light (2003). (c) Viewer position inside the talking head, similar to one display in Massaro & Light (2003). (d) Front half of the head removed, similar to the display in Badin et al. (2008). (e) Displaying the vocal tract only, similar to the display in Kröger et al. (2008).

Since we are normally unaccustomed to seeing the movements of the tongue, the use of such a display leads to several research questions. AR talking head displays have therefore been created by several research teams, in order to investigate their usefulness as a support for speech perception or for speech production practice. This chapter will first introduce and discuss the different types of augmented reality displays used (Section 2) and then present a set of studies on speech perception supported by AR talking heads (Section 3). The use for speech production practice is more briefly discussed in Section 4, before ending with a general outlook on further questions related to the use of AR talking heads in Section 5.

2. Augmented reality talking heads

Augmented reality displays of the face have been tested for both speech perception (Badin et al., 2008; Engwall, 2010; Engwall & Wik, 2009a; Grauwinkel et al., 2007; Kröger et al., 2008; Wik & Engwall, 2008) and speech production (Engwall, 2008; Engwall & Bälter, 2007; Engwall et al., 2006; Fagel & Madany, 2008; Massaro et al., 2008; Massaro & Light, 2003; 2004). These studies have used different displays to visualize the intraoral articulation, as examplified in Fig. 1 and summarized in Table 1. The list excludes the epiglottis and the larynx, which are only shown in the studies by Badin et al. (2008) and Kröger et al. (2008).

As is evident from Table 1 and Fig. 1, there are several different choices for the presentation of the AR display. It is beyond the scope of this chapter to try to determine if any set-up is superior to others, but it may nevertheless be interesting to compare the different alternatives, as it is not evident what articulators to display and how. In addition to the tongue, all studies show the jaw in some form, since it is needed as a reference frame to interpret tongue movements and since it in itself gives important information for speech reading (Guiard-Marigny et al., 1995). One could argue that all other articulators that are relevant to speech production should be displayed as well, in order to give the viewer all the available information. However, most viewers have a diffuse and superficial understanding of the intraoral anatomy and articulatory movements and may hence be confused or frightened off by too much detail in the display. Some articulators may also hide others if a full three-dimensional representation is used.

Displays that show the entire 3D palate, either fully visible or semi-transparent, may encounter problems in conveying sufficiently clear information about if and where the tongue touches the palate, which is vital in speech production. To overcome such problems, Cohen et al. (1998) proposed to supplement the face view with a separate display that shows the regions were the tongue is in contact with the palate. This additional display would however split the learner's visual attention and it has not been used in the subsequent studies by Massaro et al. The alternative opted for by Badin et al. (2008), Engwall (2010); Engwall & Wik (2009a); Wik & Engwall (2008) and Massaro et al. (2008) is to concentrate on the midsagittal outline of the palate to facilitate the perception of the distance between the tongue and the palate. Engwall (2010); Engwall & Wik (2009a); Wik & Engwall (2008) simplified the display further by showing the tongue and jaw moving inside a dark oral cavity, with the limit of the transparent skin region corresponding to the palate outline (Fig. 1(a)). This choice was made since the children who were shown a line tracing of the palate in Engwall et al. (2006) found it difficult to interpret (they e.g., speculated that it was a small tube where the air passes in the nose). Kröger et al. (2008) on the other hand presented the vocal tract movements without the surrounding face, as in (Fig. 1(e)), and avoided occluding articulators this way.

The velum has been included in some of the studies in Table 1, but the usefulness of displaying it can be discussed. Seeing tongue movements is strange for many viewers, but they are at least conscious of the appearance and proprioceptic responses of the tongue surface, whereas it is much more difficult to internally visualize the placement and movement of the velum.

	B=Badin et al. (2008) E={ E1=Wik & Engwall (2008), E2=Engwall & Wik (2009a), E3=Engwall (2010) } F=Fagel & Madany (2008), K=3D model in Kröger et al. (2008) M=Massaro et al. (2008), ML=Massaro & Light (2003), Massaro & Light (2004)
View	Side view (B, E, F, K) (Fig. 1(a)), with a small angle (M) (Fig. 1(d)) Front view (K, ML) (Fig. 1(b)) Back view (ML) (Fig. 1(c))
Face	Video-realistic. Closer half removed, remoter half a black silhouette (B) Synthetic-looking. Closer half removed (M), semi-transparent skin (F, ML), transparent skin at the oral cavity (E) No face (K) (Fig. 1(e))
Lips	3D and video-realistic (B) 3D and synthetic-looking (F, K, L) 3D for the remoter part of the face (E, M)
Tongue	Midsagittal shape (in red, B; or turquoise, M) and the remoter half (B, M) Upper tongue surface (K) 3D body (E, F, ML)
Jaw & teeth	Midsagittal shape of the incisor (in blue, B; or green, M) and the remoter half of the lower and upper jaw (B, M) Semi-transparent schematic teeth blocks or quadrangles (F, K) Semi-transparent and realistic in 3D (ML) Visible and realistic 3D jaw, lower teeth and upper incisor (E)
Palate	Midsagittal shape (in yellow, B; or green, M) and the remoter half (B, M) Uncoloured semi-transparent tube walls (K) Semi-transparent schematic (F) or realistic (ML) Upper limit of transparent part of the skin corresponds to the midsagittal contour of the palate (E, Fig. 1(a))
Velum	Midsagittal shape (B) and the remoter part (M) Part of the semi-transparent tube walls (K) As part of the palate surface (F)
Pharynx walls	Realistic remoter half (B) Non-realistic surface at the upper part of the pharynx (F, M) Semi-transparent tube wall (K) Limit of transparent part corresponds to upper pharynx walls (E)
Movements	Resynthesis of one speaker's actual movements measured with EMA (B,E2) Rule-based, but coarticulation adapted to measurements (E1, E3, K) Rule-based with coarticulation models from facial animation (F, M, ML)

Table 1. Alternative representations of the articulators in the augmented reality display.

Another simplification, used in several studies, is to present the intra-oral articulations from a side view that makes the display similar to traditional two-dimensional tracings in phonetics, even if the model is in 3D. The side-view is the one that makes different articulations most distinct (which is why this display is used in phonetics), but one may well argue that different viewers may prefer different set-ups. Massaro & Light (2003) in addition used a front (as in Fig. 1(b)) and a back (as in Fig. 1(c)) view of the head, but without attempting to investigate if any view was better than the other. As an alternative, one could choose an interactive display, in which the user can rotate the 3D structure to different view points, but there is a risk that the structure complexity in other views may hide important articulatory features. To the best of our knowledge, the side view is hence the best alternative for displaying intra-oral movements.

The studies also differ in the attempted realism of the articulator appearance, anatomy and movements. For the appearance, several researchers, e.g., Badin et al. (2008); Massaro et al. (2008) intentionally depart from realism by choosing contrasting colours for the different articulators. No user study has yet been performed to investigate whether viewers prefer easier discrimination between articulators or caricaturized realism. The meaning of the latter would be that the appearance does not have to be photo-realistic, but that the articulator colours have the expected hue. Concerning anatomy, the models were created from Magnetic Resonance Imaging (MRI) (Badin et al., 2008; Engwall, 2010; Engwall & Wik, 2009a; Wik & Engwall, 2008) or adapted through fitting of an existing geometric model to data from MRI (Fagel & Madany, 2008; Kröger et al., 2008) or three-dimensional ultrasound (Cohen et al., 1998). For the articulatory movements, Badin et al. (2008); Engwall & Wik (2009a) used actual Electromagnetic articulography (EMA) measurements of the uttered sentences, while the other studies used rule-based text-to-speech synthesis. Experiments reported in Section 3.2 indicate that this choice may have an influence on speech perception. On the one hand, prototypic or exaggerated movements created by rules may be easier to understand than real tongue movements, but on the other, real movements may be closer to the viewer's own production and therefore more easily processed subconsiously.

A final issue regarding realism concerns the appearance of the face and its correspondence with the intra-oral parts. A video-realistic face may have benefits both for pleasantness of appearance and possibly also for speech perception, since finer details may be conveyed by the skin texture. There is however a risk of the so called uncanny valley effect when the intra-oral articulation is shown within a video-realistic face. In the current scope, the uncanny valley effect signifies that users may perceive the talking head as unpleasant if the face has a close-to-human appearance, but includes non-human augmented reality, with parts of the skin removed or transparent. This question is further discussed in Section 5.

3. AR talking heads as a speech perception support

AR talking heads as a speech perception support have been investigated in several studies in the last years (Badin et al., 2008; Engwall, 2010; Engwall & Wik, 2009a; Grauwinkel et al., 2007; Kröger et al., 2008; Wik & Engwall, 2008). The studies have shown that even if the intraoral articulators give much less information than the face, at least some listeners benefit from seeing tongue movements; but only if they have received explicit or implicit training on how to interpret them.

Badin et al. (2008) tested audiovisual identification of all non-nasal French voiced consonants in symmetrical vowel-consonant-vowel (VCV) contexts with [a, i, u, y] and different levels of signal-to-noise ratio (SNR). To one group the stimuli was presented in four decreasing steps of SNR, from clean conditions to muted audio, whereas the steps were reversed with increasing SNR for the other group. The first group hence received implicit training of the relationship between the acoustic signal and the tongue movements. Four different conditions were presented to the subjects, acoustic only and three audiovisual conditions. They were a cutaway display showing the outline of the face, the jaw and palate and pharynx walls, but not the tongue (AVJ); a cutaway display that in addition also showed the tongue (AVT); and a display showing the face with skin texture instead (i.e., a realistic display, rather than AR). The main results of the study were that the identification score was better for all audiovisual displays than for the acoustic only, but that the realistic display was better than the two augmented reality displays (of which AVT was the better). The subjects hence found it easier to employ the less detailed, but familiar, information of the face. The group that had received implicit training was however significantly better in the AR conditions than the one that had not. For the first group, the AVT display was moreover better than the realistic display in mute condition.

Similarly, Grauwinkel et al. (2007) concluded that the additional information provided by animations of the tongue, jaw and velum was not, in itself, sufficient to improve the consonant identification scores for VCV words in noise. Ten German consonants in symmetric [a, i, u] context were presented in white noise at SNR=0 to two groups of subjects who saw either the external face or a semi-transparent face with movements of the tongue and velum. The audiovisual recognition scores were significantly higher than the acoustic ones, but the subject group that saw an AR face was not significantly better than the one that saw a non-transparent face, *unless* subjects had received training prior to the test. The training was in the form of a video presentation that explained the place and manner of articulation of the consonants and the movement of the articulators for all consonants in all vowel contexts in a side view display.

Kröger et al. (2008) performed a visual only test of 4 vowels and 11 consonants with German articulation disordered children. Mute video animations of the articulatory movements at half speed were displayed in a 2D- or 3D-model and the children were asked to acoustically mimic the sound they saw. One repetition was used for the 2D-model and two, with different views, for the 3D-model. The phoneme recognition rates and correct identification of articulatory features (i.e., the case when the child produced a different phoneme, but it had the same type of lip rounding, place of articulation, manner of articulation or used the same articulator, as in the stimuli) were significantly above chance level and similar for the two models.

The implications of these three studies for general speech perception are nevertheless limited, since only forced-choice identification of consonants and four isolated vowels were tested. If the articulatory display is to be used as an alternative to cued speech, a more varied and less restricted corpus needs to be tested as well. It is also of interest to explore the importance of realism of the displayed articulatory movements. Finally, the role of the training merits further investigation to determine if the subjects are learning the audiovisual stimuli as audiovisual templates or if they start to make use of already established articulatory knowledge. In order to do so, we have conducted a series of tests, focused on the use of AR talking heads as a general speech perception support (Section 3.1), on comparing speech perception with authentic and rule-generated articulatory movements (Section 3.2) and on the subjects internalized articulatory knowledge (Section 3.3).

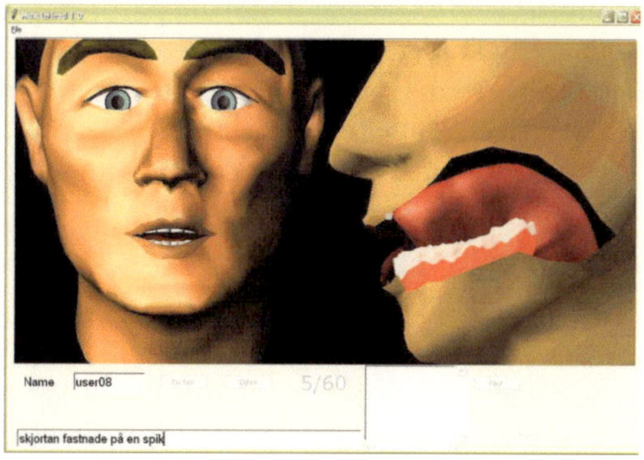

Fig. 2. The dual face display showing a normal front view and an AR side view simultaneously. The picture in addition shows the experimental display set-up with an entry frame, in which the subjects typed in the sentence that they perceived.

3.1 AR talking heads as an alternative to cued speech

In the first study, we tested a setting simulating what a hearing impaired person could use as a speech reading support. A group of listeners were presented vocoded speech accompanied by a dual display, showing a normal front view of the face and an augmented reality side view (c.f. Fig. 2). Vocoded speech is a good simulation of a hearing impairment and a dual display would be used in a speech reading support, since the front view is the best for lip reading, while the side view is better to show the articulation of the tongue.

3.1.1 Stimuli and subjects

The stimuli consisted of acoustically degraded short Swedish sentences spoken by a male Swedish speaker. The audio degradation was achieved by using a noise-excited channel vocoder that reduces the spectral details and creates an amplitude modulated and bandpass filtered speech signal consisting of multiple contiguous channels of white noise over a specified frequency range (Siciliano et al., 2003). In this chapter, the focus is placed on 30 sentences presented with a three-channel vocoder, but Wik & Engwall (2008) in addition give results for sentences presented with two channels.

The sentences have a simple structure (subject, predicate, object) and "everyday content", such as *"Skjortan fastnade på en spik"* (*The shirt got caught on a nail*). These sentences are part of a set of 270 sentences designed for audiovisual speech perception tests, based on MacLeod & Summerfield (1990). The sentences were normally articulated and the speech rate was kept constant during the recording of the database by prompting the speaker with text-to-speech synthesis set to normal speed.

The sentences were presented in three different conditions: Acoustic Only (AO), Audiovisual with Face (AF) and Audiovisual with Face and Tongue (AFT). For the AF presentation a frontal view of the synthetic face was displayed (left part of Fig. 2) and the AFT presentation in addition showed a side view, where intra-oral articulators had been made visible by making parts of the skin transparent (Fig. 2).

18 normal-hearing native subjects (15 male and 3 female) participated in the experiment. All were current or former university students and staff. They were divided into three groups, with the only difference between groups being that the sentences were presented in different conditions to different groups, so that every sentence was presented in all three conditions, but to different groups. The sentence order was random, but the same for all subjects.

3.1.2 Experimental set-up

The acoustic signal was presented over headphones and the graphical interface was displayed on a 15″ laptop computer screen. The perception experiment started with a familiarization set of sentences in AFT condition, in which the subjects could listen to and watch a set of five vocoded and five clear sentences as many times as they wanted. The correct text was then displayed upon request in the familiarization phase. When the subjects felt prepared for the actual test, they started it themselves. For each stimulus, the subjects could repeat it any number of times and they then typed in the words that they had heard (contrary to the familiarization phase, no feedback was given on the answers during the test). No limit was set on the number of repetitions, since the material was much more complex than the VCV words of the studies cited above and since subjects in Badin et al. (2008) reported that it was difficult to simultaneously watch the movements of the lips and the tongue in one side view. Allowing repetitions made it possible for the subjects to focus on the front face view in some repetitions and the augmented side view in others. This choice is hence similar to that in Grauwinkel et al. (2007), where each stimulus was repeated three times. The subjects' written responses were analyzed manually, with the word accuracy counted disregarding morphologic errors.

3.1.3 Results

The results for the two audiovisual conditions were significantly better than the acoustic only, as shown in Fig. 3(a). A two-tailed t-test showed that the differences were significant at a level of $p<0.05$. The word recognition for the two audiovisual conditions was very similar, with word accuracy 70% *vs.* 69% and standard deviation 0.19 *vs.* 0.15 for AF *vs.* AFT. Overall, the augmented reality display of the tongue movements did hence not improve the performance further compared to the normal face view, similar to the findings by Badin et al. (2008) and Grauwinkel et al. (2007). Fig. 3(a) however also shows that the performance differed substantially between the groups, with higher accuracy in AFT condition than in AF for groups 1 and 2, but lower for group 3.

The reason for this may be any of, or a combination of, differences in the semantic complexity between the sentence sets, in the phonetic content of the sentences between the sentence sets or in the distribution of individual subjects' ability between the subject groups. Sentences and subjects were distributed randomly between their three respective groups, but it could be the case that the sentences in one set were easier to understand regardless of condition, or that one group of subjects performed better regardless of condition. Since the sentence sets were presented in different conditions to the subject groups, both differences between sentence sets and subject groups can make comparisons between conditions unfair. The differences between sentence sets and subject groups were therefore first analyzed. For the sets, the average word accuracy was 71% for set 1, 59% for set 2 and 64% for set 3, where the difference between sets 1 and 2 is statistically significant at $p<0.005$, using a paired t-test, whereas the difference between sets 1 and 3 and between sets 2 and 3 is non-significant. For the groups, the average word accuracy was 66% for group 1, 62% for group 2 and 66% for group 3, and none of the intra-group differences are significant.

There is hence an artifact of set difficulty that needs to be taken into account in the following analysis. In order to be able to compare display conditions without the influence of the intra-set differences, a weighted word accuracy was calculated, in which the average score of each set was normalized to the average of the three sets (66%). The word accuracy for sentences belonging to set 1 was decreased by multiplying it by a factor 0.66/0.71=0.92, while that of sets 2 and 3 was increased by a factor 1.12 and 1.03, respectively. The weighted word accuracy for the different display conditions is displayed in Fig. 3(b). The difference between the weighted AF and AO conditions is significant at a level of $p<0.05$, while that between AFT and AO is significant at $p<0.001$. The difference between the two audiovisual conditions is still not significant.

The intra-subject differences are a natural consequence of different subjects having different multimodal speech perception abilities to make use of augmented reality displays of intraoral articulations, and this was also observed in the study by Badin et al. (2008) (personal communication). Fig. 4 shows that six subjects (1:3, 1:5, 1:6, 2:3, 2:6, 3:3) clearly benefited from the augmented reality view, with up to 20% higher weighted word accuracy scores in AFT than in AF, while three others (2:4, 3:2, 3:5) were as clearly better in the AF condition.

In future studies we plan to use an eye-tracking system to investigate if the differences between subjects may be due to where they focus their visual attention, so that subjects who have higher recognition scores in the augmented reality condition give more attention to the tongue movements. Such an evaluation has also been proposed by Badin et al. (2008).

In order to analyze how different phonetic content influenced the speech perception in different display conditions, the average word accuracy per sentence was first considered. Fig. 5 shows the weighted word accuracy, where the effect of differences in subject performance between the groups has been factored out through a normalization procedure equivalent to that described for the sentence set influence (however, contrary to the set

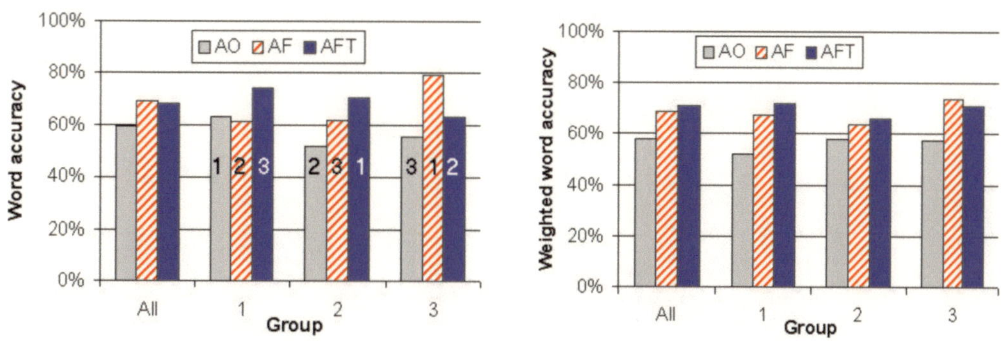

(a) Average word accuracy

(b) Average weighted word accuracy

Fig. 3. Word accuracy for all subjects and the three different groups. a) The numbers in the bars indicate which set of sentences that was presented in the different conditions. b) The weighting is a normalization, applied to factor out the influence of intra-set differences.

influence, the effect of the different subject groups was marginal, with scale factors 0.98, 0.98 and 1.05).

From Fig. 5 one can identify the sentences for which AFT was much better than AF (sentences 5, 9, 10, 17, 21, 22, 28) and vice versa (1-3, 6-8, 12, 27). A first observation concerning this comparison of the two audiovisual conditions is that of the first eight sentences, seven were more intelligible in the AF display. This suggests that the subjects were still unable to use the additional information from the AFT display, despite the familiarization set, and were initially only confused by the tongue animations, whereas the more familiar AF view could be used as a support immediately. The very low AFT score for sentence 12 is probably due to a previously unnoticed artifact in the visual synthesis, which caused a chaotic behavior of the tongue for a few frames in the animation.

The analysis of the sentences that were better perceived in AFT than in AF condition is tentative and needs to be supported by more, and more controlled, experimental data, where sentences can be clearly separated with respect to the type of articulatory features they contain. As a first hypothesis, based on the words that had a higher recognition rate in AFT condition, it appears that subjects found additional information in the AFT display mainly for the tongue dorsum raising in the palatal plosives [k, g] and the tongue tip raising in the alveolar lateral approximant [l] and the alveolar trill [r]. In addition, the fricatives [ɧ, ɕ] also seem to have been better perceived, but they appeared in too few examples to attempt hypothesizing. The animations of the tongue in particular appear to have been beneficial for the perception of consonant clusters, such as [kl, ml, pl, sk, st, kt, rd, rt, rn, dr, tr], for which the transitions are difficult to perceive from a front face view.

Note that there is a weak negative correlation (σ=-0.09) between the number of repetitions for a sentence and the accuracy rates, and the accuracy rate is hence not increased if the subjects listened to the stimuli additional times. The word accuracy decreased almost monotonously with the number of repetitions after an initial peak (at 1-2 repetitions for AO and AF and at 3 for AFT), as shown in Fig. 6. A two factor ANOVA with number of repetitions and display condition as factors indicates that there is no interaction between number of listenings and display condition for the word recognition accuracy. Fig. 6 also shows that, on average, the

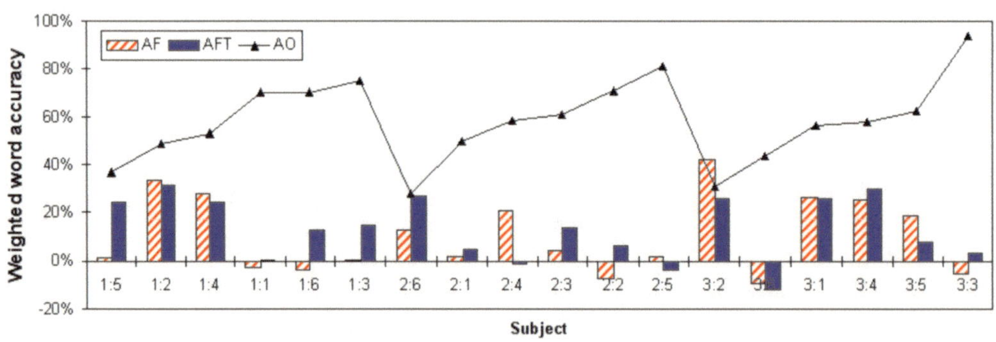

Fig. 4. Average weighted mean word accuracy per subject in the acoustic only (AO) condition and the change compared to the AO condition when the AF or the AFT display is added. Numbers on the x-axis indicate group and subject number within the group. Subjects have been sorted on increasing AO performance within each group.

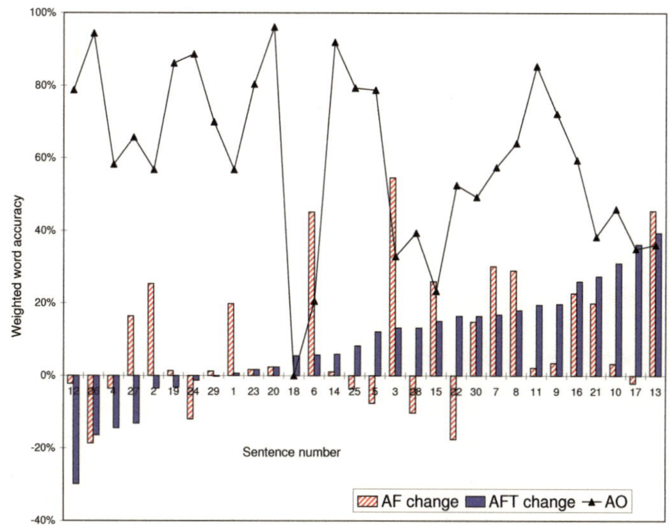

Fig. 5. The weighted mean word accuracy for each stimulus in the acoustic only (AO) condition and the change compared to the AO condition when the AF or the AFT display is added. The sentences have been sorted in order of increasing AFT change.

stimuli were mostly played two, three or more than six times. From the number of repetitions used and the corresponding word accuracy, it appears that the subjects were either certain about the perceived words after 1-3 repetitions, or they used many repetitions to try to decode difficult sentences, but gained little by doing so. Fig. 6 suggests that the additional repetition

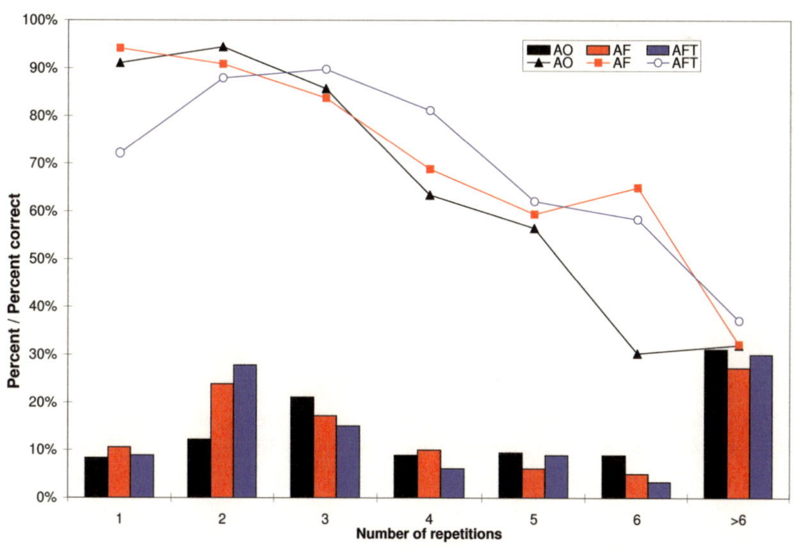

Fig. 6. Lines show the average weighted mean word accuracy in the three display conditions as a function of number of times the stimulus was repeated before the subject gave an answer. Bars show the distribution of the average number of repetitions for the different conditions.

with the AFT display allowed users to take more information from both face views into account.

Due to the rapidity of the tongue movements and the comparably low word recognition for one repetition, it seems unrealistic that the AR talking head could be used as an alternative to cued speech for real-time speech perception for an average person, at least not without large amounts of training. However, the study shows that some subjects are indeed very strong "tongue readers", and such persons could well be helped by an AR talking head display. The following two sections continue to explore how the tongue movements in the augmented reality animations are processed by the listeners.

3.2 On the importance of realism of articulator movements

As described in Section 2, both rule-based and recorded articulator movements have been used in the AR animations. Movements created from rules are more prototypic, may be hyperarticulated (i.e. more exaggerated) and have no variation between repetitions of the same utterance. Recorded movements display speaker specific traits, with variability and more or less clearly articulated words, but they are, on the other hand, *natural* movements. We have performed a study on VCV words and sentences to investigate if the difference between these two types of movements influences the perception results of the viewers. Realistic tongue movements could be more informative, because the listener can unconsciously map the displayed movements to his or her own, either through activation of mirror neurons (Rizzolatti & Arbib, 1998) when seeing tongue movements, or if the theory of speech motor control is applicable (Perkell et al., 2000). It may, on the other hand, be so that the rule-based movements give more information, because the hyperarticulation means that the articulations are more distinct. This was indeed found to be the case for the velar plosive [g], for the part of this test on VCV words (Engwall & Wik, 2009a). The consonant identification rate was 0.44 higher with animations displaying rule-based [g] movements than for those with real movements. For other consonants ([v, d, l, r, n, s ɕ, ɧ]), the difference was either small or with the recorded movements resulting in higher identification rates. For a description of the test with VCV words, please refer to Engwall & Wik (2009a), as the remainder of this section will deal with sentences of the same type as in Section 3.1.

3.2.1 Stimuli and subjects

For the animations based on recorded data (AVR), the movements were determined from measurements with the MacReflex motion capture system from Qualisys (for the face) and the Movetrack EMA (for the tongue movements) of one female speaker of Swedish (Beskow et al., 2003). For the face, 28 small reflective markers were attached to the speaker's jaw, cheeks, lips and nose, as shown in Fig. 7(a). To record the tongue movements, three EMA coils were placed on the tongue, using a placement shown in Fig. 7(b). In addition, EMA coils were also placed on the jaw, the upper lip and the upper incisor. Beskow et al. (2003) describe how the recorded data was transformed to animations in the talking head model through a fitting procedure to minimize the difference between the data and the resynthesis in the model.

For the rule-based synthesis animations (AVS), the movements were created by a text-to-visual speech synthesizer with forced-alignment (Sjölander, 2003) to the recorded acoustic signal. The text-to-visual speech synthesis used is an extension to the one created for the face by Beskow (1995) and determines the articulator movements through targets for each phoneme

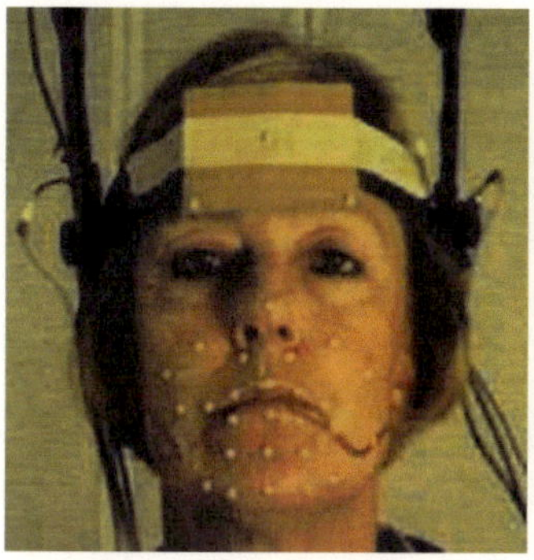

(a) Motion capture markers

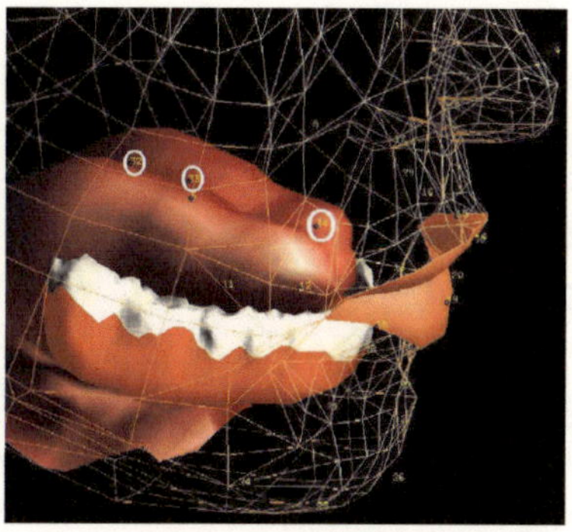

(b) EMA coil placement

Fig. 7. Set-up used to collect data for the AVR animiations. (a) Placement of the Qualisys motion capture markers. (b) The corresponding virtual motion capture markers (+) and articulography coils (circled) in the talking head model.

and interpolation between targets. The targets and the timing for the tongue movements are based on data from static MRI and dynamic EMA (Engwall, 2003), but the interpolation is the same as for the face, which might not be suitable for the tongue movements, since they are much faster and of a slightly different nature. It has been shown that the synthetically generated face animations are effective as a speech perception support (Agelfors et al., 1998; Siciliano et al., 2003), but we here concentrate on if the synthesis is adequate for intraoral animations.

The stimuli were 50 Swedish sentences of the same type (but not necessarily the same content) and with the same acoustic degradation as described in Section 3.1.1. The sentences were divided into three sets S1, S2 and S3, where S1 contained 10 stimuli and S2 and S3 20 stimuli each.

The subjects were 20 normal-hearing native speakers of Swedish (13 male and 7 female). They were divided into two groups, I and II. The sentences in S2 were presented in AVS condition to Group I and in AVR to Group II, while those in S3 were presented in AVR to Group I and in AVS to Group II. Both groups were presented S1 in acoustic only (AO) condition. To determine the increase in word recognition when adding the AR animations to the acoustic signal, a matched control group (Group III) was presented all stimuli in AO. For the comparisons below, the stimuli were hence the same as for Groups I and II, but the subjects were different in Group III. The results on set S1 were therefore used to adjust the scores of the control group so that the AO baseline performance corresponded to that of Groups I-II on S1, since inter-group differences could otherwise make inter-condition comparisons invalid.

3.2.2 Experimental set-up

The AR talking head shown in Fig. 1(a) was used to display the animations and the acoustic signal was presented over high-quality headphones. The sentence order was the same for all subjects and the display condition (AVR, AVS or AO) was random, but balanced, so that all conditions were equally frequent at the beginning, middle and end of the test.

Each sentence was presented three times before the subjects typed in their answer in five entry frames. The five frames were always active, even if the sentence contained fewer words.

Before the test, the subjects were given the familiarization task to try to identify the connection between the sound signal and tongue movements in five sentences presented twice with normal acoustic signal and twice with degraded.

3.2.3 Results

Both types of animations resulted in significantly higher word recognition rates than the acoustic only condition, when comparing the perception results for Groups I and II with those of Group III for sets S2 and S3, as shown in Table 2. When considering the two audiovisual conditions, the word recognition rate was 7% higher when the animations were based on recorded data than when they were synthesized, and the difference is highly significant, using a single factor ANOVA (p<0.005).

	AO	AVS	AVR
acc.	54.6%	56.8%	63.9%
std.	0.12	0.09	0.09

Table 2. Word accuracy rates (acc.) and standard deviation (std) when the stimuli were presented as acoustic only (AO), with animations created from synthesis (AVS) and from measurements (AVR). The differences AVR-AO and AVS-AO are significant at p<0.005, using a paired two-tailed t-test.

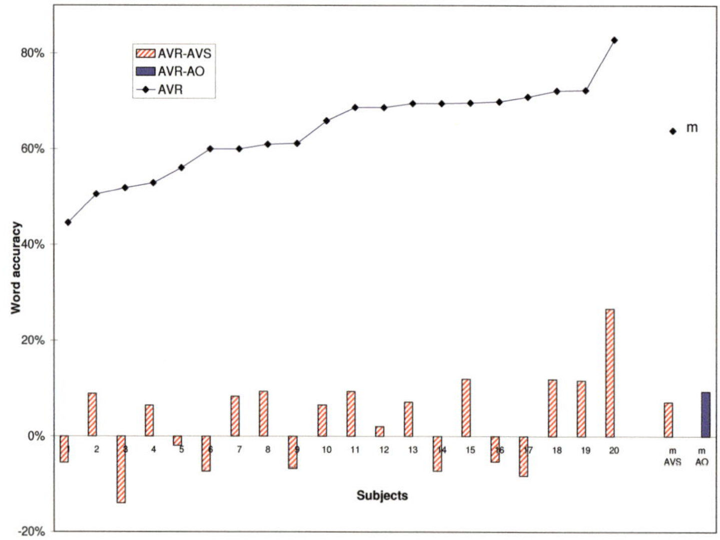

Fig. 8. Rate of correctly recognized words for animations with recorded data (AVR, black line) and difference in recognition rate between AVR and synthetic movements (AVS, striped bars) for each subject. The AVR average for the group (m) and the average improvement for the group, compared to AVS (m AVS, striped bar) and acoustic only (m AO, blue bar) is also given. Subjects are shown in order of increasing AVR score.

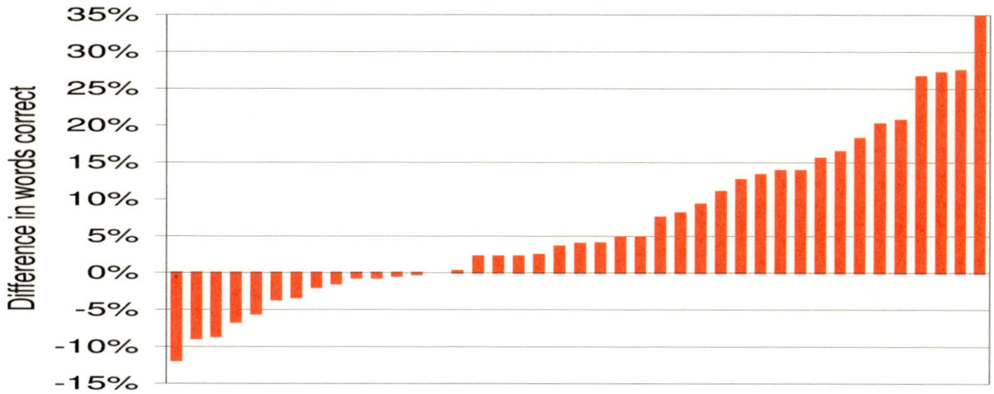

Fig. 9. Difference in recognition rate between AVR and AVS for each sentence. The sentences have been sorted in order of increasing AVR-AVS difference.

Since the same subject was not presented the same sentences in both AVR and AVS, the recognition scores were weighted, so that the average score for the two sets S2 and S3 over all subjects and both conditions AVR and AVS is the same. The scale factors were w_{S1}=0.97 and w_{S2}=1.03. As shown in Fig. 8, the accuracy rate in the AVR condition varied between 45% and 85% for different subjects, and 40% of the subjects actually performed better in AVS condition. The majority of the subjects nevertheless performed better in the AVR condition, and whereas four subjects were more than 10% better with AVR, only one was 10% better with AVS.

The word accuracy rate per sentence, shown in Fig. 9, was higher in AVR for 70% of the sentences, and for about half of these, the difference is large. For one of the sentences (*"Snön låg metertjock på marken"*, i.e. *"The snow lay a meter deep on the ground"*), the word accuracy is 35% higher in AVR, and the difference is significant at the sentence level at $p<0.0005$.

In a follow-up study, published in Engwall & Wik (2009b), it was shown that subjects (of which 11 out of the 22 were the same as in the experiment presented here) could not judge if an animation was created from real recordings or from text-to-speech synthesis. It is hence the case that even though subjects are unaccustomed to seeing tongue movements and can not consciously judge if the animations are truthful representations of the tongue movements, they are, as a group, nevertheless better if the actual articulations that produced the acoustics are displayed.

A possible explanation for this would be that there is a more direct connection between speech perception and articulatory movements, rather than a conscious interpretation of acoustic and visual information by the subjects. There are indeed several theories and evidence that could point in that direction. Skipper et al. (2007) showed that perception of audiovisual speech leads to substantial activities in the speech motor areas of the listener's brain and that the activated areas when seeing a viseme are the same as when producing the corresponding phoneme. However, the connection between visemes and speech perception could be established through experience, when seeing the speaker's face producing the viseme simultaneously with hearing the phoneme, whereas we here deal with a connection between acoustics and visual information that is not normally seen. A potential explanation could be provided by the direct realist theory of speech perception (Fowler, 2008), which states that speech is perceived through a direct mapping of the speech sounds to the listener's articulatory gestures. Hence, seeing the gestures may influence perception unconsciously. Similarly, the speech motor theory (Liberman & Mattingly, 1985) stipulates that both acoustic and visual gestures are processed in accordance with how the speaker produced them. This would explain why the AVS animations, which are realistic, but are not necessarily in accordance with the speaker's gestures, gave lower recognition rates than AVR, where acoustic and visual gestures correspond.

The above explanations are however problematic, since the speaker's and the listener's oral anatomy differ, and they would use slightly different gestures to produce the same sequence of sounds. It is hence unclear if the listener could really map the speaker's articulatory gesture's to his or her own. An alternative explanation is provided by the fuzzy logical theory of speech perception (Massaro, 1998), which argues that perception is a probabilistic decision based on previously learned templates. Acoustic and visual information is processed independently and then combined in a weighted fusion to determine the most probable match with both sources of information. While this appears to be a plausible explanation for visemes (see further the explanation of the McGurk effect in Section 3.3), it is unclear how the visual templates for the tongue movements could have been learned. In the next section, this issue of learning is investigated further.

3.3 How do people learn to "read" tongue movements?

All perception studies cited above indicated that a training phase in some form was required if the subjects should be able to use the information provided by the AR talking head. A fundamental question is then what the subjects learn during this training phase: Is it a conscious mapping of articulatory movements to corresponding phonemes in a template learning scheme? Or are tongue reading abilities pre-existing, and the role of the training phase is to make subjects sub-consciously aware of how to extract information from animations of articulatory movements?

In order to investigate this issue, the so called McGurk effect (McGurk & MacDonald, 1976) can be used. The McGurk effect describes the phenomenon that if the acoustic signal of one phoneme is presented together with the visual lip movements of another, it is often the case that a third phoneme is perceived, because of audiovisual integration. For example, if auditory [ba] is presented with visual [ga], then for the very large majority of subjects [da] is perceived. The reason is that the visual signal is incompatible with [ba] (since the lip closure is missing) and the acoustic with [ga] (the acoustic frequency pattern in the transition from the consonant to the following vowel is wrong) and the brain therefore integrates the two streams of information to perceive [da], which is more in agreement with both streams. It should be noted that this effect is sub-conscious, that the subject actually perceives [da], and that the effect appears even for subjects who know about the conflicting stimuli.

For the AR talking heads, the McGurk effect was adapted to create mismatches between the acoustic signal and the tongue movements in the AR display, rather than with face movements in a normal display. Subjects were then randomly presented either matching stimuli (the acoustics and the animations were of the same phoneme) or conflicting (McGurk stimuli). The underlying idea was that if the subjects had an existing subconscious notion of general articulatory movements, then the perception score for the matching stimuli should be higher and that some type of McGurk effect should be observed for the conflicting stimuli.

3.3.1 Stimuli and subjects

24 different symmetric VCV words, with C=[p, b, t, d, k, g, l, v] and V=[a, ɪ, ʊ], uttered by a female Swedish speaker, were presented at four different levels of white noise (signal-to-noise ratio SNR=+3dB, -6dB, -9dB and Clean speech) and three different audiovisual conditions. The stimuli were presented in blocks of 48 stimuli at each noise level, in random order between noise levels and audiovisual conditions, but in the same order for all subjects. The 48 stimuli consisted of the 24 VCV words played in acoustic only condition (AO), plus 12 of these VCV words played with the animations of the tongue matching the acoustic signal (AVM) and 12 played with animations of the tongue movements that were in conflict with the acoustics (AVC).

The conflicting animations were created by in turn combining the acoustic signal of each of the bilabials [p, b], alveolars [t, d] and velars [k, g] with tongue movements related to one of the other two places of articulation. The conflicting condition for [l] was visual [v] and vice versa. The display excluded the lip area (in order to avoid that lip movements, rather than those of the tongue, influenced the results), and the labial consonants [p, b, v] therefore constitute a special case for both AVM and AVC. Since the subjects did not see the articulation of the lips, AVM in this case signifies that there were *no conflicting* tongue movements in the animation, and AVC for acoustic [k, g, t, d, l] with the animation showing the articulation of [p, b, v] in this case signifies that there were *no supporting* tongue movements in the animation.

Subjects were divided into two groups, with the only difference between groups being that the were presented the AVM and AVC stimuli in opposite conditions. That is, Group I was presented Set 1=[ap:a, ɪd:ɪ, uk:u, ɪb:ɪ, ut:u, ag:a, up:u, ad:a, ɪk:ɪ, al:a, ɪv:ɪ, ul:u] with matched animations and Set 2=[ab:a, ɪt:ɪ, ug:u, ɪp:ɪ, ud:u, ak:a, ub:u, at:a, ɪg:ɪ, av:a, ɪl:ɪ, uv:u] with conflicting. Group II was, on the other hand, presented Set 1 with conflicting and Set 2 with matching animations. Note that Sets 1 and 2 are balanced in terms of vowel context and consonant place of articulation and voicing, i.e., if Set 1 contains a VCV word with an unvoiced consonant, then Set 2 contains the voiced consonant having the same place of articulation in the same vowel context, and this is reversed for another vowel context.

The 18 subjects (13 male and 5 female, aged 21-31 years, no known hearing impairment) had different language backgrounds. Four were native speakers of Swedish; two each of Greek, Persian and Urdu; and one each of German, English, Serbian, Bangla, Chinese, Korean, Thai and Tamil. The heterogeneous subject group was chosen to investigate if familiarity with the target articulations influenced perception results. The question is relevant in the light of the use of AR talking heads for pronunciation training of a foreign language (c.f. Section 4). The influence of the subjects' first language is further discussed in Engwall (2010), while we here deal with the general results.

The description in this chapter concentrates on the stimuli presented at SNR=-6dB, where the combination of audio and animations was the most important. An analysis of the results at the other noise levels is given in Engwall (2010).

3.3.2 Experimental set-up

Each stimulus was presented once, with the acoustic signal played over high quality headphones and the animations of the tongue movements shown on a 21" flat computer screen. AVM and AVC animations displayed the movements in an AR side view, such as

	AO	AVM	AVC
acc.	36.2%	43.1%	33.8%
std.	0.13	0.15	0.14

Table 3. Word accuracy rates (acc.) and standard deviation (std) when the stimuli were presented as acoustic only (AO), with matching animations (AVM) and with conflicting (AVC). The differences AVM-AO and AVM-AVC are significant at $p<0.05$, using a single factor ANOVA.

the one in Fig. 1(a), but translated to hide the lip area. For AO, an outside view, without any movements, was instead shown.

For the auditory stimuli, the SNR for the added white noise spectrum was relative to the average energy of the vowel parts of each individual VCV word and each VCV word was then normalized with respect to the energy level.

Before the test, a set of 9 VCV words with C=[m, n, ŋ] and V=[a, ɪ, ʊ] was presented in AVM at SNR=Clean, -6dB and -9dB, as a familiarization to the task. No feedback was given and these stimuli were not included in the test. The familiarization did hence not constitute a training phase.

A forced choice setting was used, i.e., subjects gave their answer by selecting the on-screen button for the consonant that they perceived. In the results below, accuracy is always counted with respect to the acoustic signal.

3.3.3 Results

The mean accuracy levels at SNR=-6dB are shown in Table 3. The differences between AVM and AO and between AVM and AVC are significant at $p<0.05$ using a single factor ANOVA. Note that voicing errors were disregarded and responses were grouped as [p/b], [t/d] and [k/g], giving a chance level of 20%. The reasons for this was that several subjects were from language backgrounds lacking the voiced-unvoiced distinction (such as between [t] and [d]) and that the aim was to investigate the influence of the visual information given about the tongue articulation. In the following, /p/ refers to [p, b], /t/ to [t, d] and /k/ to [k, g].

As a general result, the animations with matching articulatory movements hence gave an important support to the perception of the consonants in noise. This is all the more true if only the consonants that are produced with the tongue [t, d, k, g, l] are considered. Fig. 10 summarizes the individual and average perception scores (m_{AVM}=59%) for these consonants. The graph shows that 14 of the 18 subjects performed better with matched animations than with only audio and that 9 performed worse with conflicting animations than with audio only. Curiously, 9 subjects however performed better with conflicting animations than with audio only, indicating that one effect of presenting the animations may have been that the subjects listened more carefully to the acoustic signal than if the same acoustic signal was presented without animations. The graph also shows, just as the results for the studies presented above, that the differences between subjects were very large, with e.g., subject 18 being a particularly gifted tongue reader (100% recognition in AVM compared to 32.5% in AO)

When analyzing the responses with respect to accompanying animation shown in Fig. 11, several patterns appear, both in terms of the strength of the information given by a particular acoustic signal or articulatory movement and integration effects for conflicting acoustic and visual signals. For the acoustic signal, [l] is the most salient with over 90% correct responses already with AO and consequently only marginal improvement with AVM or decline with AVC. On the other hand, the fricative [v] is particularly vulnerable to the background noise, with the AO accuracy level being half that of the next lowest, /p/. For the visual signal, the articulatory movement of /k/ has the strongest influence: For acoustic /k/, when the movement is shown in AVM, the accuracy in the responses increases with 50%, and when it is lacking in AVC, the accuracy decreases by 25%, regardless of if the animation shows no tongue articulation (for /p/) or a conflicting movement (for /t/). Further, for /t/, a conflicting /k/ animation decreases the recognition score in AVC by 10% compared to AO.

Concerning audiovisual integration, shown in Fig. 12, the changes listed in Table 4 are the most important that can be observed. Several of these changes are similar to the McGurk effect, even if the change is much smaller (and only took place with a noisy acoustic signal).

In conclusion for this study we can argue that the subjects must have a prior knowledge of articulatory movements of the tongue, since the animations were randomly matched and conflicting and the subjects performed significantly better with the matching movements. The conflicting animations further showed that subjects integrated both signals in their perception.

We are currently planning a follow-up study with a training phase prior to the test, in order to investigate if consistency between training and test or between acoustics and articulation is the most important. In this, subjects will be divided into four groups. Group I will be shown matching audiovisual stimuli in both training and test. Group II will be shown conflicting audiovisual stimuli in both training and test, but the audiovisual combinations would be consistent between training and test. Group III will be shown conflicting audiovisual stimuli

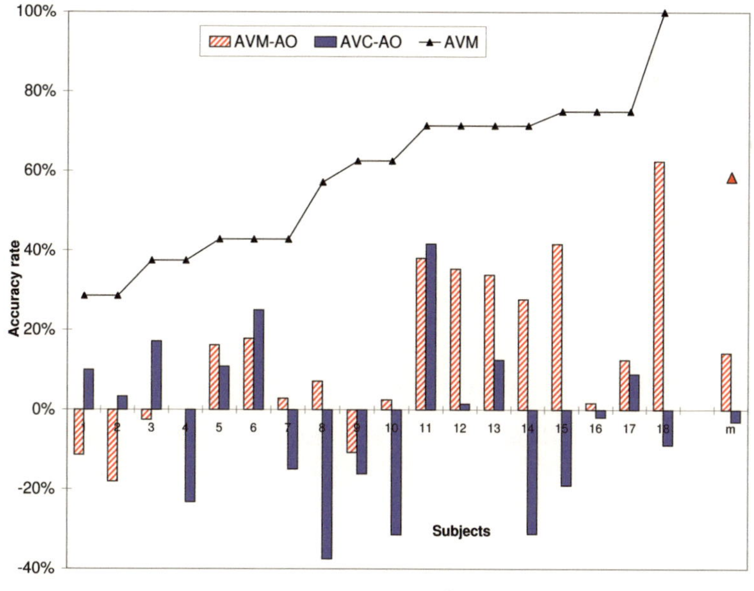

Fig. 10. The accuracy rate for [t,d,k,g,d,l] in the matched (AVM) condition (black line), and the difference between the matched AVM (red and white striped bars) or conflicting AVC (blue bars) conditions and the acoustic only (AO), for each individual subject, and for the group (m). Subjects are presented in order of increasing AVM score.

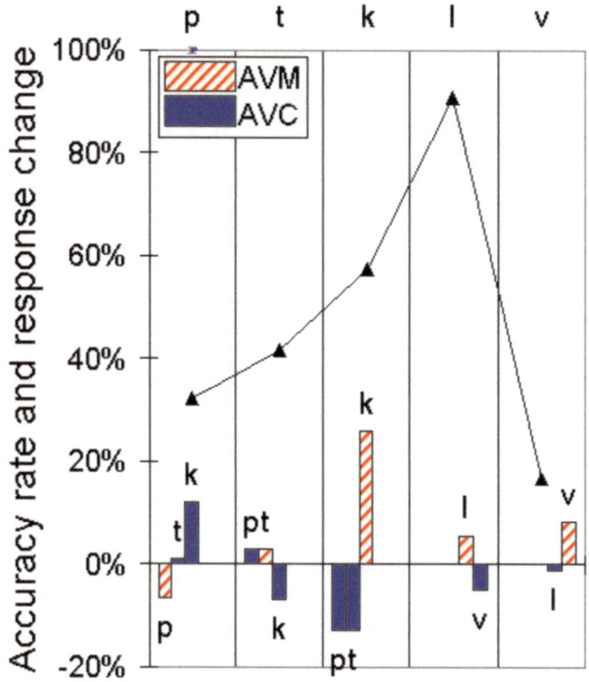

Fig. 11. The accuracy rate in acoustic only AO condition (black line), and the change (bars) when animations were added. The stimuli having the same acoustic signal ([p/b, t/d, k/g, l, v]) are grouped on the x-axis and within each group the bars indicate the difference in perception score, for that stimuli, compared to AO. Red and white striped bars signal matching condition AVM, blue bars conflicting AVC.

in the training, but matching in the test. Group IV will be shown matching audiovisual stimuli in the training, but conflicting in the test.

If match between the acoustic and visual signals is the most important, then Group I and Group III will have higher recognition scores than Groups II and IV. If, on the other hand, consistency between training and test is more important, Groups I and II will perform similarly, and better than Groups III and IV.

4. AR talking heads in speech production training

Several studies on the use of AR talking heads in pronunciation training have been performed (Engwall & Bälter, 2007; Engwall et al., 2006; Fagel & Madany, 2008; Massaro et al., 2008; Massaro & Light, 2003; 2004).

In Massaro & Light (2003), Japanese students of English were instructed how to produce /r/ and /l/ with either a normal front view of the talking face or with four different AR displays that illustrated the intraoral articulation from different views (c.f. Section 2). In Massaro & Light (2004), American hearing-impaired children were instructed how to produce consonant clusters, the fricative-affricate distinction and voicing differences in their native language, using the same four AR displays. In Massaro et al. (2008), English speakers were instructed

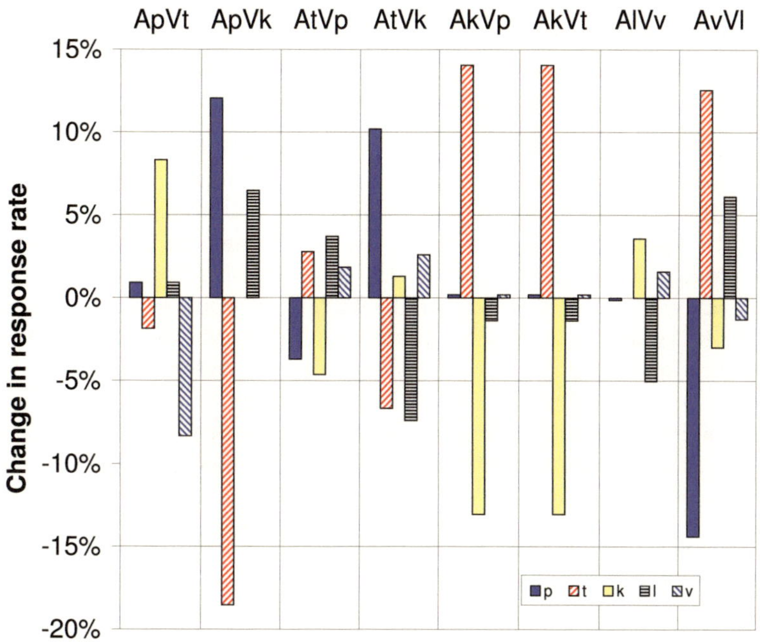

Fig. 12. The change in response rate for different consonant labels when comparing AVC with AO. The conflicting stimuli are given on the x-axis, with AxVy indicating that the acoustic signal was of consonant x and the visual signal of consonant y.

A	V	+	-	Explanation
p	t	k	v	The acoustic signal is incompatible with /t/ & the visual with /p, v/, /k/ is the most compatible with both.
p	k	p	t	The visual signal is incompatible with /t/, the jaw movement in /k/ may be interpreted as signaling a bilabial closure.
t	p		k	The visual signal is incompatible with /k/.
t	k	p	l	The acoustic signal is incompatible with /k/, the visual with /t,l/ & the jaw movement in /k/ may be interpreted as signaling a bilabial closure
k	p	t	k	The acoustic signal is incompatible with /p/ & the visual with /k/, /t/ is the most compatible with both.
k	t	t	k	The visual signal is compatible with /t/ and incompatible with /k/.
l	v		l	The visual signal is incompatible with /l/.
v	l	t	p	The acoustic signal is incompatible with /l/ & the visual with /p/, /t/ is the most compatible with both.

Table 4. Observed changes in response when a conflicting animation is added to an acoustic stimuli. The table lists the acoustic (A) and the visual (V) signals, the main increase (+) and decrease (-) in the subjects' responses compared to the AO condition and a tentative explanation on why the change takes place.

how to produce either one pair of similar phonemes in Arabic or one pair of similar phonemes in Mandarin. For the Arabic phoneme pair, the main articulatory difference was the place of contact between the tongue and the palate, while for the Mandarin pair, the difference was in the lip rounding. For the Arabic pair, a cut-away AR side-view was used to illustrate the position of the tongue, while a normal front view was used for the Mandarin pair.

These three studies did not provide any strong evidence that the AR view was beneficial, as judged by listeners rating the students production before and after the training. In Massaro & Light (2003), the students improved in both training conditions, but those who had been presented the AR displays did not improve more than those who had seen the normal face view. In Massaro & Light (2004), the children did improve, but since they were not compared with other subjects who had not been shown the AR talking heads, it can not be concluded that this was thanks to the augmented reality-based training. In Massaro et al. (2008), the group that practised the Mandarin pair with the normal face view had improved significantly more than a control group that had only been presented the auditory targets, while the group that practised the Arabic phoneme pair was not significantly better than the acoustic only control group. However, many of the subjects in the three studies reported that they really enjoyed the practise with the AR talking head and believed that it was useful.

The outcome in Fagel & Madany (2008) was somewhat better in terms of subject improvement. Children with pathological lisping were instructed how to produce [s, z] during two interactive lessons with a human teacher and the AR talking head was used as a tool to illustrate prototypic correct articulations. Listeners, who rated the degree of lisping before and after the lessons, judged that there was a significant reduction in lisping for the children as a group, but that there were large individual differences.

In Engwall et al. (2006), Engwall & Bälter (2007) and Engwall (2011), the subjects were given *feedback* on their articulation, using the AR talking head display shown in Fig. 1(a). The feedback was in the form of instructions on how to change the articulation, e.g., *"Lower the tongue tip and move the back of the tongue as far back as you can in the mouth and then slightly forward, to create a wheezing sound."* in order to change the articulation from [ʃ] to [ɧ], accompanied by animations illustrating the instructions in the AR talking heads. In the first study, the subjects were Swedish children with pronunciation disorders and in the other two, they were non-native speakers without prior knowledge of Swedish. The first two studies focused on user evaluations of the interface and the subjects' improvement in the production of the practice phoneme, the velar fricative [ɧ], was not investigated quantitatively. In the last study, the articulation change that the subjects did when they received feedback on the production of the Swedish [r] and [ɧ] was measured with ultrasound. Some subjects readily followed the audiovisual instructions, as exemplified in Fig. 13, showing two French speakers who changed their articulation from the French rhotic [ʁ] with a low tongue tip to the Swedish [r] with a raised tip, after a number of attempts and feedback. However, other subjects had great difficulties changing the articulation in the short practice session.

The studies described above indicate that it is not an easy task initially to transfer articulatory instructions to the own production. However, throughout the different studies, the subjects were positive about the usefulness of the AR talking heads. They stated that they thought that they had improved through the practise and that the feedback instructions had been helpful to change the articulation. As an example, in Engwall & Bälter (2007), subjects were asked to rate the pronunciation training system's usability on a number of aspects, using a 1-9 Likert

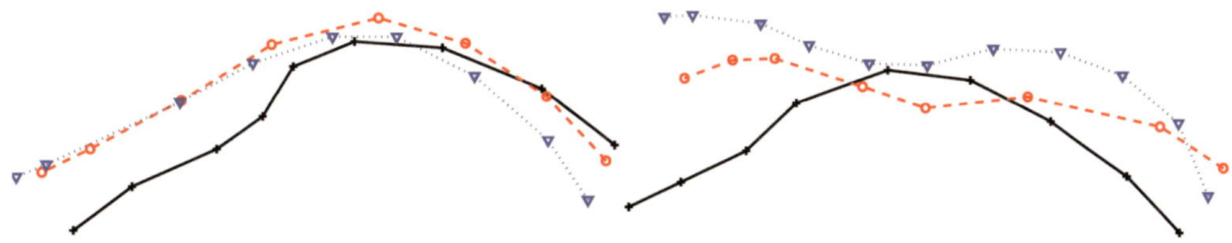

Fig. 13. Change in the tongue articulation of 'r', from a French rothic in the first attempt (black line, +) to a Swedish alveolar trill (red line, o; blue line, $\bigtriangledown$) in the sequence "rik".

scale. For the question regarding if the articulatory animations were confusing (1) or clear (9), the mean opinion score was m=7.75 with a standard deviation of ρ=1.18, and the subjects further stated that the interaction with the virtual teacher was clear (m=7.68, ρ=1.04) and interesting (m=8.06, ρ=1.31). They also thought that the practice had helped them improve their pronunciation (m=7.32, ρ=1.37). It may hence well be the case that AR talking heads could provide the learners with useful information after additional familiarization. For a more thorough discussion of the use of AR talking heads in computer-assisted pronunciation training, please refer to Engwall & Bälter (2007) or Engwall (2011).

5. Paths for future research

Many questions concerning AR talking head support remain, regarding both the large differences between subjects and for which phoneme sequences the AR animations are helpful.

It would be interesting to monitor the subjects' visual attention using an eye-tracking system to investigate if there is evidence that the subjects' viewing patterns influence their performance. That is, if subjects with higher perception rates or adequate production changes focus more on the areas on the screen that provide important information about place and manner of articulation. By analysing the looking pattern one could also look into if the important factor is where the subject looks (on what part of the display) or how (focused on the task or watching more casually).

All the studies described above have further used naive subjects, in some cases with a short explicit or implicit training prior to the perception test. An intriguing question is if long-term use would make tongue reading a viable alternative for some hearing-impaired subjects, just as normal speech reading abilities improve with practice and experience. The experiments have shown that some subjects are in fact very apt at extracting information from the AR talking head displays and it would be of interest to investigate recognition accuracy and user opinion for such subjects after several longer practice sessions.

Further, systematic larger studies are required to determine how AR talking heads may be used as a support for speech perception and in production. With larger subject groups and a larger speech material, the potentials for long term use could be more clearly evaluated.

Another question, already introduced in Section 2, concerns the realism of the AR talking head: How are the recognition rates and the subjects' impression of the interface influenced by the visual representation? That is, are recognition rates higher with videorealistic animations of the face and/or the intraoral parts or with schematic, more simplified illustrations of the most important articulatory features? We are planning for a perception study comparing the 3D AR talking head display with simplified 2D animations of the midsagittal tongue, lips and palate contours. Kröger et al. (2008) found that 5–8 year old children were as successful in mimicking vowels and consonants if they were presented a 2D- as a 3D-representation of the articulation. The authors therefore concluded that the more complex 3D view did not provide any additional information. It could however be argued that the 3D model used (only the surface of the tongue moving in a semi-transparent vocal tract tube, with no face, similar to the display in Fig. 1(e)) may not represent the full potential of AR talking heads.

Other issues that merit further consideration include user preferences for colour coding of different articulators (contrast *vs.* realism), correspondence in realism between the face and intraoral parts (potential problems of combining a videorealistic face with computer graphics for the tongue and mouth cavity) and strategy to create the Augmented Reality display (see-through or cut-away of the facial skin, or hiding the face).

For the last issue, we are interested in investigating the uncanny valley effect for Augmented Reality talking heads. The uncanny valley effect normally refers to the situation in robotics and 3D computer animation when human observers become negative towards the robot or avatar because it appears to be or act *almost* like a human, but either lack or have some aspects that one would or would not expect from a human. In the case of AR talking heads the effect could appear if the face of the avatar is so truthfully videorealistic that viewers feel uneasy about representations suggesting that the head of the avatar has been cut in half or that parts of the skin have been surgically removed. To avoid such reactions it may be suitable either to choose a less realistic face or to project intraoral information on the skin of the avatar's cheek instead. This could for example be in the form of stylized X-ray or MR Images, which many viewers are familiar with and they would hence immediately understand the analogy that these imaging techniques allow to see what is underneath the skin. With further advances in Augmented Reality display technology and response times for Automatic Speech Recognition one can also envisage that such a display could be used to provide information directly on a *real* speaker's cheek.

Even if much research is required to further investigate user reactions, preferences and performance with AR talking heads, we are convinced that they could potentially have an important role to play as a support for speech perception and production. In addition, the methods described above to illustrate tongue movements in an AR setting are also of interest for numerous other applications, such as planning for and rehabilitation after glossectomy surgery, education in phonetics, and animation in computer games and movies.

6. Acknowledgments

This work is supported by the Swedish Research Council project 80449001 Computer-Animated LAnguage TEAchers (CALATEA).

7. References

Agelfors, E., Beskow, J., Dahlquist, M., Granström, B., Lundeberg, M., Spens, K.-E. & Öhman, T. (1998). Synthetic faces as a lipreading support, *Proceedings of International Conference on Spoken Language Processing*, pp. 3047–3050.

Badin, P., Elisei, F., Bailly, G. & Tarabalka, Y. (2008). An audiovisual talking head for augmented speech generation: Models and animations based on a real speaker's articulatory data, *in* F. Perales & R. Fisher (eds), *Articulated Motion and Deformable Objects*, Springer, pp. 132–143.

Benoît, C. & LeGoff, B. (1998). Audio-visual speech synthesis from French text: Eight years of models, design and evaluation at the ICP, *Speech Communication* 26: 117–129.

Benoît, C., Mohamadi, T. & Kandel, S. (1994). Effects of phonetic context on audio-visual intelligibility of French, *Journal of Speech and Hearing Research* 37: 1195–1203.

Beskow, J. (1995). Rule-based visual speech synthesis, *Proceedings of Eurospeech*, pp. 299–302.

Beskow, J., Engwall, O. & Granström, B. (2003). Resynthesis of facial and intraoral motion from simultaneous measurements, *Proceedings of International Congress of Phonetical Sciences*, pp. 431–434.

Beskow, J., Karlsson, I., Kewley, J. & Salvi, G. (2004). Synface - a talking head telephone for the hearing-impaired, *in* K. Miesenberger, J. Klaus, W. Zagler & D. Burger (eds), *Computers Helping People with Special Needs*, Springer-Verlag, pp. 1178–1186.

Cohen, M., Beskow, J. & Massaro, D. (1998). Recent development in facial animation: an inside view, *Proceedings of International Conference on Audiovisual Signal Processing*, pp. 201–206.

Cornett, O. & Daisey, M. E. (1992). *The Cued Speech Resource Book for Parents of Deaf Children*, National Cued Speech Association.

Engwall, O. (2003). Combining MRI, EMA & EPG in a three-dimensional tongue model, *Speech Communication* 41/2-3: 303–329.

Engwall, O. (2008). Can audio-visual instructions help learners improve their articulation? - an ultrasound study of short term changes, *Proceedings of Interspeech 2008*, pp. 2631–2634.

Engwall, O. (2010). Is there a McGurk effect for tongue reading?, *Proceedings of International Conference on Auditory-Visual Speech Processing*.

Engwall, O. (2011). Analysis of and feedback on phonetic features in pronunciation training with a virtual language teacher, *Computer Assisted Language Learning* .

Engwall, O. & Bälter, O. (2007). Pronunciation feedback from real and virtual language teachers, *Computer Assisted Language Learning* 20(3): 235–262.

Engwall, O., Bälter, O., Öster, A.-M. & Kjellström, H. (2006). Designing the human-machine interface of the computer-based speech training system ARTUR based on early user tests, *Behavior and Information Technology* 25: 353–365.

Engwall, O. & Wik, P. (2009a). Are real tongue movements easier to speech read than synthesized?, *Proceedings of Interspeech*, pp. 824–827.

Engwall, O. & Wik, P. (2009b). Can you tell if tongue movements are real or synthetic?, *Proceedings of International Conference on Audiovisual Signal Processing*.

Fagel, S. & Madany, K. (2008). A 3-D virtual head as a tool for speech therapy for children, *Proceedings of Interspeech*, pp. 2643–2646.

Fowler, C. (2008). The FLMP STMPed, *Psychonomic Bulletin & Review* 15: 458–462.

Grauwinkel, K., Dewitt, B. & Fagel, S. (2007). Visual information and redundancy conveyed by internal articulator dynamics in synthetic audiovisual speech, *Proceedings of Interspeech*, pp. 706–709.

Guiard-Marigny, T., Ostry, O. & Benoît, C. (1995). Speech intelligibility of synthetic lips and jaw, *Proceedings of the International Congress of Phonetical Sciences*, pp. 222–225.

Kröger, B., Graf-Borttscheller, V. & Lowit, A. (2008). Two- and three-dimensional visual articulatory models for pronunciation training and for treatment of speech disorders, *Proceedings of Interspeech*, pp. 2639–2642.

Liberman, A. & Mattingly, I. (1985). The motor theory of speech perception revised, *Cognition* 21: 1–36.

MacLeod, A. & Summerfield, Q. (1990). A procedure for measuring auditory and audiovisual speech-reception thresholds for sentences in noise. Rationale, evaluation and recommendations for use, *British Journal of Audiology* 24: 29–43.

Massaro, D. (1998). *Perceiving Talking Faces: From Speech Perception to a Behavioral Principle*, MIT Press.

Massaro, D., Bigler, S., Chen, T., Perlman, M. & Ouni, S. (2008). Pronunciation training: The role of eye and ear, *Proceedings of Interspeech*, pp. 2623–2626.

Massaro, D. & Light, J. (2003). Read my tongue movements: Bimodal learning to perceive and produce non-native speech /r/ and /l/, *Proceedings of Eurospeech*, pp. 2249–2252.

Massaro, D. & Light, J. (2004). Using visible speech for training perception and production of speech for hard of hearing individuals, *Journal of Speech, Language, and Hearing Research* 47: 304–320.

McGurk, H. & MacDonald, J. (1976). Hearing lips and seeing voices, *Nature* 264(5588): 746–748.

Perkell, J., Guenther, F., Lane, H., Matthies, M., Perrier, P., Vick, J., Wilhelms-Tricarico, R. & Zandipour, M. (2000). A theory of speech motor control and supporting data from speakers with normal hearing and with profound hearing loss, *Journal of Phonetics* 28: 233–272.

Rizzolatti, G. & Arbib, M. (1998). Language within our grasp, *Trends Neuroscience* 21: 188–194.

Siciliano, C., Williams, G., Beskow, J. & Faulkner, A. (2003). Evaluation of a multilingual synthetic talking face as a communication aid for the hearing impaired, *Proceedings of International Conference of Phonetic Sciences*, pp. 131–134.

Sjölander, K. (2003). An HMM-based system for automatic segmentation and alignment of speech, *Proceedings of Fonetik*, pp. 93–96.

Skipper, J., Wassenhove, V. v., Nusbaum, H. & Small, S. (2007). Hearing lips and seeing voices: How cortical areas supporting speech production mediate audiovisual speech perception, *Cerebral Cortex* 17: 2387 – 2399.

Sumby, W. & Pollack, I. (1954). Visual contribution to speech intelligibility in noise, *Journal of the Acoustical Society of America* 26: 212–215.

Summerfield, Q. (1979). Use of visual information for phonetic perception, *Phonetica* 36: 314–331.

Wik, P. & Engwall, O. (2008). Can visualization of internal articulators support speech perception?, *Proceedings of Interspeech*, pp. 2627–2630.

6

Mobile Mixed Reality System for Architectural and Construction Site Visualization

Charles Woodward and Mika Hakkarainen
VTT Technical Research Centre of Finland, Finland

1. Introduction

The Architecture, Engineering and Construction (AEC) sector is widely recognized as one of the most promising application fields for Augmented Reality (AR). Building Information Models (BIM) and in particular the Industry Foundation Classes (IFC) data format are another main technology driver increasingly used for data sharing and communication purposes in the AEC sector (Koo & Fischer 2000). For example, the Finnish state owned facility management company Senate Properties demands use of IFC compatible software and BIM in all their projects (Senate 2007).

At some advanced construction sites, 3D/4D Building Information Models are starting to replace paper drawings as reference media for construction workers. Thus, workers can check daily work tasks using BIM systems installed at site offices, sometimes with remote connections to BIM databases, and even annotate the virtual model with information relating to the construction site. However, the model data is mostly hosted on desktop systems in the site office, which is situated far away from the target location and not easily accessible. Combined with mobile Augmented Reality and time schedules, 4D BIMs could facilitate on-the-spot comparisons of the actual situation at the construction site with the building's planned appearance and other properties at the given moment.

Besides augmented visualization, the related camera tracking technologies open up further application scenarios, enabling mobile location-based feedback from the construction site to the CAD and BIM systems. Such feedback possibilities include adding elements of reality such as images, reports and other comments to the virtual building model, correctly aligned in both time and space. Our discussion thus addresses the complete spectrum of Mixed Reality as defined by (Milgram and Kishino 1994), with real world augmented with virtual model data, and digital building models augmented with real world data.

Shin and Dunston (2008) evaluated 17 classified work tasks in the AEC industry. They concluded that eight of them (layout, excavation, positioning, inspection, coordination, supervision, commenting and strategizing) could potentially benefit from the use of AR. Additionally, related application areas would be communication and marketing prior to construction work, as well as building life cycle applications after the building is constructed.

Among previous work, the first mobile AR system was developed by Feiner et al. (1997). Their application was to present an AR view of campus information at Columbia University.

Gleue and Thaene (2001) presented the Archeoguide system to provide tourists an AR view to historical and cultural sites. More recently, Reitmayr and Drummond (2006) presented a robust feature based and hybrid tracking solution for outdoor mobile AR. Among the first to address practical AEC applications, (Schall et al. 2008) presented a mobile handheld AR system Vivente for visualizing underground infrastructure. Their work was extended with state-of-the-art sensor fusion methods for outdoor tracking in (Schall et al. 2009). For further references on mobile AR with building construction models, see the thesis by Behzadan (2008) and the review article (Izkara et al. 2009).

However, little research has been done to integrate mobile AR with real world building models, often containing millions of triangles and being hundreds of megabytes in size. Integrating the time component to mobile AR solutions is another topic that is seldom addressed in previous literature. Among non-mobile solutions, however, let us note the impressive work (Goldparvar-Fard et al. 2010). They provide off-line still image based tools to compare the situation at construction site against 4D plans, based on 3D reconstruction of the construction site created from photographs taken of the site.

Our long term research goal has been to prove the technical validity of bringing real world BIM models to the construction site, for augmenting with lightweight mobile devices. Our work on mobile AR dates back to 2003 with the client-server implementation on a PDA device (Pasman & Woodward 2003). The next generation implementation (Honkamaa et al. 2005) produced a marker-free UMPC solution by combining the building's location in Google Earth, the user's GPS position, optical flow tracking and user interaction for tracking initialization. This work lead to the first version of the current system architecture (Hakkarainen et al. 2009) to handle arbitrary OSG formats and IFC (instead of just Google Earth's Collada), 4D models for construction time visualization (instead of just 3D), and mobile feedback from the construction site to the design system ("augmented virtuality"). The system was further extended in (Woodward et al. 2010) to cover more accurate map representations, mobile interaction, operation with data glasses, efficient client-server architecture, tracking methods, as well as discussion on photorealistic visualization for mobile AR.

This article gives an overall presentation of our software system, its background, current state and future plans. Among the most recent developments, we present: the client implementation on mobile phones, based on a lightweight optical tracking solution; results of our field trials in different pilot cases, including application during the construction work and comparing previous visualization results with the appearance of a partially ready building; as well as conclusions of the present status of the research.

The article is organized as follows. Section 2 explains the general implementation and functionality of the core software modules. The mobile phone implementation is discussed in Section 3. Our lightweight feature-based tracking solution is presented in Section 4. The photorealistic rendering functionality for mobile AR is described in Section 5. Results from our field trials are presented in Section 6. Items for future work are pointed out in Section 7 and concluding remarks are given in Section 8.

2. System overview

This Section presents the general implementation of the system. The discussion is given mainly from functional point of view, while a more detailed discussion is provided in (Woodward et al. 2010).

2.1 Software modules

Our system is divided into three parts; 4DStudio, MapStudio and OnSitePlayer. The Studio applications fulfill the authoring role of the system and are typically used at the office, while OnSitePlayer provides the augmented reality view and mobile feedback interface at the construction site. OnSitePlayer can be operated either as a stand-alone, or as a client-server solution, distributing heavy 3D computation to the OnSiteServer extension, and tracking and rendering to the OnSiteClient extension. See Figure 1.

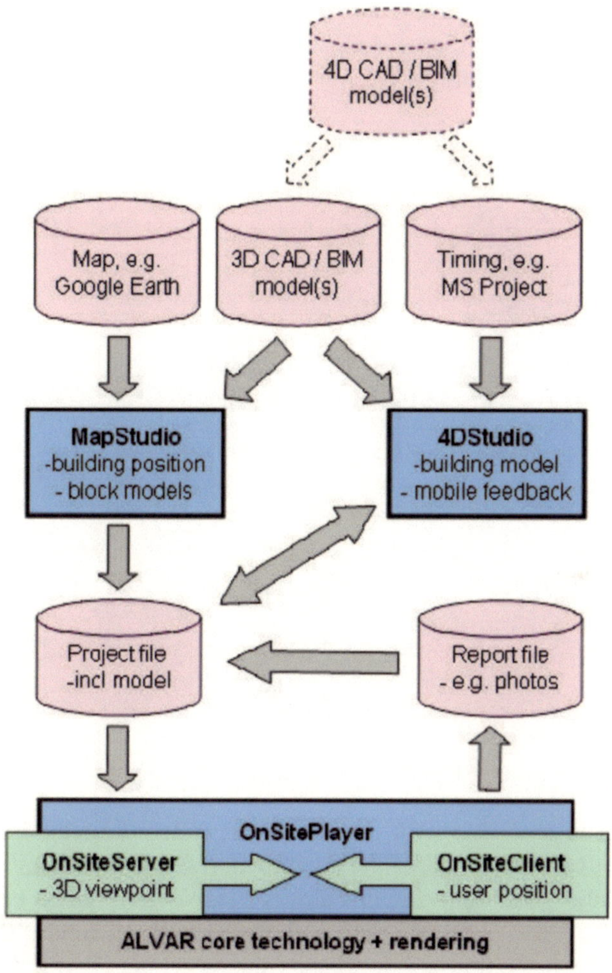

Fig. 1. System architecture.

The tracking algorithms are based on our software library ALVAR - A Library for Virtual and Augmented Reality (VTT 2011), and the OpenCV computer vision library. The GUI is built using the wxWidgets framework. For rendering, the open-source 3D graphics library OpenSceneGraph (OSG) version is used. The applications can handle all OSG supported file formats via OSG's plug-in interface (e.g. OSG's internal format, 3DS, VRML). The TNO IFC Engine3 (TNO 2010) is used as a platform to process IFC building model files.

2.2 4D studio

The 4DStudio application takes the building model (in IFC or some other format) and the construction project schedule (in MS Project XML format) as input. 4DStudio can then be used to link these into a 4D BIM. 4D IFC models defined with Tekla Structures can also be read directly by 4DStudio. Once the model has been defined, 4DStudio outputs the project description as an XML file.

4DStudio has a list of all the building parts and project tasks, from which the user can select the desired elements for visualization. For interaction, 4D Studio provides various tools to select elements for visualization, user definable color coding, clip planes, and viewing the model along the time line. See Figure 2.

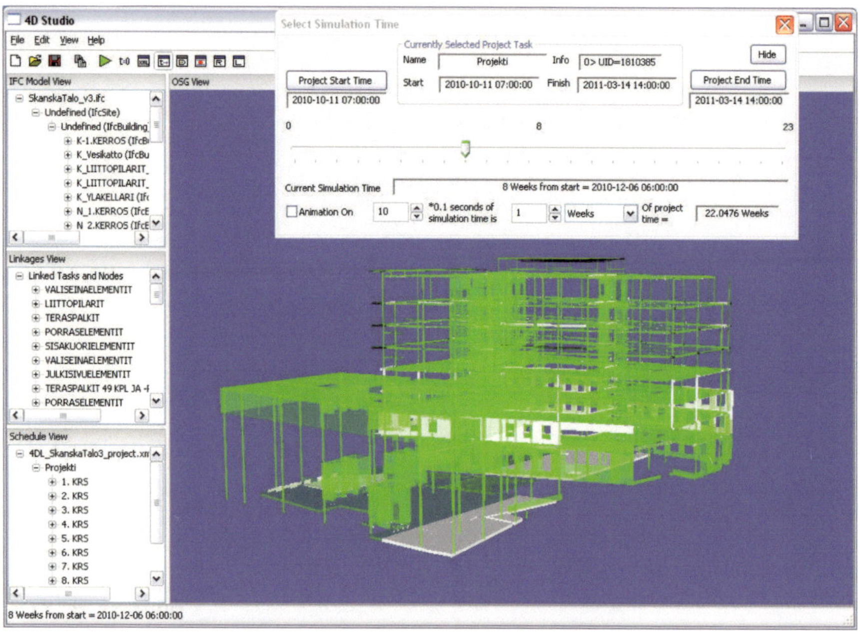

Fig. 2. Building model with construction schedule in 4DStudio.

Feedback report items generated with the mobile AR system describe for example tasks or problems that have been observed at the construction site by workers. These can also be viewed with 4DStudio. Each item contains a title, a task description, a time and location of the task, and optionally one or several digital photos. Selecting a report item in the list takes the 4D building model to the time and location of the report item in question.

2.3 MapStudio

The MapStudio application is used to position the models into a geo coordinate system, using an imported map image of the construction site. The geo map can be imported from Google Earth, or for more accurate representations geospatial data formats like GeoTiff. The image import is done using the open source Geospatial Data Abstraction Library (GDAL).

The models are imported from 4DStudio, and can be any OSG compatible format or IFC format. The model can either be a main model or a so-called block model, which is used to enrich the AR view, or to mask the main model with existing buildings. The system can also be used to add clipping information to the models, for example the basement can be hidden in the on-site visualization.

The user can position the models on the map either by entering numerical parameters or by interactively positioning the model with the mouse (see Figure 3). Once all the model information has been defined, the AR scene information is stored as an XML based scene description, ready to be taken out for mobile visualization on site.

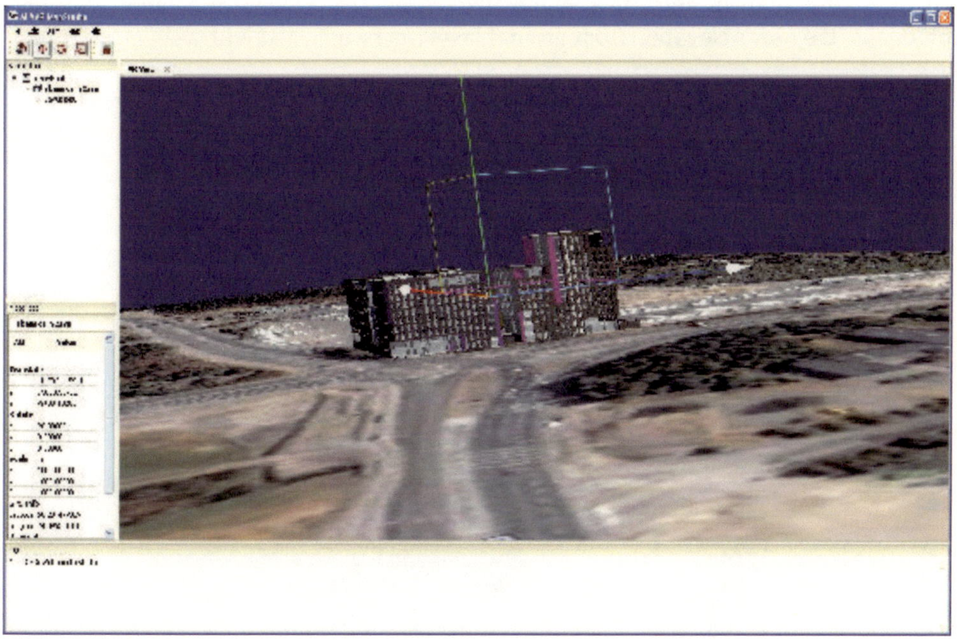

Fig. 3. Building placed in geo coordinates with MapStudio.

2.4 OnSitePlayer

OnSitePlayer is launched at the remote location by opening a MapStudio scene description, or by importing a project file containing additional information. The application then provides two separate views in tabs; a map layout of the site with the models including the user location and viewing direction (see Figure 4) and an augmented view with the models displayed over the real-time video feed (see Figures 5 and 6).

The user is able to request different types of augmented visualizations of the model based on time, for example defining the visualization start-time and end-time freely, using clipping planes, and/or showing the model partially transparent to see the real and existing structures behind the virtual ones. OnSitePlayer also allows for storing augmented still images and video of the visualization, to be later reviewed at the office.

With OnSitePlayer, the user can also create mobile feedback reports consisting of still images annotated with text comments. Each report is registered in the 3D environment at the user's location, camera direction, and moment in time. The reports are attached to the BIM via XML files and are available for browsing with 4DStudio, as explained above.

2.5 Interactive positioning

As GPS positioning does not always work reliably (e.g. when indoors) or accurately enough, we provide the user with the option to indicate his/her location interactively. The system presents the user the same map layout as used in the MapStudio application. The user is then able to zoom into the map and place the camera icon to the his/her currently know location. Note by the way that by using manual positioning, possible errors in the model's and user's positioning are aligned and thus eliminated from the model orientation calculation. Additionally, the user's elevation from ground level can be adjusted with a slider.

Fig. 4. User position and placemark shown in OnSitePlayer.

Compass (if any) does not always provide sufficient grounds for automatic tracking initialization. As backup, interactive means are provided for model alignment. After the model is properly aligned the system switches to feature-based tracking.

The interactive alignment of the video and the building models can be achieved in several ways (Woodward et al. 2010). As one option, block models that represent existing buildings can be used as a reference for the inital alignment. However, this approach requires modeling parts of the surrounding environment which might not always be possible or feasible.

As a more generally applicable approach (Wither et al. 2006), known elements of the real world are marked in MapStudio as "placemarks" (see Figure 4). The mobile user then selects any of the defined placemarks with the "viewfinder" to initialize real time tracking (see Figure 5). Real time augmented view (Figure 6) is produced as the user "shoots" the placemark by pressing a button on the mobile device.

Fig. 5. OnSitePlayer view showing viewfinder for the placemark.

Fig. 6. Building model augmented with OnSitePlayer, at two different locations.

2.6 Client-Server Implementation

Virtual building models are often too complex and large to be rendered with mobile devices at a reasonable frame rate. This problem is overcome with the client-server extension for the OnSitePlayer application. The client extension, OnSiteClient, is used at the construction site while the server extension, OnSiteServer, is running at the site office or at some other remote location. Data communication between the client and server can be done using either WLAN or 3G.

The client and server applications were basically obtained with relatively small modifications to the OnSitePlayer code. The client and server share the same scene description as well as the same construction site geospatial information. The client is responsible for gathering position and orientation information, but instead of rendering the full 3D model, the client just passes the user location and viewing direction to the server. The server uses this information to calculate the correct model view, which is then sent to the client for augmenting on the mobile device.

In our implementation, the view is represented as a textured spherical view of the virtual scene surrounding the user. The sphere is approximated by triangles. An icosahedron was chosen since it is a regular polyhedron formed from equilateral triangles, therefore simplifying the texture generation process. The icosahedron also provides a reasonable tradeoff between speed (number of faces) and accuracy (resolution of images).

As the scene is rendered into the sphere representation, alpha values are used to indicate transparent parts of each texture image. If some image does not contain any part of the 3D model to be rendered, the whole image can be discarded and not sent to the client. See (Woodward et al. 2010) for further implementation details.

The client augments the scene by aligning the sphere to the virtual camera coordinates according to the user's position and camera direction, and renders the alpha textured sphere over the video image. Camera tracking keeps the 2D visualization in place and the user may pan/tilt the view as desired.

The same sphere visualization can be used as long as the user remains at the same location. Our solution generally assumes that the user does not move about while viewing. This is quite a natural assumption, as viewing and interacting with a mobile device while walking would be quite awkward or even dangerous, especially on a construction site. The user is still free to rotate around 360/360° and view the entire sphere projection.

3. Mobile phone implementation

In the PC based client-server implementation (Woodward et al. 2010), the client and server extensions were obtained by direct modifications to the OnSitePlayer application. With the mobile phone implementation this was not feasible due to the difference of platforms. Also, to create as lightweight solution as possible, we implemented a whole new client application for the Nokia N900 smart phone (see Figure 7).

The mobile phone client still supports the network connection and data stream provided by the original server on the PC. The application framework is built using Qt SDK 1.0 and Qt Mobility. Rendering is done with OpenGL ES 2.0. The network connection is ad-hoc WLAN.

Fig. 7. OnSiteClient running on N900 phone.

The functionality of our first mobile phone version is restricted to architect's visualization models, without time component or other advanced features. Positioning is done using the integrated GPS module, without any user interaction. On the other hand, the N900 does not have a compass so the user is responsible for defining the viewing direction.

All the user interactions are done via the touch screen. The viewing direction is defined with a slightly modified version of the PC based viewfinder approach. On the mobile phone we show all of the pre-defined viewfinder positions (authored in MapStudio) first in arbitrary direction. The user is then able to swipe the screen and choose the valid viewfinder(s) for the final aligning. After locking the model in the correct position, the viewfinder images are removed from the view and tracking is started.

Model rendering is based on the sphere projection method, as described above. Downloading the sphere images from the server depends on the number of images (triangles) required. New sphere initialization typically takes some 5 seconds, though in the worst case scenario (20 images, model all around the user) it takes up to 30 seconds. The initialization phase could be improved (up to some 50 %) by compressing the raw images and also packing multiple images in one texture. Alternatively, "hot spot" viewing positions can be defined at office using OnSitePlayer. In this case the sphere images are stored beforehand in the OnSiteClient's scene description and no downloads or even connection to the server are required.

4. Tracking

We have developed altogether three vision based tracking methods to be used in different use cases. Two solutions were developed for the OnSiteClient application, one for PC and one for mobile phone. These solutions assume the user stands at one position, at least a few meters away from the target object, and explores the world by panning with the mobile device (camera). A separate solution was developed for the stand-alone OnSitePlayer on PC, allowing the user also to move freely while viewing. While the PC based tracking solutions have been described in our previous article (Woodward et al. 2010), the implementation on mobile phone is new and is described in the following.

4.1 Tracking on mobile phone

Our light-weight markerless tracking solution designed for the mobile phone client application is based on rotation-invariant fast features (RIFF) (Takacs et al. 2010) and the FAST interest point detector (Rosten & Drummond 2006). The implementation follows closely the tracking logic of (Takacs et al. 2010) with the following modification. Instead of matching detected RIFF descriptors between two consecutive frames, we maintain a set of 3D features and assign one descriptor for each 3D feature. For each camera frame we select a sub-set of these 3D features by projecting the features using a predicted camera orientation and choosing features evenly across the image. To maintain real-time performance, only a limited number of features are selected. For each selected feature, matching descriptors are then searched around the projected feature positions. We use the same search radius of 8 pixels as in (Takacs et al. 2010).

Since descriptor matching gives correspondences between image corners and 3D features, the camera orientation is estimated simply by minimizing the re-projection error of the features. We use the Levenberg-Marquardt optimization routine for orientation estimation as in our previous implementation. We process each image pyramid level separately and the optimized orientation of the previous pyramid level is used as the initial camera orientation for the next pyramid level. For the first pyramid level, the final result of the previous frame is used instead.

Once all image pyramid levels have been processed, the set of 3D features is updated. First, outliers are detected from the residual re-projection errors. Feature quality values are increased for inliers and decreased for outliers. Once the quality value of a feature drops below a threshold, the feature is completely removed from the feature set. New 3D features are created by choosing strong FAST corners and back-projecting the corners into a surface of a sphere centered at the camera. New features are created only in image regions where there are no existing features.

Compared to our previous lightweight implementation (Woodward et al. 2010), the use of RIFF descriptors and FAST corners gives two clear benefits. Firstly, detecting FAST corners is much faster than the previously used interest point detector (Shi & Tomasi 1994). With a carefully optimized implementation we are able to reach a real-time performance of 30 FPS on the N900 mobile phone. Secondly, by tracking features using descriptor matching instead of the optical flow method of Lucas and Kanade (1981), we gain some ability for local recovery. The orientation of the camera is not updated if the tracker fails to match enough feature descriptors. If the tracker fails to match enough feature descriptors, the user can rotate the camera to bring more inlier features back into the camera view, thus restoring the previously found orientation.

5. Rendering

On-site visualization of architectural models differs somewhat from general purpose rendering (Klein & Murray 2008), (Aittala 2010) and the methods should be adapted to the particular characteristics of the application for optimal results. The following special characteristics typical for mobile architectural visualization were identified in (Woodward et al. 2010):

- Uneven tesselation of 3D CAD building models
- Shadow mapping methods, related to the previous
- Complex and constantly changing lighting conditions
- Aliasing problems with highly detailed building models
- Sharp computer graphics vs. web camera image quality

We have experimented with the rendering and light source discovery methods described in (Aittala 2010) and integrated them into the OnSitePlayer application. Figure 8 shows an example of applying our rendering methods with a pilot project. The present implementation of the rendering methods covers: determining of sun light direction based on GPS, date and time of day; interaction with sliders to adjust day light intensities; screen-space ambient occlusion; soft shadows based on shadow maps; and adjusting the rendered image quality to web camera aberrations.

Fig. 8. Photorealistic AR rendering with OnSitePlayer.

Automatic lighting acquisition from the real scene (Aittala 2010) has not been integrated into our system yet, and the current implementation has been done for the stand-alone OnSitePlayer system only. We plan to implement more advanced features also with the client-server solution, using separate feedback mechanisms for interaction and passing of lighting conditions of the real world scene to the server.

6. Field trials

Several iterations of field trials have been performed with three pilot cases. The first mobile use experiments were done with a laptop PC device in summer 2009. We used the 4D model of the Koutalaki hotel in Lapland as an example and augmented it behind our Digitalo offices in Espoo. The experiment enabled us to verify that most of the intended functionality was already operational, including e.g. visualizing the building in various modes and along the timeline, masking the virtual model with the real one, creating and viewing of mobile feedback reports, etc. However some problems were noticed with the user interface; especially the PC screen brightness was far from sufficient in bright day light. Also, the poor accuracy of the compass as well as GPS was noticed to be a major problem in practice. This stimulated our decision to develop interactive positioning methods as backup for the sensors.

A second round of experiments was carried out in fall 2009 in a case of the Forchem oil refinery in Sweden, with the purpose of augmenting new equipment to be installed, using Sony Vaio UX as mobile device (see Figure 9). Video of these experiments is available in (VTT 2010a).

Fig. 9. Mobile AR view of Forchem factory on a UMPC.

In the Forchem case we relied completely on our 3D feature based tracking solution without sensors (Woodward et al. 2010). Tracking was initialized manually by having the user indicate point correspondences between the video image and the 3D model of the factory. As hypothesis for future work, we believe this initialization step could be avoided by first roughly aligning the video and the model using compass information, and based on that, finding the actual point correspondences automatically.

Our most comprehensive field tests were conducted in a series of experiments with the new Skanska offices in Helsinki 2010-2011. In summer 2010 before the building work started, we compared AR visualization of the planned building with different display devices: laptop PC on a podium, attached data glasses, and UMPC client. The two first devices were used in stand-alone mode while the UMPC was used in client-server mode. For rendering, we compared standard computer graphics without adjustments against our photorealistic rendering methods to account for light direction, intensity and other visual properties. See Figures 2-8 and video (VTT 2010b).

In October 2010 when the construction work had already started, we finally received the complete 4D model of the Skanska building (IFC model size 60 MB) and went out to try it at the construction site. We could then verify that our solution also worked in practice with this rather demanding experiment. With some user interaction, we were able to augment the complex model on site, and display the construction elements to be installed at different time frames and from various view points. With respect to tracking initialization, managing altitude information interactively was considered to be the biggest problem. Stand-alone laptop PC version was used in these experiments. See Figure 10 and video (VTT 2010b).

Fig. 10. Mobile AR during construction work.

Harsh winter interrupted our field tests for almost half a year. The most recent experiments with the Skanska pilot were done in May 2011 when the back part of the building was already completed and also the first version of our mobile phone implementation was ready. In these experiments we were able to verify that our mobile phone solution using the new tracking method and pre-defined placemarks on the scene provided a stable augmented view of the building (see Figure 7). Comparison of the OnSitePlayer view which we had computed nine months earlier (Figure 8) against the real situation at the site (Figure 11) also validated the quality of our photorealistic rendering methods.

Fig. 11. Photo of the Skanska building partly ready.

7. Future work

For practical reasons, we still have a number of stand-alone OnSitePlayer features yet to be integrated in the client-server solution. Also, integration of our feature based tracking methods with sensor data as well as photorealistic rendering technology into the AR system is still under way. Some near term plans for interaction, tracking and rendering enhancements were discussed above, and previously in (Woodward et al. 2010). Positioning accuracy could also be improved by applying more accurate methods, e.g. differential GPS, Real Time Kinematics (RTK) and other measurement tools that are routinely employed at construction sites.

In future, we look forward also to obtaining feedback from different user groups. The first formal user studies with the system will be performed in our next outdoors visualization project in September 2011. Handing out the system to actual end users will certainly bring up various proposals and wishes for improvements to the system. Instead of adding new functionality however, we anticipate a general request to simplify the user interface and limit it to the most essential features.

8. Conclusions

In this article, we have described a software system for mobile mixed reality interaction with complex 4D Building Information Models. Our system supports various native and standard CAD/BIM formats, combining them with time schedule information, fixing them to accurate geographic representations, using augmented reality with feature based tracking to visualize them on site, applying photorealistic rendering, with various tools for mobile user interaction and feedback. The client-server solution is able to handle complex models on mobile devices, and an efficient tracking solution enables implementation also on mobile phones.

While there is still some way to go until the technology is in daily use at real construction sites, and there are some general concerns for applicability such as weather conditions, we believe that we have proven the technical validity of the concept. In particular, mobile AR visualization of architectural models is already quite manageable with the present system. We look forward to evaluating our system with user tests in the future, and eventually to bringing our solutions to real production use.

9. Acknowledgements

The main body of this work was conducted as part of the "AR4BC" project (2008-2010), with Skanska, Tekla, Pöyry, Buildercom, Adactive and Deskartes as industrial partners. The mobile phone implementation was done as part of the "DIEM3/MMR" project (2010-2011) with Nokia as industrial partner. The main funding for these projects was provided by Tekes (Finnish Funding Agency for Technology and Innovation).

Tuomas Kantonen was responsible for developing and implementing the feature-based tracking solution for mobile phones. Alain Boyer gave a valuable contribution in making the AR loop run efficiently on the Nokia N900 device. We also thank our colleagues Kari Rainio, Otto Korkalo and Miika Aittala who have been involved earlier in the implementation.

10. References

Aittala M. (2010). Inverse lighting and photorealistic rendering for augmented reality. *The Visual Computer*. Vol 26, No. 6-8, pp. 669-678.

Behzadan A.H. (2008). *ARVISCOPE: Georeferenced Visualisation of Dynamic Construction Processes in Three-Dimensional Outdoor Augmented Reality*. PhD Thesis, The University of Michigan.

Feiner S., MacIntyre B., Höllerer T., and Webster A. (1997). A touring machine: prototyping 3D mobile augmented reality systems for exploring the urban environment. In *Proc. ISWC'97*, Cambridge, MA, USA, October 13, 1997.

Gleue T. and Daehne P. (2001). Design and implementation of mobile device for outdoor augmented reality in the Archeoguidee project. *Proc. of the 2001 Conference on Virtual Reality, Arceology and Cultural Heritage*, ACM, Glyfada, Greece, pp. 161-168.

Goldparvar-Fard M., Pena-Mora F. and Savarese S. (2010). D4AR - 4 dimensional augmented reality - tools for automatred remote progress tracking and support of decision-enabling tasks in the AEC/FM industry. In *Proc. of The 6th Int. Conf. on innovations in AEC*, State College, PA, Jun 9-11, 2010.

Hakkarainen M., Woodward C. and Rainio K. (2009). Software Architecture for Mobile Mixed Reality and 4D BIM Interaction. In *Proc. 25th CIB W78 Conference*, Istanbul, Turkey, Oct 2009.

Honkamaa P., Siltanen S., Jäppinen J., Woodward C. and Korkalo O. (2007). Interactive outdoor mobile augmentation using markerless tracking and GPS. *Proc. Virtual Reality International Conference (VRIC)*, Laval, France, April 2007, pp. 285-288.

Izkara J. L., Perez J., Basogain X. and Borro D. (2009). Mobile augmented reality, an advanced tool for the construction sector. *Proc. 24th CIB W78 Conference*, Maribor, Slovakia, June 2009, pp. 453-460.

Klein G. and Murray D. Compositing for small cameras. (2008). *Proc. The 7th IEEE International Symposium on Mixed and Augmented Reality (ISMAR 2008)*, Cambridge, UK, September 2008, pp. 57-60.

Lucas B.D. and Kanade T. (1981). An iterative image registration technique with an application to stereo vision. *Proc. of the 7th International Joint Conference on Artificial Intelligence (IJCAI '81)*, April 1981, pp. 674-679.

Milgram P. and Kishino F. (1994). A taxonomy of mixed reality visual displays. IEICE Transactions on Information Systems, Vol E77-D, No 12, December 1994

Pasman W. and Woodward C. (2003). Implementation of an augmented reality system on a PDA. *Proc. The Second IEEE and ACM International Symposium on Mixed and Augmented Reality (ISMAR 2003)*, Tokyo, Japan, October 2003, pp. 276-277.

Reitmayr G. and Drummond T. (2006). Going out: robust, model based tracking for outdoor augmented reality. *Proc. The Fifth IEEE and ACM International Symposium on Mixed and Augmented Reality (2006)*, Santa Barbara, USA, 22-25 October 2006, pp.109-118.

Rosten E. and Drummond T. (2006). Machine learning for high-speed corner detection. *European Conference on Computer Vision*, May 2006, pp. 430-443.

Schall G., Mendez E. and Schmalstieg D. (2008). Virtual redlining for civil engineering in real environments. *Proc. The 7th IEEE International Symposium on Mixed and Augmented Reality (ISMAR 2008)*, Cambridge, UK, September 2008, pp. 95-98.

Schall G., Wagner D., Reitmayr G., Taichmann E., Wieser M., Schmalstieg D. and Hoffmann-Wellenhof B. (2008). Global pose estimation using multi-sensor fusion for outdoors augmented reality. *Proc. 8th IEEE International Symposium on Mixed and Augmented Reality (ISMAR 2008)*, Orlando, Florida, USA, October 2008, pp. 153-162.

Senate (2007). Senate BIM Guidelines. http://www.senaatti.fi/document.asp?siteID =2&docID=588.

Shi J. and Tomasi C. (1994). Good features to track. *Proc. 1994 IEEE Conference on Computer Vision and Pattern Recognition (CVPR'94)*, pp. 593-600.

Shin D.H. and Dunston P.S. (2008). Identification of application areas for augmented reality in industrial construction based on technological suitability. *Automation in Construction* 17, pp. 882-894.

Takacs G., Chandrasekhar V., Tsai S.S., Chen D.M., Grzeszczuk R. and Girod B. (2010). Unified real-time tracking and recognition with rotation-invariant fast features. *Proc. The Twenty-Third IEEE Conference on Computer Vision and Pattern Recognition, (CVPR 2010)*, San Francisco, CA, USA, June 13-18, 2010, pp. 934-941.

TNO (2010). TNO IFC Engine. http://www.ifcbrowser.com/ifcenginedll.html.

VTT (2010a). Video on the Forchem pilot. http://youtu.be/xpZDXih9zLg.

VTT (2010b). Video on the Skanska pilot. http://youtu.be/rVt86NGXQv4.

VTT (2011). ALVAR. www.vtt.fi/multimedia/alvar.html.

Wither J., DiVerdi S. and Höllerer T. (2006). Using aerial photographs for improved mobile AR annotation. *Proc. The Fifth IEEE and ACM International Symposium on Mixed and Augmented Reality (2006)*, Santa Barbara, USA, 22-25 October 2006, pp.159-162.

Woodward C., Hakkarainen M., Korkalo O., Kantonen T. Aittala M., Rainio K. and Kähkönen K. (2010). Mixed reality for mobile construction site visualization and communication. *Proc. 10th International Conference on Construction Applications of Virtual Reality (CONVR2010)*, Sendai, Japan, Nov 4-5, 2010, pp. 35-44.

7

NeuAR – A Review of the VR/AR Applications in the Neuroscience Domain

Pedro Gamito[1,2,3], Jorge Oliveira[1,2], Diogo Morais[1,2], Pedro Rosa[1,2,4] and Tomaz Saraiva[1]
[1]*Universidade Lusófona de Humanidades e Tecnologias,*
[2]*Centro de Estudos em Psicologia Cognitiva e da Aprendizagem,*
[3]*Clínica S. João de Deus,*
[4]*ISCTE-IUL/CIS*
Portugal

1. Introduction

Since the 1980's, computational applications based on virtual reality (VR) aimed at treating mental disorders and rehabilitating individuals with cognitive or motor disabilities have been around. They started off by focusing on simple phobias like acrophobia (Emmelkamp et al., 2002) and agoraphobia (Botella et al., 2004), fear of flying (Rothbaum, Hodges, Smith, Lee & Price, 2000), and evolved to fear of driving (Saraiva et al., 2007) or posttraumatic stress disorder (PTSD) (Gamito et al., 2010), schizophrenia (Costa & Carvalho, 2004) or traumatic brain injuries (Gamito et al., 2011a), among many others (Gamito et al., 2011b).

VR holds two chief properties that enable patients to experience the synthetic environment as being real: immersion and interaction. The first relates to the sensation of being physical present and perceptually included in the VR world. The second stands for the ability to change the world properties, i.e. the environment and its constituents react according to participants actions. Along with imagination, interaction and immersion concur to create the so called "sense of being there" or presence.

This characteristic of VR settings has been acknowledged by the psychotherapists as a media to expose patients with anxiety disorders (AD) to anxiogenic cues within an ecologically sound and controlled environment. VR designed for therapeutic purposes can replicate any of the ansiogenic situations, enabling a better approximation to the ansiogenic world and inducing higher levels of engagement when compared to traditional imagination exposure (Riva et al., 2002). Hyperrealistic threatening stimuli provided by VR lead to higher attention, and subsequent encapsulation, which means, once the fear system is activated the participant perceives the synthetic world as being real (Hamm & Weike, 2005). Also, VR reduces the decalage between reality and imagination, by diminishing potential distraction or cognitive avoidance to the threatening stimuli (Vincelli & Riva, 2000). These and other studies revealed that VR exposure therapy (VRET) may be an alternative to *in vivo* and imagination exposure.

In fact, Parsons and Rizzo (2008), on a meta-analysis found an average size effect of 0.96, reflecting a large effect for VRET on the decrease of negative affective symptoms of the six affective domains studied (PTSD, Social Phobia, Arachnophobia, Acrophobia, Panic Disorder with Agoraphobia and Aerophobia). Also, Powers and Emmelkamp (2008), on another meta-analysis, observed a large mean effect size for VRET, when compared with *in vivo* and control conditions (waiting list, attention control, etc.).

In this way, VRET as a form of a psycotherapeutic approach presents some advantages when compared with the two traditional exposure techniques: *in vivo* and imagination exposure. Concerning the first, VRET is able to replace real traumatic events, such as, war scenarios or motor vehicles accidents, eliciting traumatic emotions as if the patient were really there. The interactive simulation that VR encloses ensures a rich full sensorial experience similar to an *in vivo* occurrence.

Regarding the last, in VRET the therapeutic environment is controlled by the therapist, something that does not occur when a patient is asked to imagine the anxiogenic situation as occurs during imagination exposure. Both typology and intensity of cues can be managed by the therapist. For instance, Rizzo and colleagues (2006), in a VR world devised to treat veterans with PTSD from Iraqi war, have included a console in which scenario's assets such as alternation between day and night, night vision, fog, helicopter coming in, spawn of enemies, among others functions, can be placed, as requested, in the VR world.

Concerning rehabilitation, its three core pillars: repetition, feedback and motivation may gain from the use of VR (Holden, 2003). In rehabilitation, one of the most common procedures is the repeated and systematic training of the impaired functions (Allred et al., 2005). In agreement to the review from Sveistrup (2004), VR can provide training environments where visual and auditory feedback can be systematically manipulated according to individual differences. Furthermore, the use of 3D (3 dimensions) virtual environments offers the possibility of real-time feedback of subject's position and progression (Sveistrup, 2004). For Levin and colleagues (2005) the use of VR applications in rehabilitation can be effective because of the 3D spatial correspondence between movements in the real world and movements in the virtual worlds which, in turn, may facilitate real-time performance feedback. Cirstea and Levin (2007) referred that performance feedback can provide information regarding impaired motor movements. For example, Feintuch and colleagues (2006) developed a haptic-tactile feedback system that, when integrated on a video-capture-based VR environment, enables patients to feel a vibration on their fingers whenever they "touch" a ball on the VR world. Viau and colleagues (2004) analyzed movements performed by participants with hemiparesis with virtual objects in VR and real objects in real environments. These authors found no differences between performances in VR and real environments and suggested that this VR technique can be an effective training for rehabilitation.

The repetitive practice is also an important aspect in motor and cognitive training as it improves performance in disabled patients (Chen et al., 2004). These authors used VR environments in children with cerebral palsy and observed that the repetitive practice of a particular motor aspect enables the coordination of a specific muscular system.

And because VR is usually presented on a multimodal platform with several sorts of immersive cues, such as images and sounds, patients are more willing to engage and pursue with the exercise. Bryanton and colleagues (2006) found that when compared to conventional exercise, children with cerebral palsy had more fun and tended to repeat more often at home ankle dorsiflexion and long-sitting VR exercises.

VR seems, during hospitalization, to promote a more intensive and program supportive approach to the execution of the exercise, providing appropriate feedback to the patient. Also, exercises may be displayed with an adapting degree of difficulty, making possible the use of non-invasive forms of physiological monitoring. VR, in addition, gives therapist the ability to individualize treatment needs, while providing the opportunity for repeated learning trials and offer the capacity to gradually increase the complexity tasks while decreasing therapist support and feedback (Weiss & Katz, 2004). VR is a promising response to shorter hospitalization and foster homecare (Giorgino et al., 2008).

Studies on VR rehabilitation are usually focused on motor rehabilitation following brain damage and on training people with intellectual disabilities (Attree et al., 2005). However, VR has been also applied to rehabilitate patients that had suffered traumatic brain injuries (TBI). Slobounov and colleagues (2006) found VR to be useful as a tool to assess brain concussion. A VR system was developed to inspect the temporal restoration of the effect of visual field motion on TBI's subjects with short term and long term balance anomalies. The study of memory and attentional problems is important for many patients with a history of TBI, even when they are not a primary problem. Wilson and colleagues (2006) stressed that the automaticity of basic movement skills is often learned in controlled environments. Once the patient is required to apply skills in real-world settings, demands on attention and on working memory often exceed their processing and response capabilities. Also, skills' compliance in the previous stages of rehabilitation is inhibited by disruptions to attention and working memory processes. Patients with acquired brain injuries may find it tricky to train both a primary task (e.g. walking) and a simultaneous secondary task (e.g. signal detection). During the skill learning phase, the function of attention and memory can be supported by visual and verbal cues that can signal attention to obstacles and forthcoming events.

In-between "real" reality and virtual reality rests, according to Milgram's continuum (Milgram & Kishino, 1994), another form of interaction with the real world coined by Caudell and Mizell (1992) as augmented reality (AR). This technique, as mentioned in previous chapters, consists (through at least three different approaches, video see-through, optical see through or projection) on superimposing a computer generated object onto a real world setting.

As a result, it is expected participant's perception to be tricked so that the virtual object should be perceived as being part of the real world. But this perquisite is not sufficed. Also, real time interaction and 3D registration are required (Azuma et al., 2001). Likewise in VR, interaction is a key feature. In order to guarantee that the user recognizes the synthetic object as being part of the real world, it is paramount that he or she may interact with it as if it is a real entity. Interaction is perceived by many authors (Witmer & Singer, 1998; Riva et al., 2002) as the cornerstone of any virtual or close to virtual experience as it promotes the immersion on the synthetic world. Also, the precise alignment between the real world and the plan where the 3D image is placed is essential so that the illusion of non-real and real coexistence may take place. AR properties will be fully discussed in the next section.

These characteristics of AR were adopted by practitioners and researchers of the area of neurosciences. Similarly to VR, also AR applications were developed to treat anxiety disorders and to rehabilitate individuals with cognitive and motor impairments, following the same VR principles of application referred above. The upcoming sections of the chapter will focus on the work of several research groups that employ AR as a media to treat mental disorders and to rehabilitate patients with acquired central nervous injuries. But first, a fly over the "techy" bits and bites of AR.

2. Art – Augmented reality technology

Despite the several approaches that can be used to achieve the augmentation effect, the AR systems' architecture relies essentially on the combination of two components: the visual display and the tracking system. The visual display is decisive on the immersive ability of the system, while an efficient tracking is required to reach an optimal alignment of virtual and real objects, also known as registration (Zlatanova, 2002).

2.1 Visual display

The visual display is an image-forming system responsible for how the virtual content is combined with the real one and presented in the user's line of sight. The type of display is a product of the combination of the technology with the positioning of the display relatively to the user (Van Krevelen & Poelman, 2010). Currently there are four different available technologies: optical see-through (OST); video see-through (VST); virtual retinal display (VRD) and projective display.

2.1.1 Visual display technology

2.1.1.1 Optical See-through (OST) vs. Video See-through (VST)

With the OST technology the user sees the real world through optical combiners, usually half-silvered mirrors or transparent LCD displays. These allow an unobstructed view of the real world while supporting the superimposition of virtual content (Azuma, 1997).

The VST technology consists in overlaying the virtual content on a live video feed of a real environment. The real world is captured in real-time by one or two video cameras and the virtual content is digitally blended into the original recording (Van Krevelen et al., 2010) using video keying techniques or pixel-by-pixel depth comparison (Azuma, 1997). The main difference between these systems consists in the nearly intact real world view provided by the OST technology as opposed to the live video feed replacement created by the VST.

Preserving the real world view allows a higher resolution on OST in comparison to VST displays. While on the optical method the user looks through a thin lens that leaves the real-world resolution intact, the video method clamps it to the maximum resolution supported by the display or video source (Rolland et al., 1994). The OST method is also safer than VST. In power failure incidents, the OST only loses the virtual overlay, while in the video replacement such an incident would leave the user completely blind, which could be critical in medical or military applications (Azuma, 1997). The OST is also a parallax free method. In the OST displays the view of the world corresponds exactly to the viewpoint of the eye, while in the VST there is a mismatch in the viewpoint information. The users' view of the world is provided by the cameras which are not perfectly aligned with the eyes' position. This incongruity may lead to disorientation resulting from the eye offset (Biocca & Rolland, 1998). However, the VST display is able to create more compelling experiences than its optical counterpart (Azuma, 1997). Despite being a replacement of the real view, the video live feed introduces several advantages on the augmentation process.

In order to provide a realistic AR experience it is imperative an optimal level of registration. Virtual objects must appear perfectly aligned with the real ones in order create a believable experience. An obstacle to this registration is the delay in time, between the moment when the position of the object is measured and the moment when the digitized imaged is presented. Using an OST display, the user has an immediate view of the real world but a slightly delayed view of the virtual overlay. This gives the impression that virtual objects are not fixed in the environment, something referred as a swimming effect (Azuma & Bishop, 1994). Solutions have been developed, from using predictive tracking to optimizing the system for low latency (Azuma et al., 1994). While this is a serious limitation in the optical method, with the VST technology it is possible to take advantage of having two video feeds, the real and the virtual. As demonstrated by Bajura and Neumann (1995) it is possible to enforce registration, matching both views by delaying the original video in order to equal the presentation of the synthetic objects. This way, both feeds are matched and the objects appear perfectly aligned (Rolland et al., 1994).

One of the most important advantages of the VST technology is related to how it deals with occlusion. Depth cues are extremely important when creating realistic environments and occlusion is one of the strongest. Occlusion depth cue consists in how an object is hidden by another one which is closer and in front of it relatively to the users' line of sight. The optical method is limited when dealing with occlusion (Azuma, 1997). The optical combiners receive light simultaneously from real and virtual world, which makes it impossible to obscure completely the real objects with the virtual ones. In this way, the virtual objects appear as semi-transparent, affecting the sense of occlusion and therefore the overall realism of the experience. On the other hand the VST technology can deal perfectly with occlusion. While using a digitized version of the reality it is possible to obscure completely the real, the virtual or to blend both using a pixel-by-pixel comparison. In the same way this method allows a better matching between real and virtual brightness and contrast, which is not possible on optical methods.

The VST technology also benefits from additional tracking methods that enhance the alignment of real and virtual objects. Using a video feed of the real scene it is possible to employ additional registration methods based on image processing techniques. The same methods are unavailable on OST displays, which can only rely on tracking information from the users' body movement.

One last issue regarding these technologies is the Field-of-View (FOV). Both systems present limited FOVs. OST displays support a 20° to 60° overlay FOVs but provide a close match to our eyes' natural real-world FOV, since the peripheral vision is available to look around the device. On the other hand, the VST displays may support overlay FOVs similar to the viewing optics but the peripheral FOV is occluded, resulting in a smaller real-world FOV. This limitation can affect applications where situation awareness is necessary since the users need to perform larger head movements when scanning the environment (Rolland et al., 1995).

2.1.1.2 Virtual retinal display

In addition to OST and VST technologies, more recent methods are being developed. One method is called Virtual Retinal Display (VRT) (Pryor et al., 1998; Kollin, 1993; Lewis, 2004). Although being analogous to the OST display, since it preserves the real world view, it is a screen free method. The virtual overlay is drawn directly on the retina using low-power lasers discarding the need of a screen (Kollin, 1993).

Although being still in development, the VRT shows promising advantages. According to Kollin (1993), these are low-profile portable displays that allow also wider FOVs. Since its technology its independent of pixel size, it allows a much brighter and higher resolution virtual overlays (Van Krevelen et al., 2010). However, it still presents some drawbacks. Most systems are monocular and monochromatic (red), do not support stereoscopic vision and provide fixed focal length (Bimber & Raskar, 2006). However, Schowengerdt and colleagues (2004) are developing a full colour, low-cost, light-weight binocular version with dynamic refocus.

2.1.1.3 Projective display

There is also the possibility to use projective technology, which consists in using virtual overlays being directly projected onto real objects instead of being presented on a plane or surface on the users' line of sight (Van Krevelen et al., 2010).

The main advantages of this technology are related with the absence of special eye-wear in order to see the virtual overlay. Projecting the synthetic information directly on the real environment decreases the incongruity of accommodation and convergence usually present on the other methods and also allows for a wider FOV (Bimber et al., 2006). However, it lacks on providing a reasonable occlusion effect and it is restricted to indoor use, since the projected images have low brightness and contrast (Van Krevelen et al., 2010).

2.1.2 Visual display positioning

In addition to the display technology it is fundamental to decide about the display positioning: head-mounted displays (HMD); handheld displays; spatial displays. Each type of positioning has specific advantages and limitations and should be chosen in regard to the application requirements and the technologies supported.

2.1.2.1 Head-Mounted Displays (HMDs)

The HMDs require the user to wear the display connected to his/her head. This type of display supports the optical and video see-through technologies, the virtual retinal display (VRD) and the projection method.

Relatively to the optical/video see-through HMD and VRD, technology limitations aside, this type of display positioning also lacks in mobility since it requires to be connected to a laptop which battery life is rather limited (Van Krevelen et al., 2010). It is also quite difficult to find a balance between display quality and ergonomics, since most systems vary from high quality cumbersome displays to low quality ergonomic ones (Bimber et al., 2006). Another issue related to HMD is the incidence of simulator sickness during fast head movements (Patrick et al., 2000).

Besides the regular HMDs, there are also available head-mounted projective displays (HMPD) and projective HMD. The HMPD use a mirror beam-splitter to project the synthetic images onto retro-reflective surfaces (Hua et al., 2005), while the projective HMD beam the virtual overlay onto the ceiling and then integrate those images onto the users' visual field using two half-silvered mirrors (Kijima & Ojika, 1997).

In comparison to the regular HMDs, these provide a wider FOV and prevent disorientation resulting from viewpoint information mismatch. However, they present specific limitations regarding the synthetic objects' brightness. The HMPD require special display surfaces in order to display the objects with an adequate level of brightness, while on projective HMD it depends on the environmental light conditions (Bimber et al., 2006).

2.1.2.2 Handheld displays

The handheld displays are the best solution for mobile applications since they integrate on a single device the graphics, display and interaction technology which support unrestrained handling (Bimber et al., 2006). It supports video/optical and projective technologies. Although, the video method is preferred, there are also optical devices, such as the real time tomographic reflection of Stetten and colleagues (2001) or projection handheld solutions as demonstrated by Bimber and colleagues (2000).

Since handheld devices use common technologies such as Tablet PCs, PDAs and mobile phones, its main advantages are related with the mass diffusion of AR technology, low production costs and ease of use applications (Van Krevelen et al., 2010). The use of such ordinary technologies has also its shortcomings (Bimber et al., 2006). Low-end devices cannot provide enough processing power for AR applications resulting in system delay and very low frame rates in addition to limited image quality resultant from their integrated cameras. The screen-size may also limit the FOV. However this effect may be counteracted by the occurrence of a perception effect known as Parks Effect. In a nutshell, when moving a display over a stationary scene, the virtual display actual size becomes larger than its physical size because of the persistence of the image in the retina (Parks, 1965). In comparison to HMD, these types of devices don't allow a complete hands-free experience.

2.1.2.3 Spatial displays

The spatial displays are positioned on fixed places in the environment and therefore are completely detached from the user. It supports optical, video and projective technologies - respectively, screen-based video see-through display, spatial optical see-through display and projection-based spatial displays. The screen-based video see-through displays are the most cost-effective AR technology. They are similar to the video see-through HMDs but instead of presenting the images on a head-attached device, it uses a regular computer monitor. This simple setup has several limitations. It provides a small FOV, because it depends on the screen size and a low resolution of the real environment since it needs to be adapted to the system specifications. It does not support direct interaction with the environment being more a system for remote viewing than a proper see-through technology (Bimber et al., 2006).

According to the same authors, the spatial optical see-through displays use a diverse range of optical combiners (planar or curves mirror beam splitters, transparent screens and optical holograms) in order to generate images aligned within the real environment. Besides the optical technology limitations this kind of systems are not appropriated for mobile applications and the applied optics restrict the number of simultaneous users.

For Bimber and colleagues (2006), projection-based spatial displays use front projection to display the virtual overlay directly on the physical objects. This technique presents several limitations. On the one hand the front projection method limits the interaction since the interacting users and other physical objects may cast shadows on the display. There are also restrictions on the display area. Since the synthetic images are projected directly onto the physical objects, their surfaces become the display and therefore it is constrained to their size, shape and colour.

2.2 Tracking system

The other fundamental component, maybe even more important than the visual display, is the tracking system. Without tracking the system cannot know what, when or where to display the virtual overlay. In order to correctly present the synthetic information, the system must acknowledge the position and relative movement of the users' viewpoint in the real world, so that virtual objects may appear exactly where they should be. There is a vital relationship between the tracking systems and the level of registration (Van Krevelen et al., 2010).

However, to this day, a perfect single solution is still missing and so several approaches and possible combinations are still in study. Currently, two main categories of tracking may be defined: sensor-based and vision-based tracking techniques (Zhou et al., 2008).

2.2.1 Sensor-based techniques

Sensor-based techniques acquire tracking information from a diverse range of sensors such as ultrasonic, optical, inertial, mechanical and magnetic. Each of these sensors present advantages and limitations as demonstrated in Rolland and colleagues (2001).

The ultrasonic sensors measure movement and orientation through acoustic pulse propagation. Essentially, these sensors are able to acquire the distance between emitter/receivers attached to reference positions and a moving target, by measuring the time of propagation of pulsed signals between those features. As upsides, these sensors are small, light and with no distortion. As downsides they provide low update rate, are sensitive to environment conditions (temperature, pressure, humidity) and to physical obstacles. Optical sensors are able to track position and orientation using cameras to acquire the shape of the target features. In contrast to the ultrasonic sensors, these provide a good update rate, but are sensitive to optical noise, spurious light, ambiguity of surface and physical obstacles.

The principle of the inertial sensors is based on the inertia principle. Any physical object tends to resist to a possible change in its state of motion or rest. Measuring the variation between an initial and final position/rotation it is possible to determine the movement of the target feature. Gyroscopes are used to measure orientation and accelerometers to measure position. The main advantage of these methods is the absence of a reference point while its main limitation is related with an increase in error with time due to relative measurements (measurements are relative to the previous ones). Mechanical sensors are based on the variation of the angles in mechanical linkages. This type of tracking provides a good accuracy and precision, update rate and lag. However, in order to achieve such measurements there is a great downside in terms of movement freedom.

The magnetic sensors measure orientation and position using magnetic fields to obtain the distance between emitters and receivers. These type of tracking is not sensitive to physical obstacles, provides a great update rate, low lag, is inexpensive and small. However, it works on small areas and is quite sensitive to electromagnetic noise and metallic objects. Most of these tracking systems are dominant in virtual reality environments. However, in AR, studies using only sensor-based tracking techniques are rare (Zhou et al., 2008). In order to achieve the necessary tracking precision on AR environments, most setups tend to combine the use of sensors with the vision-based tracking techniques (Pinz et al., 2002).

2.2.2 Vision-based techniques

In comparison to sensor-based tracking, the vision-based methods are more accurate since provide dynamic correction of tracking errors (Bajura et al., 1995) and the possibility for a pixel-perfect registration of virtual objects (Van Krevelen et al., 2010). Vision-based tracking techniques may be divided into an earlier fiducial-based approach and more recent model-based and feature-based techniques (Pressigout & Marchand, 2006). The fiducial-based approach places recognizable artificial markers or LEDs (light emitting diodes) on the scene in order to compute in real time the position and orientation of the camera. These fiducial markers are placed in known locations and have certain properties (shape or colour) that allow the camera to easily recognize and extract them from a video frame. By identifying exactly the position of the markers, it is also possible to perfectly align the virtual and real objects on the scene enhancing the level of registration.

The fiducials have the advantage of being cheap, customizable for greater efficiency (identification and extraction by the camera) and can be place arbitrarily on the scene (Park, You & Neumman, 1998). Even though this approach is quite efficient in small and prepared environments, it is not useful when considering large environments or even multiple instances of the same setting. In this way, markerless tracking approaches emerged.

The feature-based approach is based on identifying 2D natural features (points, lines, edges or textures) in the environment in order to provide a robust and markerless vision-based tracking (Pressigout et al., 2006). The system is able to detect natural features on each image frame and to achieve the correspondence through images using a feature tracking algorithm. Therefore the image coordinates and their estimated 3D positions may be used to track the camera position in space (Park et al., 1998). This approach is quite sensitive to changes in illumination (Pressigout et al., 2006).

The model-based approach instead of using 2D natural features of the environment is based on a model constructed of the features of the tracked object. This can be a CAD (computer assisted design) model or a 2D template built from the indistinguishable features of the target object (Zhou et al., 2008). This method is considered more robust then the feature-based. This approach may adopt an edge-based or a texture-based method to construct the feature model. The edge-based method is more commonly used since edges are easier to identify and quite robust to light changes. The texture-based method is usually applied as a complementary method in order to reinforce the tracking accuracy (Zhou et al., 2008).

According to Van Krevelen and colleagues (2010), despite being necessary more robustness and lower computational costs on these methods, they demonstrate very promising results.

3. AR applications on psychotherapy

3.1 Traditional therapeutic approaches

Surprisingly or not, many people still think that mental illnesses are not treatable, being the main reason for not seeking mental health treatment (Sussman et al., 1987). A large *palette* of efficacious treatments is available to ameliorate symptoms. In fact, for most mental disorders, there is generally not just one but a range of treatments of proven efficacy. Most treatments fall under two general categories, non-pharmacological and pharmacological (Gazzaniga & Heatherton, 2006).

Among non-pharmacological treatments, cognitive–behavioural therapy (CTB) is the gold standard. CBT seeks to change faulty biased cognitions and replace them with thoughts and self-statements that promote adaptive behavior (Beck et al., 1976). For instance, CBT tries to replace self-defeatist expectations ("I can't do anything right") with positive expectations ("I can do this right"). CBT has gained such ascendancy as a means of integrating cognitive and behavioral views of human functioning, being empirically validated and a common approach in anxiety disorders (Hofmann & Smits, 2008), mood disorders (Gloaguen et al., 1998) and schizophrenia (Wykes et al., 2007).

Under CBT approach, exposure therapy (ET) is the most common psychotherapeutic technique for the treatment of anxiety disorders (Foa et al., 2000). Particularly for phobias and PTSD, ET is an effective therapeutic technique which involves the exposure to the feared stimulus or context without any danger while the psychotherapist helps patients relieving their anxiety (e.g. Cooper et al., 2008; Rothbaum & Schwartz, 2002).

3.2 Psychotherapy powered by technology: AR as a 3T (Therapeutic Technological Tool)

As seen on the introductory section the advance of technology brought about new approaches and new computational applications. One of those is virtual reality exposure therapy (VRET). This human–computer interaction system is a medium in which patients can be immersed within a virtual anxiogenic environment where the fear structure is effectively elicited and the emotional processing of fears fired-up (Rothbaum et al., 1995). In VRET patients are immersed within a computer-generated simulation or virtual environment, bypassing, as previously mentioned, some limitations of imagination and *in vivo* exposure (e.g., the risks of distressing patients). VRET is a better-quality technique to control potential distracters and cognitive avoidance to threatening stimuli when imagination exposure or *in vivo* exposure is compromised (Vincelli & Riva, 2002). In VRET, cues of events which are not replicable in real-life situations can be reproduced *ad infinitum* in the therapist' room (Gamito et al., 2010, 2011a). When a patient is immersed in a synthetic world, he/she can be systematically exposed to specific feared stimuli integrated in a relevant context.

In AR, patients see an image made up of a real image and virtual elements that are superimposed over it. The most relevant aspect in AR is that the virtual elements add relevant and helpful information to the real scene. Although VR and AR share and present some advantages over traditional approaches (e.g. improving acceptance and therapy duration), AR in some cases also presents additional advantages over VR. (Botella et al., 2004). First, in VRET is expensive to create different areas of high level of detail (LOD). Second in VRET one can include for instance avatars that simulate patients' bodies; however patients cannot see their own body (arms, hands, etc.) as can be seen in augmented reality exposure therapy (ARET). Third, animated avatars with close-to-real artificial intelligence are difficult to find. On the other hand, with ARET a delicate issue arouses. The integration of real and virtual elements should fit perfectly and remain during the entire length of exposure. Otherwise when an error is perceived, patients will not get the sense that the two worlds blend into one, decreasing the sense of being there (Milgram et al., 1994).

In ARET patient sees the real world "augmented" by virtual elements, which means that, AR attempts to improve the reality and not to replace it (Azuma, 1997). The basis of ARET is that the virtual elements add information to the physical details of the real world. For instance, a therapist can present certain information by imposing virtual stimuli (such as personalized threatening snake) over real objects and environments. In ARET, the patient can see images that are merged in both real and virtual elements. Whereas in VRET the patient is in a totally artificial environment, in AR patients are *de factum* in a real world, with the essential difference that virtual elements are fused with real ones in a composite image (Milgram et al., 1994).

AR applications are already available in the areas of education (Arvanitis et al., 2007; Kerawalla et al., 2006; Squire & Klopfer, 2007; Squire & Mingfong, 2007) and medicine (Wörn et al., 2005). In the domain of psychotherapy, however, there are not many studies around. The ones that were conducted confirmed the benefits of ARET in the treatment of specific animal phobias, namely cockroaches (Botella et al., 2005; Botella et al., 2010) and spiders and in the treatment of acrophobia (Juan et al, 2005).

In cockroach phobia, Botella and colleagues (2005) conducted a one-session ARET, following the guidelines developed by Öst (1989). In a more recent study, ARET was applied in the short and long term (three-, six- and twelve-month follow-up) using a multiple baseline design across individuals (Botella et al., 2010). In both studies ARET was capable of inducing fear and all the participants showed an improvement on the outcome measures in the post-treatment assessment (less fear and less avoidance). In addition, the results were maintained at follow-up periods. In the study of acrophobia (Juan et al., 2005), ARET was conducted using immersive pictures (180° view) with encouraging results. In these studies, ARET induced high sense of presence probably due to a hyperrealist merged context, leading to a higher attention and subsequent fear encapsulation (Hamm & Weike, 2005).

Given that ARET may lead to high sense of presence the emotional processing of the phobia-related information is facilitated and the access to the patient's fear memory structure promoted (Foa & Kozak, 1986). Under this view, the higher level of presence, better the therapeutic results are.

Both the three studies demonstrate how effective ARET is and can be a motivating factor to develop applications not only on specific phobias, but other mental illnesses as well. ARET which is in its infancy when it comes to psychotherapeutic applications may spark a change of paradigm, not only in the way how ET is conducted, but also in the therapeutic project itself, being a new challenge for future clinical applications.

4. AR applications on neuro-rehabilitation

4.1 Principles of neuro-rehabilitation

The consequences of acquired brain injury (ABI) can be very severe and depending on the etiology and distribution, the effects are seen immediately after brain injury or at long term as a result of metabolic disturbances of the primary neural damage (Sohlberg & Mateer, 2001). The etiology of brain injury varies from infectious (e.g., encephalitis) and degenerative diseases (e.g., Alzheimer's) to brain tumors, stroke or traumatic brain injury. The nature of the neurological disease determines specific patterns of disability, being associated with different syndromes of impaired physical, cognitive, behavioral and emotional domains.

In agreement with Wilson (2003), neuropsychological rehabilitation can be defined as a set of techniques to restore and/or compensate for acquired physical or intellectual disability. The techniques used for physical and functional rehabilitation are aimed to assist and promote the natural recovery process, decreasing the development of maladaptive patterns (e.g. disrupting behaviors) and implementing physical, pharmacological, cognitive and behavioral interventions to facilitate the functional recovery of these patients.

ABI may result in motor and/or cognitive impairment. In this context, neuropsychological rehabilitation can be classified into two broad categories, motor and cognitive rehabilitation. Motor rehabilitation plans rely on the assumption that flexion and extension exercises are important to enhance muscle functioning, while cognitive rehabilitation approaches consider that training basic, instrumental or complex tasks of daily living will improve overall adjustment.

The scientific literature is more extensive regarding the neuropsychological interventions for stroke or traumatic brain injuries (TBI). Previous work from Sohlberg and Mateer (1989) suggest that early interventions after severe brain injury are directed essentially to environmental management to control the level of stimulation provided to these patients. During spontaneous recovery, the first signs of change are shown by involuntary responses to environmental stimuli, where cognitive skills such as self-orientation and memory are being partially recovered. According to these authors, this phase is the focus of rehabilitation, with emphasis on training in self-care activities, usually involving motor training to work muscle tone and postural control. Cognitive training is also applied during this stage, aimed at improving communication, attention and memory deficits (Sohlberg et al., 2001).

The conventional rehabilitation plans for motor and cognitive rehabilitation consider that repeated and massive practice of a predetermined function can actually affect neural reorganization, allowing for synaptic reconnectivity and neural reorganization (Butefisch et al., 1995). Previous work from Taub and colleagues (1999) suggests that motor recovery may be possible when training is used to stimulate a specific motor activity. These authors claim that even after damage to the central or peripheral nervous system, implicit information regarding motor schemes may persist in the central nervous system (CNS). In this way, the stimulation of the impaired motor functions benefit the functional reorganization of the CNS, in which, the intact neural systems may reorganize to achieve a given motor act.

4.2 Neuro-rehabilitation using AR technology

Survivors of acquired brain injuries live with minor to severe functional impairments (Merians et al., 2002). These deficits, such as loss of range motion in upper or lower limbs along with lack of organization and motor planning are associated to decreased autonomy and independence on activities of daily living. Occupational Therapy can be applied to patients with upper or lower limb disabilities in order to promote their functional ability. Traditional occupational sessions are carried out in rehabilitation centers where the patients are instructed on how to manage basic motor skills (Alamri et al., 2010). Repetitive practice is considered to be helpful for effective therapy, even after discharge from the rehabilitation's hospital. However, the vast majority of the patients with brain injury are not able to travel to rehabilitation centers located essentially in urban areas for maintenance sessions. The contribution of the new information technologies by means of using VR settings for neuro-rehabilitation could offer opportunities for neuropsychological rehabilitation. On one hand, the use of on-line virtual environments as a form of tele-rehabilitation may increase the accessibility to training environments, enabling home training for patients that are far from the rehabilitation centre (Gamito et al., 2011b). On the other hand, Correa and colleagues (2006), suggest that novel VR applications in a form of an augmented reality (AR) system could offer new possibilities for motor and cognitive training of patients with acquired brain injury. For Leitener and colleagues (2007) the use of AR in rehabilitation allows patients to touch and move the objects in a natural way and without the use of electronic input devices (e.g., mouse, keyboard or gamepads), which may improve interaction and the sense of presence when performing the predetermined tasks. Luo and colleagues (2005), consider that one advantage of AR over VR is that disabled patients following stroke are less disoriented when performing the exercises in AR than in immersive VR environments.

There is increasing interest in the use of AR/VR technology in motor and cognitive rehabilitation (Riva, 2005). The use of interactive AR/VR environments may also help the transfer of the learned skills during training. Although, the transfer process of skills from virtual to real worlds are poorly understood, rehabilitation paradigms using AR/VR techniques should be based on previous assumptions of neuroplasticity, that effective rehabilitation is achieved mainly through repetition, rewarding or reinforcing adaptive skill acquisition. The AR/VR environments for rehabilitation offer the opportunity to include naturalistic challenges that are important for adjustment in real-world activities (Rizzo et al., 2004). The use of this technology in rehabilitation has the advantage of simulating the learning of real tasks in a controlled reality, where training repetition and intensity can be gradually increased in function of patients' achievements. In addition, the visual correspondence between motor or cognitive exercises in AR training allow real time feedback of performance, providing well suited and personalised applications for function based training.

4.2.1 Motor rehabilitation

For Edmans and colleagues (2006), an important question is whether the difficulties that affect a task in the real world are similar to those in the virtual world or whether the errors committed in the virtual world are the same of an analogous task in real world.

Furthermore, several experiments undertaken by Kosslyn and collaborators (2001) have suggested the mental imagery of movement may activate cortical regions involved in planning and execution of movements. These findings may also encourage the use of AR/VR systems in rehabilitation, specifically the use of AR environments that promote mental practice of a desired motor movement may stimulate the activation of wider neural networks.

Alamri and colleagues (2010) are developing an AR based Rehabilitation (AR-REHAB) system to provide motor training in activities of daily living. These authors used several virtual objects in a real kitchen setup, where the patients were able to interact with virtual and real objects. Preliminary results from fifteen healthy male participants are promising and support the use of AR applications in neuropsychological rehabilitation.

According to Kahn and colleagues (2001), motor training can be facilitated through the use of mechanical devices in an AR setup, such as haptic gloves or even body accelerometers. Luo and colleagues (2005), highlight that the use of AR/VR may be beneficial when combined with assistive devices for kinematics. For these authors, the combination of these different technologies in rehabilitation training provides new possibilities that are not possible in conventional rehabilitation programmes. They have developed a training environment that combines AR and assistive devices. This system comprised an assistive device to provide assistance for finger extension. The preliminary results of one case study showed user acceptance along with an improvement in finger extension of the impaired hand after 6 weeks of training.

Riess (1995) developed an AR system to decrease the maladaptive patterns of movement (akinesia) in Parkinson disease, by superimposing virtual images to the real world. This system was designed to compensate for paradoxical motion or kinesis paradoxa, which describes the incapacity for walk without the presence of visual cues. The author suggest that the use AR with visual cues can help the patients to start walking by themselves, however the results are unclear and should be more fully explored.

Baram and colleagues (2002) describe a similar system that combines an AR portable technology with body accelerometers, allowing the generation of a virtual tiled floor to provide a greater sense of reality. These authors tested this system in a sample of fourteen Parkinson patients and found that walking speed and stride length can be effectively manipulated through the use of virtual visual cues.

The AR/VR systems also incorporate game elements that increase motivation to participate in training plans. Commercial video games like Nintendo Wii or Sony PlayStation EyeToy are being used for motor recovery. Yavuzer and colleagues (2008) studied a small sample of disabled patients with the use of conventional therapy sessions combined with AR with PlayStation Eye-Toy. The results showed a significant enhancement of range motion of movements and satisfaction with training in the experimental group using AR in comparison to a control group without AR. Similar results were observed by Deutsch and colleagues (2009) using Wii technology.

In agreement with Kirner and colleagues (2007) the AR games allow an enhanced and wider environment that stimulates perception and spatial orientation. In addition, the new interaction systems developed by the video game industry can also be beneficial for rehabilitation since these mechanisms require 3 axis based movements, similar to those performed in real world situations.

4.2.2 Cognitive rehabilitation

A separate literature defines two general approaches in cognitive rehabilitation, an intervention specifically targeted for rehabilitation and compensation of acquired cognitive deficits, and more recently the focus on a more global and holistic approach with a growing interest in other individual variables at personal, emotional and social levels and their relations to cognitive functioning (Sohlberg et al., 2001). Actually, the literature on this topic is not consistent on whether neuropsychological rehabilitation should focus on the process of cognitive training or the overall adjustment of ABI patients (Clare & Woods, 2004). Several forms of cognitive interventions are described in the literature, however the distinction between cognitive stimulation and training in some cases is unclear and rather confusing. Clare and colleagues (2004) describe cognitive stimulation as a form of cognitive intervention to maintain an adequate level of cognitive functioning when deficits are related to diffuse and progressive brain injury such as in degenerative brain diseases (e.g. Alzheimer). Cognitive stimulation aims at improving the patient's everyday living activities and seeks the management of its cognitive deficits, rather than the recovery of brain function.

When cognitive interventions refer to restoration or recovery of a specific function, neuro-rehabilitation should be considered as training since these are based in a cognitive retraining rationale as suggested earlier. The most frequent cases of cognitive training are related to memory, attention and executive functioning. These deficits are in most cases associated with focal brain injury after a traumatic brain injury or acute stroke episodes.

There are other interesting systems in development as alternatives to cognitive recovery. An example is provided by Sandor and Klinker (2006) that are developing an AR system, termed as Mixed Reality Kitchen, to train organization and planning functions in activities of daily living (e.g., making breakfast). The authors studied a stroke patient in their own environment when performing specific routines. After a five-session training, a decreased time spent on task and decreased location errors were reported when transferring the exercises to the real world.

Nevertheless, one of the most interesting AR systems in cognitive training is the ARVe (Augmented Reality to Vegetal field) - (Richard et al., 2007). The ARVe is an educational environment to assist cognitive disabled children in decision making process. This system consists of a book with several sorts of virtual markers, each of them representing a type of vegetable (leaves, flowers, fruits and seeds). The main goal of this application is to match vegetable entities according to their functions shown on a reference page. The authors found that cognitive disabled children in the AR condition were more motivated to complete the exercises than other children in the control condition.

In sum, the studies reported here for motor and cognitive rehabilitation are promising and may encourage the use of AR/VR applications for function based training. In fact, as suggested before, the use of this technology has the key advantage of being an ecological valid application, where generalization or transfer of learned skills from virtual to real world may be improved, augmenting functionality and overall adjustment in disabled patients.

5. How much more can we augment reality? Future applications and present limitations

5.1 Augmented hardware – Future prospects and issues concerning psychotherapy and neuro-rehabilitation

As has been discussed in this chapter, AR has a part to play in the neurosciences area, namely on psychotherapy and neuro-rehabilitation. This role derived from the technological evolution in the last decade. One of the clearest signs of this evolution rests upon two pillars that are usually related to any new technology that strolled from research labs into households' living-room: price and availability.

If it is true that prices have significantly decreased in most of the equipments needed to deploy AR applications to clinicians, therapists and other caregivers, it is also clear that some of these technologies will never have a large audience since their technical specs are just too obscure for daily-life personal use. Be as it may, technology prices tend to decrease overtime as production increases and become optimized. And, of course, as the market demands for better and easy-to-use applications new and superior products will emerge. In fact, AR is already in our living-room. Examples can be found in some game console applications (Playstation 3 has some videogames, like EyePet and Eye of Judgment, that can take AR into our homes for roughly 30€) and more is on the way if we consider the technological development surrounding portable videogame devices and tablets PCs.

The development of these technologies is, as usually, associated with the investment made in the military, entertainment and medical research since these are industries that attract considerable amounts of investment and have the spending power to promote major advances in a very short time (Gamito et al., 2011b). These advances have helped surpassing most of the constraints associated with the use of AR in therapy and rehabilitation. For example, HMDs, which still are the most common devices to display VR and AR worlds, saw some of their limitations such as weight and ergonomic characteristics resolved. But further work is still needed on addressing technical matters, such as resolution, FOV, registration and occlusion. As discussed before, OST displays have some advantages as they rely mainly on the optical apparatus that constitutes the human eye. On the other hand, VST displays have some features that are appealing when compared to OST. Most recent technologies like projective displays and VRT show great prospect in solving most of the shortcoming concerning displays in AR technology. Nevertheless, and to our best knowledge, even these two state-of-the-art solutions have some limitations. The fact is the ideal solution will probably come from some new technology that it is able to combine the most features present in all of these types of displays, or a significant evolution in one of these, even though it seems at the moment that projective technology is the way to move forward.

Beyond the discussion about displays, it is also important to understand current issues in positioning. As has been shown in this chapter, some positioning solutions have received more attention to specific ends like rehabilitation. HMDs are still used frequently even with all the obvious constraints they pose. However, handheld devices are becoming increasingly popular and are receiving closer attention from both scholars and solution providers in rehabilitation technologies. The future will probably bring forth a solution where handheld devices can work with projection technologies to ensure that hands are available for interaction while AR is in use (Zhou et al., 2008). Current research shows, however, that there are still not enough rehab applications using such combination, even though it has been proved to be a cost-efficient response.

5.2 Augmented Reality Exposure Therapy (ARET) contribution to psychotherapy and neuro-rehabilitation: How to explore its full potential?

Bearing in mind that some applications mentioned in this chapter concerns mental illness, ARET is only a slight improvement on more spread forms of VRET use. If a closer look is taken at phobia treatment using CBT with VRET, ARET's major contribution can be attributed to its ability to insert virtual objects in the real worlds which is an excellent substitute for *in vivo* exposure, since it also addresses ecological validity issues. Maybe it is wiser to insert virtual elements in the real world than to draw people entirely into the VR scenario. Moreover, ARET simplifies the need for world/scenario construction since it uses real places with superimposed objects, making it less time-consuming. Therefore, ARET seems to be able to be used as a coadjutant or as a substitute to VRET in CBT's approach using exposure therapy.

This is also true for another important field of application: rehabilitation. Since one of the key aspects of rehabilitation is repetition, VR/AR solutions may represent a clear path to swifter recoveries. AR also provides a more realistic environment where the individual can practice while being motivated by the insertion of virtual elements. Additionally, solutions where videogame consoles are being used can also serve as an added bonus since prices of off-the-shelf products are becoming more accessible. On the other hand, videogames bring in the fun of a game. Videogame based solutions also guarantee top notch CGI (computer graphic imaging) and, more importantly, the products that are market leaders all have motion detection hardware that can easily be used to rehabilitation. But some fences are still needed to be crossed as the available applications were designed for entertainment and must be adapted for these specific ends.

One aspect that is shared by both rehabilitation and mental illness fields of research when addressing AR is that this technology ensures a smoother transition from therapy to real life as it removes most mediated elements, ensuring a more proximal experience to real objects and situations. This is probably one of the most essential aspects of AR versus VR and constitutes a major opportunity for AR based applications. Knowledge transfer between mediated environments and real-life situations is still an issue and more research is needed to dissipate all doubts about the efficacy of VR/AR in competence development.

A collateral issue to the full and unrestricted use in both rehabilitation and mental health is the need to gain the support of more clinical practitioners. There is still some reserve from many mental health professionals about the use and the advantages that these technology-based solutions have to offer. For that reason, a bigger effort on education and results dissemination is the way to get more support for these applications development.

For all the above mentioned reasons, AR solutions have a bright future ahead in deploying exciting and fruitful solutions for some serious issues. And with the continuous development of exciting new technological solutions, AR based solutions may be available in every home in just a few years.

6. References

Alamri, A., Cha, J., & Saddik, A. (2010). AR-REHAB: An Augmented Reality Framework for Poststroke-Patient Rehabilitation. *IEEE Transactions on Instrumentation and Measurment,* pp. (1-10).

Allred, R.P., Maldonado, M.A., Hsu, J.E. & Jones, T.A. (2005). Training the "lessaffected" forelimb after unilateral cortical infarcts interferes with functional recovery of the impaired forelimb in rats. *Restor Neuroly Neuroscience,* 23, pp. (297-302).

Arvanitis, T. N., Petrou, A., Knight, J. F., Savas, S., Sotiriou, S., Gargalakos, M., et al. (2007). Human factors and qualities pedagogical evaluation of a mobile augmented reality system for science education used by learners with physical disabilities. *Personal and Ubiquitous Computing,* 11, pp. (1–8).

Attree, E.A., Brooks, B.M., & Rose, F.D. (2005). Virtual environments in rehabilitation and training: international perspectives. *Cyberpsychology & Behavior,* 8, 3, pp. (187–188).

Azuma, R. & G. Bishop (1994). Improving static and dynamic registration in an optical see-through HMD. *Proceedings SIGGRAPH '94,* pp. (197-204).

Azuma, R. T. (1997). A survey of augmented reality. Presence: Teleoperators and Virtual Environments, 6, 4, pp. (355-385).

Azuma, R., Baillot, Y., Behringer, R., Feiner, S., Julier, S. & MacIntyre, B. (2001). Recent Advances in Augmented Reality. *IEEE Computers Graphics & Applications,* pp. (1-15).

Bajura, M. & Neumann, U. (1995). Dynamic Registration Correction in Video-Based Augmented Reality Systems. *IEEE Computer Graphics and Applications,* 15, 5, pp. (52-60).

Baram, Y., Aharon-Peretz, J., Simionovici, Y. & Ron, L. (2002). Walking on virtual tiles. *Neural Processing Letters,* 16, pp. (227-33).

Beck, A.T. (1976). *Cognitive therapy and emotional disorders.* New York: International Universities Press.

Bimber, O. & Raskar, R. (2007). Modern approaches to augmented reality . In *ACM SIGGRAPH 2007 Courses* (San Diego, California, August 05 - 09, 2007). SIGGRAPH '07. ACM, New York, NY.

Bimber, O., Encarnação, L.M., & Schmalstieg, D. (2000). Augmented Reality with Back-Projection Systems using Transflective Surfaces. *Proceedings of EUROGRAPHICS 2000 - EG'2000,* 19, 3, pp. (161-168).

Biocca, F.A. & Rolland J.P., (1998). Virtual eyes can rearrange your body-adaptation to visual displacement in see-through, head-mounted displays. *Presence,* 7, 3, pp. (262–277).

Botella C., Villa, H., García-Palacios, A., Baños, R., Perpiñá, C., & Alcañiz. M. (2004). Clinically Significant Virtual Environments for the Treatment of Panic Disorder and Agoraphobia. *CyberPsychology & Behavior,* 7, 5, pp. (527-535).

Botella, C., Baños, R., Quero, S., Perpiñá, C., & Fabregat, S. (2004). Telepsychology and self-help: The treatment of phobias using the internet. *CyberPsychology&Behavior,* 7, pp. (272–273).

Botella, C., Bretón-López, J., Quero, S., Baños, R. M., & García-Palacios, A. (2010). Treating cockroach phobia with augmented reality. *Behavior Therapy,* 41, 3, pp. (401-413).

Botella, C., Juan, M. C., Baños, R., Alcañiz, M., Guillén, V., & Rey, B. (2005). Mixing realities? An application of augmented reality for the treatment of cockroach phobia. *CyberPsychology & Behavior,* 8, pp. (162–171).

Bryanton, C., Bossé, J., Brien, M., Mclean, J., McCormick, A., Sveistrup, H. (2006). Feasibility, Motivation, and Selective Motor Control: Virtual Reality Compared to Conventional Home Exercise in Children with Cerebral Palsy. *CyberPsychology & Behavior*, 9, 2, pp. 1(23-128).

Butefisch, C., Hummelsheim, H., Denzler, P. & Mauritz, K.H. (1995). Repetitive training of isolated movements improves the outcome of motor rehabilitation of the centrally paretic hand. *Journal of the Neurological Sciences*, 130, pp. (59–68).

Caudell, T. & Mizell, D. (1992) Augmented reality: An application of heads-up display technology to manual manufacturing processes. *Proceedings Hawaii International Conference on Systems Sciences*, pp. (659–669).

Chen, Y., Kang, L.J., Chuang, T.Y., Doong, J.L., Lee, S.J. & Tsai, M.W. (2004). Use of Virtual Reality to Improve Upper-Extremity Control in Children With Cerebral Palsy: A Single-Subject Design. *Physical Therapy*, 87, 11, pp. (1441-1457).

Cirstea, M.C. & Levin, M.F. (2007). Improvement in arm movement patterns and endpoint control depends on type of feedback during practice in stroke survivors. *Neurorehabilitation & Neural Repair*, 21, pp. (1-14).

Clare, L. & Woods, R. T. (2004). Cognitive training and cognitive rehabilitation for people with early-stage Alzheimer's disease: A review. *Neuropsychological Rehabilitation*, 14, 4, pp. (385-401).

Cooper, R.A., Dicianno, B.E., Brewer, B., LoPresti, E., Ding, D., Simpson, R., Grindle, G. & Wang, H. (2008). A perspective on intelligent devices and environments in medical rehabilitation. *Medical Engineering & Physics*, 30, pp. (1387–1398).

Correa, A. G., Klein, A. N., Lopes, R. D. (2009). Augmented Reality Musical System for Rehabilitation of Patients with Duchenne Muscular Dystrophy. In Kheng T.Y. (Eds.) *Rehabilitation Engineering*. InTech, Publishing, pp. (2–36).

Costa, R. & Carvalho, L. (2004). The acceptance of virtual reality devices for cognitive rehabilitation: a report of positive results with schizophrenia. *Computer Methods and Programs in Biomedicine*, 73, 3, pp. (173-182).

Deutsch J.E., Robbins D., Morrison J. & Bowlby P. G. (2009). Wii-based compared to standard of care balance and mobility rehabilitation for two individuals pot-stroke. *Virtual Rehabilitation International Conference*. Haifa, Israel. pp. (11-129).

Edmans, J.A. Gladman, J.R., Cobb, S., Sunderland, A., Pridemore, T., Hilton, D. & Walker, M. (2006). Validity of a virtual environment for stroke rehabilitation. *Stroke*, 37, 11, pp. (2770-5).

Emmelkamp, P.M., Krijn, M., Hulsbosch, A.M., de Vries, S., Schuemie, M.J., & van der Mast, C.A. (2002). Virtual reality treatment versus exposure in vivo: A comparative evaluation in acrophobia. *Behavior Research and Therapy*, 40, 5, pp. (509-516).

Feintuch, U., Raz, L., Hwang, J., Yongseok, J., Josman, N., Katz, N., Kizony, R., Rand , D., Rizzo, A.A., Shahar, M. & Weiss, P.L. (2006). Integrating haptic-tactle feedback into a video capture based VE for rehabilitation. *CyberPsychology & Behavior*, 9, 2, pp. (129-135).

Foa, E. & Kozak. M.(1986). Emotional processing of fear: exposure to corrective information. *Psychological Bulletin*, 99, 1, pp. (20-35).

Foa, E., Keane, T, & Friedman M. (2000). *Effective treatments for PTSD: practice guidelines from the International Society for Traumatic Stress Studies*. Guilford Press, Guilford Press.

Gamito P., Oliveira J, Morais D., Rosa P. & Saraiva T. (2011b). Serious Games for Serious problems: from Ludicus to Therapeuticus. In J. J. Kim (Ed.) *Virtual Reality*. InTech, Publishing, pp. (527 - 548).

Gamito, P., Oliveira, J., Pacheco, J., Morais, D., Saraiva, T., Lacerda, R., Baptista, A., Santos, N., Soares, F., Gamito, L & Rosa, P. (2011a). Traumatic Brain Injury memory training: a Virtual Reality online solution. *International Journal on Disability and Human Development*, 10, 3, pp. (309-312).

Gamito, P., Oliveira, J., Rosa, P., Morais, D., Duarte, N., Oliveira, S. & Saraiva, T., (2010). PTSD Elderly War Veterans: A Clinical Controlled Pilot Study. *Cyberpsychology, Behavior, and Social Networking*, 13, 1, pp. (43-48).

Gazzaniga, M.S. & Heatherton, T.F. (2006). *The Psychological Science: Mind, Brain, and Behavior* (2nd edition). New York: W.W. Norton & Company

Giorgino, T., Tormene, P., Maggioni, G., Cattani, B., Pistarini, C. & Quaglini, S. (2008). My Hearth's Neurological Rehabilitation Concept - Technologies for Post-Stroke Treatment. *Cybertherapy & Rehabilitation*, 1, pp. (17-19).

Gloaguen, V., Cottraux, J., Cucherat, M., Blackburn, I. (1998). A meta-analysis of the effects of cognitive therapy in depressed patients. *Journal of Affective Disorders*, 49, pp. (59-72).

Hamm A, & Weike A. (2005). The neuropsychology of fear-learning and fear regulation. *International Journal of Psychophysiology*, 57, pp. (5–14).

Hofmann, S. & Smits, J. (2008). Cognitive-behavioral therapy for adult anxiety disorders: a meta-analysis of randomized placebo-controlled trials. *Journal of Clinical Psychiatry, 69*, 4, pp. (621-32).

Holden, M. (2003). Virtual Environments for Motor Rehabilitation: Review. *Cyberpsychology & Behaviour*, 8, 3.

Hua, H., Gao, C., Brown, L., Ahuja, N. & Rolland, J.P. (2005). Using a head-mounted projective display in interactive augmented environments. In *Proceedings IEEE and ACM International Symposium on Augmented Reality*, pp. (217–223).

Juan, M. C., Alcañiz, M., Monserrat, C., Botella, C., Baños, R. & Guerrero, B. (2005). Using augmented reality to treat phobias. *IEEE Computer Graphics and Applications*, 25, pp. (31–37).

Kahn, L. E., Averbuch, M., Rimer, W. Z. & Reinkensmeyer, D. J. (2001). Comparison of robot-assisted reaching to free reaching in promoting recovery from chronic stroke. In *International of Assisted Technology in the Information Age*, IOS Press, Amsterdam: pp. (39–44).

Kerawalla, L., Luckin, R., Seljeflot, S. & Woolard, A. (2006). Making it real: exploring the potential of augmented reality for teaching primary school science. *Virtual Reality*, 10, pp. (163–174).

Kijima, R. and Ojika, T. (1997). Transition between virtual environment & workstation environment with projective head-mounted display. *Proceedings of IEEE Virtual Reality Annual International Symposium*, pp. (130- 137).

Kirner, C., Gonçalves, T. & Zorzal, E.R. (2007). Collaborative Augmented Reality Environment for Educational Applications. *Proceedings of the 9th International Conference on Enterprise Information Systems*. Lisboa: INSTICC, pp. (257-262).

Kollin, J.A. (1993). Retinal Display For Virtual-Environment Applications. In *Proceedings of SIDInternational Symposium Digest of Technical Papers.*

Kosslyn, S.M., Thompson, W.L., Wraga, M. & Alpert, N.M. (2001). Imagining rotation by endogenous and exogenous forces: distinct neural mechanisms for different strategies. *NeuroReport*, 12, pp. (2519–25).

Leitener, M., Tomitsch, T., Koltringer, T., Kappel, K. & Grechenig, T. (2007). Designing Tangible Tabletop Interfaces for Patients in Rehabilitation. *Proceedings of Conference & Workshop on Assistive Technologies for People with Vision and Hearing Impairments: Assistive Technology for All Ages*. M. Hersh (Eds.), Spain. pp. (1-7).

Levin, M. F., Musampa, N. K., Henderson, A. K. & Knaut, L. A. (2005). New approaches to enhance motor function of the upper limb in patients with hemiparesis. *Hong Kong Physiotherapy Journal*, 23, pp. (2-5).

Lewis, J.R. (2004). In the eye of the beholder. *IEEE Spectrum*, pp. (16-20).

Luo, X., Kline, T., Fischer, H., Stubblefield, K., Kenyon, R. & Kamper, D. (2005). Integration of Augmented Reality and Assistive Devices for Post-Stroke Hand Opening Rehabilitation. *Proceedings of the IEEE Engineering in Medicine and Biology 27th Annual Conference in Shanghai*, pp. (1-4).

Merians, A. S., Jack, D., Boian, R., Tremaine, M., Burdea, G. C., Adamovich, S. V., Recce, M. & Poizner, H. (2002). Virtual Reality–Augmented Rehabilitation for Patients Following Stroke. *Physical Therapy*, 82, 9, pp. (898-915).

Milgram, P., Kishino, F. (1994). A Taxonomy of Mixed Reality Visual Displays. *IEICE Trans. Information Systems*. 77, 12, pp. (1321-1329).

Öst, L. G. (1989). One-session treatment for specific phobias. *Behaviour Research & Therapy*, 27, pp. (1–7).

Öst, L. G. (1997). Rapid treatment of specific phobias. In G. C. L. Davey (Ed.), *Phobias: A handbook of theory, research, and Treatment*. pp. (227–247). New York: Wiley.

Park, J., You, S. and Neumann, U. (1998). Natural feature tracking for extendible robust augmented realities. *In IWAR '98*.

Parks, T.E. (1965). Post Retinal Visual Storage. *American Journal of Psychology*, 78, pp. (145-147).

Parsons & Rizzo (2008). Affective Outcomes of Virtual Reality Exposure Therapy for Anxiety and Specific Phobias: A Meta-Analysis. *Journal of Behavior Therapy & Experimental Psychiatry*, 39, 3, pp. (250-261).

Patrick, E., Cosgrove, D., Slavkovic, A., Rode, J.A., Verratti, T., & Chiselko, G. (2000). Using a Large Projection Screen as an Alternative to Head-Mounted Displays for Virtual Environments. *Proceedings of CHI' 2000*, 2, 1, pp. (479-485).

Pinz, M. Brandner, H. Ganster, A. Kusej, P. Lang, P. & Ribo, M. (2002). Hybrid tracking for augmented reality. *ÖGAI Journal*, 21, 1, pp. (17-24).

Powers, M. & Emmelkamp, P. (2008). Virtual reality exposure therapy for anxiety disorders: A meta-analysis. Journal of Anxiety Disorders, 22, 3, pp. (561-569).

Pressigout, M. & Marchand, E. (2006). Hybrid tracking algorithms for planar and non-planar structures subject to illumination changes. *ISMAR '06*, pp. (52-55).

Pryor, Homer L., Furness, Thomas A. & Viirre, E. (1998). The Virtual Retinal Display: A New Display Technology Using scanned Laser Light. *Proceedings of Human Factors and Ergonomics Society in the 42nd Annual Meeting*, pp. (1570-1574).

Richard, E., Billaudeau, V., Richard, P. & Gaudin, G. (2007). Augmented Reality for rehabilitation of cognitive disabled children: A preliminary study. *Virtual Rehabilitation*, pp. (100-106).

Riess T. (1995). Augmented reality in the treatment of Parkinson's disease. In K. Morgan, M. Satava, HB Sieburg, R Mattheus & JP Christensen (Eds.). *Interactive technology and the new paradigm of healthcare*. Amsterdam: IOS Press: pp. (298-302).

Riva G. (2005). Virtual reality in psychotherapy: review. *CyberPsychology & Behavior*, 8, pp. (220 -230).

Riva, G., Molinari, E. & Vincelli, F. (2002). Interaction and presence in the clinical relationship: virtual reality (VR) as communicative medium between patient and therapist. *IEEE Transactions on Information Technology in Biomedicine*, 6, 3, pp. (198-205).

Rizzo, A., Schultheis, M. Kerns, K.A. & Meteer, C. (2004). Analysis of assets for virtual reality applications in neuropsychology. *Neuropsychological Rehabilitation*, 14, 2, (207-239).

Rizzo, A., Pair J., Graap K., Manson, B., McNerney, P., Wiederhold, B., Wiederhold M. & Spira J. (2006). A Virtual Reality Exposure Therapy Application for Iraq War Military Personnel with Post Traumatic Stress Disorder: From Training to Toy to Treatment. In: M. Roy. (Eds.). *NATO Advanced Research Workshop on Novel Approaches to the Diagnosis and Treatment of Posttraumatic Stress Disorder*. IOS Press, Washington D.C., pp. (235-250).

Rolland, J. P., Davis L. & Baillot. Y. (2001). A survey of tracking technology for virtual environments. In Barfield & Caudell (Eds.). *Fundamentals of Wearable Computers and Augmented Reality*. Mahwah, NJ, pp. (67-112).

Rolland, J.P., Biocca, F., Barlow, T. & Kancherla, A. (1995). Quantification of Perceptual Adaptation to Visual Displacement in See-Through Head-Mounted Displays. *Proceedings IEEE VRAIS'95*, pp. (56-66).

Rolland, J.P., Holloway, R.L. & Fuchs, H. (1994a). A comparison of optical and video see-through head mounted displays. *SPIE Telemanipulator and Telepresence Technologies*, pp. (293-307).

Rothbaum, B. & Schwartz, A. (2002). Exposure therapy for posttraumatic stress disorder. *American Journal of Psycotherapy*, 56, pp. (59-75).

Rothbaum, B., Hodges, L., Smith, S., Lee, J. & Price, L. (2000) A controlled study of virtual reality exposure therapy for the fear of flying. *Journal of Consulting and Clinical Psychology*, 68, 6, pp. (1020-1026).

Sandor, C. & Klinker, G. (2006). Lessons Learned in Designing Ubiquitous Augmented Reality User Interfaces. In M. Haller, M. BillingHurst, B. Thomas (Eds.). *Emerging Technologies of Augmented Reality: Interfaces and Design*, Idea Group Publishing, USA, pp. (218-235).

Saraiva,T., Gamito, P., Oliveira, J., Morais, D., Pombal, M. Gamito, L. & Anastácio, M. (2007). VR exposure: reducing acute stress disorder derived from motor vehicle accidents. In Wiederhold et al. (Eds.). Interactive Media Institute. *Annual Review of Cybertherapy & Telemedicine*, 5, pp. (199-206).

Schowengerdt, B.T, Seibel, E.J. Silverman, N.L. & Furness, T.A. (2004). Stereoscopic retinal scanning laser display with integrated focus cues for ocular accommodation. A.J. Woods, J.O. Merritt, S.A. Benton, & M.T. Bolas (Eds.). Stereoscopic Displays and Virtual Reality Systems XI. *Proceedings of SPIE-IS&T Electronic Imaging*, SPIE 5291, pp. (366–376).

Slobounov, S., Slobounov, E. & Newell, K. (2006). Application of Virtual Reality Graphics in Assessment of Concussion. *Cyberpsychology & Behavior*, 9, 2, pp. (188–191).

Sohlberg, M. M. & Mateer, C. A. (1989). *Introduction to cognitive rehabilitation : theory and practice*. New York: Gildford Press.

Sohlberg, M. M. & Mateer, C. A. (2001). *Cognitive rehabilitation: An integrative neuropsychological approach*. New York: Gildford Press.

Squire, K., & Klopfer, E. (2007). Augmented reality simulations onhandheld computers. *Journal of the Learning Sciences*, 16, pp. (371–413).

Squire, K., & Mingfong, J. (2007). Mad city mystery: Developing scientific argumentation skills with a placebased augmented reality game on handheld computers. *Journal of Science Education and Technology*, 16, pp. (5–29).

Stetten, G., Chib, V., Hildebrand, D., & Bursee, J. (2001). Real Time Tomographic Reflection: Phantoms for Calibration and Biopsy, In *Proceedings of IEEE/ACM International Symposium on Augmented Reality (ISMAR'01)*, pp. (11-19).

Sussman, L. K., Robins, L. N., & Earls, F. (1987). Treatment-seeking for depression by black and white Americans. *Social Science and Medicine*, 24, pp. (187–196).

Sveistrup, H. (2004). Motor rehabilitation using virtual reality. *Journal of NeuroEngineering and Rehabilitation*, pp. (1-10).

Taub, E., Uswatte, G. & Pidikiti, R. (1999). Constraint-induced movement therapy: A new family of techniques with broad application to physical rehabilitation—a clinical review. *Journal of Rehabilitation Research and Development*, 36, pp. (237–251).

Van Krevelen, D.W.F. & Poelman, R. (2010). A Survey of Augmented RealityTechnologies, Applications and Limitations. *The International Journal of Virtual Reality*, 9, 2, pp. (1-20).

Viau, A., Levin, M.F., McFadyen, B.J. & Feldman, A.G. (2004). Reaching in reality and in virtual reality: a comparison of movement kinematics. In *Proceedings of the 15th International Society of Electrophysiology and Kinesiology Congress*, 51.

Vincelli F, Riva G (2000). Virtual reality as a new imaginative tool in psychotherapy. *Studies in Health Technologies and Informatics*, 70, pp. (356-358).

Vincelli, F. & Riva, G. (2002). Virtual Reality: a new tool for panic disorder therapy. *Expert Review of Neurotherapeutics*, 2, 3, pp. (89-95).

Weissman, M., Markowitz, J. & Klerman G. (2000). *Comprehensive guide to interpersonal psychotherapy*. New York: Basic Books.

Weiss, P.L. & Katz, N. (2004). Guest Editorial: The Potential of Virtual Reality for Rehabilitation. *Journal of Rehabilitation Research & Development*, 41, 5, pp. (7-10).

Wilson, B. (2003). *Neuropsychological rehabilitation : theory and practice*. Swets & Zeitlinger Publishers.

Wilson, P., Thomas, P., Sum, D., Duckworth, J., Gugliemetti, M., Rudolph, H, Mumford, N. & Eldridge, R. (2006). A multilevel model for movement rehabilitation in Traumatic Brain Injury (TBI) using Virtual Environments. *IEEE, 5th International Workshop of Virtual Rehabilitation* (IWVR 2006).

Witmer, G. & Singer M. (1998). Measuring Presence in Virtual Environments: A Presence Questionnaire. *Presence: Teleoperators and Virtual Environments*, 7, 3. pp. (225-240).

Wörn, H., Aschke, M., & Kahrs, L. A. (2005). New augmented reality and robotic based methods for head-surgery. *International Journal of Medical Robotics and Computer Assisted Surgery*, 1, pp. (49–56).

Wykes, T., Reeder, C., Landau, S. , Everitt, B., Knapp, M., Patel A. & Romeo, R. (2007). Cognitive remediation therapy in schizophrenia. Randomised controlled trial. *British Journal of Psychiatry,* 190, pp. (421-427).

Yavuzer G., Senel A., Atay M.B. & Stam H. J. (2008). Playstation eyetoy games' improve upper extremity-related motor functioning in subacute stroke: a randomized controlled clinical trial. *European Journal of Physical and Rehabilitation Medicine*, 44, pp. (237-44).

Zhou, F., Duh, H.B.L. & Billinghurst, M. (2008) Trends in Augmented Reality Tracking, Interaction and Display: A Review of Ten Years of ISMAR. Cambridge, UK: 7th IEEE and ACM International Symposium on Mixed and Augmented Reality (ISMAR 2008), pp. (15-18).

Zlatanova, S. (2002). Augmented Reality Technology. *GISt Report,* 17, pp. (1-76).

8

Augmented Reality Assisted Upper Limb Rehabilitation Following Stroke

Kimberlee Jordan and Marcus King
Industrial Research Ltd.
New Zealand

1. Introduction

Stroke is a rapidly developing loss of brain function(s) resulting from lack of blood flow caused by either a blockage, or a hemorrhage (Sims & Muyderman, 2009). Common motor impairments after stroke include muscle weakness, reduced reaction time, loss of joint range of motion and disordered movement organization: hemiparesis or weakness on one side of the body is common. It is widely regarded as a leading cause of disability in the developed world (Adamson et al., 2004). For survivors of stroke, these impairments can severely limit daily activities and participation in social and family environments (Merians et al., 2002; Werner & Kessler, 1996). The upper limb (UL) in particular remains problematic post stroke. Whereas up to 83% of stroke survivors learn to walk again (Skilbeck et al., 1983), it is estimated that only 5 to 20% of stroke survivors attain complete functional recovery of their affected UL (Kwakkel et al., 2003). This may be in part because the high costs of standard therapy mean that treatment frequently ceases once patients are released from acute care and long term outcomes are often poor (Feys et al., 1998; Carter et al., 2006). Another possibility is that it is possible for the patient to learn to use their unaffected arm almost exclusively for most activities of daily living, whereas the patient has no choice but to use both legs for walking (Feys et al., 1998; Kwakkel et al., 1999). Additionally, significant loss of hand function may cause some people to abandon any residual function in that hand through learned non-use (Sterr et al., 2002).

Best practice rehabilitation requires multiple trained personnel up to 30 hours of therapy a week (anon, 2007), but this is seldom achieved and outcomes of conventional therapy are poor (Feys et al., 1998). Evidence suggests that repetitive training of functional UL motor tasks (Van Peppen et al., 2004; Kwakkel et al., 1999; van der Lee, 2001); intensity of practice, and functional relevance of the motor tasks (French et al., 2009; Butefisch et al., 1995) are the critical components of successful UL rehabilitation. Neuroplasticity is the process by which neural circuits in the brain are modified by experience, learning and/or injury (e.g. Nudo, 2003) that allows for motor-relearning and recovery after stroke. A large number of repetitions of the same movement pattern forms the physiological basis of motor learning and is thus an essential component of motor-relearning (Butefisch et al., 1995). Animal studies indicate that as many as 400 to 600 repetitions per day may be required to induce changes in neuroplasticity following stroke (Nudo et al., 1996). But repeated motor activity on its own is not sufficient however to promote recovery: the specificity and functionality of the repeated task is also an important consideration associated with functional recovery (Butefisch et al., 1995; Nudo et al., 1996; Plautz et al., 2000).

Subjective well-being is reduced one year post stroke and this is mainly attributed to poor arm function (Wyller et al., 1997). However, improvements in outcomes can be seen up to 3 years post stroke (Stinear et al 2007), well past the point at which standard rehabilitation therapy stops (Stein et al., 2009). There is, therefore, a clear need for effective UL rehabilitation tools that provides large repetition of functional movements and can be used in a home setting without the constant supervision of a therapist.

2. Robot assisted rehabilitation therapy

From the stand point of the therapist, the large number of repetitions necessary for effective rehabilitation is very labour intensive. Robot-assisted physiotherapy (e.g. robotic or automated exercise machines) can help in alleviating therapist work load by providing autonomous training where patients can engage in repeated and intense practice of goal-directed tasks (Prange et al., 2006). For example, Krebs et al (2008) describe a 2 DOF robot, the MIT Manus, that trained shoulder and elbow movements in a horizontal plane, although robots can be used for "teaching a trajectory" or "enabling a movement through minimal assistance", the amount of guidance for maximising recovery is not known (Adamovich, 2009). Robotic-assisted therapy devices can also provide an objective and reliable means of monitoring patient progress, and can be used in conjunction with computer-based augmented or virtual reality environments, leading to improvements in motor function (Fasoli et al., 2003; Krebs et al., 2002; Kwakkel et al., 2008).

Reports indicate that robotic therapy can improve motor control in stroke survivors to a greater extent than conventional therapy and results of clinical trials using these systems to rehabilitate the UL are positive (Prange et al., 2006). However, this is likely to be due primarily to the greater intensity of practice that can be achieved using these devices (Kwakkel et al., 2008).

There is a crucial need to improve the cost-to benefit ratio of robot-assisted therapy and their effectiveness in rehabilitation of the impaired arm (Johnson et al., 2007). The rehabilitation interventions described in Kwakkel et al. (2008) require patient time on the devices of an average of 48 min per day for 8 weeks. A 6-axis robot can be expected to cost about US$60,000 and deployment (e.g., training, programming, adding tools etc.) may cost another US$200,000. Such a capital item, with a depreciation rate of say 15%, operating 40 h per week, would need to be charged at US$19/h, meaning that robotic arm treatment of one patient's rehabilitation programme will cost US$800 in capital depreciation alone, regardless of maintenance, running or therapist costs (King et al., 2010). Peattie et al. (2009) describe a reaching training robot, based on an armskate (Fig 1), using a personal computer as the controller. If a low-cost (under US$1000) peripheral device for a personal computer can supply a beneficial therapy, the cost-effectiveness of such therapies would be significantly improved and clinical uptake will be expedited.

3. Virtual reality rehabilitation

Virtual reality (VR) allows the user to interact with a simulated "real" environment via dedicated computer hardware and software (Holden & Dyer, 2002). It potentially provides a

Fig. 1. Robotic armskate with PC controller for UL rehabilitation.

user with a disability a stimulating experience, engaging and motivating to the practice of UL movements as the user manipulates the interface device (Sviestrup, 2004). VR allows the creation and control of dynamic 3-dimensional, ecologically valid stimulus environments within which behavioral response can be recorded and measured, therby offering clinical assessment and rehabilitation options not available with traditional methods (Schultheis & Rizzo, 2001).

Studies have reported increased participant motivation, enjoyment or perceived improvement in physical ability following the inclusion of VR into stroke rehabilitation (Broeren et al., 2008; Housman et al., 2009; Yavuzer et al., 2008). Importantly, computer games can improve compliance with prescribed rehabilitation exercises (Kwakkel et al., 2008).

Assistive devices may be combined with virtual reality in order to provide a valuable rehabilitation experience for stroke survivors. For example Pyk et al. (2008) describe a combination of data gloves and virtual reality for UL rehabilitation in children with motor deficits.

3.1 The Able-X

Industrial Research Ltd (IRL) developed the Able-X for UL rehabilitation of stroke survivors who are able to move their arm against gravity, but have minimal strength or control over their actions (Hijmans et al., 2011). It is a light-weight handlebar (Fig 2) which contains a motion sensitive game controller (CyWee Z, Taiwan) that interfaces with a PC. The Able-X couples the arms so that the unaffected arm can assist movement of the hemiparetic arm.

A suite of computer games provided a graduated series of physical challenges, from target hitting games, to faster sports games, as well as some casual and puzzle games.

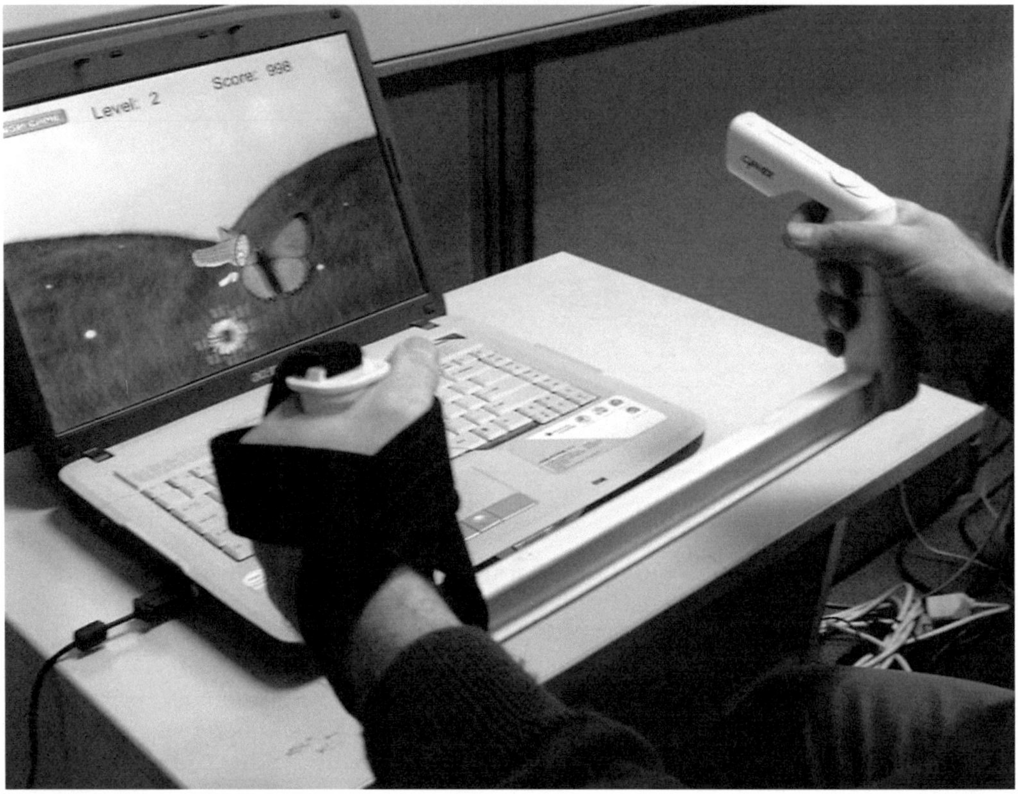

Fig. 2. Against-gravity bilateral exercise device that interacts with computer games.

3.2 Able-X pilot study

3.2.1 Able-X participants

To trial the system fourteen participants with post-stroke UL hemiparesis were recruited: their mean age was 71 years (range 47-85); nine were male, five female; time since stroke one to six years; eight had a stroke in their left hemisphere and six in their right and in nine participants the dominant hand was affected while in five it was the non-dominant.

3.2.2 Able-X assessment, outcome measures and Intervention

Assessments were conducted after enrolment in the study (T0). A 2.5 week sham-intervention was provided which consisted of playing mouse based computer games on a personal computer using their unaffected arm for eight to ten sessions, each lasting at least 45 minutes. Following this, participants were re-assessed (T1). There was a 2 ½ week period where no intervention was provided, after which participants were again re-assessed (T2). The 2.5 week intervention was then performed and consisted of playing computer games with the Able-X for eight to ten therapist supervised sessions lasting 45 to 60 minutes. Game difficulties were adjusted to mach the ability of the participant and progressed as participant ability improved. Finally the participants were reassessed (T3). The Fugl Meyer Upper Limb assessment (FMA-UL) (Fugl-Meyer, 1975) was the primary outcome measure. Additional outcome measures were the DASH (Disabilities of the Arm, Shoulder and Hand), a questionnaire for self reported symptoms and abilities in certain activities (Beaton et al., 2001) and the WOLF test (Wolf Motor Function Test for functional movement (Wolf & Catlin, 2001)).

3.2.3 Able-X results

The Able-X intervention resulted in a significant improvement in UL motor performance as measured by the FMA-UL (Table 1). The mean improvement post intervention (T3) ranged from 4.2 (compared to T2) to 5.2 (compared to T1). These results are especially encouraging in light of the fact that the group comprised adults with chronic stroke and the cohort was heterogeneous (FMA-UL ranged from 14 to 65 at inclusion). Post-intervention focus groups showed that participants enjoyed the experience and reported perceived gains in UL movement, concentration and balance.

	T0	T1	T2	T3	F	p
FMA-UL (n=13)	44.2±17.9	44.0±17.2	45.0±16.2	49.2±16.6	10.41	<0.001
WMFT (n=13)	32.7±50.4	32.4±50.6	31.5±50.9	30.5±51.2	2.74	0.06
DASH (n=13)	51.8±21.5	54.5±23.4	55.0±24.4	55.6±23.2	0.66	0.58

Table 1. Means ± standard deviation of the outcome measures pre-control (T0), post-control/ pre-washout (T1), post-washout / pre-intervention (T2), and post-intervention (T3).

3.3 Able-X home care pilot study

To test use of the system in an unsupervised home situation, three participants from the above trial were asked to use the system at home for 8 weeks. Participants were assessed prior to the intervention (T1); the systems were left with them for up to 61 days; after which they were reassessed (T2). As patient self-reports are suggested as the best method of evaluating adherence to home-based physiotherapy (Bassett, 2003), participants diaries of usage and the Intrinsic Motivation Inventory (McAuley, 1987) were the outcome measures.

Participant	J	D	W
IMI: average	70%	70.5%	49%
Diary: number of sessions in intervention	44 / 55 days	46 / 58 days	49 / 61 days
Diary: Average session duration (minutes)	46	35	38
Diary: Average sessions per week	5.5	5.5	4.5

Table 2. IMI and diary results for unsupervised homecare therapy using Able-X.

The diaries (Table 2) indicated that all of participants continued therapy at a rate of from 4.5 to 5.5 sessions per week and maintained that throughout the 8 week period. The IMI results suggest that the therapy successfully motivated the participants. Patient motivation and compliance with prescribed exercise/practice is a key component of successful home-based therapy or telerehabilitation. We have shown this can be provided with a computer game therapy system that did not rely on regular therapist prompting to exercise.

4. Augmented reality rehabilitation

In contrast to VR, Augmented Reality (AR) superimposes a computer-generated image on a user's view of the real world, thus providing a composite view, which has significant advantages over VR for neurorehabilitation. Neurological injuries, such as stroke, cause considerable environmental impoverishment due to the stroke survivor's either limited ability or inability to interact physically with their environment (Stein et al., 1995). There is substantial literature on the negative impact of impoverished environments and their effects on the cortex in rats and primates (Renner & Rosenzweig, 1987). Similarly there is evidence to suggest that enriching an environment has a beneficial effect on both behavioural and cognitive function in brain damaged animals. Although more research on humans is necessary, there is general agreement that this holds for humans too (Rose et al., 1998). There is widespread agreement amongst clinicians that the reduction of interaction with the physical environment resulting from stroke is detrimental to recovery of function (Rose et al., 2005). Thus a key factor in successful stroke rehabilitation is whether the patient's level of interaction with their environment can be dramatically increased.

Augmented environments offer a unique rehabilitation solution for stroke survivors in that the information within the environment and the way in which patients interact with this information can be controlled very specifically (Levin, 2011; Rose et al., 1998). Many of the physical issues giving rise to a stroke-induced impoverished environment can be solved or circumvented using augmented environments. For example, a given sensory aspect or modality can be emphasised or augmented to make up for other sensory loss. If a patient is unable to walk through their physical environment, VR or AR can be combined concurrently with a robotic walking aid, e.g. Hocoma Locomat, therapy to provide visual flow and thus the overall sensation of moving through an environment. In fact the computer technology underlying AR is ideally suited to delivering an enriched environment to humans with disabilities as it is generally possible to cater for whatever motor capability an individual may have. Similarly the particular sensory aspects of an environment may be augmented to offset partial sensory loss.

Because of the above, augmented environments have the potential to be highly engaging for patients undergoing rehabilitation, leading to greater levels of compliance. Approximately 65% of patients are likely to be non-adherent to physical therapy rehabilitation programmes, to varying degrees (Bassett, 2003). Additionally, Tinson (1989) found that stroke patients within a rehabilitation unit spent 30 - 40% of their time in "disengaged and inactive tasks" and only 30-60 minutes per day in formal therapy. It is crucial that a person engaged in rehabilitation following neurological injury is engaged in their therapy and an augmented reality rehabilitation has the potential to fill some of the patient "down-time" with valuable therapeutic activity.

AR environments and the skills practiced or learned within them can be tailored according to a patient's impairment(s) in terms of task complexity, required response(s), sensory presentation, type and amount of feedback provided (Holden, 2005). Particular elements can be enriched or downplayed as required to exploit principles of motor learning and plasticity (Rose et al., 2005; Levin 2011). Particular elements of a task can be shown selectively to highlight the relevant information. For example, the specifications for reaching movements are determined from observation of the end point trajectory of a moving limb. This can therefore be highlighted to focus the attention of the patient onto the relevant information. Effectively this reduces the complexity of the environment in terms of clutter and unnecessary information that may distract and/or frustrate the patient.

Feedback is a critical component to motor learning which is easily manipulated in an augmented environment and can be delivered in a variety of different ways. Holden (2005) suggests creation of a virtual teacher for demonstration of movements. The virtual teacher has the advantage that they can perform an unlimited number of repetitions (unlike a human therapist). Many studies have investigated the VR environment for stroke rehabilitation, but few have shown effective transfer of training to the real world. Pridmore et al. (2004) discussed how moving VR environments closer to the real world will ease the transfer of rehabilitation activities into daily life. This means moving to the right of the continuum shown in fig 3, i.e. making use of AR. Rand et al. (2005) found that older adults prefer a head-mounted display to seeing an image projected on a screen, which is an example of elderly users requiring the environment to be closer to reality than younger people do.

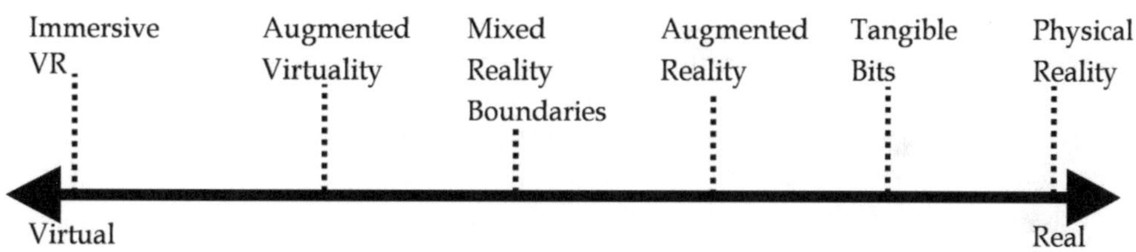

Fig. 3. Technologies across the virtual divide (Pridmore et al., 2004).

A significant advantage of AR is that it provides for activation of mirror neurons, thought to be the basis of imitative learning. A mirror neuron is one that fires when someone either acts or observes a goal directed action performed by another (Rizzolatti & Craighero, 2004). However, they do not fire when a simple movement is executed or observed, so a task must be associated with the movement (Gallese et al., 1996). Mirror neurons have a direct input to the motor cortex and a role for these neurons in recovery from stroke has been suggested by several authors (Eng et al., 2007; Ramachandran & Altschuler, 2009; Sathian et al., 2000). Human fMRI and TMS studies have shown increased mirror neuron activity and formation of motor memories during learning of new motor tasks by imitation or action-observation (Buccino et al., 2004; Stefan et al., 2005).

Observation of another individual performing a motor training task (action observation) results in increased cortical excitability of the primary motor cortex and can enhance the beneficial effects of motor training on motor memory formation in patients with chronic stroke (Celnik et al., 2008). The mirror system plays the role of 'movement organizer' and is sensitive therefore to observation and thereon action. Preliminary data indicate that the action / observation approach may produce significant clinical results (Ertelt et al., 2007). The action/observation/execution mechanism requires the stroke survivor to view their hemiparetic arm carrying out the task, even though it may be too weak to function independently and this can stimulate the cortical mirror neurone system.

A related treatment, mirror box therapy has been shown to be effective in UL stroke therapy (Sütbeyaz et al., 2007; Yavuzer et al., 2008). Mirror box therapy, was originally developed to reduce phantom pain in amputees by Ramachandran et al. (1995). The patient places their stump into a box which has mirrors arranged so that the image of the good limb appears to be superimposed onto the stump of the amputated or phantom limb. When the patient moves their good limb, it appears as if their lost limb is also moving and through the use of this artificial visual feedback it becomes possible for the patient to "move" the phantom limb, and to unclench it from potentially painful positions. This demonstrates a real-world attempt to create an AR environment for rehabilitation.

4.1 The Able-B: an AR mirror box for stroke rehabilitation

AR therapy may be utilised to stimulate a similar experience to mirror box therapy and we have developed the Able-B (Figure 3) based on these principles as well as bilateral UL exercise therapy (Caraugh et al., 2005; McCombe-Waller et al., 2008). This device is designed to facilitate re-learning of reaching movements for patients who are either unable or have great difficulty moving their hemiparetic arm. The patient can use the strength of their unaffected arm to assist the hemiparetic arm as required while observing the mirrored movement of the impaired arm through the AR system. The patient sits with both arms in the moulded forearm supports, held in place using padded velcro straps. The hands rest on either a palmar mound or a joy-stick style handle, depending on user preference. The Able-B provides a platform for high repetition, intense bilateral exercise within a relatively low-cost package that decreases therapist supervision requirements and allows persons with more severe UL hemiparesis to exercise independently (Sampson et al., 2011).

4.2 The software

It is necessary to create a specific set of games for rehabilitation of stroke survivors, who are generally over 65 years old. Stroke often results in reduced attention span, short term memory and problem solving skills (anon, 2009) and most computer games are very fast and provide negative feedback when losing (IJsselsteijn, 2007). We have developed a suite of computer games to provide a graduated series of physical challenges, from stationary target hitting games, to strategic target hitting games, to moving target hitting games. These games always provide positive feedback for actions performed and do not have significant memory or problem solving challenges. The graphics are large sized, in high contrast colours and the movements do not require fast reactions. Use of sound is maximised, so that every time an object appears and every time an interaction occurs, a sound is provided.

All games required large cursor movements in both horizontal and vertical directions. The games are presented using a simple AR environment using a web camera and conventional computer monitor as display. The computer game characters were superimposed over the image of the stroke-affected arm and hand (fig 5) to create an action/observation/ execution scenario within an affordable and easy to implement AR environment.

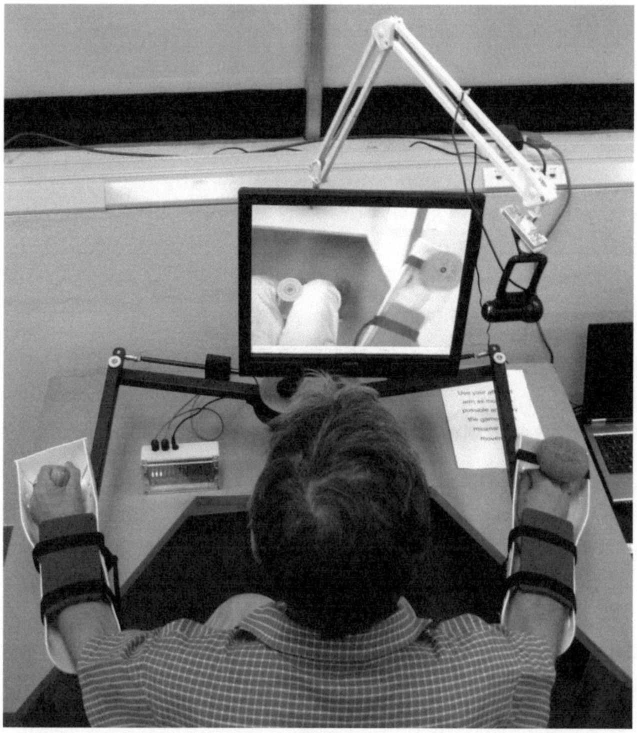

Fig. 4. Able-B to allow an individual to exercise their hemiparetic right arm, using AR to show their hemiparetic arm interacting with a computer game.

A web camera is used to display the hemiparetic arm (Fig 3) on the monitor such that it appears to interact with the computer games. Using color-tracking software, a colored patch attached to the hand acts as a "computer mouse" to play specially designed games.

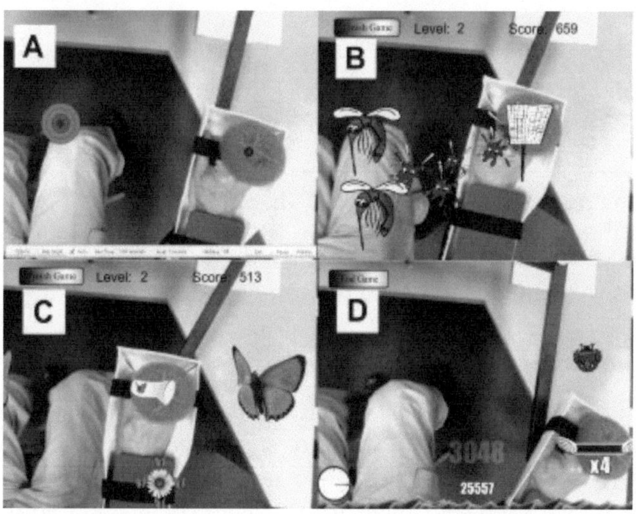

Fig. 5. The series of computer images of the four AR games used for arm reaching exercises.

4.3 Able-B case study

4.3.1 Able-B participants

To test the efficacy of the Able-B, five post-stroke participants with UL hemiparesis were recruited: their mean age was 61.8 years (range 45 - 76 years); 3 were male, 2 were female; all were right dominant with 3 participants having right hemiparesis and 2 having left hemiparesis. The mean time post stroke that the intervention was started was 45.2 weeks (range 9 - 64 weeks) and participants were free of other neurological deficits.

4.3.2 Able-B assessment, Outcome measures and Intervention

Assessors conducted blinded assessments of the trial participants, in the week prior to the start of intervention (T0) and in the week following the cessation of interventions (T1). The FMA-UL was the primary outcome measure and participant motivation was assessed using the Intrinsic Motivation Inventory (IMI) after the intervention.

Participants completed 6 weeks of Able-B + AR intervention consisting of therapist supervised, 45 minute sessions, 4x/week. Game difficulties were adjusted to match the ability of the participant and progressed as participant ability improved.

4.3.3 Able-B results

Overall the results indicate a positive effect from intervention using the Able-B system (Table 3), with the FMA-UL score increase ranging from 1 to 5 points after 6 weeks of therapy.

Fugl-Meyer Upper extremity scores (/66)

Participant	T0 (Wk 0)	T1 (Wk 7)	Change
1	16	21	5
2	15	18	3
3	7	11	4
4	19	20	1
5	7	9	2

Table 3. FMA-UE scores before and after Able-B therapy.

The results of the IMI ranged from 80% for participant 4 to 95% for participant 2, indicating that all participants were highly motivated to comply with the Able-B therapy.

4.4 AR rehabilitation using a polished board

Polished board or armskate exercising is designed for patients who have some ability to move their hemiparetic arm, provided they are supported against gravity e.g. by sliding their arm across a polished table top. King et al. (2010) describes an affordable, computerised table-based exercise system using AR in conjunction with such an exercise regime (fig 6).

Fig. 6. AR arm rehabilitation using polished board, showing the virtual butterfly net superimposed on the image of the hand.

4.5 AR and polished board case study

4.5.1 AR and polished board: participants

To test the concept of integrating AR with a simple reaching exercise, four participants with UL hemiparesis as a result of stroke were recruited. The age ranged from 55 to 85; time since stroke ranged from 2 to 12 years; three were male and one female; two were left side hemiparetic, and all were right hand dominant; all participants were free of other neurological deficits.

4.5.2 AR and polished board: assessment, outcome measures and intervention

The FMA-UL was the primary outcome measure, but additional outcome measures were the WOLF and the DASH. Assessors conducted pre- (T0) and post-intervention (T1) assessments.

Participants completed 4 weeks of AR and polished board intervention consisting of 8 supervised sessions which lasted 45 minutes each. An overhead mounted web camera using the computer vision algorithm ARToolkit (HIT Lab, University of Canterbury, NZ), tracked the position of a fiducial marker attached to the user's hand. A computer game showed a butterfly net superimposed over the user's hand. The user placed the marker on a cross marked in the centre of the screen to start the game. Virtual butterflies "flew" from eight evenly spaced different directions, starting at the outer edge of the screen and traveling towards the centre at a fixed speed. The user's task was to move their hand to the outside of the screen to "catch" the butterfly in the net (Figure 6). After the butterfly was caught, the user moved back to the centre cross and the next butterfly appeared. After all 8 butterflies had been caught, the time taken, and therefore the distance moved in each direction was shown with a graph.

4.5.3 AR and polished board case study results

This study indicated a positive effect of the therapy (Table 4) with two participants increasing their FMA-UL scores and Wolf times significantly. Interestingly their self-reported standard of life as shown by the DASH, showed a decrease for two participants, possibly as a result of the focus of attention on their arm impairment.

	Fugl-Meyer (/44)			Wolf, average time / task (sec)			DASH (/100)		
No	T0	T1	Change	T0	T1	Change	T0	T1	Change
1	33	33	0	34.3	24.5	-9.8	33.3	34.2	0.9
2	10	17	7	84.0	77.0	-7.0	67.5	71.7	3.2
3	31	31	0	43.4	44.4	1.0	-	-	-
4	36	42	6	4.2	4.1	-0.1	21.7	40.0	18.3

Table 4. Results of the outcome measures pre and post ARS intervention for the 4 participants.

5. A computer assisted upper limb rehabilitation system for stroke

We have developed a computer assisted UL rehabilitation system which combines the advantages of both AR and VR with three assistive devices that provide a lower cost alternative to rehabilitation robotics for training of shoulder and elbow reaching. The Able-X and Able-B described above are suitable for people with severe and mild arm movement impairments. A third device, the Able-M has been designed to enable the delivery of the AR with polished board exercises in a rehabilitation setting.

5.1 The able-M

The Able-M is designed for patients who have some ability to move their hemiparetic arm, provided they are supported against gravity. It is based on a traditional arm-skate or sliding board to provide gravity support while practising reaching exercises across a tabletop. The Able-M (Fig 7) interacts with the computer in the same way as a wireless computer mouse, controlling the cursor of the PC. A button, which acts as the mouse clicker switch, is flexibly mounted to position it around the dorsal side of the hand or fingers, hence requiring finger or wrist extension exercises to operate.

5.2 The suite of devices

The assistive devices allow people with hemiparesis to interact with a computer during rehabilitation exercises, providing a system which can are aligned to the degree of

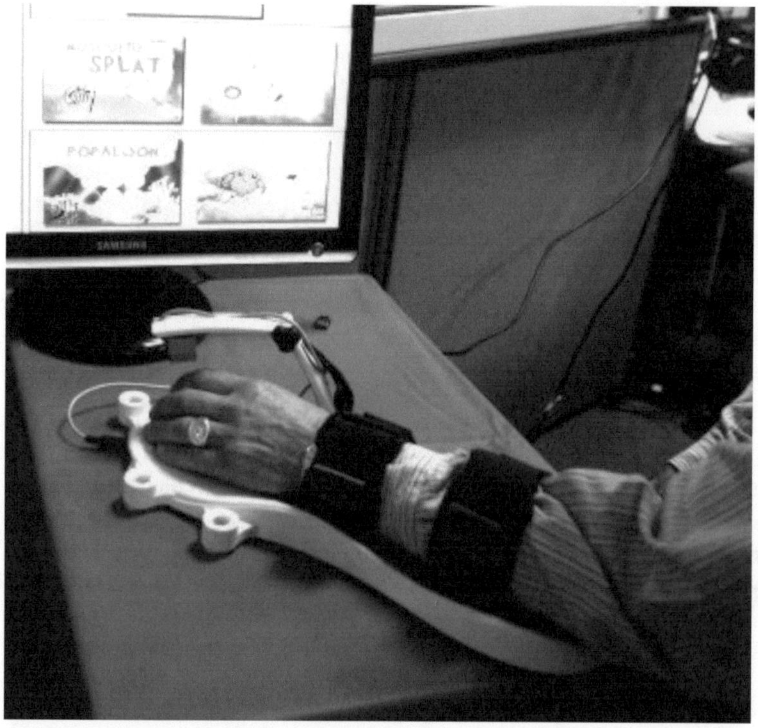

Fig. 7. Able-M, a gravity supported arm exercise device that interacts with computer games.

impairment, or weakness presented by the patient. Fig 8 shows the relationship of the components of the system to the patient's strength as measured by the Oxford scale of muscle strength (Parkinson, 2000).

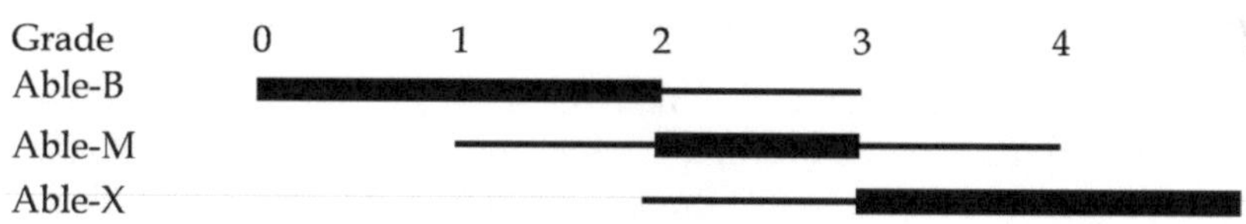

Grade 0	No Contraction
Grade 1	Flicker or trace of contraction
Grade 2	Active movement with gravity eliminated
Grade 3	Active movement against gravity
Grade 4	Active movement against gravity and resistance
Grade 5	Normal power

Fig. 8. IRL devices aligned to level of strength.

6. Discussion

There is significant amount of evidence to show that learning in a virtual environment can transfer to the real environment. However, there is also evidence that transfer of rehabilitation training into real world activities of daily living is easier if the training is carried out in as close to the real environment as possible. Therefore, the AR environment has potential for better rehabilitation outcomes than a VR environment.

Mirror neurons were first described in 1992 so the use of mirror therapy is relatively new. AR seems to be an ideal method for bringing mirror therapy to people with a variety of disabilities or injuries. The development of a suite of devices that can bring this technology into a homecare situation, for people to rehabilitate themselves, with minimal supervision from clinicians, has potential to allow delivery of rehabilitation to a large numbers in a cost effective manner. The operating range of the three IRL devices is wide enough to provide smooth transition and overlap from one to the next, thereby allowing a person to exercise at their own rate until they are able to "graduate" from one to the next. The suite demonstrates the application of a systems approach to the rehabilitation of the UL.

Although the quantity of UL repetitions per session were not recorded, they were estimated (conservatively based on the game parameters set during sessions) to range from 600 to 1000 per 45 min session for each of the 3 devices, depending upon which games were used. Lang et al. (2009) found that in typical stroke rehabilitation units, 32 UL repetitions per session was typical, so this is greater than many conventional UL therapy sessions and would compare favourably with other non-robotic platforms with or without AR or VR. The Able-X results are comparable to more intensive robotic-aided therapies reported previously, with improvements on the FMA-UL of between 3 and 6 (Prange et al., 2006).

Computer game play has been shown to be very motivating for stroke survivors to undertake as part of a rehabilitation programme, even without supervision. However, it is important that the game play actually constitutes task-based movements, because the mirror neuron system is only activated when task are undertaken, rather than when passive movements are made. Further research is required to ensure that AR gameplay activates these neural regions, leading to learning and recovery.

7. Future directions / considerations

Our research has been carried out with small numbers in pilot trial situations. Larger randomised, controlled trials across multiple centres are necessary for clinical validation of these devices. Future clinical research should be aimed at developing protocols for rehabilitation using the range of devices and software or games that may be used with the devices. Additionally, for delivery of a rehabilitation service to stroke survivors, products must meet medical devices standards.

Brain imaging (e.g. fMRI, EEG) should be incorporated into future research programme. This will allow clinicians to determine which patients will benefit most from specific treatments (e.g. bilateral therapy vs. unilateral therapy or AR versus VR environments). The importance of including information on lesion size and location in the planning of stroke treatment trials has also been highlighted. Incorporation of brain imaging can assist with the planning and prescription of rehabilitation (Hamzei et al., 2006). The development of functional imaging promises major advances within neuroscience and there is significant potential for combining these methods with virtual environments. The combination of neuroimaging and activity in virtual environments could be used to investigate the extent to which interaction with virtual and real environments is cognitively equivalent.

A comparison should be made between the use of VR with avatars, versus AR in a stroke affected population. Adamovich et al. (2009) suggested that VR avatars can create an observation condition and hence it may be possible to use avatars, rather than real time images of a person's limbs, to provide positive rehabilitaion outcomes. The authors have recorded anecdotal statements from study participants that they do not like viewing their stroke-affected limb, due to it's "old look".

The acute phase of stroke recovery is the optimal period for maximum recovery following stroke and so research must move into that area. Currently most researchers work with participants who are in the chronic stage of their stroke recovery, due to their stable baseline and the lack of interference with medical interventions by research protocols.

AR rehabilitation has a large potential for benefit to stroke survivors and the community as it can be delivered in a home environment. But it is necessary to integrate these systems with homecare, using telerehabilitation services, to ensure adherence to the programme and tailoring the service to the individual's requirements. Such systems must be robust for home installation by non-specialised technicians (e.g. physiotherapists) and daily use by the individual who may have a cognitive disability as a result of the injury.

It is not yet clear what mix of cognitive and physical rehabilitation challenges should be provided for optimal recovery following stroke. For example Schimmelpfennig (2000) found that, following orthopaedic or phlebological procedures, patients who underwent mental activation training, showed a greater motivation in rehabilitation and recovered their movement coordination quicker. This area is an ideal research opportunity for AR therapies.

Environmental enrichment, in addition to being beneficial in its own right, can optimise other treatments designed to restore function following brain damage. There is evidence of enrichment induced neuroplastic change in primates and it would be interesting to see how this translates to humans, especially in relation to an AR environment.

8. Conclusions

Neurological injury leads to environmental impoverishment and AR provides the ability to enrich the environment and increase a stroke survivor's interaction / experiences, leading to beneficial effects in terms of engagement and rehabilitation outcomes.

Improvements in UL function and isometric strength were observed during studies of augmented physical therapy utilising a combination of assistive devices and AR that allow people with UL disabilities that range from very severe hemiparesis to almost able-bodied.

Engaging in AR therapy using simple assistive devices seems to be a cost effective alternative to other forms of therapy such as robotic therapy, catering for repetitive self-supported UL exercises. It also can integrate easily with conventional physiotherapy.

Overall these studies suggest that further research on a larger sample size and range of stroke survivors with UL hemiparesis is warranted to provide a greater level of clinical evidence as to the effect of the system for people with UL hemiparesis.

The system has the potential to provide a calibrated range of exercises which can be selected to suit the physical and cognitive abilities of a patient ranging from severe hemiparesis to almost able-bodied or integrated as a systems approach to UL rehabilitation.

9. Acknowledgements

The authors wish to thank the stroke survivors and clinicians who willingly gave their time and thoughts during development of the interventions described here. All studies involving human participants were approved by the University of Otago, NZ Human Ethics Committee or by the NZ Health and Disabilities, Upper South A, Regional Ethic Committee. We thank Im-Able Ltd., New Zealand, for supporting this research through the supply of Able-X and Able-M devices.

10. References

Adamovich, S.; August, K.; Merians, A. & Tunik, E. (2009). A virtual reality-based system integrated with fmri to study neural mechanisms of action observation-execution: A proof of concept study. *Restorative Neurology and Neuroscience*, Vol.27, No.3, pp. 209-223, ISSN 0922-6028

Adamovich, S.; Fluet, G.; Merians, A.; Mathai, A. & Qiu, Q. (2009). Incorporating haptic effects into three-dimensional virtual environments to train the hemiparetic upper extremity. *IEEE Transactions on Neural Systems and Rehabilitation Engineering*, Vol.17, No.5, pp. 512-20, ISSN 1534-4320

Adamson, J.; Beswick, A. & Ebrahim, S. (2004). Is stroke the most common cause of disability? *Journal of Stroke and Cerebrovascular Diseases*, Vol.13, No.4, pp. 171-177, ISSN 1052-3057

Anon. (2007). *Post-Stroke Rehabilitation Fact Sheet.* National Institute Of Neurological Disorders And Stroke. Available from http://www.ninds.nih.gov/disorders/stroke/poststrokerehab.htm

Anon. (2009). *Recovery After Stroke: Thinking and Cognition.* National Stroke Association. available from http://www.stroke.org/site/DocServer/NSAFactSheet_Cognition.pdf?docID=986

Bassett, S. (2003). The assessment of patient adherence to physiotherapy rehabilitation. *New Zealand Journal of Physiotherapy*, Vol.31, No.2, pp. 60-66, ISSN 0303-7193

Beaton, D.; Davis, A., Hudak, P. & McConnell S. (2001). The DASH (Disabilities of the Arm, Shoulder and Hand) outcome measure: what do we know about it now? *British Journal of Hand Therapy*, Vol.6, No.4, pp. 109-117, ISSN 1758-9983

Broeren, J.; Claesson, L.; Goude, D.; Rydmark, M. & Sunnerhagen, K. (2008). Virtual rehabilitation in an activity centre for community-dwelling persons with stroke: The possibilities of 3-dimensional computer games. *Cerebrovascular Diseases*, Vol.26, No.3, pp. 289-296, ISSN: 1015-9770

Buccino G.; Vogt, S.; Ritzl, A.; Fink, G.; Zilles, K.; Freund H. & Rizzolatti G. (2004). Neural Circuits Underlying Imitation Learning of Hand Actions: An Event-Related fMRI Study. *Neuron*, Vol.42, pp 323–334, ISSN1748-2968

Bütefisch, C.; Hummelsheim, H.; Denzler, P.; & Mauritz, K. (1995). Repetitive training of isolated movements improves the outcome of motor rehabilitation of the centrally paretic hand. *Journal of the Neurological Sciences*, Vol.130, No.1, pp. 59-68, ISSN 0022-510X

Carter, K.; Anderson, C.; Hacket, M.; Feigin, V.; Barber, P.; Broad, J. & Bonita, R. (2006). Trends in ethnic disparities in stroke incidence in Auckland, New Zealand, during 1981 to 2003. *Stroke*, Vol.37, No.1, pp. 56-62, ISSN 00392499

Cauraugh, J. & Summers J. (2005). Neural Plasticity and bilateral movements: A rehabilitation approach for chronic stroke. *Progress in Neurobiology*, Vol.75, pp. 309-320, ISSN: 0301-0082

Celnik, P.; Webster, B.; Glasser, D. & Cohen, L. (2008). Effects of action observation on physical training after stroke. *Stroke*, Vol.39, No.6, pp. 1814-1820, ISSN 00392499

Eng, K.; Siekierka, E.; Pyk, P.; Chevrier, E.; Hauser, Y.; Cameirao, M.; Holper, L.; Hägni, K.; Zimmerli, L.; Duff, A.; Schuster, C.; Bassetti, C.; Verschure, P. & Kiper, D. (2007). Interactive visuo-motor therapy system for stroke rehabilitation. *Medical & Biological Engineering & Computing*, Vol.45, No.9, (September), pp. 901-7, ISSN: 0140-0118

Ertelt, D.; Small, S.; Solodkin, A.; Dettmers, C.; McNamara, A.; Binkofski, F. & Buccino, G. (2007). Action observation has a positive impact on rehabilitation of motor deficits after stroke. *NeuroImage*, Vol.36, No.2, pp. 164-73, ISSN: 1053-8119

Fasoli, S.; Krebs, H.; Stein, J.; Frontera, W. & Hogan, N. (2003). Effects of robotic therapy on motor impairment and recovery in chronic stroke. *Archives of Physical Medicine and Rehabilitation*, Vol.84, No.4, pp. 477-482, ISSN 0003-9993

Feys, H.; De Weerdt, W.; Selz, B.; Cox Steck, G.; Spichiger, R.; Vereeck, L.; Putman, K. et al. (1998). Effect of a therapeutic intervention for the hemiplegic upper limb in the acute phase after stroke: A single-blind, randomized, controlled multicenter trial. *Stroke*, Vol.29, No.4, pp. 785-792, ISSN 00392499

French, B.; Thomas, L.; Leathley, M.; Sutton, C.; McAdam, J.; Forster, A.; Langhorne, P. et al. (2009). Repetitive task training for improving functional ability after stroke. *Stroke*, Vol.40, No.4, pp. 98-99, ISSN 00392499

Fugl-Meyer, A.; Jääskö, L.; Leyman, I.; Olsson, S. & Steglind, S. (1975). The post-stroke patient: 1. A method for evaluation of physical performance. *Scandinavian Journal of Rehabilitation Medicine*, Vol.7, pp. 13-31, ISSN 0036-5505

Gallese, V.; Fadiga, L.; Fogassi, L. & Rizzolatti, G. (1996). Action recognition in the premotor cortex. *Brain*, Vol.119, pp. 593-609, ISSN 0006-8950

Hamzei, F., Liepert, J., Dettmers, C., Weiller, C., & Rijntjes, M. (2006). Two different reorganization patterns after rehabilitative therapy: An exploratory study with fMRI and TMS. *NeuroImage*, Vol.31, No.2, pp. 710-720, ISSN: 1053-8119

Hijmans, J.; Hale, L.; Satherley, J.; McMillan, N. & King, M. (2011). Bilateral upper limb rehabilitation after stroke using a movement based game controller. Accepted for publication in Journal of Rehabilitation Research and Development

Feys, H.; De Weerdt, W.; Selz, B.; Cox Steck, G.; Spichiger, R.; Vereeck, L.; Putman, K. & Van Hoydonck, G. (1998). Effect of a Therapeutic Intervention for the Hemiplegic Upper Limb in the Acute Phase After Stroke. *Stroke*, Vol.29, pp. 785-792, ISSN 00392499

Holden, M. (2005). Virtual environments for motor rehabilitation: review. *Cyberpsychology & Behavior: The Impact of the Internet, Multimedia and Virtual Reality on Behavior and Society*, Vol.8, No.3, pp. 187-211; discussion pp. 212-219, ISSN: 1094-9313

Housman, S.; Scott, K. & Reinkensmeyer, D. (2009). A randomized controlled trial of gravity-supported, computer-enhanced arm exercise for individuals with severe hemiparesis. *Neurorehabilitation and Neural Repair*, Vol.23, No.5, pp. 505-514, ISSN 1545-9683

IJsselsteijn, W.; Nap, H.; de Kort, Y.; & Poels, K. (2007). Digital Game Design for Elderly Users, In *Proceedings of Futureplay 2007.* (Toronto, Canada, 14-18 November 2007), pp. 17-22, ISBN 978-1-59593-943-2

Johnson, M.; Feng, X.; Johnson, L. & Winters, J. (2007). Potential of a suite of robot/computer-assisted motivating systems for personalized, home-based, stroke rehabilitation. *Journal of NeuroEngineering and Rehabilitation,* Vol.4, pp. 6, ISSN: 17430003

King, M.; Hale, L.; Pekkari, A.; Persson, M.; Gregorsson, M. & Nilsson, M. (2010). An affordable, computerized, table-based exercise system for stroke survivors. *Disability and Rehabilitation Assistive Technology*, Vol.5, No.4, (July), pp. 288-93, ISSN: 1748-3107

Krebs, H. I., Volpe, B. T., Ferraro, M., Fasoli, S., Palazzolo, J., Rohrer, B., Edelstein, L., et al. (2002). Robot-aided neuro-rehabilitation: From evidence-based to science-based rehabilitation. *Topics in Stroke Rehabilitation*, Vol.8, No.4, pp. 54-70, ISSN: 1074-9357

Krebs, H.; Mernoff, S.; Fasoli, S.; Hughes, R.; Stein, J. & Hogan, N. (2008). A comparison of functional and impairment-based robotic training in severe to moderate chronic stroke: a pilot study. *NeuroRehabilitation,* Vol.23, No.1, pp. 81–87, ISSN 1053-8135

Kwakkel, G.; Wagenaar, R.; Twisk, J.; Lankhorst, G. & Koetsier, J. (1999). Intensity of leg and arm training after primary middle-cerebral-artery stroke: A randomised trial. *Lancet,* Vol.354, No.9174, pp. 191-196, ISSN: 0140-6736

Kwakkel, G.; Kollen, B.; Van der Grond, J. & Prevo, A. (2003). Probability of regaining dexterity in the flaccid upper limb: Impact of severity of paresis and time since onset in acute stroke. *Stroke, 34*(9), 2181-2186, ISSN 00392499

Kwakkel, G.; Kollen, B. & Krebs, H. (2008). Effects of Robot-assisted therapy on upper limb recovery after stroke: A Systematic Review. *Neurorehabilitation and neural repair,* Vol.22, No.2, pp. 111-121, ISSN: 1545-9683

Lang, C.; MacDonald, J.; Reisman, D.; Boyd, L.; Kimberley, T.; Schindler-Ivens, S.; Hornby, G.; Ross, S. & Scheets, P. (2009). Observation of amounts of movement practice provided during stroke rehabilitation. *Archives of Physical Medicine and Rehabilitation,* Vol.90, No.10, (October), pp. 1692–1698, ISSN 0003-9993

Levin, M. (2011). Can virtual reality offer enriched environments for rehabilitation? *Expert Review of Neurotherapeutics,* Vol.11, No.2, (February), pp.153-5, ISSN: 1473-7175

Merians, A.; Jack, D.; Boian, R.; Tremaine, M.; Burdea, G.; Adamovich, S.; Recce, M. et al. (2002). Virtual reality-augmented rehabilitation for patients following stroke. *Physical Therapy,* Vol.82, No.9, pp. 898-915, ISSN 0031-9023

McAuley, E.; Duncan, T. & Tammen, V. (1987). Psychometric properties of the Intrinsic Motivation Inventory in a competitive sport setting: A confirmatory analysis. *Research Quarterly for Exercise & Sport,* Vol.60, pp. 48-58, ISSN 0270-1367

McCombe-Waller, S. & Whitall, J. (2008). Bilateral arm training: Why and who benefits? *NeuroRehabilitation,* Vol.23, pp. 29-41, ISSN 1053-8135

Parkinson, M. (ed.) (2000). *Aids to examination of the peripheral nervous system.* 4th ed. W. B. Saunders, ISBN0-7020-2512-7, Edinburgh, United Kingdom

Peattie, A.; Korevaar, A.; Wilson, J.; Sandilands, B.; Chen, X. & King, M. (2009). Automated Variable Resistance System for Upper Limb Rehabilitation, *Proceedings of Australasian Conference on Robotics and Automation 2009,* ISBN 978-0-9807404-0-0 Sydney, Australia, December 2-4, 2009

Prange, G.; Jannink, M.; Groothuis-Oudshoorn, C.; Hermens, H. & Ijzerman, M. (2006). Systematic review of the effect of robot-aided therapy on recovery of the hemiparetic arm after stroke. *Journal of Rehabilitation Research and Development,* Vol.43, No.2, pp. 171-183, ISSN 0748-7711

Pridmore, T.; Hilton, D.; Green, J.; Eastgate, R. & Cobb, S. (2004). Mixed reality environments in stroke rehabilitation: interfaces across the real/virtual divide. *Proceedings of International Conference on Virtual Reality, Disability and Associated Technologies.* ISBN-10: 0704911426 Oxford, United Kingdom, September 20-22, 2004

Pyk, P.; Wille, D.; Chevrier, E.; Hauser, Y.; Holper, L.; Fatton, I.; Greipl, R.; Schlegel, S.; Ottiger, L.; Rückreim, B.; Pescatore, A.; Meyer-Heim, A.; Kiper, D. & Eng, K. (2008). A Paediatric Interactive Therapy System for Arm and Hand Rehabilitation. *Virtual Rehabilitation 2008,* pp. 127-132, ISBN 978-1-4244-2700-0 Vancouver, Canada August 25-27, 2008.

Ramachandran, V.; Rogers-Ramachandran, D. & Cobb, S. (1995). Touching the phantom., *Nature,* Vol.377, pp. 489–490, ISSN 0028-0836

Ramachandran, V. & Altschuler, E. (2009). The use of visual feedback, in particular mirror visual feedback, in restoring brain function. *Brain,* Vol.132, No.7, pp. 1693-1710, ISSN 0006-8950

Rand,D.; Kizony, R.; Feintuch, U.; Katz, N.; Josman, N.; Rizzo, A. & Weiss, P. (2005). Comparison of Two VR Platforms for Rehabilitation: Video Capture versus HMD. *Presence Teleoperators and Virtual Environments,* Vol.14, No.2, pp. 147-160, ISSN 1054-7460

Renner, M. & Rosenzweig, M. (1987). *Enriched and Impoverished Environments.Effects on Brain and Behavior.* Springer-Verlag, New York, ISBN 978-3540965237

Rizzolatti, G. & Craighero, L. (2004). The mirror-neuron system. *Annual Review of Neuroscience,* Vol.27, pp. 169–192, ISSN 0147-006X

Rose, F.; Attree, E.; Brooks, B. & Johnson, D. (1998). Virtual Environments In Brain Damage Rehabilitation: A Rationale From Basic Neuroscience, In *Virtual Environments in Clinical Psychology and Neuroscience.* Riva, G.; Wiederhold, B. & Molinari, E. (Eds.) Ios Press: Amsterdam, Netherlands, ISBN-10 905199429X

Rose, F.; Brooks, B. & Rizzo, A. (2005). Virtual Reality in Brain Damage Rehabilitation: Review. *CyberPsychology & Behavior,* Vol.8, No.3, pp. 241-262, ISSN 1094-9313

Sampson, M.; Shau, Y. & King, M. (2011). Bilateral Upper Limb Trainer with Virtual Reality for poststroke rehabilitation: case series report. *Disability and Rehabilitation: Assistive Technology.* (doi:10.3109/17483107.2011.562959), ISSN 1748-3107

Sathian, K. Greenspan, A. & Wolf, S. (2000). Doing it with mirrors: a case study of a novel approach to neurorehabilitation. *Neurorehabilitation and Neural Repair,* Vol.14, pp. 73-76, ISSN 1545-9683

Schimmelpfennig, L. (2000) Ohne Kopf geht`s nicht. Geistig Fit. Vol.2, pp. 6-9, ISBN 3211836756

Schultheis, M. & Rizzo, A. (2001). The application of virtual reality technology in rehabilitation. *Rehabilitation Psychology,* Vol.46, No.3, pp. 296–311, ISSN 0090-5550

Sims, N. & Muyderman, H. (2009). Mitochondria, oxidative metabolism and cell death in stroke. *Biochimica et Biophysica Acta,* Vol.1802, No.1, pp. 80–91, ISSN 0006-3002

Stefan, K.; Cohen, L.; Duque, J.; Mazzocchio, R.; Celnik, P.; Sawaki, L.; Ungerleider, L. & Classen, J. (2005). Formation of a motor memory by action observation. *Journal of Neuroscience,* Vol.25, pp. 9339–9346, ISSN 0270-6474

Stein, D.; Brailowski, S. & Will, B. (1995). *Brain Repair,* Oxford University Press, ISBN 0195076427, New York

Stein, J.; Harvey, R.; Macko, R.; Winstein, C. & Zorowitz, R. (2009). *Stroke recovery and rehabilitation,* Demos Medical Publishing. ISBN 978-1933864129, New York

Sterr, A.; Freivogel, S. & Schmalohr, D. (2002). Neurobehavioral aspects of recovery: Assessment of the learned nonuse phenomenon in hemiparetic adolescents. *Archives of Physical Medicine and Rehabilitation,* Vol.83, No.12, pp. 1726-1731, ISSN 0003-9993

Stinear, C.; Barber, P.; Smale, P.; Coxon, J.; Fleming, M. & Byblow, W. (2007). Functional potential in chronic stroke patients depends on corticospinal tract integrity. *Brain,* Vol.130, pp. 170–180, ISSN 0006-8950

Sütbeyaz, S.; Yavuzer, G.; Sezer, N. & Koseoglu B. (2007). Mirror Therapy Enhances Lower-Extremity Motor Recovery and Motor Functioning After Stroke: A Randomized Controlled Trial. *Archives of Physical Medicine and Rehabilitation,* Vol.88, pp. 555-559, ISSN 0003-9993

Sveistrup, H. (2004). Motor rehabilitation using virtual reality. *Journal of NeuroEngineering and Rehabilitation,* Vol.1, pp. 10, ISSN 17430003

Tinson, D. (1989). How stroke patients spend their days: An observational study of the treatment regime offered to patients with movement disorders in hospitals following stroke. *International Disability Studies,* Vol.11, pp. 45-49, ISSN:0259-9147

van der Lee, J.; Snels, I; Beckerman, H.; Lankhorst, G.; Wagenaar, R. & Bouter, L. (2001). Exercise therapy for arm function in stroke patients: A systematic review of randomized controlled trials. *Clinical Rehabilitation,* Vol.15, No.1, pp. 20-31, ISSN 0269-2155

Van Peppen, R.; Kwakkel, G.; Wood-Dauphinee, S.; Hendriks, H.; Van der Wees, P. & Dekker, J. (2004). The impact of physical therapy on functional outcomes after stroke: What's the evidence? *Clinical Rehabilitation,* Vol.18, No.8, pp. 833-862, ISSN 0269-2155

Werner, R. & Kessler, S. (1996). Effectiveness of an intensive outpatient rehabilitation program for postacute stroke patients. *American Journal of Physical Medicine and Rehabilitation,* Vol.75, No.2, pp. 114-120, ISSN 08949115

Wolf, S. & Catlin, P. (2001). Assessing Wolf Motor function Test as outcome measure for research in patients after stroke. *Stroke,* Vol.32, pp. 1635-1639, ISSN 00392499

Wyller, T.; Sveen, U.; Sedring, K.; Pettersen, A. & Bautz-Holter, E. (1997). Subjective well-being one year after stroke. *Clinical Rehabilitation,* Vol.11, No.2, pp. 139-145, ISSN 0269-2155

Yavuzer, G.; Selles, R.; Sezer, N.; Sutbeyaz, S.; Bussmann, J.; Koseoglu, F.; Atay, M. et al. (2008). Mirror therapy improves hand function in subacute stroke: a randomized controlled trial. *Archives of Physical Medicine and Rehabilitation,* Vol.89, No.3, pp. 393–398, ISSN 0003-9993

9

Post-Biological Agency in Real-Time Mixed Reality Data Transfer

Julian Stadon
Curtin University of Technology, Australia

1. Introduction

This research offers a contribution, through art theory and practice, to an emerging culturally orientated discourse regarding mixed reality interaction. It seeks to deconstruct and analyse syncretic, hybridized agency, particularly in mixed reality data transfer systems. Recent developments in bridging autonomous relationships with digital representation, through mixed reality interfacing, have brought about the need for further analysis of these new 'post-biological', hybridized states of being that traverse traditional paradigms of time and space. Roy Ascott's reconceptualisation of syncretic dialogues may facilitate further understanding of multi-layered world views, both material and metaphysical, that are emerging from our engagement with such pervasive computational technologies and post-biological systems. Syncretism has traditionally been regarded as an attempt to harmonise and analogise disparate or opposing veiwpoints (Ascott, 2010). Citing recent examples of research, this will discuss what Deleuze and Guattari have called the 'deterritorialisation' of the human body through its dispersion into multiple reality manifestations, in relation to how mixed reality data transfer might constitute a 'reterritorialising' effect on our syncretic understanding of post-biological digital identity (Delueze and Guatarri, 1980).

The research analyses systems that allow for the bridging of the body with its virtual incarnations, through unique transfers of biological and physical data, such as 3D bio-imaging, biofeedback data, motion tracking and bio/nano microscopy. These processes involve interfacing that allows for biological and physical data to be transferred into a (digitally mediated) mixed reality state. Giannachi calls this 'hypersurfacing' (Giannachi, 2008) and recent technologies provide further opportunity for hypersurfaced systems to be substantially developed. It is a popular belief that we are now, through a media convergent, participatory culture (that is integrated socially through a sub network of platforms) creating what was first coined in 1997 as *collective intelligence* by Pierre Lévy (Levy, 1997), which exists in a global society of knowledge (data) transfer. This perspective evades traditional (mythologically based) notions of anthropomorphic interaction as it moves beyond the individual and into a universal model of (hypersurfaced) open access. Networked agency destabilises traditional orthodoxies of thought through challenging notions of representation, confronting materialism, accelerating and smoothing social engagement and most importantly, demanding participation in these open systems of collaborative engagement. This has redefined our understandings of consciousness and presence in way that requires rethinking everything from spirituality, time and space, esotericism, agency, emergence, quantum coherence through to eroticism (Ascott, 2010). This fusion of real and representation, linking cyber and real worlds constitutes mixed reality interaction as experienced by humans in the physical world, their avatars, agents, and virtual humans.

Remote Procedure Call Interfaces (RPCI) and real-time data transfer enhance the experience of the hypersurface for the audience beyond any previous virtual media types, such as, hypertext, HTML, VRML, virtual reality, etc. Unlike traditional sites for communication and cultural exchange, virtual platforms rely on actions and conversations to shape not only the social and cultural environments, but also the spatial environment. XML RPC interfaces further this to (re)include the physical environment, from the perspective of the viewer. The following research scopes unique autonomous relationships between authors and agents, through augmenting biological and virtual (natural and technical) information into mixed reality states that allow for their mediation through networked systems interfacing. Such systems allow participants to physically interact with virtual biological components through real-time data transfer and mediate through physical engagement, rather than entering traditional text or numerical based data sets and command sequences.

Previously, the majority of research in mixed reality focused on specific technical aspects of the field encompassing computer science, cognitive science, robotics, etc. with arts, media and humanities only recently contributing to a mixed reality knowledge base. Along with several examples from computer science, I will primarily discuss three recent projects: *Organtrader2010, Promethean Alchemist* and *Terra(socio)sonica:Pouvoir/Poussanse* which use innovative mixed reality data transfer methods, in a culturally positioned way in order to demonstrate the 'deterritorialisation' (Deleuze and Guatarri, 1980) of the human body and its' 'reterritorialising' effect on postbiological digital identity construction. The examples chosen deconstructs the notion of 'post-biological' digital identity through creating innovative actualisation examples. Through increasing the level of physical and social involvement that viewers have in the creation of a mixed reality system of exchange, the works included demonstrate a new model of representation and experience that stretches, disperses and merges the position of both artwork and viewer in order to question post-biological identity and the body

2. Background

Current research in mixed reality and interactive workspaces that use the concept of a bridge for visual data transfer have continued the development of new knowledge in this emerging field, however the majority of previous research in this area has been in the field of computer science. The rigorous application of cultural and philosophical discourse to recent developments in screen based technologies and software applications will suggest new modes of representation, that are concerned with the affective capacities of art in a way that articulates a sense of dispersed embodiment.

Unlike traditional sites for communication and cultural exchange, digital platforms rely on actions and conversations to shape not only the social and cultural environments, but also the spatial environments. Such systems allow participants to physically interact with virtual (deterritorialised) biological representations and mediate (reterritorialise) through physical engagement (rather than entering traditional text or numerical based data sets and command sequences). A good example for mixed reality would be would be the Layar application for smartphones. This application, available for free download to any smartphone user, provides an advanced augmented reality platform capable of reliably delivering many different AR experience, though largely focusing on using geolocation to augment the user's physical surroundings. For example, Manifest.AR, an international artist's collective working with emergent forms of augmented reality as public art, use the technology to transform public space for users. They install virtual objects and artworks that respond to and overlay the configuration of located physical meaning. The application uses geolocation software to superimpose computer generated three-dimensional art objects, enabling the public to see the work integrated into the physical location as if it existed in the real world (Manifest.AR, 2011). Thus, the Layar application reterritorialises information primarily through geolocating individuals, in order to provide a richer engagement with their physical surrounds through the layering of virtual content over real time video.

Massively Multi User Online Worlds (MMOs) are another example of an open virtual environment that allows for the contribution to and manipulation of private and publicly owned virtual space through a variety of methods. The content of these environments is dependent on the participants, due to this open interaction, and therefore relies on the quality of information transfer methods being used. Through collaborative creative production MMOs facilitate social engagement and further collaborative production by its participants. Spatial developments define the environments and the (real or virtual) individuals inhabiting such spaces through their participation in and response to them. The collective construction of such virtual meeting sites, for remote interpersonal interaction acts as an instrument of location and orientation, referential to the real world of knowledge. Implementing biological and physical data into MMOs through augmented reality, contributes new knowledge in regards to bridged mixed reality states, under a paradigm of post-biological deterritorialisation and reterritorialisation of the body. Deleuze and Guatarri discuss deterritorialisation in terms of dispersed resemblance and identity. In *Difference and Repetition* Deleuze introduces the notion of deterritorialisation (through dispersion) as a "dark precursor" that "relates heterogeneous systems and even completely disparate things (Deleuze, 1993)." In order for deterritorialisation to occur there must be some form of agent that can remain constant and self-referent. Deleuze and Guatarri state that: "The alignment of the code or linearity of the nucleic sequence in fact marks a threshold of deterritorialisation of the "sign" that gives it a new ability to be copied and makes the organism more deterritorialised than a crystal: only something deterritorialised is capable of reproducing itself (Deleuze and Guatarri, 1980)."

Virtual reality's hybridization with physical and biological architecture is constructed by the methods used to connect the environments. The combination and cohesion of heterogeneous elements is generally problematic, particularly when a three dimensional space is primarily viewed on a two dimensional plane. The integration of virtual elements and physical environments relies on bridging the two spaces with dynamic interfaces that are simultaneously accessible and able to be openly engaged with, edited and developed. To create integration systems that network physical and virtual data 'shared locations' are required in order to represent the data in a meaningful way that is inclusive of both environments.

For the construction and exploration of mixed reality to occur interfacing is required to bridge the virtual environment with the physical so that both spaces can be mediated in an autonomous manner. The hypersurface is the site on which bridges are built: where the real and virtual, material and textual, author and agent can meet and interact with each other. Performance technology theorist Gabriella Giannachi states that, "The hypersurface is a zone of exchange between consciousness (language and text) and levels of the inorganic… Able to present dichotomous relationships, between representation and matter, inside and outside, organic and inorganic, the hypersurface is the site of virtual performance (Giannachi)." For the construction and exploration of mixed reality to occur interfacing is required to bridge the virtual environment with the physical so that both spaces can be mediated in an autonomous manner. The hypersurface is the site on which bridges are built: where the real and virtual, material and textual, author and agent can meet and interact with each other.

2.1 Examples from computer science

The earliest example of a research project that proposed a hypersurfaced system for data transfer using mixed reality was in 1999. Butz et al. proposed a drag and drop technique between an augmented reality space to a screen space within the EMMIE system. Using a mirror metaphor, virtual objects would change representation and dimensionality by passing through screen boundaries, with the approach focused on transferring documents.

Recently Lang et al. (Lang et al., 2008) from Georgia Tech University modified Second Life to create mixed reality experiences the purpose being the creation of a novel augmented reality environment for entertainment. This example bridged reality states in a way that facilitated a further inquiry into the socio-cultural implications of such systems, but was never addressed in the research publications.

The VTT Technical Research Center Finland has also recently worked with hypersurfacing Second Life avatars within physical experience through the *Meeting Avatars* joint project with IBM and Nokia (Kantonen et al., 2010). By using the Second Life engine, virtual avatars had the same appearance and behavior as in the virtual world but in their context be represented in a physical meeting room

Barakonyi and Schmalstieg (2008) created two pilot systems in order to facilitate proactive multi-user interface adaptation and user interface migration. The system was developed in order to migrate tasks across a range of autonomous agents and a number of users, rather than a single avatar being used by each individual. The goal was to increase the versatility of ubiquitous agency through mixed reality data bridging (hypersurfacing). By increasing the number of agents (in various reality states) that can autonomously perform tasks set by users, the bridge defines a dedicated space where the viewer can transfer objects and images between worlds, spaces, and contexts

Koleva et al (2006) explored navigation between real, augmented and virtual worlds by establishing "mixed reality boundaries" and proposed a model of how space, boundaries can be represented. Schnädelbach et al (2006) further generalized the concept to any architectural construct, how collaboration and communication can be established in this type of environment. Finally, Grasset et al proposed a general conceptual model on how to represent spaces, navigation and the different steps of a transition between contexts (Grasset et al. 2005) (Grassett et al 2006).

These research examples articulate a range of different solutions that have been proposed for technological developments in the field of computer science, and often neglect the philosophical and theoretical impact of such technologies on human subjectivity, representation, identity and social discourse. The collaboration between computer science and art establishes a transdisciplinary practice, that is capable of traversing disparate fields, such as: biology, cybernetics, philosophy, spirituality, nanotechnology, distributed cognition, robotics, game theory, virtual environments and aesthetics. This produces a syncretic dialogue orientated towards existence and consciousness that is (potentially) more thorough and rigorous than any previous methodology relating to our engagement with digital systems. Emerging technologies often develop faster than we have the ability to understand them. When these technologies, particularly imaging systems across science and lived experience become creative mediums, they redefine the ways by which we define humanity.

3. Examples from artistic practice

Art and science have, of course shared a long history of collaboration, particularly in the medical, biological and astrological sciences. Historically, scientific findings have been represented to society through artistic representation, for example anatomy of the body, drawings of the galaxy (via telescopes), or that which was accessed (beyond natural vision) through the microscope. It is important to note here that representation has historically been further facilitated by technology that enables us to see beyond the limitations of the body. Whether due to the technicization of scientific imaging or academia's need to quantify/qualify research under set paradigms, the significant (collaborative) involvement of artists in scientific inquiry became quite a rare occurrence for some years. In recent times we have seen artists become much more flexible and adventurous with the mediums they use and this has seen a return to sciencific methods and technologies. Unlike previously where the artists' role primarily was to document proceedings, today artists are much more likely to collaborate with a scientist/team in order to produce outcomes that traverse the respective fields in order to question the cultural impact such technologies and scientific fields have on society.

An example of a researcher that creates shared mixed reality systems of exchange under a cultural predisposition is telematic artist Paul Sermon. Sermon's early work explored the emergence of user-determined narrative by bringing remote participants together in a shared telepresent environment. Through the use of live chromakey and video conferencing technology, two public rooms or installations and their audiences are joined in a virtual duplicate that turns into a mutual space of activity. Currently Sermon's practice examines the concepts of presence and performance within Second Life and what he calls 'first life', and attempts to bridge these two spaces through mixed reality techniques and interfaces (Sermon and Gould, 2009). The notion of telepresence is explored through a blurring between 'online' and 'offline' identities, and the signifiers and conditions that make us feel present in this world. His research questions how subjectivity is articulated in relation to embodiment and disembodiment. Sermon creates hypersurfaces through which data can oscillate between two reality states in an autonomous way: present and telepresent. The development of such a method of data exchange creates an interesting situation where both the user and an autonomous agent (their avatar) can now affect visual data in a mixed reality environment. The important aspect to this exchange is that Sermon does not privilege either the online agent or the physical beings that participate, thus alluding to a post-biological system of engagement where traditional hierarchies between the body and virtual agents are redefined.

3.1 Terra(socio)sonica: Pouvoir/Puissance

Terra(socio)sonica: Pouvoir/Puissance, by Julian Stadon (in collaboration with Steven Berrick) realises a sonic soundscape constructed via the movements of communities that inhabit two current landscape realities that constitute the University of Western Australia (UWA) cultural precinct. Through the translation of movement into sound in both the physical and virtual realms, the work explores the notion of unspoken 'silent dialogues' under a paradigm of social engagement. Individuals and large clusters of people produce amplified sounds and shadows based on their oscillating movements within a defined social landscape.

The work uses real-time motion-tracking technologies with a unique pipeline application to create a mixed-reality soundscape. This audio environment is mediated through interactions between the viewer, the physical environment, and other participants within a hypersurfaced mixed-reality feedback loop. As visitors negotiate a traditional public environment -the entrance and surround to the Somerville Auditorium at UWA- data regarding their movements and interaction with others present is gathered and translated into sonic outputs, both in the physical and virtual environments. In the physical, the output is via stereo speakers installed in the space and in the virtual, a three dimensional representation shadows and echoes sonic and visual traces of the real-time dialogues into UWA's Second Life Environment. In this case the physical augments into the virtual and the virtual into the physical in an ongoing representational archive of what has occurred in that shared space.

Fig. 1. Second Life view of virtual 'shadows' from physical data.

The individual experiences an intimate interaction with the work and social environment where they control the soundscape through their actions, thereby conducting their own personal song. Meanwhile, each community that forms also produces unique tones. Movements of individuals between groups result in a sonic symphony of social interaction that shifts dynamically according to the social dialogues that occur in the space. The audience movement in the space produces stepped tonal outputs, for example a stroll to the right will cause the pitch to drop with each step. The pace of the movement determines the speed of the notes; lingering conversations produce long lingering sounds while the rush of busy passersby results in fleeting melodies that come and go just as quickly.

The work is inspired by previously discussed Deleuzian notions of deterritorialisation, with particular regards to second-order cybernetic feedback systems (within the context of mixed reality social interaction). Deleuze and Guatarri discuss deterritorialisation in terms of dispersed resemblance and identity. In order for deterritorialisation to occur there must be some form of agent that can remain constant and self-referent and in this case it is the audience that acts as agent and the self referent being the various resulting feedback (mixed reality image and sound). This feedback affects physical participation with the installation and therefore facilitates a second-order cybernetic feedback loop.

In practice, the work models global deterritorialisation by destabilising established social groups through intuitive interaction with virtual space, reconfiguring them in the soundscape. The work also investigates the relationship between traditional (postcolonial) socio-technic hierarchies, and those developing in current evolving cyber cities

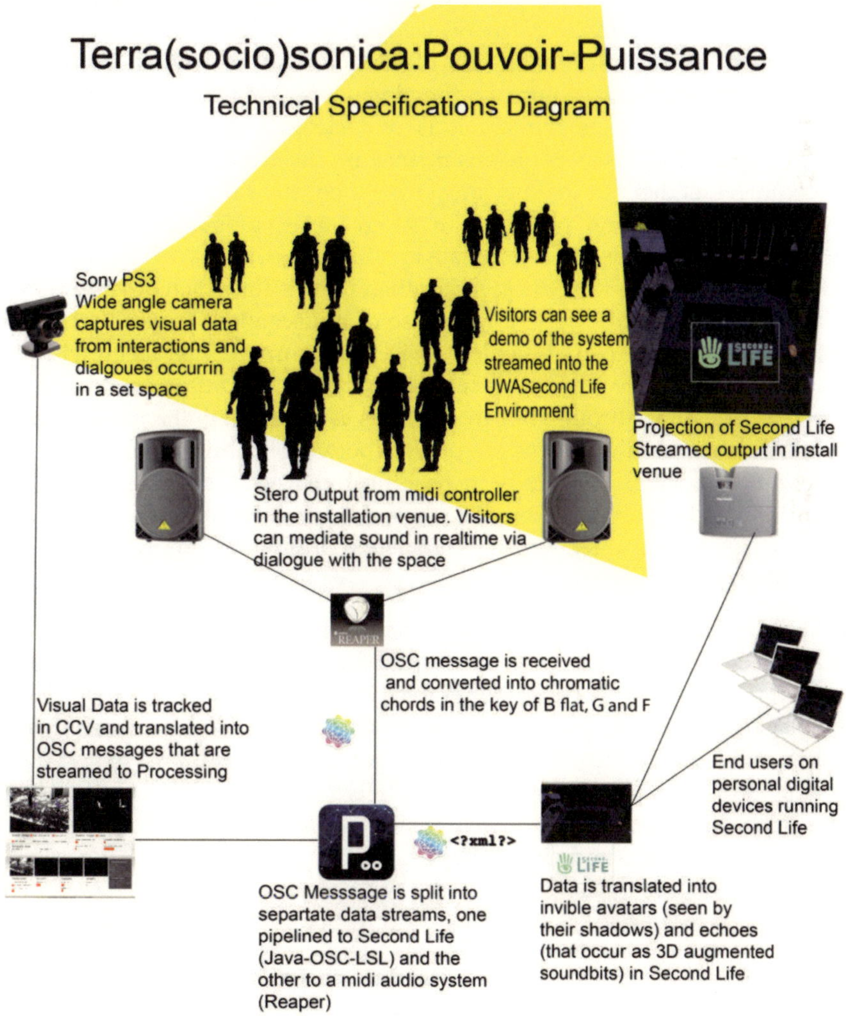

Fig. 2. Technical specifications diagram.

Conceptually, the work attempts to explore Bernard Steigler's historicisation of technical objects and western philosophy in a way that embraces Deleuze's translation of Bergsonism, particularly regarding intuitive method. For Deleuze, intuitive thought is more like a narrative than an instantaneous 'eureka' moment. In order to understand Deleuzian intuition it is important to situate it within the Bergsonian departure from a structuralist notion of reality in terms of space, in favour of the metaphysical idea that reality should be understood in terms of time. In contrast to Descartes' 'instantaneous glance' or moment of clarity-distinctness that separates the intuitive idea, Deleuzian intuition is rather a "progressive description of the whole," more like a multi-lateral trajectory than a moment of illumination. For Deleuze, intuition "reconcatenates thought to beings as the co-presence of a being of the simulacrum and of a simulacrum of Being" (Deleuze, 1991).

Deleuze's concept of intuitive thought is in line with Bernard Steigler's notion of technics defining what it is to be human. As mentioned earlier, Steigler has posited the important contribution to metaphysical thinking that it is technics -the artificial realm of symbols, systems, tools, etc.- that makes humans functional, speaking, meaning-making creatures; that is, what makes humans human. It is in Deleuze's distinction between different degrees of 'power' that I see Bergsonism, that is, the intuitive method, and Steigler's technics coming together. In looking at 'power' one must distinguish between the two French words puissance and pouvoir. "In social terms, puissance is immanent power, power to act rather than power to dominate another; we could say that puissance is praxis (in which equals clash or act together) rather than poiesis (in which others are matter to be formed by the command of a superior, a sense of transcendent power that matches what pouvoir indicates for Deleuze)." (Stiegler, 1998). Our intuitive interaction with technology is, as demonstrated by the hypersurface, the enactment of puissance, that is, immanent power to create meaning through our interactions as opposed to the passing-down of pre-established ideas through transcendent power (pouvoir). Intuitive interaction challenges the academy model, which essentially treats education as transcendent power, the passing on of information by solving problems that already have answers. Instead, intuitive interaction creates opportunity for true knowledge production; an instance of power that puissance indicates for Deleuze.

It is through observing human intuitive interaction with technologies that one might theorize a plausible post-human or postbiological digital identity. As summarized by Daniel Smith and John Protevi, "Here we see the empiricist theme of the 'externality of relations': in an assemblage or consistency, the 'becoming' or relation of the terms attains its own independent ontological status. In Deleuze's favourite example, the wasp and orchid create a "becoming" or symbiotic emergent unit." In *Terra(socio)sonica:Pouvior/Puissance,* human interaction with the hypersurfaced mixed-reality feedback loop becomes an emergent unit in the soundscape, physical and virtual worlds.

3.2 Organtrader2010

organtrader2010 is a novel mixed reality interface that allows for the transfer of real CT scanned organs into augmented reality and Second Life. Using the metaphor of organ trade to allude to traditional gallery hierarchies, organtrader2010 allows the participant to donate, sell, buy or steal virtual organs across platforms including an interactive mixed reality system, standard Second Life interfaces and mobile platforms. **organtrader2010** uses the organ trade metaphor to question the meaning of ownership and the relationship between content and property. In regards to (unregulated) machines of production and the subversion of power hierarchies, organtrader2010 examines the roles of media artist/supplier, gallery/distributor and participant/trader. In doing so, this project also explores deterritorialisation of the body and post-biological identity in mixed realities.

organtrader2010 uses a narrative representational structure in a mixed reality context where a participant, wearing a camera mounted HMD (head mounted display) can transfer real CT scanned organs to an augmented organ 'trader.' This augmented Second Life avatar can exist in both physical and virtual space simultaneously, so when the participant hands over one of their organs to the 'augmented trader' they are also giving their organs unsuspectingly to the 'in-world avatar.' This avatar is linked to a network of organ trader avatars that all have ownership permissions to clone and steal organs from the augmented trader and sell them to other Second Life avatars.

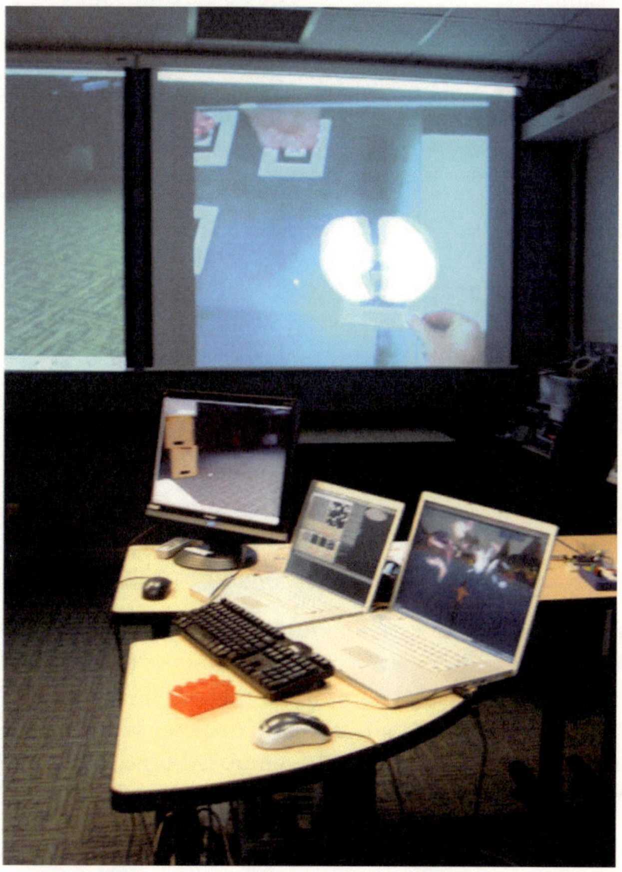

Fig. 3. Installation setup at Banff New Media Institute (2010).

As mentioned above, the organs in **organtrader2010** are obtained through real CT scans and are made by converting data into a 3D model, then converting this model to Open Scene Graph. They are then included in a Python-based application that uses the OSGSWIG python wrapper for the ARToolkit to enable the augmented reality system to occur. To bridge this application with Second Life, data is streamed in to the Linden Scripting Language via the PHP server using XML. PHP provides the potential to extend the application network to include mobile devices and multiple reality environments with the system. The actual **organtrader2010** application can even be installed to Python enabled platforms for multiple mixed reality participation.

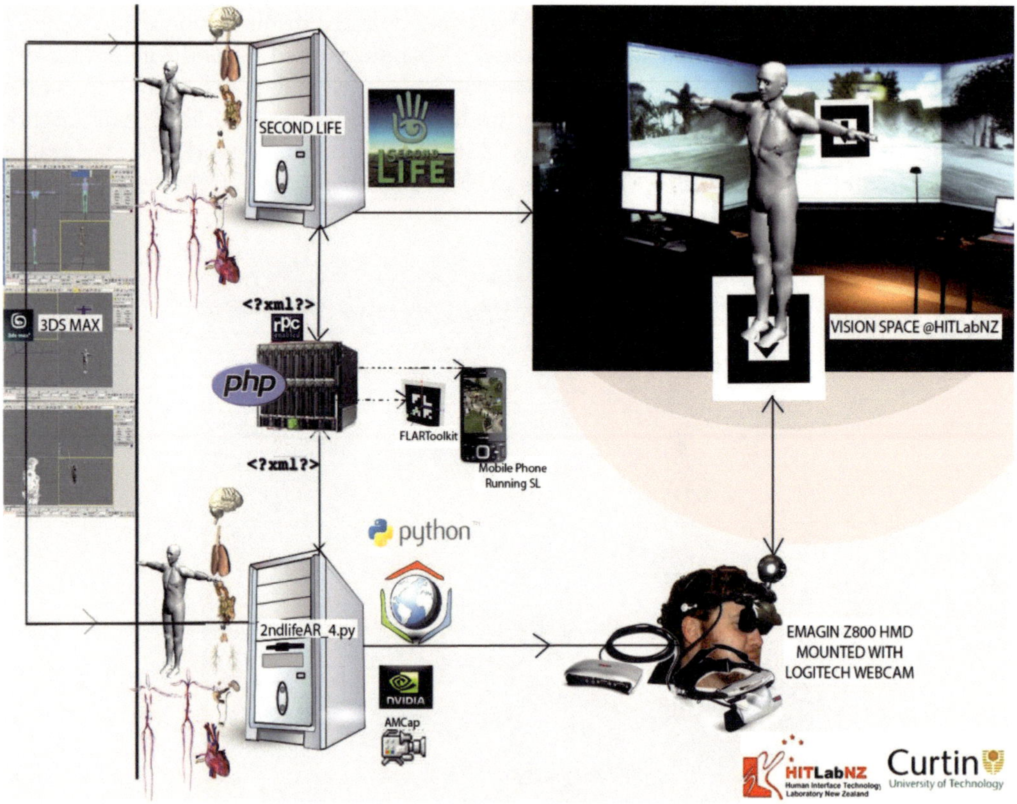

Fig. 4. Technical overview diagram for **organtrader2010**.

The system uses an XML RPC to link an augmented reality application with Second Life via a PHP server. This pipeline allows for a method of real-time transfer of 3D visual material, linking the body with the augmented and virtual representations of it. The use of real CT scanned organs with fiducial marker and proximity tracking adds to the viewer's experience of agency within the processes involved in the simulated organ trade and in the process of media art creation, display and dissemination.

While being more technically advanced than the previous example, this project challenges the same ideas under a more specific paradigm of the body. Here the work was designed to engage the viewer in a fictitious situation where they participate in a system of monetary exchange for virtual organs. This quite literally questions the value society places on biological elements within virtual and mixed reality systems as the audience dictates the market.

3.3 Promethean alchemist

Perhaps most explicitly exemplifying this mixed reality structure is *Promethean Alchemist.* This project was conceptualized during the Liminal Screens Co-Production Residency at the Banff New Media Institute (BNMI), The Banff Centre, Canada, and is currently under development. *Promethean Alchemist* is a mixed-reality interactive data transfer system that engages participants in mythological creation and DNA sequencing. Biological DNA is translated into computer data using DNA sequencing technology, which is further manipulated into 2D and 3D visual graphic appearance in the ARToolkit. The visualization form is the classic DNA double helix, which re-enters the physical world through an XML RPC (Remote Procedure Call) interface. When two sections of DNA are brought into close proximity, the system recognizes their proximity and 'splices' (combines) the data set into one.

Thus, wearing a HMD (Head Mounted Display) and using these cards, participants are able to pick up segments of DNA in mixed-reality space and throw them into the 'mixing pot' (visualized as a brazier burning with Promethean Fire) to create constantly evolving artificial life forms. Participants are able to create life in an augmented environment and then retrieve their creation in the virtual. Here they can export the form to 3D printing or animation platforms.

Promethean Alchemist is an artistic rendition of the implications of DNA code translated into the Deleuzian 'fold'. That is, the in-betweenness of spaces; "able to represent dialectical opposites, such as organic and inorganic, inside and outside."(Deleuze, 1993). The viewers' participation in the layers of code, which constitutes the work, implicates them in a complex exchange between organic and inorganic information where the differences between the two dissolve. The *Promethean Alchemist* is therefore an example of Giannachi hypersurface: "Able to present dichotomous relationships, between representation and matter, inside and outside, organic and inorganic, the hypersurface is the site of virtual performance." (Giannachi, 2008). My participation in the exchange is the threefold translation from organic DNA to computational code to visual representation in the ARToolkit. The viewer pushes this further by becoming the 'alchemist' stirring a virtual primordial soup. While the viewer in firmly planted in the physical realm, they still experience the dissolve between the organic and inorganic, humanity and technology.

Promethean Alchemist pays homage both visually and conceptually to the Ancient Greek creation myth of Prometheus and Epimetheus, which philosopher Bernard Stiegler references in his text *Technics and Time 1* (Stiegler, 1998). His text seeks to define technics -a technical entity arising out of, but distinct from, mechanical and biological entities- and to delineate the relationship between technics and humans. In the Greek creation story, Prometheus and Epimetheus were given the task of allotting suitable powers to all mortal creatures. Epimetheus did the initial distribution, which was then to be reviewed by Prometheus. Epimetheus set about giving creatures equal shares of positive and negative traits (small beings were given flight, weaker beings speed, etc); "Thus he made his whole distribution on a principle of compensation, being careful by these devices that no species should be destroyed." (Stiegler, 1998). However, when Prometheus came to inspect the work, he realized that Epimetheus had forgotten humans and had nothing left to bestow upon the naked, unshod, and unarmed creatures. Distraught, Prometheus stole from the

Gods the gifts of skill in the arts and fire, for without fire there was no way to use the skill. Thus through kinship with the Gods by their possession of such God-like powers, humans were able to create things such as clothing, shoes and weapons and could obtain food from the earth.

Thus what constitutes humanity is something that is outside of humanity itself: imagination, discovery and realization through technics; what could be called *Promethean Fire*. While animals are granted predestination in their origin, humans must create their qualities, "Humanity is without qualities, without predestination: it must invent, realize, produce qualities, and nothing indicates that, once produced these qualities will bring about humanity that they will become *its* qualities; for they may rather become those of technics." (Stiegler, 1998). In other words, humanity *is* its inventions, its tools, its technology. *Promethean Alchemist* demonstrates this concept in that each entity that exists in the virtual environment of the system is a translation and an archive of a particular moment in the evolution of humanity mediated between genetic and computational code.

It is through this definition of being in the divine gift of Promethean Fire that humans experience their mortality. "To partake in the lot of immortals means to endure one's mortality by the fact of being in (privative) relation with immortality." (Stiegler, 1998). Indeed, *Promethean Alchemist* represents, in a literal way, the desire of many scientists and philosophers to locate immortality in humanity's technological existence. The translation of DNA code into computational code and re-created in the augmented environment of the digital realm, demonstrates an instance of, 'transcendence through technology.' (Hayles, 1991). The ability to manipulate DNA mediated through the hypersurface represents the hope of many scientists to, in essence, dupe Zeus once again by locating the essence of humanity *within* that which defines it: in technics, thereby attaining immortality.

This hope has practical grounding, for example, in conservation biology. Currently, many scientists are extracting DNA samples from endangered animal species bred in captivity and preserving them for a future time when the organism might be safely reintroduced into its restored habitat, or even into another ecosystem on another planet. The assumption is that organisms can be preserved intact in DNA to be re-substantiated in physical form at a later time; the organism is thought to exist in essence in its DNA. Immortality is gleaned through the ability to store and preserve the organism in this way indefinitely. *Promethean Alchemist* actively uses the kind of technology that further abstracts and compresses the organism. That the viewer can only retrieve their creation through the limited methods of 3D printing or animation platforms, rather than re-substantiating into living tissue is a testament to the current limitations of translating from biological to virtual environments and back.

Alchemy is, ostensibly, the precursor to modern medicine and science, though its methods may have been closer to magic than scientific method. Sixteenth and Seventeenth Century scientists and swindlers dabbled for years in an alchemical obsession, the search for the philosopher's stone — the long-sought agent for transmuting lead to gold and unlocking other material and spiritual secrets. The stone was the unified theory of everything in that time, including the search for immortality and ways to keep the body young. [5] In *Promethean Alchemist* the viewer becomes the alchemist searching for immortality in the primordial soup of virtual DNA, combining and recombining combinations of computational 'DNA' code to create immortal virtual life forms. The metaphor of the modern digital alchemist points to the ways in which fruitless occult pursuits can sometimes evolve into transformative practices unforeseen in the former utopian, self-deluded view.

4. Syncretic post biological identity

At the recent First International Conference on Transdisciplinary Imaging at the Intersections between Art, Science and Culture (TIIC) Roy Ascott gave a keynote in which he described Syncretism as a possible method by which to classify mixed reality interaction (Ascott 2010). He used Second Life as an example of a metaverse that allowed for an embodied syncretic participatory experience.

Second Life, like all virtual environments uses an avatar (agent) to navigate users through the space. While these agents are, usually controlled by the user (avatars can be automated and left on their own, plus there are bots being regularly created and used), they function as independent to their 'master' and are therefore autonomous. Looking to social media and the examples of Facebook, LinkedIn and YouTube to name only three, this can also be said for user profiles on all platforms. Who we represent ourselves as on social networks is not necessarily a true articulation of our identity by any means and therefore it is autonomous. Avatars represent a transient, continually altered identity, usually that of its author and acts as an agent, through which users can engage with virtual platforms. This becomes particularly interesting in unique autonomous systems where participants can physically interact with a virtual deterritorialised 'self' and mediate it through physical engagement. The dispersion of multiple autonomous virtual agents via mixed reality constructs and expands deterritorialisation to include reterritorialisation, by facilitating a dispersive relationship between the body and its virtual self-referent. In the same way that a digital device deterritorialises and reterritorialises information through binary code, the augmentation of an autonomous agent into a shared space with the body, creates new opportunities for investigation into technology, the body and identity.

Critical literary theorist Donna Haraway relates the body's augmentation through digital technology to the notion of the cyborg. In *A Cyborg Manifesto* she argues that the body can be viewed as a conglomerate where its components can be separated, combined with new elements and put together again in ways that violate its traditional boundaries Haraway, 1991). This rhetoric implies a fractured identity that articulates a 'cyborg' reality. *In Chaos Bound,* literary theorist N. Katherine Hayles refers to the notion of dispersed self in light of virtual bodies and narrative, arguing that by turning bodiless information into narratives, the teleology of disembodiment is replaced with contests with ambiguous outcomes: "As I have argued, human being is first of all embodied being, and the complexities of this embodiment mean that human awareness unfolds in very different ways than intelligence in cybernetic machines (Hayles, 1999)."

The advent of nanobiology has called for a rethinking of Hayles and Harraways' post-human discourse through it shifting our perception of organisms from micro to nano scale. Charles Ostman suggests: "[T]he very definition of life itself may be perched on the edge of the next great revolution in medicine- nanobiology. What is emerging now are technologies and applications in the arenas of biomolecular 'components' integrated into microscale systems, . . . synthetically engineered quasi-viral components, modified DNA and related pseudoproteins, biomolecular prosthetics, and biomolecular organelle component 'entities' .

. . [that] will redefine the very essence of what is commonly referred to as 'life'." (Ostman 2003). Critical theorist Colin Milburn relates nanotechnology to virtual environments, stating: "Nanotechnology thrives in the realm of the virtual. Throughout its history, the field has been shaped by futuristic visions of technological revolution, hyperbolic promises of scientific convergence at the molecular scale, and science fiction stories of the world rebuilt atom by atom." (Milburn, 2008). Today nanotechnology exists as a living sensation of the future of human existence: In Milburn's words, "[A] bodily registration of potential for global change."(Milburn, 2008). Brian Massumi states, "The body,sensor of change, is a transducer of the virtual." Through existing in these virtual representations, that are directly linked to living bio-systems, we effectively sense, feel and think in a way that hybridizes the virtual with scientific inquiry, and therefore we require a discourse that addresses whether this does in fact make us post-biological (Massumi, 2002).

5. Conclusion

Art has historically had a strong preoccupation with the body and with consciousness. When dealing with such a massive area of inquiry there is a need to look to a wide variety of fields, As Ascott has stated, "[H]owever eccentric or esoteric, any culture, immediate or distant in space or time, any technology, ancient or modern, to find ideas and processes that allow for the navigation of mind and its open-ended exploration."(Ascott, 2008). Roy Ascott proposes a syncretic approach to this issue: "Just as cybernetics analogizes differences between systems, so syncretism finds likeness between unlike things. Syncretic thinking breaches boundaries and subverts protocols. Thinking out of the box, testing the limits of language, behaviour and thought puts the artist on the edge of social norms but at the centre of human development."(Ascott, 2008). Second-order cybernetics did very well to explain our early relationships with machines in terms of interactivity and connectivity, however the incorporation of more open networked systems of autonomous/anthropomorphic based interactions have created a less physical and paradigmatic situation. Networked agency destabilises traditional orthodoxies of thought through challenging notions of representation, confronting materialism, accelerating and smoothing social engagement and most importantly, demanding participation in these open systems of collaborative engagement.

As art is fundamentally an articulation of the human condition it can therefore be said that syncretism is also a valid method for analysing identity within the post-biological discourse. If we are indeed post-biological then we must exist in syncretic mixed reality state. The hybridisation of augmented reality and virtual environments with physical/biological systems calls for a rethinking of not only posthuman ideologies, but also the way that cybernetic systems function. This paper has scoped a range of examples from varying fields of inquiry that have influenced the author's own practice, which is articulated in order to provide a range of practical outcomes to what has been discussed. Through the creation of systems that engage the viewer in a hybridized participatory interaction with mixed reality data transfer, these notions of deterritorialisation, reterritorialisation, syncretism and post biological identity can be explored in a more intuitive and involved fashion.

Mixed Reality data transfer allows for the oscillation between different realities in a way that is seamless and intuitive as it incorporates traditional paradigms of physical engagement to occur, situated though, in an entirely digitally mediated environment. The projects discussed serve as practical research outcomes that present an investigation into the social and cultural impacts of such systems, through the utilisation of traditional explanations of how we integrate ourselves as individuals in a greater social context. The works serve to function as social experiments that propose questions without answers, in order to allow viewers to investigate these ideologies from a personally discursive position. Mixed reality environments exist as mirrors for society and as such should represent the current state of human existence within such networked systems of social and cultural exchange. The ability to incorporate real-time date transfer methods into such systems redefines our very understanding of what constitutes identity and humanity

6. References

Ascott, R. (2008). Cybernetic, Technoetic, Syncretic : The Prospect for Art), *Leonardo* Vol.41, No.3, (June 2008) pp. 204.

Ascott, R. (2010). Syncretic Dialogues: Keynote address at Proceedings of The First International Conference on Transdisciplinary Imaging at the Intersections between Art, Science and Culture, pp. 4, ISBN: 978-0-9807186-6-9, Sydney Australia, November 2010

A. Butz, T. H¨ollerer, S. Feiner, B. MacIntyre, and C. Beshers. (1999). Enveloping Users and Computers in a Collaborative 3d Augmented Reality. *IWAR'99: Proceedingsof the 2nd IEEE and ACM International Workshop on Augmented Reality,* page35, Washington, DC, USA, 1999.

Deleuze, G. (1993, original 1968) *Difference and Repetition.* Columbia University Press, New York.

Deleuze, G. (1991, original 1966) *Bergsonism.* Zone Books, Brooklyn, NY.

Deleuze, G. and Guatarri, F. (1987, original 1980) *A Thousand Plateaus: Capitalisim and Schizophrenia.* University of Minnesota Press, Minneapolis, MN.

Giannachi, G. (2008) *Virtual Theatres: An Introduction,* Routledge, London and New York.

Grasset, R. Lamb, P. Billinghurst, M. (2005). Evaluation of Mixed-Space Collaboration. In *Proceedings of the 4th IEEE/ACM International Symposium on Mixed and Augmented Reality* (ISMAR '05). IEEE Computer Society, pp. 90-99, Washington, DC, USA,.

Grasset, R. Looser, J and Billinghurst, M. (2006). Transitional Interface: Concept, Issues and Framework. In *Proceedings of the 5th IEEE and ACM International Symposium on Mixed and Augmented Reality* (ISMAR '06). IEEE Computer Society, pp. 231-232,Washington, DC, USA.

Haraway, D.1(991,) Simians Cyborgs and Women, The Reinvention of Nature, Routledge, New York. Hayles, N.K. (1990). Chaos Bound: Orderly Disorder in Contemporary Literature and Science. Cornell University Press, Ithaca, NY Kantonen T. Woodward C., Katz N. (2010) *Mixed reality in virtual world teleconferencing. Proceedings IEEE Virtual Reality 2010.* pp. 179-182 Waltham, Massachusetts, USA, March 20 - 24,

Koleva, B. Schndelbach, H. Benford, S. and Greenhalgh, C.(2000) Traversable interfaces between real and virtual worlds. In *Proceedings of the SIGCHI Conference on Human Factors in Computing Systems* (CHI '00), pp. 233-240.ACM, New York, NY, USA, 2000.

Lang, T. MacIntyre, B. and Zugaza, I. (2008). Massively Multiplayer Online Worlds as a Platform for Augmented Reality Experiences. Virtual Reality Conference, 2008 (VR'08 IEEE), March 8-12 2008.

Levy, P. (1997), *Collective Intelligence.* trans. Bononno, R. Perseus Books, Cambridge, Brian Massumi, B. (2002) *Parables for the Virtual: Movement, Affect, Sensation.* Duke University Press, Durham, NC, McLuhan, M. (1994) *Understanding Media.* Massachusetts. MIT Press

Milburn, C. (2008). Atoms and Avatars: Virtual Worlds as Massively-Multiplayer Laboratories. *Spontaneous Generations.* University of Toronto

Ostman,O. (2003). Nanobiology? Where Nanotechnology and Biology Come Together. www.biota.org/ostman/nanobio.htm (accessed June 3, 2004)

Sermon, P and Gould, C (2011). Liberate your Avatar: The Revolution Will Be Socially Networked , *Creating Second Lives* , pp. 15-31 Routledge, Taylor & Francis Group, New York, USA.

Stiegler, B. (1998). *Technics and Time, 1: The Fault of Epimetheus,* trans. Richard Beardsworth & George Collins Stanford University Press, 1998

10

Intraoperative Visual Guidance and Control Interface for Augmented Reality Robotic Surgery

Rong Wen, Chee-Kong Chui and Kah-Bin Lim
National University of Singapore,
Singapore

1. Introduction

Minimally invasive surgery (MIS) with its small artificial incisions imposed on the patient skin for operation is becoming a preferred surgical treatment comparing with the conventional open surgery. The open surgeries usually create large traumas on the patient bodies to expose their internal anatomy for operational access. The MIS offers its distinct advantages of small injuries, less blood loss and pain and faster recovery during the surgery procedures (Puangmali et al., 2008). However, the indirectly accessed operating causes problems such as restricted vision and difficult hand-eye coordination through the small key holes. The recent development of the modern optics, computer graphics, computer vision and robotics provides possible chances to resolve the problems described above.

Virtual Reality (VR) is a technology providing users an artificial environment to simulate the physical world and objects for displaying, training or gaming etc. Users are allowed to interact with the VR environment through human-computer interface that consists of computer graphic models and various sensors. The major applications of virtual reality in surgery can be divided into three areas: virtual humans for training, virtual telemedicine shared decision environments for training of multiple players and the fusion of virtual humans with real humans for performing surgery (Rosen et al., 1996). VR can create individualized treatment needs and training protocols by providing an environment in which the intensity of feedback and training can be systematically manipulated and enhanced (Anderson et al., 2002; Wang et al., 1999; Cai et al., 2003). VR simulators also allow users to compare their performance with that of their peers (Pearson et al., 2002; Watterson et al., 2002). VR assisted surgical planning facilitates preoperative and postoperative diagnosis with sufficient details of 3-D medical models which are commonly constructed from the computed tomography (CT) or magnetic resonance (MR) images. For example, surgical planning was conducted using a three-dimensional VR based interface to provide a quantitative osteotomy-simulated bone model and prediction of postoperative appearance with photorealistic quality (Xia, et al., 2001). Additionally, there were medical researches based on VR technology specifically conducted to assist surgeons during neurologic, orthopedic, arthroscopic, and urologic surgery (Akay & Marsh, 2001; Burdea et al., 2000; Heng et al., 2004; Kuo et al., 2001; Chui et al., 2006). Recently, there is an increasing emphasis on data fusion involving integration of virtual patient with real patient as a navigational aid in surgery (Rosen et al., 1996; Wen et al., 2010).

Augmented reality (AR) does not rely solely on artificially created virtual environments but expands the virtual computer-generated models with real world environment. AR is characterized as being a fusion of real and virtual data within a real world environment (Milgram et al., 1994). Medical augmented reality is proposed to create the virtual scenes on the related physical tissues, organs or patient skin to assist surgeons visualizing the internal anatomy or invisible surgical planning such as operational distance, trajectories etc.. Due to the advancement in tracking, visualization and display technology, computer-aided medical procedure based AR solutions was examined in the context of minimally invasive surgery (Navab et al., 2007). AR system has been developed to enhance the endoscopic or laparoscopic view to extend surgeons' visibility of hidden anatomical structures that were beneath the then surgical scene. This augmentation facilitates the surgical operation to avoid risk regions like arteries and nerves. On the other hand the pathology regions are easily to be reached. The needle's insertion happened within the target organ was guided to reach the tumor volume (Konishia et al., 2005; Thoranaghatte et al., 2008; Lee et al., 2010). Thus a more intuitive visual assistance during the surgery procedure is provided for surgeon's response. Integration of laparoscopic and 3D-ultrosound images that provided anatomical information inside the target organs was studied by Konishia et al. (Konishia et al., 2005). With head-mounted display (HMD) based AR interface, numerous studies have demonstrated the potential efficiency of MRI-guided tumour extraction and therapy (Liao et al., 2010). Projector-based visualization system for clinically intraoperative navigation was reported (Hoppe, 2003). Grimson et al. (Grimson et al., 1996) showed its potentials to surgical navigation systems that enhance physical scenes with the augmentation of overlaying virtual internal structures. Another medical application of marking the surgical object with a virtual-pen was based on direct AR interface (Seo et al., 2007). It was proposed to supersede the ink pen which was widely used in the surgical environment. With the virtual-pen, the surgical markings were achieved by directly projecting them onto human body. The introduction of AR to surgical treatment creates a virtual medium between preoperative plan and intraoperative environment.

In order to enhance manual dexterity and accuracy of instrument manipulation, robotic assistance has been introduced in the MIS to solve operation constraint problems. The da Vinci™ Surgical System, a master–slave integrated robot, has been applied for treating a range of surgical conditions improving operational flexibility and accuracy (Guthart & Salisbury, 2000). For the sophisticated minimally invasive operations like coronary artery bypass and mitral valve repair, robot assisted surgery is expected to achieve satisfying clinical outcomes (Devernay et al., 2001). Surgical robot also demonstrated its distinct advantages in speed, accuracy and consistency for the larger liver tumor treatment with RFA. Yang et al. investigated design and implementation of a novel robotic system for RFA considering both kinematics and clinical requirements (Yang et al., 2010). Other advantages offered by the robotic RFA include minimizing radioactive exposure and overcoming visual restriction as well as spatial constraint for minimally invasive approaches like the laparoscopic or percutaneous surgical procedure. Integrating the imaging guidance and the surgical robot assistance into minimally invasive operation brings the preoperative planning and intraoperative manipulation into perspective.

2. Spatial AR interface for robot assisted MIS

Depending on different ways of augmenting the environment, there are three approaches in AR display devices: Optical See Through devices, Video See Through devices, and Direct Augmentations. Direct Augmentations is also called spatial augmented reality (SAR) using projector-camera system to present the virtual information directly in the 3D real world environment (Raskar et al., 2001; Bimber & Raskar, 2004). Based on the above different approaches of augmentations, four kinds of AR platform are popularly used in present surgical simulation and treatment: head-mounted display (HMD) based AR (Cakmakci & Rolland, 2006), semi-transparent mirror based AR (Liao et al., 2010) and projector based AR (Bimber & Raskar, 2004).

Comparing with the other augmentation approaches, SAR offers the distinct advantages that allow users not wearing heavy helmet, overcoming the limited vision area, sharing the AR intraoperative information and communicating freely with their fellow users. The projector-based AR, which is considered to be the most natural way combining the virtual environment and real environment together, is expected to serve as an effective integrated interface to overcome the aforementioned constraints of the MIS. In addition, the surgical robot and interactive hand gesture operation, considered as dynamic components in the real environment, can be easily integrated in this AR interface for robot assisted MIS surgery.

The general work flow using this advanced user interface is illustrated in Fig. 1. It first involves the handling of 3D models that can be derived from the CT images and the preoperative surgical planning. The construction of the static 3D AR environment includes

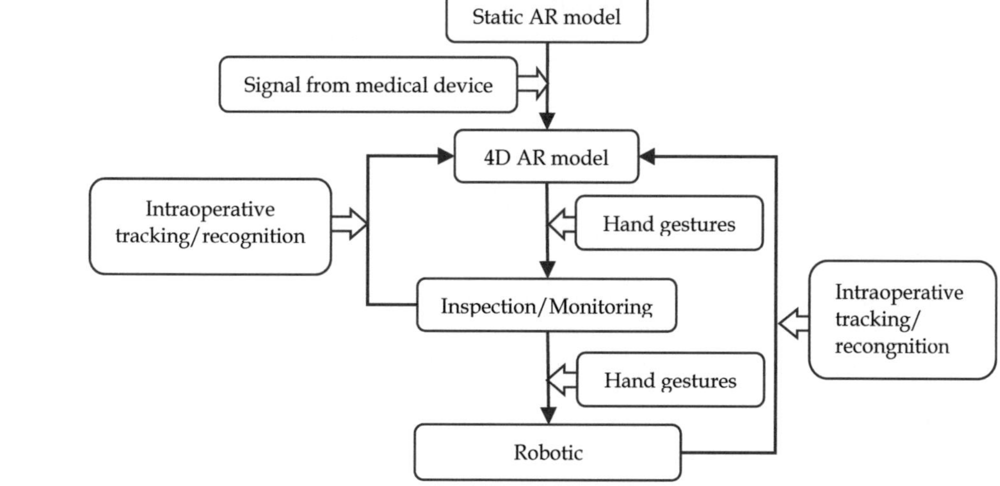

Fig. 1. Work flow of the advanced interface for augmented reality surgery.

registration, geometric and radiometric correction. There is an iterative process with AR real-time model rendering and feedback from the real world environment, including hand gesture interaction with the AR model, surgical robot and the feedback of signal from related medical devices during the surgical operation. When the AR model, displayed over the real organ of the patient by the projector-camera system, receives any "stimulus" from the real environment, there will be changes responding in real time on the model to guide the surgeons' decisions and operation.

3. Registration

Registration is a main challenge in AR technology (Pablo et al., 2010). Correct and consistent registration method plays an important role in estimating the position of either the virtual objects relative to the object in the real world or of the virtual objects relative to a common coordinate system. A number of registration methods have been developed ranging from analysis of the real world environment to evaluations of intentionally introduced fiducials (Massoptier & Casciaro, 2008; Teber et al., 2009).

Marker based methods are commonly used to aid intraoperative registration in robot assisted surgeries (Yang et al., 2010). A marker based registration method for projector-camera system is introduced in this chapter. With the markers attached onto the patient's skin, spatial relationship between the markers and target organ can be derived from CT image of the patient. As shown in Fig. 2, three markers M_1, M_2, M_3, are attached onto the patient body to construct a space reference fame T. This marker based frame is used to construct the spatial relationship that connects the stereovision frame, world coordinate and CT image frame. The spatial relationship enables the virtual model displayed by the projector-camera system to register with the target organ within the patient body. The two steps to overlay a virtual model of the target organ precisely on the patient with correct position, scale and angle in the projector-camera system are described as follows.

The first step involves establishing the spatial relationship between the markers M_i (i=1, 2, 3) and the target organ O. CT imaging of the patient with three markers attached is performed prior to the surgery. Appropriate markers deployment is important. The markers should facilitate the registration and avoid inconveniencing the surgery. Their deployment is dependent on the following considerations. Firstly, the surgical tools' motion should not be obstructed by the markers. The surgical path or motion is given a higher priority in preoperative planning compared to that of markers' deployment. Since the markers are used primarily for constructing the space reference frame T, this can be achieved as long as the stereovision system can detect the markers during registration. Preoperative planning including obstruction prevention will be discussed in section 5.1. Secondly, the markers should be placed beyond the expected projection region to avoid violating the projected virtual model.

For the second step, the initial calibration of projector-camera system has been described by Bimber & Raskar (Bimber & Raskar, 2004). It establishes the correspondence between the pixels in camera and projector as a lookup table. With the stereo vision system, the reference frame T consisted of three markers is achieved from the estimation of space coordinate of the three markers. As mentioned above the spatial relationship between the markers and the target organ based on the image coordinate is derived from the CT images. In this case, the spatial relationship between target organ and the projected virtual model is established as Eq. (1):

$$R_0^T = R_{m_i}^T \times R_o^{m_i} \quad (1)$$

Since the coordinate of the top-left corner L_2 of the projected image is easily detected, the position of L_2 can be adjusted to its expected coordinate. Assume that the L_1 and L_3 are the top-left corner of the source image and the captured image respectively, and $L_1'(x, y)$ and $L_3'(x, y)$ are the expected position of the top-left corner of the source image and the captured image respectively. The expected coordinates of the projected image can be acquired by calculating the spatial relationship with the homography between the camera and the world coordinate. The relationship between $L_1'(x, y)$ and $L_3'(x, y)$ is shown as Eq. (2) and Eq. (3):

$$L_3 = \mathbf{M_A} L_3', \quad (2)$$

$$L_1' = \mathbf{H_p H_c^{-1}} L_3', \quad (3)$$

where $\mathbf{M_A}$ is a affine transformation. A testing projection is conducted to detect the differences between L_3 and L'_3. With the piecewise linear method described above, $\mathbf{M_A}$ and $\mathbf{H_p H_c^{-1}}$ can be replaced by the $\mathbf{M_{A_i}}$ and $\mathbf{H_{p_i} H_{c_i}^{-1}}$ for corresponding piecewise regions.

Suppose that the patient is lying on a surgical bed and the camera is placed along the vertical axis from the target organ relative to the surgical bed. A virtual organ model with the same size and angle located as the real one is expected to be projected on the patient body. This bird-eye view of the image of the virtual model can be derived from the CT images. Finally, the geometric correction for the projected image is conducted to register the virtual model with the real target organ.

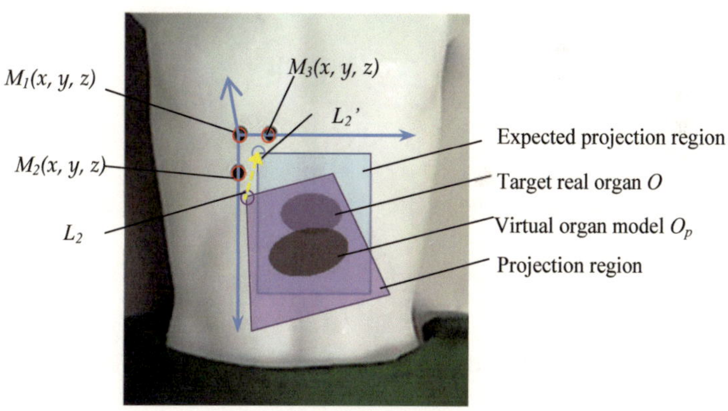

Fig. 2. Marker based registration for SAR (M_1, M_2, M_3 are three markers attached onto the phantom's body.)

4. Correction for projection

In order to create an overall projected image that appears correct and seamless on arbitrary surfaces in the real world, geometric correction plays an important role in construction of the SAR environment. This task is challenging for projector-based displays because of the following problems:

1. Perspective distortion arising from projection.
2. Geometric distortion arising from lens distortion, arbitrary physical surfaces, etc..
3. Real-time geometric correction. This is a challenging problem and it may occur during the dynamic projection in spatial space in which screen surface is changing in real-time because of variance of projector's location or angle.

In addition, the display quality of the projected image is modulated by the colored and textured arbitrary surface sacrificing its photometric quality. Human eyes are sensitive to this artifact. Radiometric correction can be used to relax this restriction with the SAR system by compensating the spatially varying reflectance.

4.1 Geometric correction

Assume the screen surface is planar and projection light is perpendicularly to the surface. The projection on the screen surface appears hardly distorted to the observers in front of the screen. When an image is projected on a planar screen surface that is not perpendicular to it, the projective distortion corrupts the projected image. When an image is projected onto a screen surface with irregular unevenness, geometric factor of the screen surfaces also affects distortion of the projected image.

For a planar projection, homography is used to represent the transformation from the source image to the projected image in the world coordinate, from the projected image to the captured image in the camera as Eq. (4) and Eq. (5):

$$\begin{pmatrix} p_x \\ p_y \\ 1 \end{pmatrix} = \mathbf{H_p} \begin{pmatrix} w_x \\ w_y \\ 1 \end{pmatrix}, \tag{4}$$

$$\begin{pmatrix} c_x \\ c_y \\ 1 \end{pmatrix} = \mathbf{H_c} \begin{pmatrix} w_x \\ w_y \\ 1 \end{pmatrix}, \tag{5}$$

$(w_x, w_y, 1)^T$ is an image point projected on a planar surface. $(p_x, p_y, 1)^T$ and $(c_x, c_y, 1)^T$ are the corresponding points located in the projector's and camera's respectively. From H_p and H_c, a relation from the source image to the captured image can be established in Eq. (6):

$$\begin{pmatrix} p_x \\ p_y \\ 1 \end{pmatrix} = \mathbf{H_p H_c^{-1}} \begin{pmatrix} c_x \\ c_y \\ 1 \end{pmatrix}, \tag{6}$$

The geometric correction process is illustrated in Fig. 3. There are two types of correction models: viewer dependent and viewer independent. For viewer-dependent correction, the source image should be pre-wrapped as $T^{-1}S$, where S is the source image and T is the mapping function between the source image and the captured image. For viewer-independent correction, the source image should be wrapped as $P^{-1}S$, where P is the mapping function between the source image and the projected image. Eq. (7) and Eq. (8) illustrate the correction process:

$$PC\left(T^{-1}S\right) = PC\left(C^{-1}P^{-1}\right)S = S, \tag{7}$$

$$P\left(P^{-1}S\right) = P\left(CT^{-1}\right)S = S. \tag{8}$$

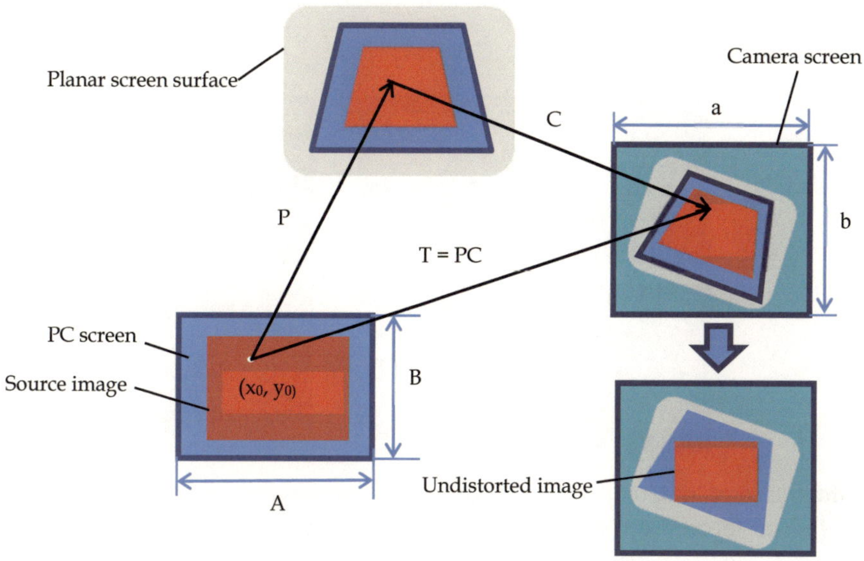

Fig. 3. Viewer-dependent geometric correction.

Although Eq. (6) is not directly applicable when the screen is non-flat, the function $\mathbf{H_pH_c}^{-1}$ can be found easily. An idea of replacing $\mathbf{H_pH_c}^{-1}$ by piecewise linear mapping function that relates the camera and the projector is proposed in this research. With the piecewise linear method, the source image can be marked piecewise by defined feature points. Consequently, the source image can be operated "piece" by "piece", in which the correction of projected image on non-planar screen surface is approximated by connecting all these piece regions. Quadrilateral piece is used as unit region to compute the homography between source image and projected image, captured image and source image. The region connection could be compensated by bilinear interpolation.

The point-correspondence between the image pairs could be acquired from the result of registration. For every piece region, four feature points are established with the respective relationship defined by Eq. (9), (10) and (11). i is the ith piecewise region in the source image, projected image and the captured image. The other parameters have the same meaning as that of the equation (4), (5), (6).

$$\begin{pmatrix} p_{i_x} \\ p_{i_y} \\ 1 \end{pmatrix} = \mathbf{H}_{\mathbf{p}_i} \begin{pmatrix} w_{i_x} \\ w_{i_y} \\ 1 \end{pmatrix}, \tag{9}$$

$$\begin{pmatrix} c_{i_x} \\ c_{i_y} \\ 1 \end{pmatrix} = \mathbf{H}_{\mathbf{c}_i} \begin{pmatrix} w_{i_x} \\ w_{i_y} \\ 1 \end{pmatrix}, \tag{10}$$

$$\begin{pmatrix} p_{i_x} \\ p_{i_y} \\ 1 \end{pmatrix} = \mathbf{H}_{\mathbf{p}_i} \mathbf{H}_{\mathbf{c}_i}^{-1} \begin{pmatrix} c_{i_x} \\ c_{i_y} \\ 1 \end{pmatrix} \tag{11}$$

An example of piecewise geometric correction for chessboard projection is shown as Fig. 4. From Fig. 4, we can observe that the number and location of the selected feature points play important role on the final result.

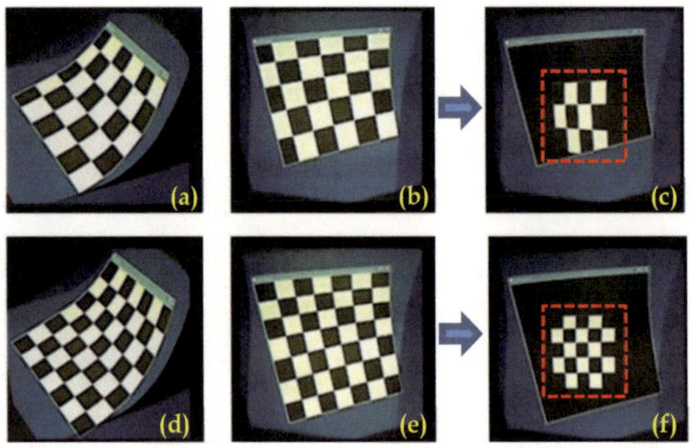

Fig. 4. Geometric correction on the curved surface with a chessboard pattern ((a) and (d) are side views. (b) and (e) are front views. (c) and (f) are the corrected projection for (a) and (d) respectively from the front views).

4.2 Radiometric correction

Radiometry distortion is due to angle of projection, screen texture and the environment lightings. Photometric models of interaction with spectra reflectance between projector and camera were proposed by S. K. Nayar et al. (Nayar et al., 2003) and K. Fujii et al. (Fujii et al., 2005). Based on the photometric models, a practical method to apply radiometric compensation by the projector-camera system is presented in this section. Image $\mathbf{C} = [C_R \;\; C_G \;\; C_B]^T$ acquired by camera from the projected image $\mathbf{P} = [P_R \;\; P_G \;\; P_B]^T$ is affected by surface reflectance and environment lighting. Assume projector and camera each have three color channels (R, G, B). The equation (12) illustrates the radiometric transformation from projector to camera via the screen surface based on the above photometric models:

$$\mathbf{C} = \mathbf{F}(\mathbf{E} + \mathbf{MP}), \tag{12}$$

where :

$$\begin{bmatrix} C_R \\ C_G \\ C_B \end{bmatrix} = \begin{bmatrix} F_R E_R \\ F_G E_G \\ F_B E_B \end{bmatrix} + \begin{bmatrix} F_R M_{RR} & M_{RG} & M_{RB} \\ M_{GR} & F_G M_{GG} & M_{GB} \\ M_{BR} & M_{BG} & F_B M_{BB} \end{bmatrix} \begin{bmatrix} P_R \\ P_G \\ P_B \end{bmatrix}.$$

The vector **F** is the reflectance of surface. **E** is the contribution of the environment lighting to the captured image. The color mixing matrix **M** describes the radiometric interaction between the projector and the camera.

In comparison with the brightness of environment lighting, projector is considerably brighter when performing the projection on the textured and colored surface (Fujii et al., 2005). The color mixing matrix **M** can be derived by projecting two gray images with gray values of 255 and 0 respectively for monotonic radiometric calibration. To compute the **M** for the color case, normalization of the elements in the **M** is conducted to eliminate the influence of the surface reflectance. The diagonal elements in the **M** are evaluated to unity, $M_{dd} = 1(d = \mathrm{R, G, B})$. By comparing of images with differences in one of the three channels, the other elements in the M_{ij} are acquired for the corresponding channel:

$$M_{Rk_1} = \Delta C_{k_1} / \Delta C_R \;\; (\mathrm{k}_1 = \mathrm{G, B}), \tag{13}$$

$$M_{Gk_2} = \Delta C_{k_2} / \Delta C_G \;\; (k_2 = \mathrm{R, B}), \tag{14}$$

$$M_{Bk_3} = \Delta C_{k3} / \Delta C_B \;\; (k_3 = \mathrm{R,G}). \tag{15}$$

Based on the piecewise linear method described in the section A, the matrix **F**, **E** and **M** can be replaced by $\mathbf{F}_i$, $\mathbf{E}_i$ and $\mathbf{M}_i$ as (9), (10) and (11).

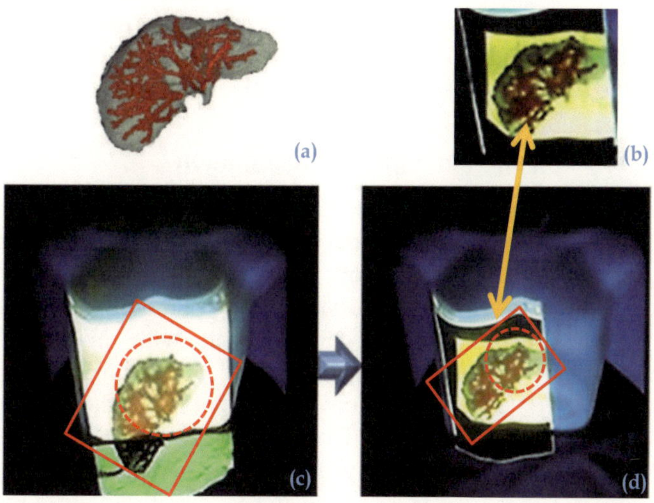

Fig. 5. Projected correction for Augmented Reality environment construction ((a) is a source image of liver model. (c) is the distorted image projected on a phantom body. (b) and (d) are the corrected images.)

5. Intraoperative surgical intervention based on the AR interface

5.1 Therapeutic model design

The dynamic augmented virtual model displayed on the AR interface during surgery is derived from the therapeutic model developed in the preoperative phase. The preoperative plan is based on medical diagnosis, and includes the therapeutic model and surgical planning. The therapeutic model is a stereoscopic cyber-graphic model reconstructed from CT images with relevant organs and tissues segmented. Besides the three dimensional profile of the target tumour and blood vessels, other important circumjacent tissues and organs around the interested region are included in the model as specified by the surgeons. Additionally, markers deployment should also be examined for this therapeutic model design to make sure they are beyond the surgical working path.

For the therapeutic model design based on the robot assisted surgery, optimization algorithms are usually applied to enhance the efficiency of robotic implementation and to decrease complexity during the surgery. For example, an ablation model with a "Voxel Growing" algorithm (Yang et al., 2009) is applied for a prototyped robot assisted radiofrequency ablation (RFA) surgery. This algorithm automatically adapts the different tumour's irregular 3-D profile to produce the ablation points. In order to further reduce the number of required ablation and minimize burning of healthy tissue, the "grown region" is optimally aligned to best fit the geometry of the target region. The input for the ablation model is the surface data of the tumour, which are acquired from CT scan in advance. Surgical path planning is another important consideration for the preoperative planning. This method involves the construction of spherical elements defined by inscribed cubes. Each sphere represents the ablation area, and its inscribed cube represents a voxel element. Voxel elements propagate layer by layer along defined directions according to its surface edges of the present layer, covers the entire tumour area coinciding with its contour. As voxel elements grow, the coordinates of centres of every voxel elements are produced and being assigned as the ablation coordinates. After the therapeutic model and the surgical plan are prepared, the model is projected onto the patient in the spatial AR environment.

5.2 Intraoperative tracking and hand gesture recognition

Intraoperative tracking is to establish the real-time spatial awareness of medical instrument navigation and hand motion necessary for visual guidance and intraoperative control during the surgery. Intraoperative tracking of the operating trajectory of the medical instrument provides surgeons real-time feedback of the operation procedure. This real-time feedback information is usually analysed and dealt with in consideration of the intraoperative process as well as the previous medical preplanning. For example in RFA surgery, when the RFA needle is inserted into the patient body, the distal end of needle is tracked to detect the needle's trajectory. The AR environment is updated in real-time producing a virtual needle part, which is projected on the patient surface, following the needle's treatment plan. The surgeon can visualize the operation within the patient's body and surgical processes.

Numerous tracking methods have been developed for surgical environment including vision based tracking and magnetics based tracking. (Dutkiewicz et al., 2004; Felfoul et al., 2008). After taking into consideration the consistent surgical luminance, distinct background content and usability, a vision-based approach based on Continuously Adaptive Mean-Shift (CamShift) algorithm (Ling et al., 2010) is adopted for intraoperative tracking. CamShift algorithm is built upon the Mean-Shift algorithm to track objects based on probability distribution (Wen et al., 2010; Mustafa & Kalajdziski, 2007). Back projection is a way to find the extent to which the pixel distribution of a region coincides with a histogram model. It can be used to compute the probability distribution image from the original image with the colour histogram. The pixel values in the input image are scaled using the values in the corresponding bin of the color histogram and stored in the probability distribution image. The function computes the probability of each element value according to the empirical probability distribution represented by the histogram. If C is the color of the pixel and F is the probability that a pixel belongs to the object being tracked, then the probability map gives $P(C|F)$. The probability distribution image is used in the algorithm for tracking.

The procedure of the Mean-Shift tracking algorithm is described as follows::

1. An initial location of a search window is chosen.
2. Compute the mean location or centroid in the window based on the probability distribution image. The centroid (x_c, y_c) is calculated as follows:
   Firstly, the zeroth and first moments of the image are calculated as:

$$M_{20} = \sum_x \sum_y x^2 I(x,y), \tag{16}$$

$$M_{02} = \sum_x \sum_y y^2 I(x,y), \tag{17}$$

$$M_{11} = \sum_x \sum_y xyI(x,y), \tag{18}$$

   where *I(x, y)* is the probability value at coordinate (x, y) in the image, ranging over the entire search window. The coordinates of the centroid are then computed from the moments as Eq. (19) and Eq. (20).

$$x_c = M_{10} / M_{00}, \tag{19}$$

$$y_c = M_{01} / M_{00}, \tag{20}$$

3. Move the center of the window to the location derived from the previous step.
4. Return to Step 2 until convergence is achieved.

The CamShift algorithm also has the ability to update the size of the search window to fit the object being tracked as the frames change (Ling et al., 2010).

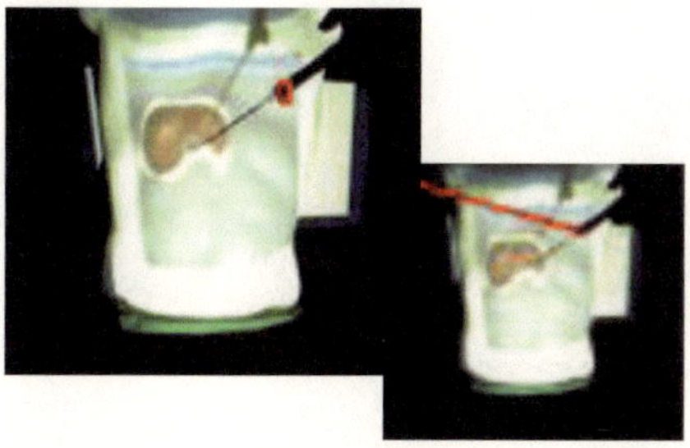

Fig. 6. RFA needle is tracked based on an AR environment.

For intraoperative interaction, hand gesture is adopted to control display of the AR model and robotic device. Surgeon's hand gestures are detected by a stereovision system over or beside the AR environment. This interface has advantage on sterilization which is an important requirement in operating room. The vision based hand gesture can be integrated into the AR system using projector-camera system or conventional tracking device. The AR model projected on the patient surface can be scaled and rotated using hand gestures. Additionally, hand gestures can also be used to guide robotic execution.

In order to enhance the speed and accuracy of hand gesture recognition, an innovative 3D model based method is introduced. This method is based on the analysis of model features produced by a space palm plan and 3D convex hull points. Users are allowed to pose the defined hand gestures without wearing markers or data glove. Due to human hand's flexibility, stereovision system is used to resolve ambiguity on recognizing the hand features.

As shown in Fig. 7, the 3D model is constructed including the space palm plan which is relatively stable, and a brace model of five fingers with the key joints and finger tips. Before starting the hand gestures recognition, the 3D hand model is initialized by characterizing the model with the specific hand parameters such as palm size, fingers layout of different users. This initialization can be achieved by directly measuring the key parameters of the user's hand under the vision system with a defined pose. These key parameters include hand length and width, the ratio between the palm and the fingers, and the palm's location relative to the stereovision system. Palm plan can be acquired by regression of the hand palm coordinates shown as Fig.7 (b). There are several possible ways of tracking the user's hands (Mahmoudi & Parviz, 2006). In consideration of the background of hand operation based on this AR interface is covered by the surgical cloth which is green in color. CamShift based method used for medical instrument tracking can also be integrated with hand tracking. When the hand tracking is implemented, the palm plan is invoked to change its pose in the space coordinate. Following with the hand tracking, the 3D hand model is attached to the user's hand wherever the hand moves. In this case the parameters of the 3D hand model are analysed in real-time and the hand gesture recognition is achieved in real-time.

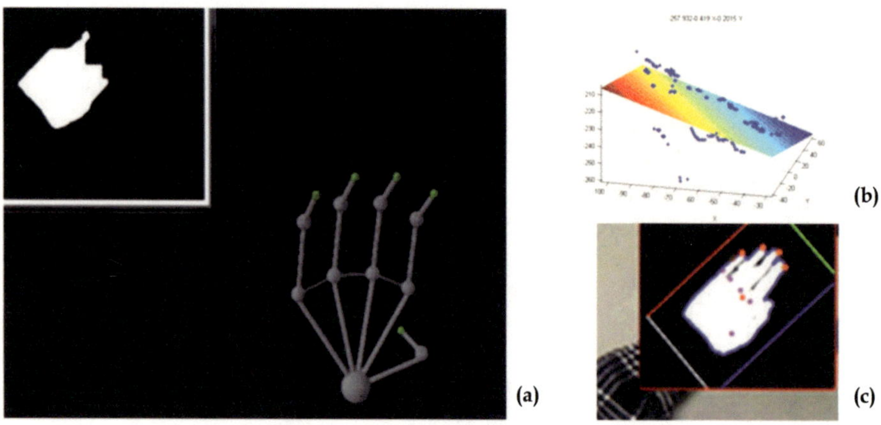

Fig. 7. 3D model based hand gesture recognition.

5.3 Robotic implementation

While the introduction of AR in computer aided surgery enhances visualization of preoperative surgical plan, it alone does not necessarily translate to precision and accuracy in intraoperative execution. In the case of minimally invasive surgery, the surgeon is not only deprived of direct visual information but also subjected to dexterous constraints in the manoeuvring of laparoscopic tools or percutaneous ablation devices. Performing such operation manually even with AR guidance can be non-trivial and often expose to uncertainties and inconsistent outcomes. For instance, the challenges in large tumor treatment with percutaneous ablation technique have been discussed (Abolhassani et al.,2007; Choi, et al., 2000; Goldberg, et al., 1998). This lack of intraoperative consistency poses a serious bottleneck for the effectiveness surgical outcome. Robotic assistance provides the necessary augmentation in dexterity to provide precision and accuracy even in space constraint situation (Hyosig & Wen, 2001; Kuo & Dai, 2009; Stoianovici et al., 1998; Taylor & Stoianovici, 2003; Taylor, 2008). The Transcutaneous Robot-assisted Ablation-device Insertion Navigation System (TRAINS) is developed for ablation treatment in liver tumor (Chang et al., 2011; Yang et al., 2010). Technical details and demonstrate the implementation of robotic modules for AR robotic system are presented as follows.

The integration of the robotic modules requires establishment of the spatial relationship between the multi-body system and surgical field. It begins with the construction of a kinematic model for the manipulator and frame assignments to the various entities for the AR applications. Frame assignment of the multi-body robotic mechanism can be established based on the Denavit-Hartenberg (D-H) convention described by (Fu, 1987). Fig. 8 (left) illustrates the D-H frame assignments for TRAINS prototype. The joint variables and link parameters tabulated in Table 1.

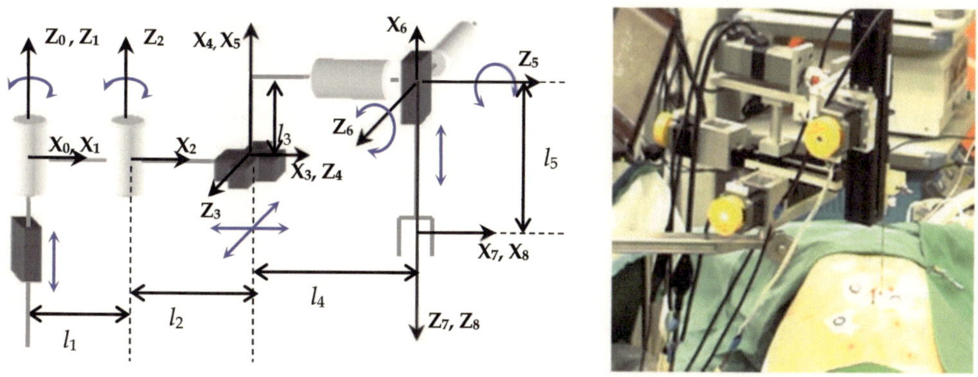

Fig. 8. Denavit-Hartenberg frame assignments for TRAINS prototype (left); Robotic needle insertion for ablation treatment (right).

	θ	D	a	a
${}^0T_1$	0	q_1	0	0
${}^1T_2$	q_2	0	l_1	0
${}^2T_3$	q_3	0	l_2	90°
${}^3T_4$	90°	q_4	0	90°
${}^4T_5$	0	q_5	0	0
${}^5T_6$	q_6	l_4	-90°	-90°
${}^6T_7$	q_7	0	0	90°
${}^7T_8$	0	q_8+l_5	0	0

Table 1. Denavit-Hartenberg table for manipulator (q_i stands for ith joint variable).

The kinematic model can subsequently be expressed in homogenous transformation matrix as shown in Eq. (21). which represents the orientation and position of the end effector as a function of joint variables from their respective axis of control.

$$ {}^0T_c = \begin{bmatrix} {}^0R_8 & {}^0P_8 \\ \bar{0} & \bar{1} \end{bmatrix}, \quad (21) $$

where

$$
{}^{o}R_{8}=\begin{bmatrix} s_{23}s_{6}c_{7}-c_{23}s_{7} & s_{23}c_{6} & s_{23}s_{6}s_{7}+c_{23}c_{7} \\ -c_{23}s_{6}c_{7}-s_{23}s_{7} & c_{23}c_{6} & -c_{23}s_{6}s_{7}+s_{23}c_{7} \\ c_{6}c_{7} & -s_{6} & c_{6}s_{7} \end{bmatrix}, \tag{22}
$$

$$
{}^{o}P_{8}=\begin{bmatrix} s_{23}s_{6}s_{7}\left(q_{8}+l_{5}\right)+c_{23}[c_{7}\left(q_{8}+l_{5}\right)+l_{4}]+q_{5}c_{23}+q_{4}s_{23}+l_{1}c_{2}+l_{2}c_{23} \\ -c_{23}s_{6}s_{7}\left(q_{8}+l_{5}\right)+s_{23}[c_{7}\left(q_{8}+l_{5}\right)+l_{4}]+q_{5}c_{23}-q_{4}s_{23}+l_{1}s_{2}+l_{2}s_{23} \\ c_{6}c_{7}\left(q_{8}+l_{5}\right)l_{3}q_{1} \end{bmatrix}, \tag{23}
$$

where s_j=sin (q_i), c_{ij}=cos(q_i), sij=sin (q_i+q_j) and c_{ij}=cos(q_i+q_j).

Direct vision is usually absence in minimally invasive surgery or percutaneous interventional procedure. Hence registration between diagnostic medical images, surgical field and its entities has to be done. Preoperative image coordinates can be readily transformed to spatial coordinates based on the system configuration of the imaging module. Intraoperative spatial information however, requires a tracking and navigation system. TRAINS uses a vision-based system for tracking and navigation purpose. Light emitting fiducial markers are used for the registration of entities in the real world to the interventional plan. Fig. 8 (right) depicts the robotic setup in a porcine surgery.

6. Discussion

The use of the intraoperative visual guidance and AR control interface in surgical procedures provide surgeons with a very exciting viewable integrated information platform. With this platform, the surgeon can concurrently conduct an intraoperative diagnosis, surgical operation and collection of patient's medical information on a single interactive augmented interface. This augmented reality based interactive interface allows surgeons to not only experience a new type of technology that extends their visibility without looking at any other screen or wearing any head-mounted device during the surgery, but also perform the operation with the combination of preoperative and intraoperative medical information. With regards to the surgical robot, not only does it contribute to higher accuracy of the surgical operation and optimizes the procedural flow, it is also easy for this intraoperative AR interface to incorporate the surgical robot assistance into the surgery, which includes the display of the robotic operation inside the patient and interactive control by the surgeons.

Although interactive spatial AR interfaces have been used for some applications such as games and advertisements, the intraoperative visual guidance and interactive AR interface for surgery is still a challenging problem. The reasons for this are as followed. First of all, an accurate display of the human organs and tissues is essential in surgery. The visual corrections, including geometric corrections of a projected virtual organ model, are important steps in constructing the spatial augmented reality environment, especially when projecting on an arbitrary surface. Other than the influence of irregular geometric surfaces, the projection is also affected by dynamic motions in the AR environment such as the patient's aspiration, unexpected surface motions or occlusions etc. Secondly, registration of an AR model with the real organ is especially difficult because of the non-rigid soft tissue. Thirdly, in usability tests with the medical tool, the ablation needle is as assumed to be a rigid needle without bending during the insertion. However, this assumption may not always be true. Therefore, other than vision-based tracking technology, other types of intraoperative feedback such as real-time CT scanning etc. are needed to generate more reliable surgical information. Additionally, in order to realize a dynamic observational perspective from any location around the AR environment, more projectors and cameras are required.

7. Conclusion and future work

The intraoperative visual guidance and control AR interface is an attempt to integrate the preoperative diagnostic information with real-time augmented visual information produced by the patient's reactions, surgeon's decisions, and robotic implementation. This interface provides surgeons with a mean to extend a person's visual limitations during the MIS and to engage interactively during the surgical robot assisted surgery. Augmented reality technology has the potential as a therapeutic intervention which combines the virtual augmented physical model with locally detected real-time medical information including geometric variance and respiration rate. The interface is coupled with the augmented physical model, surgeon's operation, and robotic implementation through vision based tracking and hand gesture recognition.

This intraoperative AR interface will benefit from a stereoscopic vision system with higher accuracy and higher frame rate which plays an important factor in vision based tracking and recognition. While the current tracking algorithm worked satisfactorily at the workstation used for testing, users still had problems with robustness when operating in an environment with a colourful background. In addition, this interface could be expanded to assimilate with more medical devices and equipments such as ultrasound that would integrate more real-time augmented medical information. In this scenario, the interface is a powerful integrated medical AR platform centralized in the network of all the other medical devices and equipment in the operating room.

8. References

Abolhassani, N.; Patel, R. & Moallem, M. (2007). Needle insertion into soft tissue: A survey. *Medical Engineering & Physics*, Vol.29, No.4, pp. 413-431, ISSN 1350-4533.

Akay, M. & Marsh, A. (2001). Neuro orthopedic rehabilitation and disability solutions using virtual reality technology information technologies in medicine. *Rehabilitation and Treatment*, Vol. 168, No. 2, pp.1–18, ISSN 1530-437X.

Anderson, J.H.; Chui, C.K.; Cai, Y.; Wang, Y.P.; Li, Z.R.; Ma, X.; Nowinski, W.L.; Solaiyappan, M.; Murphy, K. & Gailloud, P. (2002). Virtual reality training in interventional radiology: The Johns Hopkins and Kent Ridge Digital Laboratory Experience. *Seminars in Interventional Radiology*, Vol. 19, No. 2, pp. 179-185, ISSN 0739-9529.

Bimber, O. & Raskar, R. (2004). Spatial Augmented Reality: merging real and virtual worlds. ISBN 9781568812304, Wellesley, MA : A K Peters, 2004.

Burdea, G.; Popescu, V.; Hentz, V. & Colbert, K. (2000). Virtual reality-based orthopedic telerehabilitation. *Rehabilitation Engineering, IEEE Transactions*, Vol.8, No.3, pp.430–432, ISSN 1063-6528.

Cai, Y.; Chui, C.K.; Ye, X. & Anderson, J. (2003). VR simulated training for less invasive vascular intervention. *Computers & Graphics*, Vol. 27, No.2, pp. 215-221.

Cakmakci, O. & Rolland, J.(2006). Head-worn displays: a review. *Display Technology*, Vol. 2, No.3, pp.199-216, ISSN 1551-319x.

Chang, S.K.Y.; Hlaing, W.W.; Yang, L., & Chui, C.K. (2011). Current technology in navigation and robotics for liver tumours ablation. *Ann Acad Med Singapore*, Vol.40, No.5, pp.231-236, May, 2011.

Choi, D.; Lim, H.K.; Kim, S.H.; Lee, W.J.; Jang, H.J. & Lee, J.Y. (2000). Hepatocellular carcinoma treated with percutaneous radio-frequency ablation: usefulness of power doppler us with a microbubble contrast agent in evaluating therapeutic response. *Preliminary Results1. Radiology*, Vol. 217, No.2, pp.558-563.

Chui, C.K.; Ong, JSK.; Lian, Z.Y.; Yan, C.H.; Wang, Z.; Ong, SH.; Teo, JCM.; Zhang, J.; Wang, SC.; Wong, HK.; Teo, C.L. & Teoh, S. H. (2006) Haptics in computer mediated simulation: training in vertebroplasty surgery. *Simulation & Gaming*, Vol. 47, No. 4, pp. 438-451, ISSN 1552-826X.

Devernay, F.; Mourgues, F.& Coste-Maniere, E. (2001). Towards endoscopic augmented reality for robotically assisted minimally invasive cardiac surgery. *Proceedings of the International Workshop on Medical Imaging and Augmented Reality (MIAR '01)*, pp.16-20, ISBN 0-7695-1113-9, Shatin, N.T., Hong Kong, Jun. 2001.

Dutkiewicz, P.; Kielczewski, M. & Kowalski, M. (2004). Visual tracking of surgical tools for laparoscopic surgery. *Proceedings of the Fourth International Workshop on Robot Motion and Control*, pp.23-28 , ISBN 83-7143-272-0, Zielona Gora Univ., Poland, June, 2004.

Felfoul, O.; Mathieu, J.-B.; Beaudoin, G.; Martel, S. (2008). In vivo mr-tracking based on magnetic signature selective excitation. *IEEE Transactions on Medical Imaging*, Vol.27 , No.1, pp. 28 – 35, ISSN 0278-0062.

Fu, K.S. (1987). Robotics: control, sensing, vision, and intelligence, Vol. 280227, McGraw-Hill, New York, 1987.

Fujii, K.; Grossberg, M.D. & Nayar, S.K. (2005). A projector-camera system with real-time photometric adaptation for dynamic environments. *Computer Vision and Pattern Recognition*, Vol. 2, pp.1180, ISSN 1063-6919.

Goldberg, S.N.; Gazelle, G.S.; Solbiati, L.; Livraghi, T.; Tanabe, K.K. & Hahn, P.F.(1998). Ablation of liver tumors using percutaneous RF therapy. *AJR Am J Roentgenol*, Vol. 170, No.4, pp.1023-1028 , ISSN 1023-1028.

Grimson, W.E.L.; L. T.; Wells, W.M.; Ettinger, G.J.; White, S.J. & Kikinis, R. (1996). An automatic registration method for frameless stereotaxy, image guided surgery, and enhance reality visualization. *IEEE Transactions on Medical Imaging*, (April 1996), Vol. 15, No. 2, pp.129-140. , ISSN 0278-0062.

Guthart, G.S. & Salisbury, J.K.Jr. (2000). The intuitive™ telesurgery system: Overview and application, *Robotics and Automation*, pp.618-621, ISBN 0-7803-5886-4, San Francisco, CA , USA, Apr.2000.

Heng, P.A.; Cheng, C.Y.; Wong, T.T; Xu, Y.; Chui, Y.P.; Chan, K.M. & Tso, S.K. (2004). A virtual-reality training system for knee arthroscopic surgery. *Information Technology in Biomedicine, IEEE Transactions*, Vol. 8, No.2, pp. 217-227, ISSN 1089-7771.

Hoppe, H.; Eggers, G.; Heurich, T.; Raczkowsky, J.; Marmulla, R.; Worn, H.; Hassfeld, S. & Moctezuma, J.L. (2003). Projector-based visualization for intraoperative navigation: first clinical results. *Proceedings of the 17th International Congress and Exhibition*, pp.771, ISBN 0-444-51731-6, London, Jun. 2003.

Hyosig, K. & Wen, J.T. (2001). Robotic assistants aid surgeons during minimally invasive procedures. *Engineering in Medicine and Biology Magazine*, IEEE, Vol.20, No.1, pp.94-104, ISSN 0739-5175.

Konishia K.; Hashizumeb M.; Nakamotod M.; Kakejib Y.; Yoshinoc I.; Taketomic A.; Satod Y.; Tamurad S. & Maehara Y. (2005). Augmented reality navigation system for endoscopic surgery based on three-dimensional ultrasound and computed tomography: Application to 20 clinical cases. *CARS 2005: Computer Assisted Radiology and Surgery*, Vol. 1281, pp. 537-542. Berlin, Germany, Jun. 2005.

Kuo, C.H. & Dai, J.S. (2009). Robotics for minimally invasive surgery: a historical review from the perspective of kinematics. *International Symposium on History of Machines and Mechanisms*, ISBN 978-1-4020-9484-2, pp.337-354.

Kuo, R.L.; Delvecchio, F.C.& Preminger, G.M. (2001). Virtual Reality: Current Urologic Applications and Future Developments. *Journal of Endourology*, Vol. 15, No. 1, pp. 117-122, ISSN 0892-7790.

Lee, S.L.; Mirna, L.; Vitiello, V.; Giannarou, S.; Kwok, K.W.; Visentini-Scarzanella, M. & Yang, G.Z. (2010). From medical images to minimally invasive intervention: Computer assistance for robotic surger. *Computerized Medical Imaging and Graphics*, Vol. 34, No. 1, pp. 33-45, ISSN .

Liao, H; Inomata, T; Sakuma, I & Dohi, T (2010). Three-dimensional augmented reality for mri-guided surgery using integral videography auto stereoscopic-image overlay. *IEEE Transactions on Biomedical Engineering*, Vol.57, No.6, pp.1476-1486, ISSN 15582531.

Ling, Y.; Zhang, J. & Xing, J. (2010). Video object tracking based on position prediction guide CAMSHIFT. *Proceeding of Advanced Computer Theory and Engineering (ICACTE)*, pp. V1-159 - V1-164, ISBN 978-1-4244-6539-2, Chengdu, China, Aug. 2010.

Mahmoudi, F.& Parviz, M. (2006). Visual hand tracking algorithms. *Proc. of GMAI 2006, IEEE Computer Society press*, ISBN 0-7695-2604-7, pp.228–232, London, UK, July 2006.

Massoptier, L. & Casciaro, S. (2008). A new fully automatic and robust algorithm for fast segmentation of liver tissue and tumors from CT scans. *European Radiology*, Vol.18, No.8, pp.1658-1665, ISSN 1432-1084.

Milgram, P.; Takemura, H.; Utsumi, A.; & Kishino, F. (1994). Augmentedreality:a class of displays on the reality-virtuality continuum in proc. *Telemanipulator Telepresence Technology*, Vol. 2351, pp.282–292.

Mustafa, B. & Kalajdziski, S. (2007). Spherical mapping based descriptors for 3D object matching. *The International Conference on Computer as a Tool*, pp. 361-368, ISBN 978-1-4244-0813-9, Warsaw, Poland, Sept. 2007.

Navab, N.; Traub, J.; Sielhorst, T.; Feuerstein, M. & Bichlmeier, C. (2007). Action- and workflow-driven augmented reality for computer-aided medical procedure. *Computer Graphics and Applications*, Vol.27, No.5, pp. 10–14, ISSN 0272-1716.

Nayar, S.K.; Peri, H.; Grossberg, M.D. & Belhumeur, P.N. (2003). A Projection System with Radiometric Compensation for Screen Imperfections. *Proceeding of IEEE Int'l Workshop Projector-Camera Systems*, pp.97-108 , ISBN 1077-2626, Nov.2007.

Pablo L.; Wajid A.; Alicia C.; Jordi C.; Jerome D.; Ole J.E.; Adinda F.; Hugo F.; Denis K.; Edvard N.; Eigil S.; Patricia S.G.; Francisco M.S.M.; Dieter S.; Mauro S.; Thomas S.; Jos V.S. & Enrique J.G. (2010). Augmented reality for minimally invasive surgery: overview and some recent advances. *Augmented Reality*, pp.1-26, In: InTech, Available from: http://www.intechopen.com/articles/show/title/augmented-reality-for-minimally-invasive-surgery-overview-and-some-recent-advances.

Pearson, A.M.; Gallagher, A. G.; Rosser, J. C.; & Satava, R. M. (2002). Evaluation of structured and quantitative training methods for teaching intracorporeal knot tying. *Surgical Endoscopy*, Vol. 16, No. 1, pp.130–137, ISSN 1432-2218.

Puangmali, P.; Althoefer, K.; Seneviratne, L.D.; Murphy, D. & Dasgupta, P. (2008). State-of-the-art in force and tactile sensing for minimally invasive surgery. *Sensors Journal*, Vol. 8 , No. 4, pp. 371 - 381, ISSN 1530-437X.

Raskar, R.; Welch, G. & Low, K.L. (2001). Shader Lamps: Animating Real Objects With Image-Based Illumination. *Eurographics Workshop on Rendering Techniques*, ISBN 3-211-83709-4, London, Jun.2001.

Rosen, J.M.; Soltanian, H.; Redett, R.J. & Laub, D.R. (1996). Evolution of virtual reality [Medicine] *Engineering in Medicine and Biology Magazine*, Vol.15 , No.2, pp. 16-22, ISSN 0739-5175.

Seo, B.K.; Lee, M.H.; Park, H.; Park, J.I. & Kim, Y.S. (2007). Direct-projected ar based interactive user interface for medical surgery. *Artificial Reality and Telexistence*, ISBN 0-7695-3056-7, Esbjerg, Jylland, Nov.2007.

Stoianovici, D.; Whitcomb, L.; Anderson, J.; Taylor, R. & Kavoussi, L. (1998). A modular surgical robotic system for image guided percutaneous procedures. *Medical Image Computing and Computer-Assisted Interventation – MICCAI'98*, pp.404-410, ISBN 978-3-540-65136-9, Chicago, USA, October 1998.

Taylor, R.H. & Stoianovici, D. (2003). Medical robotics in computer-integrated surgery. *IEEE Transactions on Robotics and Automation*, Vol. 19, No.5, pp.765-781, ISSN 1042-296X.

Taylor, R.H. (2008). Medical robotics and computer-integrated surgery. *32nd Annual IEEE International Computer Software and Applications*, pp.1-1, ISBN 978-0-7695-3262-2, Turku, Finland, July-August 2008.

Teber, D.; Baumhauer, M.; Simpfendoerfer, T.; Hruza, M.; Klein, J. & Rassweiler, J. (2009). Augmented reality a new tool to improve surgical accuracy during laparoscopic partial nephrectomy. *European Urology Supplements*, Vol. 7, No. 3, (March 2008), pp. 258, ISSN 1569-9056.

Thoranaghatte, R.U.; Giraldez, J.G. & Zheng, G. (2008).Landmark based augmented reality endoscope system for sinus and skull-base surgeries. *Engineering in Medicine and Biology Society*, 2008, ISBN 978-1-4244-1814-5, Vancouver, BC, Aug.2008.

Uranues, S.; Maechler, H.; Bergmann, P.; Huber, S.; Hoebarth, G.; Pfeifer, J.; Rigler, B.; Tscheliessnigg, K.H. & Mischinger, H.J (2002). Early experience with telemanipulative abdominal and cardiac surgery with the Zeus™ Robotic System. *European Surgery*, Vol. 34, No. 3, pp. 190–193, ISSN 1682-4016.

Wang, Y.P.; Chui, C.K.; Lim, H.L.; Cai, Y. & Mak, K.H. (1999). Real-time interactive simulator for percutaneous coronary revascularization procedures. *Computer Aided Surgery*, Vol. 3, No. 5, 1999, ISSN 1097-0150.

Watterson, J.D; Beiko, D.T.; Kuan, J.K.; & Denstedt, J.D. (2002). Randomized prospective blinded study validating acquisition of ureteroscopy skills using computer based virtual reality endourological simulator. *International braz j urol official journal of the Brazilian Society of Urology*, Vol.168, No.5, pp.1928–1932, ISSN 00225347.

Wen, R.; Yang, L.; Chui, C.K.; Lim, K.B. & Chang, S. (2010). Intraoperative visual guidance and control interface for augmented reality robotic surgery. *IEEE International Conference on Control and Automation*, pp.947-952, ISBN 978-1-4244-5195-1, Xiamen, China, Jun. 2010.

Xia, J.; Ip, H.H.S.; Samman, N.; Wong, H.T.F.; Gateno, J.; Wang, Dongfeng; Yeung, R.W.K.; Kot, C.S.B. & Tideman, H. (2001). Three-dimensional virtual-reality surgical planning and soft-tissue prediction for orthognathic surgery. *Information Technology in Biomedicine, IEEE Transactions*, Vol. 5, No. 2, pp. 97- 107, ISSN 1089-7771.

Yang, L.; Chui, C.K. & Chang, S. (2009). Design and Development of an Augmented Reality Robotic System for Large Tumor Ablation. *International Journal of Virtual Reality*, Vol. 8, No.1, pp.27-35, ISSN 1741-1882.

Yang, L.; Wen, R.; Qin, J.; Chui, C.K.; Lim, K.B. & Chang, S.K.Y. (2010). A robotic system for overlapping radiofrequency ablation in large tumor treatment. *IEEE/ASME Transactions on Mechatronics*, Vol. 15, No. 6, pp.887-897, ISSN 1083-4435.

Part 3

Novel AR Applications in Daily Living and Learning

11

Augmented Reality Platform for Collaborative E-Maintenance Systems

Samir Benbelkacem[1], Nadia Zenati-Henda[1], Fayçal Zerarga[1], Abdelkader Bellarbi[1], Mahmoud Belhocine[1], Salim Malek[1] and Mohamed Tadjine[2]
[1]*Development Centre of Advanced Technologies*
[2]*Polytechnic National School*
Algeria

1. Introduction

One of the recent design goals in Human-Computer Interaction is the extension of the sensory-motor capabilities of computer systems enabling a combination of the real and the virtual in order to assist the user in performing his task in a physical setting. Such systems are called Augmented Reality (short: AR). The growing interest of designers for this paradigm is due to the dual need of users to benefit from computers and interact with the real world.

AR is a new interactive approach, where virtual objects (such as texts, 2D images and 3D models) are added to real scenes in real time by using sensing and visualization technology. The computer generated digital information is overlaid on the user's physical environment so that he can perceive currently important information where needed.

Augmented Reality (AR) is derived from Virtual Reality (VR) in which the user is completely immersed in an artificial world. In VR systems, there is no way for the user to interact with objects in the real world. Using AR technology, users can thus interact with mixed virtual and real worlds in a natural way (Zhong & Boulanger, 2002).

AR research is of major interest in several domains. Azuma gives a description of various applications of AR systems in (Azuma, 1997) including medical visualisation, manufacturing and repair, robot path planning, entertainment and military aircraft.

AR application is an excellent domain for maintenance tasks in industrial environment (Changzhi et al, 2006). AR allows the user to see virtual objects increased upon real world scenes through display devices such as PCs, Laptops, Pc-Pockets, Video-projectors or Head Mounted Displays (HMD). The technician can interact with the virtual world and may dispose of additional information in various forms; for instance additional maintenance tasks instructions may be given in the form of texts, images, video or audio augmentations.

Several maintenance platforms based on AR have been developed. ARVIKA (Marsot et al., 2009) introduces AR in the life cycle of industrial products, AMRA implements a mobile AR system in an industrial setting (Didier & Roussel, 2005), STARMATE (Schwald et al., 2001) assists the operator during maintenance tasks on complex mechanical systems, ULTRA (Riess & Stricker, 2006) has developed a software architecture that enables production of augmented reality manuals and on-site support of (mobile) maintenance workers. Also, A prototype of automobile maintenance (BMW) based on AR are presented in (Platonov et al., 2006) using see through system. More recently, the project ARMAR (Henderson et al., 2010) has been interested in exploring the extent to which AR can increase the productivity, the precision and safety of maintenance personnel.

These platforms provide many advantages for repair task improvement, but not sufficiently. In some cases, technicians cannot repair equipments even with AR means. This occurs when a new failure appears, in which case, the corresponding scenario does not exist in the database. The main solution is to contact remote experts (with required qualification level) to provide maintenance procedures through collaboration with the field technician.

In recent years, systems supporting remote collaborative work for industrial maintenance have appeared. But, increasing importance is given more to collaborative principles (Bangemann et al., 2006) rather than maintenance and AR aspects (Bottecchia et al., 2010).

In (Zhong & Boulanger, 2002) a prototype is presented in which operators equipped with display devices are supervised by an expert. This latter can only provide audio indications. Sakata and Kurata (Sakata et al., 2003), (Kurata et al., 2004) developed the Wearable Active Camera/Laser (WACL) which allows the remote instructor not only to independently look into the worker's task space, but also to point to real objects in the task space with the laser spot (Alem et al., 2011). In (Bottecchia et al., 2010) a maintenance collaborative system entitled CAMEKA is described, which enables the expert to give visual indications to an operator with an AR display device fitted with a camera. What the camera sees is sent to the expert who can "capture" an image from the video flow, add notes, then send back the enriched image to the operator's display device.

Existing AR systems are based on a single technician who repairs a single machine. Others are based on a local collaboration through available on-site experts. This situation does not guarantee direct task assistance. In some cases, the experts are not available while in others, the existing local experts lack sufficient competence. It, then, is necessary to call onto a remote expertise for the technician's performances improvement. Also, the capitalization of expert's know-how is guaranteed.

Our area of interest is the establishment of a distributed platform allowing collaboration between technicians and remote experts based on AR benefits. Two main aspects are studied and developed in our case. The first aspect addresses a new collaboration strategy based on Service Oriented Architecture (SOA) which offers efficient solutions in terms of information transfer and exchange, data heterogeneous management, etc. The second aspect ensures the virtual objects (maintenance procedures) transfer from the remote expert in real time. The result is a visual space shared by the technician and the remote expert.

The content of this chapter is organised as follows. In section 2, a collaborative platform supporting AR interaction is presented. Section 3 describes a global industrial maintenance scenario. Implementation and results are presented in section 4. Finally, in the last section, a conclusion and perspectives are given.

2. E-maintenance platform based on augmented reality concept

In this section, the collaborative platform supporting AR interaction is built. The expert should be able to insert augmentation into video stream to increase the operator's view in real time, so that he understands the tasks to be achieved.

To address this need, we have developed concepts concerning the data transfer (augmented 2D/3D objects) and the remote collaboration.

2.1 Tracking system and virtual objects transfer

Tracking is a very important research subject in the field of augmented reality (Fiala, 2004), (Comport et al., 2005), and the vision-based tracking method is usually appropriate. Tracking methods use cameras that capture real scene as sensing devices. So, to apply AR to maintenance support, the positions and orientations of users in real time must be measured with high accuracy. Among the tracking technologies proposed in previous studies (Comport et al., 2005), marker-based tracking, which uses image processing technique to measure the relative position and orientation between a camera and markers (transformation matrix marker/camera), seems to be appropriate to industrial maintenance context. In fact, the most popular tracking method, which uses square markers, is ARToolkit (Kato & Billinghurst, 1999).

ARToolkit (Augmented Reality Toolkit) is an open-source software library used to develop augmented reality applications. It was developed by "The Human Interface Technology Laboratory" (HIT Lab) at Washington University. It uses vision techniques to calculate position and orientation of the camera relative to markers. The programmer can use this information to draw the 3D object and to insert it correctly in the real scene.

ARToolkit guarantees the virtual object tracking when the camera (or user) changes position. The "ARToolkit" library has several types of markers (Kato & Billinghurst, 1999) (see Fig. 1).

Fig. 1. Examples of ARToolkit's markers.

The markers are in a black square form with a code inside. This marker is a simple form that can easily be identified for the insertion of a virtual object. The position and orientation of the camera can be calculated by identifying the markers in a video stream.

However, like other vision-based tracking, the tracking with ARToolkit suffers from the lack of robustness. In this case, our team proposes (Bellarbi et al., 2010(b)) a new version of ARToolkit called i-ARToolkit (improved ARToolkit) that gives solutions to ARToolkit problems.

The first problem of ARToolkit is the use of static thresholding method that cannot adapt to changing environmental parameters (brightness level). i-ARToolkit applies dynamic thresholding approach to guarantee markers recognition even if environmental properties change.

The second problem concerns the virtual objects instability in the real scene. This is due to the uncertainty of the transformation matrix. i-Artoolkit proposes an approach which takes into account this uncertainty.

In summary, i-ARToolkit tracking system performs the following steps (Bellarbi et al., 2010(b)):

Step1: Open a video stream

Step2: For each captured image:

2.1 Calculate the optimal threshold value from the captured image using Otsu method (Otsu, 1979).
2.2 Transform the captured image to a binary image using the calculated threshold value.
2.3 Detect black squares markers in the binary image.
2.4 Calculate the camera's position and orientation (calculate the transformation matrix).
2.5 Apply the stabilization algorithm (Bellarbi et al., 2010(a)).
2.6 Superimpose the virtual objects upon the captured image (using the calculated transformation matrix).

Another problem usually appears when applying AR in maintenance; it is the non-detection of markers when the technician works in a large space. This occurs when the camera is far from the marker. Fig. 2 shows an estimation of the maximum detection distance of i-ARToolkit markers.

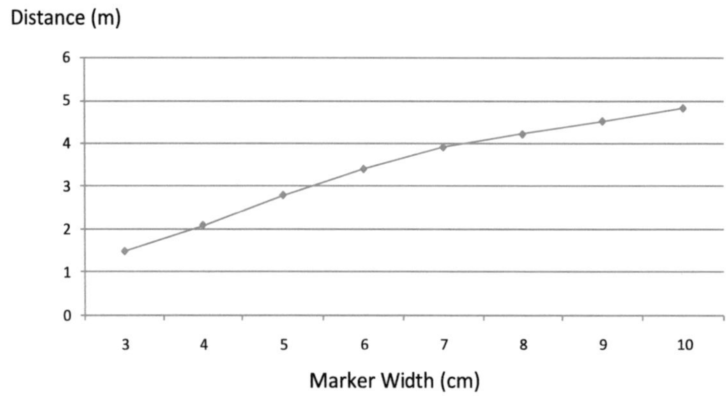

Fig. 2. Detection distance vs marker width

The proposed solution, inspired from (Hirotake et al., 2010), is to establish a relationship between a number of detected markers in the captured image and the distance between the camera and the markers.

Fig. 3.a shows that the detected markers become very numerous and the size of each marker on the image becomes very small when the distance between the camera and the markers is long. It therefore becomes difficult to calculate the transformation matrix for each marker. The markers size on the image is too small. In this case, a global transformation matrix is calculated to encompass the transformation matrices of the detected markers. This principle enhances the stability of inserted object.

On the other hand, as shown in Fig. 3.b, when the distance between the camera and the markers is short, the number of the detected markers becomes small and the markers sizes on the image become very large. In this case, it becomes possible to obtain more stable transformation matrix since the marker size on the captured image is sufficiently large.

Once the transformation matrix between the marker and the camera is calculated, augmented objects which represent maintenance procedures are easily inserted.

a. Image captured by a camera at a long distance.

b. Image captured by a camera at a short distance.

Fig. 3. Example of car engine with markers

The configuration given in Fig.3 allows the technician to view maintenance scenarios even if he changes position. A number of markers attached to preregistered locations in the area of a repair could serve as anchor points for labels, instructions, and other virtual content. In most cases, maintenance units could install these markers permanently without interfering with system components. For cases when this was not possible, technician could affix temporary markers to predetermined mount points prior to a repair sequence.

In most cases, the technician has difficulties to place the markers in adequate and precise position. For that, it is recommended to choose particular preregistered locations (example: corners) to perform easily markers placement.

To resolve the placement's marker problem, the best solution is to replace printed markers with natural features (such as visually unique parts of an engine), making possible markerless tracking (Bleser et al., 2005), (Comport et al., 2005). In our future work we plan to develop a markerless based method for maintenance field.

2.1.1 Virtual objects transfer

When a technician performs a difficult task, he can be assisted by a remote expert. The difficulty lays in how to send the augmented scene from remote the expert to the technician's visual scene. For this reason, two approaches are proposed. The first one consists in computing the technician's position (transformation matrix marker/camera) from the captured images. The captured images and the transformation matrix are both transmitted to the remote expert (see Fig. 4).

As observed in the above figure (Fig. 5), the technician just sends the captured images. The expert should have a tracking system to detect the makers and to calculate the transformation matrix. The remote expert's tracking system takes an additional time to perform the different operations. In addition, to calculate the transformation matrix, the images must be sent to the remote expert without being compressed. The markers detection in the compressed images gives poor results.

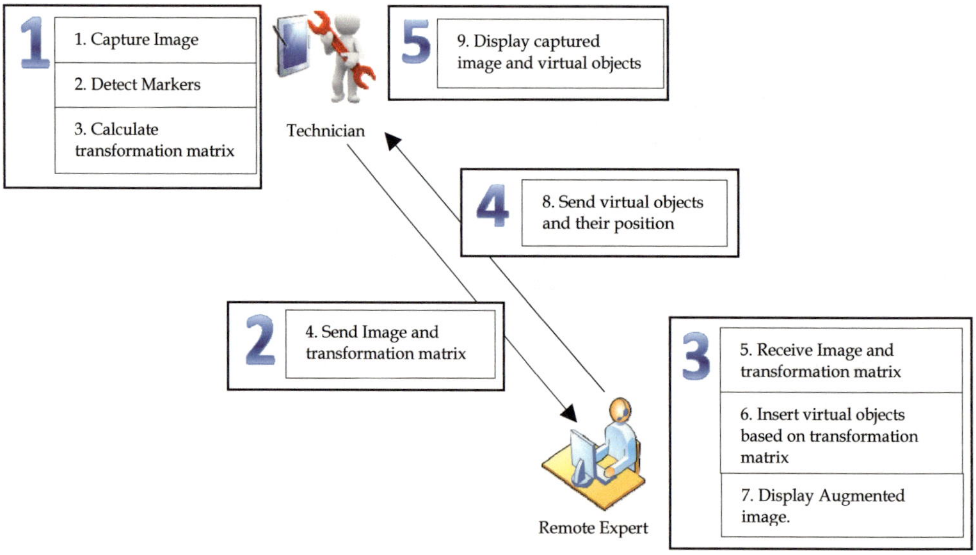

Fig. 4. Essential steps of the first method.

The second approach consists in sending the captured images alone, from the technician to the remote expert. Besides the technician, the transformation matrix is also computed at the remote expert, (see Fig. 5).

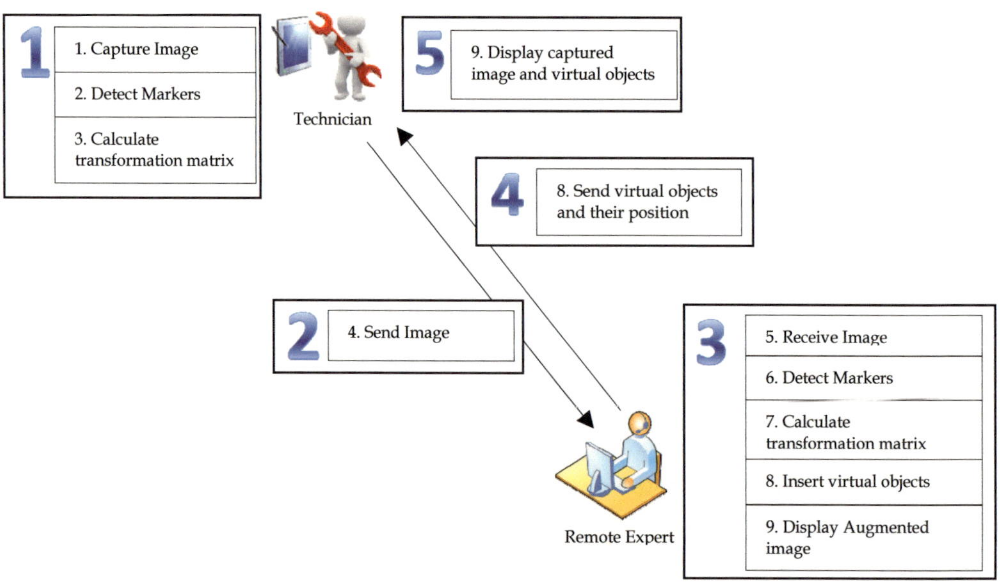

Fig. 5. Essential steps of the second method.

The first method gives better results since the markers detection is performed at the technician's device. The transformation matrix and the images are transferred to the remote expert's computer. With this approach the expert does not need a tracking system to calculate the required parameters. Also, the images can be sent to the remote expert in compressed form. So, the computing time is reduced.

According to this comparison, the first method is adopted to guarantee the best data exchange between the actors. The next section gives more details about the data exchange principle in a collaborative context.

2.2 Remote collaboration

In this section, our aim is to develop approaches for remote collaboration based essentially on the Web Services concept. In this case, we are interested in developing a communication module (for chat, file, image and augmented video transfer) to take into account the heterogeneity problem between different hardware (Pc-Pocket and PC-Tablet) and software platforms (operating systems, programming languages...). The use of Web Services ensures the interoperability between the applications of different actors.

2.2.1 Distributed and mobile e-maintenance platform

When the technician lacks competence to repair broken down equipment he contacts a remote expert to obtain appropriate solutions. A distributed platform is then required to facilitate this collaboration.

A distributed system is a set of interconnected devices which collaborate to perform a set of tasks. The tasks are called by a remote services exposed in a web server. Based on Web Services, this system can manage heterogeneous applications geographically dispersed.

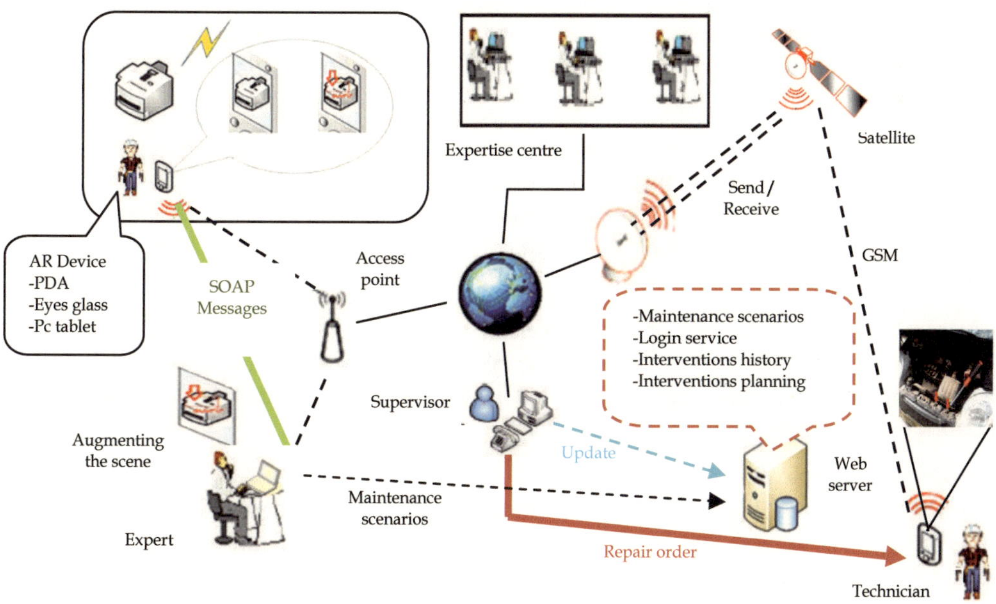

Fig. 6. ARIMA platform configuration.

In order to build infrastructure for data exchange via services, we adopt "SOA" (Service Oriented Architecture) concept which is a paradigm that allows organizing and exploiting distributed capabilities that may be under the control of different ownership domains (Nickul, 2007). Based on this architecture, we have developed our platform named ARIMA (Augmented Reality and Image processing in Maintenance Application).

Fig.6 shows a distributed and mobile platform allowing a dialogue between technicians using mobile devices (such as PDA, Pc-tablet, eye glass...) and remote experts.

2.2.2 Web services for e-maintenance

The interaction between actors (experts and technicians) requires communication platforms. Despite the advantages of the existing technologies, it cannot effectively manage the heterogeneous running environment especially when using various communication tools such as Pc-Pocket, Pc-Tablet, HMD and others. The Web Service presents efficient solution to resolve this problem. The main role is to facilitate data transfer between actors using the Internet network.

A Web Service is a software module which performs a set of discrete tasks. It is a set of services which can be invoked through a network, especially the World Wide Web, accessible via standard Internet protocols (Booth et al., 2004). A Web Service has an interface described in a WSDL (Web Service Description Language) format which exposes the method to be invoked by a web server (binding, port, services). Other systems interact with the Web Service by sending SOAP (Simple Object Access Protocol) messages to the web methods. These messages use HTTP with an XML serialization in conjunction with other Web-related standards. In other words, a Web Service is a set of related application methods that can be remotely accessed through a network (such as a corporate Intranet or Internet itself). WDSL documents are indexed in searchable Universal Description Discovery and Integration (UDDI) Business Registries, so that developers and applications can locate the Web Services.

Web Services are both characterized by the reuse facilitation. They are independent from used platforms (Windows, UNIX...) and programming languages (C #, JAVA, VB...). This interoperability form makes Web Services one of the most used technologies to design distributed applications (Leymann, 2003). In our case, Web Services principle is adopted to establish a distributed mobile maintenance platform.

As a most important concept of Web Services, we are interested to use WCF (Windows Communication Foundation). It is a new feature of Dot NET Framework version. It supports the sending of HTTP data. HTTP protocol facilitates the communication in the Internet network (Scott, 2007).

The actors consume Web Services by sending SOAP file. The services are described in a WSDL file and distributed through a UDDI registry. This allows easy collaboration between actors to resolve several technicians' task. The actors communicate by exchanging SOAP files through a service provider in order to run web methods. These web methods are described in WSDL file which is hosted in the service broker. Fig. 7 shows an example of a Web Service requested by two experts and one technician in a collaboration context.

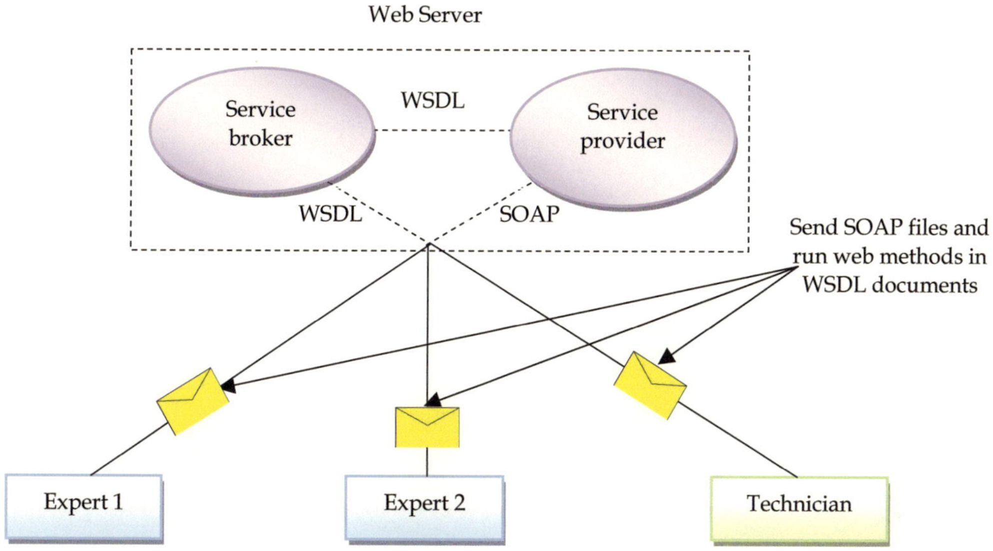

Fig. 7. Collaboration principle between actors.

2.3 Internal operation of ARIMA platform

Initially, the technician receives an alarm about failed equipment. He proceeds to a first analysis and tries to formulate a diagnosis. When he is unable to repair, he contacts a remote expert using internet network. The essential aspect is to guarantee the reliable data exchange using SOAP file through an access point in Internet network.

The data transfer process is described as follows (see Fig 8): the technician captures a video of failure's location. For every captured frame, a tracking system detects the markers and calculates a transformation matrix. Both captured video and transformation matrix are transmitted to the remote expert. The expert adds virtual objects (scenarios) according to the scene. The inserted virtual objects and their positions are sent to the technician. The virtual objects are received and displayed according to their positions affected by the remote expert.

The data transfer is based on a client/server architecture. Each user must authenticate to the system. For that, the user runs a login method "login (username, password)". The data is encapsulated in a SOAP messages. The server checks the username and the password in the database and sends the answer to the user. For video transfer, the technician runs the web method "send(image, transformation matrix)" to send the captured frame and the calculated transformation matrix to the web server. The expert performs the web method "receive(image, markers)" to retrieve the captured frame and the transformation matrix. Then, he adds augmentations. The expert returns the result to the technician by running the method "sendObject(objectPostion, Object)". The technician runs the web method receiveObject "(objectPostion, Object)" to receive and displays the virtual objects (see Fig. 8).

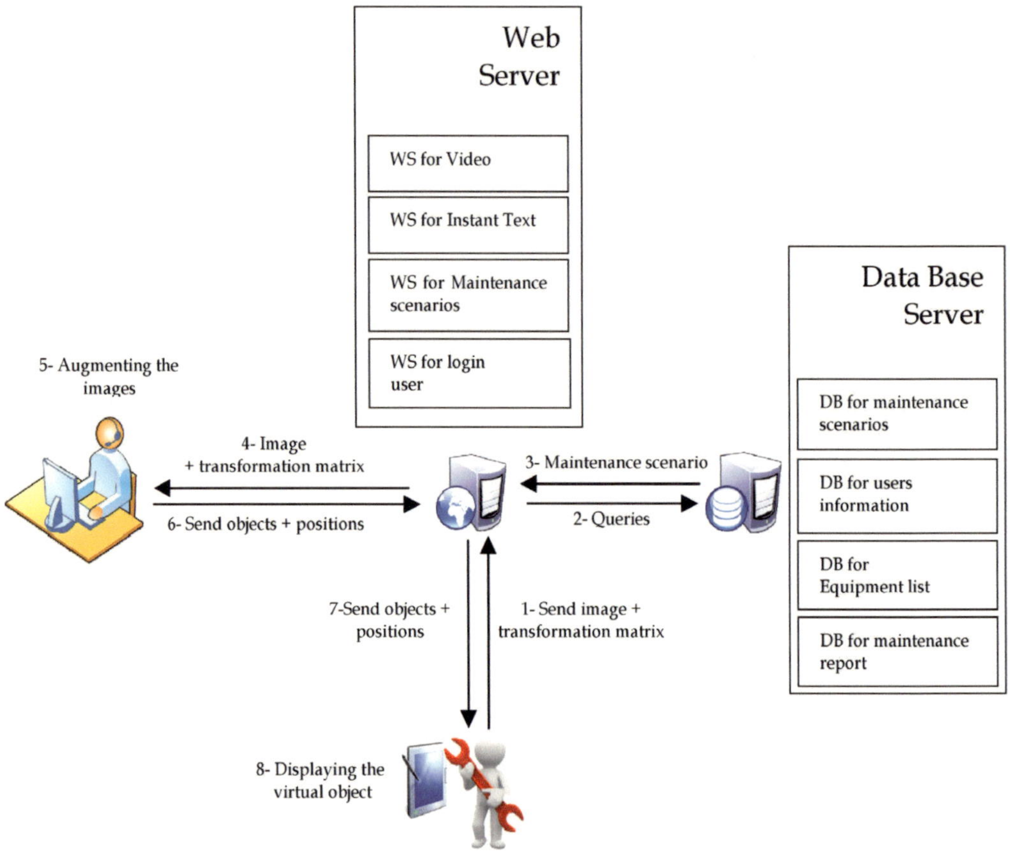

Fig. 8. Collaboration between expert and technician.

3. Global industrial scenario

ARIMA platform operation is based on a set of scenarios which are given as follows:

First, the supervisor (or team leader) sends the repair order to the technician who checks his schedule.

When the failure is identified, a maintenance scenario is then displayed in "augmented" form (see table 1) through the technician's output device.

As for the technician, due to the lack of competence, he collaborates with a remote expert. The server establishes a link between the expert and the technician. A dialogue is then performed between the two actors in order to identify the failure. To obtain more information, the expert can request documentation and/or the previous maintenance reports. Once the failure is analysed, the expert sends the augmented maintenance procedure to the technician's display device.

When the intervention is achieved, the technician fills out a maintenance report which contains all the information pertaining to the failure and the intervention procedure. This report is transmitted to the supervisor (for validation) and then stored in the interventions history database.

Augmentation	Function
Texts	Indicates the components name or the maintenance scenarios
Pointing arrows	Indicates the components or how to execute the maintenance scenario
Tools	Shows the tool type to perform the operation
Sound	Guides the technician through voice indications

Table 1. Types of augmentations.

4. Implementation and results

In this section, a maintenance application using ARIMA platform is implemented. Our tests are performed on a car engine (see Fig. 9).

Fig. 9. Example of equipment (car engine).

The technician observes that the engine has failed, but he cannot identify the problem. So, he contacts a remote expert in order to perform a detailed diagnosis. The two actors collaborate by exchanging data: chat, files, images and videos.

In our case, two failure types are treated. So, two maintenance scenarios are proposed. For the first failure, the collaboration is essentially based on a video exchange data. This requires the use of i-Artoolkit tracking system. For the second failure, we use images for exchange data (no video transfer). In this case, the tracking system is not necessary.

First case study: the engine makes much noise

The technician uses his Pc-Tablet, captures the video scene and sends it to the expert. He indicates, by chat, that the engine makes much noise. The expert views the video scene and proposes a maintenance procedure (check the oil level). The expert uses the augmentation editor to insert corresponding 3D augmentations (text and arrows) in the viewed scene. The augmented video is then transmitted to the technician (see Fig. 10). The collaboration continues until the engine is repaired.

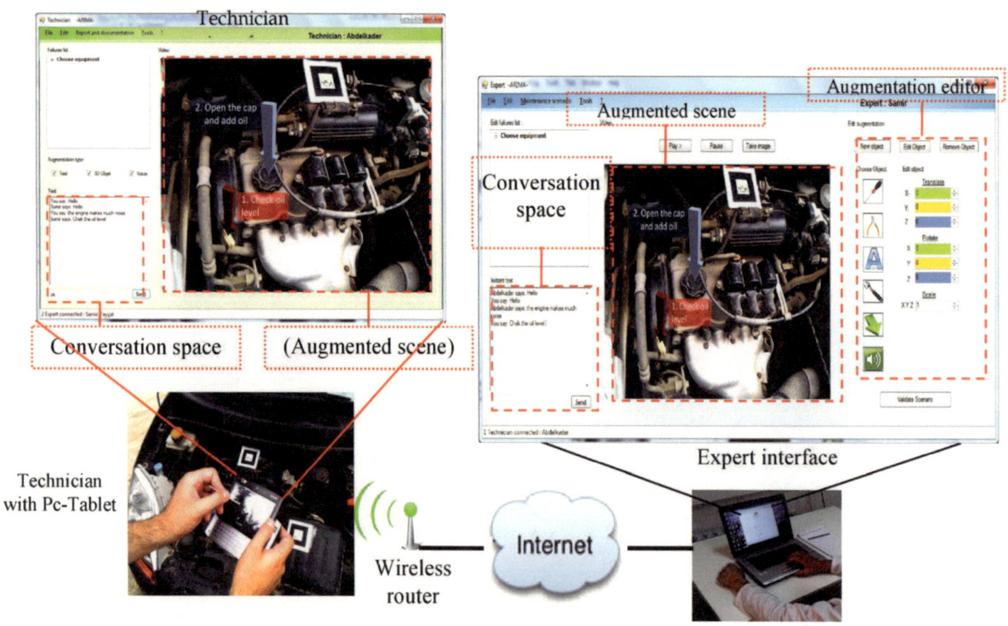

Fig. 10. Example of maintenance collaboration (first case study).

Second case study: the engine overheats

Using a Pc-Pocket, the technician captures an image (photo) of the scene (failure's location), and sends it to the expert. The failure concerns the engine temperature. Besides the chat, the expert uses a simple editor to insert 2D augmentations (screwdriver and arrows) that show the maintenance procedure (check the radiator) (see Fig. 11). The enhanced image is transmitted to the technician's Pc-Pocket.

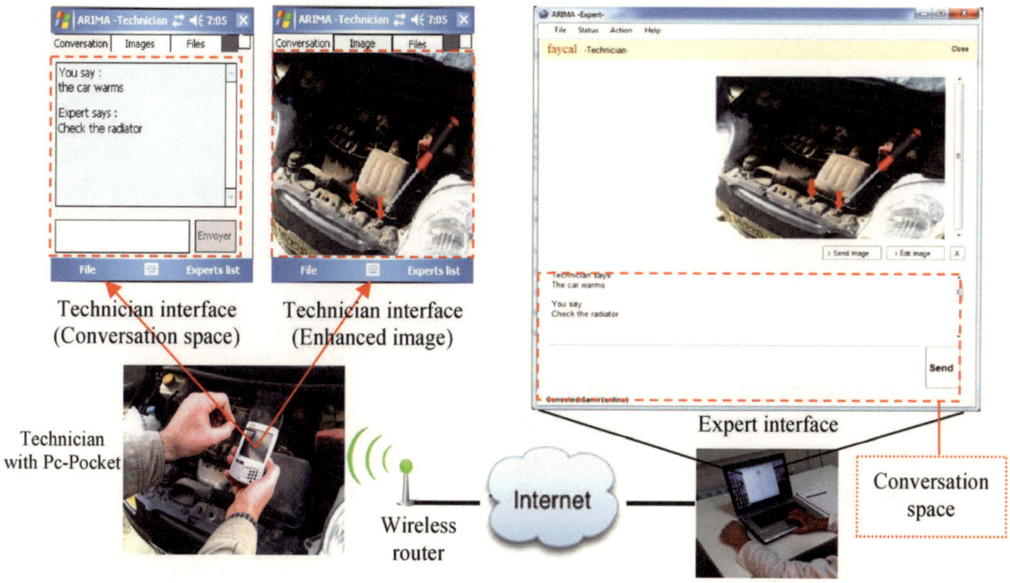

Fig. 11. Example of maintenance collaboration (second case study).

For hardware environment, technicians use a Pc-Pocket (HP, Windows mobile 5 with a video camera and internet connection) or a Pc-Tablet (Sony VAIO UX 280P, Windows XP, video camera and internet connection). Remote experts use a Laptop (Dell, Windows XP, Wi-Fi and camera). The collaboration is performed through access points which support wireless 802.11.

5. Conclusion

An AR e-maintenance platform design is presented in this paper. The aim is to help a technician during his intervention. As a result, we are focused on synchronous and remote collaboration between technicians and experts to complete maintenance and repair tasks by giving augmented information on the user's field of view.

Two principal concepts are treated and developed: remote collaboration based on Web Services and virtual objects transfer. The adopted strategy allows the technician to collaborate easily with a remote expert. Also, he can receive the augmented 3D scene in real time even if he moves.

This platform is applied in the case of a car engine repair. The maintenance operation is performed by a technician who collaborates with a distant expert to obtain maintenance scenarios displayed on the user's viewed scene. The results show the benefits of remote collaboration and AR for maintenance assistance (security, flexibility, saving time ...).

For future work, we aim to improve the proposed prototype in various ways. The user and interaction method need enhancement to make visualisation and manipulation of graphical objects easier. Also, the user's equipment weight can be reduced by using HMD. Moreover, sensors network installation is necessary to provide the equipment's state.

6. References

Alem, L., Tecchia, F. and Huang, W. (2011). ReMoTe: A tele-assistance system for maintenance operators in mines. *Proceedings of 11th Underground Coal Operators Conference (COAL2011)*. Wollongong University.

Azuma, R. T. (1997). A Survey of Augmented Reality. *Presence: Teleoperators and Virtual* Environments, Vol 6, pp.355-385.

Badard, T. (2006). Geospatial Service Oriented Architectures for Mobile Augmented Reality. *Proceedings of the 1st International Workshop on Mobile Geospatial Augmented Reality*. Banff, Canada, pp. 73-77.

Bangemann, T., Rebeuf, X., Reboul, D., Schulze, A., Szymanski, J., Thomesse, J-P., Thron, M., Zerhouni, N. (2006). PROTEUS—Creating distributed maintenance systems through an integration platform. *Computers in Industry Journal, Elsevier*, Vol 57, pp.539-551.

Bellarbi, A., Benbelkacem, S., Malek, M., Zenati-Henda, N., Belhocine, M. (2010 (a)). Amélioration des performances d'ARToolKit pour la réalisation d'applications de réalité augmentée. *International Conference on Image and Signal Processing and their Applications, ISPA'2010*, Biskra, Algeria.

Bellarbi, A., Benbelkacem, S., Malek, M., Zenati-Henda, N., Belhocine, M. (2010 (b)). Dynamic thresholding technique for ARToolKit recognition markers. *International Conference on Electrical Engineering, Electronics and Automatics, ICEEEA'10*, Bejaia, Algeria.

Bleser, G., Pastarmov, Y., Stricker, D. (2005). Real-time 3D Camera Tracking for Industrial Augmented Reality Applications. *Proceedings of International Conference in Central Europe on Computer Graphics, Visualization and Computer Vision*, Plzen - Bory, Czech Republic, pp. 47-54.

Booth, D., Haas,H., McCabe, F., Newcomer, E., Champion, M., Ferris, C., Orchard, D. (2004). Web Services Architecture. In: *W3C Working Group*. Available from: <http://www.w3.org/TR/ws-arch>.

Bottecchia, S., Cieutat, J-M., Merlo, C., Jessel, J-P. (2009). A new AR interaction paradigm for collaborative teleassistance system: the POA. *International Journal on Interactive Design and Manufacturing, Springer*, Vol. 3 N. 1.

Bottecchia, S., Cieutat, J.-M., Jessel J.-P. (2010) T.A.C: Augmented Reality System for Collaborative Tele-Assistance in the Field of Maintenance through Internet. *Augmented Human (AH'2010)*, Megève, France.

Changzhi, K., Bo, K., Dongyi C., Xinyu, L. (2006) .An Augmented reality based Application for Equipment Maintenance. *Book Chapter, Advances in Artificial Reality and Tele-Existence*, Springer, Vol. 4282.

Comport, A. I., Kragic, D., Marchand, E., Chaumette, F. (2005). Robust real-time visual tracking: comparison, theoretical analysis and performance evaluation. *In IEEE*

International Conference on Robotics and Automation (ICRA'05), pp.2841-2846, Barcelona, Spain.

Didier, J., Roussel, D. (2005). Amra: Augmented reality assistance in train maintenance tasks. *Workshop on Industrial Augmented Reality (ISMAR'05)*, Vienna (Austria).

Fiala, M. (2004). Artag, An improved marker system based on ARToolkit. *National Research Council*, Canada.

Henderson,S., Feiner, Steven. (2010). Exploring the Benefits of Augmented Reality Documentation for Maintenance and Repair. *IEEE Transactions on Visualization and Computer Graphics*, 16(1), pp.4-16.

Hirotake, I., Zhiqiang, B., Hidenori, F., Tomoki, S., Toshinori, N., Akihisa, O., Hiroshi, S., Masanori, I., Yoshinori, K., Yoshitsugu, M. (2010). Augmented Reality Applications for Nuclear Power Plant Maintenance Work. *The 3rd International Symposium on Symbiotic Nuclear Power Systems for 21st Century (ISSNP2010)*, Harbin, Heilongjiang, China.

Kato, H., Billinghurst, M. (1999). Marker tracking and hmd calibration for a video-based augmented reality conferencing system. *Proceedings of ACM/IEEE Workshop on Augmented Reality (IWAR 1999)*, pp.85–92.

Kurata, T., Sakata, N., Kourogi, M., Kuzuoka, H., Billinghurst, M. (2004). Remote collaboration using a shoulder-worn active camera/laser Wearable Computers. ISWC 2004. *Proceedings of Eighth International Symposium on Wearable Computers*, Arlington, Virginia, USA, pp. 62-69.

Leymann, F. (2003). Web Services: Distributed Applications without Limits. *Proceedings of 10th Conference on Database Systems for Business.*

Nickul, D. (2007). Service Oriented Architecture (SOA) and Specialized Messaging Patterns. *Adobe Systems Incorporated*, San-Jose, USA.

Marsot, J., Gardeux, F., Govaere, V. (2009). Réalité augmentée et prévention des risques : apports et limites. *Revue of Hygiène et sécurité du travail*, INRS, Paris pp. 15-23.

Otsu, N. (1979). A Threshold Selection Method from Gray-Level Histograms. *IEEE Transactions on Systems, Man, and Cybernetics*, Vol.9, pp. 62–66.

Platonov, J., Heibel, H., Meyer, P. and Grollmann, B. (2006). A mobile markless AR system for maintenance and repair. *Mixed and Augmented Reality (ISMAR'06)*, pp. 105–108.

Riess, P., Stricker, D. (2006). AR on-demand: a practicable solution for augmented reality on low-end handheld devices. *AR/VR Workshop of the Germany Computer Science Society*. Coblence, Germany.

Sakata, N., Kurata, T., Kato, T., Kourogi, M., Kuzuoka, H. (2003). WACL: supporting elecommunications using - wearable active camera with laser pointer Wearable Computers. *Proceedings of Seventh IEEE International Symposium on Wearable Computers*, New-York, USA, pp 53-56.

Schwald, B. and all. (2001). STARMATE: Using Augmented Reality technology for computer guided maintenance of complex mechanical elements. *E-work and E-Commerce, IOS Press*, Vol. 1, pp. 17-19, Venice, Italy.

Scott, K. (2007). Professional WCF Programming: .NET development with the Windows communication foundation. *Amazon Edition, 430 pages.*

Zhong, X., Boulanger, P. (2002). Collaborative augmented reality: A prototype for industrial training. *21th Biennial Symposium on Communication,* Canada.

12

The Design and Implementation of On-Line Multi-User Augmented Reality Integrated System

Hsiao-shen Wang and Chih-Wei Chiu
National Taichung University of Education/ Hyweb Technology Co., Ltd.
Taiwan

1. Introduction

Today's technological advancements, many innovative applications continue to emerge, and in supporting education and learning has brought many changes. With these changes, the application of using virtual reality technology has greatly different on the educational learning way compared to the traditional computer-assisted instruction. Such as abstract concepts simulation, virtual object manipulation, and interactive 3D gaming system, etc.

Through innovative technology-based learning, many learners do produce effective learning, and based on this learning effectiveness, more and more different kinds of technology-transfer medium system were requested to support learners more realistic environment in their computer-based learning system. Therefore, Augmented Reality (AR) technology gains attention in educational use because of its feature of combing real-life situation and the characteristics of virtual objects.

AR technology, through the heavy helmet display, until using the webcam and markers directly to display the result, the combing of real-life scenes and the virtual objects, on the screen, is a mature technology can be applied to assist students with learning. However, as the fixed correspondence of each maker and virtual object in AR learning system, the development of each learning courseware based on AR technology is time-consuming. Thus, how to apply software engineering methods, combined with the AR technology in education to promote more effective use of AR-based learning programs, is a subject can't be ignored.

Cooperative learning is an important way of learning in a modern educational environment. Remote cooperative learning is also an inevitable way of learning in today's internet era. Collaborative learning, from the past face to face discussions to the current Internet remote distance learning, is constantly changing, but the key is how learners can really communicate with each other between the meaning of sharing and the achievement of interaction. Based on this critical factor, many Internet-based collaborative learning systems were proposed. These systems are common, mainly through the use of the real environment among learners or the share of the virtual world generated by the system, to allow learners to engage in a dialogue between the real scenes and common virtual objects for discussion.

However, in VR-based collaborative environments, each of the client location includes a real scene and each virtual objects generated by its VR system. How to make virtual objects of each AR system could be able shown between learners in a collaborative environment is a key problem of Cooperative learning. Thus, the purpose of the paper is to propose an on-line multi-user augmented reality integrated system (OMARIS) to enhance students learning in AR collaborative environment.

2. Related work

Using technology-based application to overcome student learning difficulties is one of important and innovative ways in education environment. Because of its virtual interactive and simulative features, the applications of using Virtual Reality (VR) technology have been widely to use and to enhance several subject domains learning effect in school, such as computer assembly, art appreciation, emotional expression, medical training and geological science (Wang, 1999, 2000,; Basori et al., 2009; Deng & Zhou, 2009; Ni et al., 2009). With the same application of technology benefits, Augment Reality (AR) also plays a significant substantial advantage in education.

By seamlessly combining the real world with the various virtual materials, AR technology provides intuitive interaction experience to the learners. The various virtual materials, including graph, image, text, or animation, are superimposed on the reality scene based on the instructional design. With the characteristic of AR tehnology, Shelton and Hedley (2002) successfully applied the intuitive features in the nine planets learning activities which allowed students to construct and manipulate virtual objects through reality scene, and to establish their abstract scientific concepts. In recent years, AR technology has been applied in medical procedures (Rosenblum & Julier, 2007; Samset et al, 2008), assembly design and planning (Ong, Pang, Nee, 2007), mathematical education (Lee & Lee, 2008), Physics (Beaney & Namee, 2008), PCDIY (Chiang et al., 2011), city maps(Jiang et al., 2011) etc. Kaufman(2006) indicated that whether teachers or students are very interested in the AR-based geometry learning activities and have positive attitude to use AR-related software in the future curriculum. However, the creation of each AR application is very time-consuming, and therefore how to reuse developed materials, including markers and virtual objects, to create a new suitable AR courseware is one of must be addressed problems for the substance of the school curriculum needs.

In AR environment, students create their understanding of the learning content through the fusion of reality scene and virtual objects, and share and discuss with other students to strengthen the significance of domain knowledge. AR simply can provide a collaborative interactive AR environment for school setting, where students can interact naturally and intuitively. AR collaboration approach can be effectively used to develop face to face interfaces. There are two kinds of AR collaborative environments which are co-located collaborative AR and remote collaborative AR (Silva, Giraldi & Oliveira, 2003). The characteristic of co-located collaborative AR is that multiple users manipulate virtual objects within an augmented reality space in the same physical environment, and through the speech, gestures, eye contact and other means of communication of each other to share their meaning and reach the purpose of discussion.(Fig. 2.1, Fig.2.2)

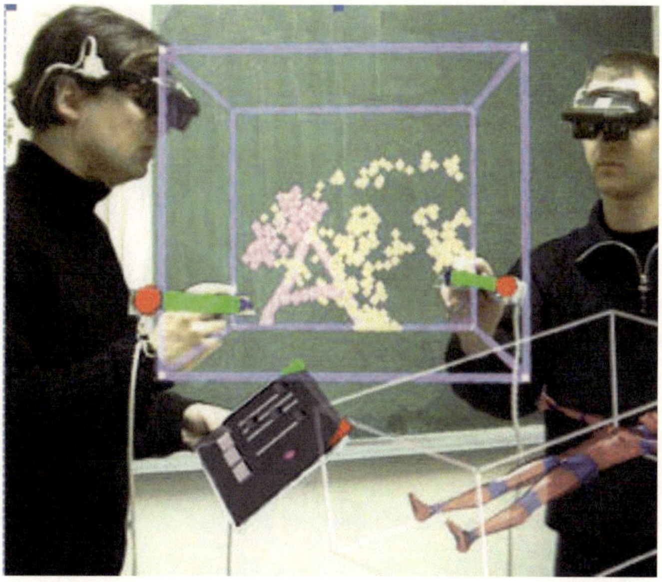

(retrieved from http://studierstube.icg.tu-graz.ac.at)

Fig. 2.1 Co-located collaborative AR.

(Billinghurst et al. , 2003)

Fig. 2.2 Co-located collaborative AR2.

While remote collaborative AR allows people in different spaces to using AR technology to share their idea for some specific virtual objects. The teachers, for instance, can use augmented reality in the remote system to guide students learning or solving problems, the students can also in different places at the same time on a specific topic of virtual objects to discuss and share their idea in the use of AR systems (Fig. 2.3).

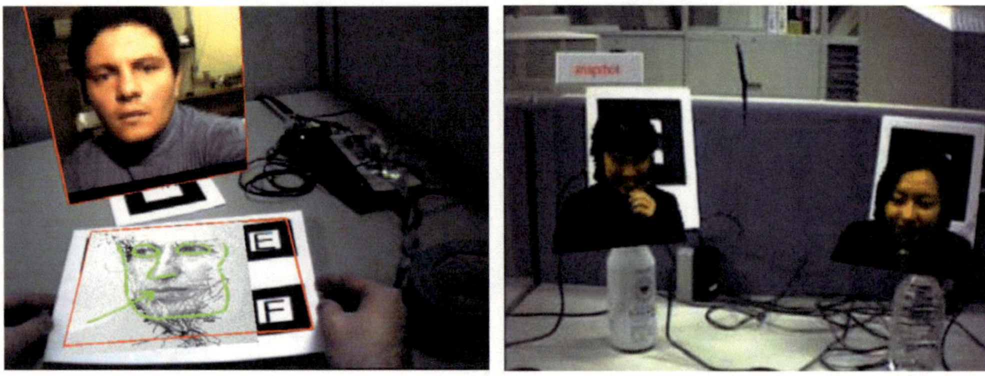

(Kato and Billinghurst, 1999)

Fig. 2.3 Remote collaborative AR.

AR has been successfully used in many learning environments, especially in cooperative interactive learning is to play its effectiveness (Lievonen et al.,2009; Shen,Ong & Nee,2008; Quy et al.,2009; Nilsson,Johansson & Jonsson, 2009; Godet-Bar,Rieu & Dupuy-Chessa, 2010; Li, 2010; Dierker, Pitsch & Hermann, 2011; Morrison et al.,2011). However, in the applications of AR collaborative environment, the learners are mostly to look from the same virtual view with an AR environment, or remote in video-conference or a network to watch and interact on a same reality scenee. How to really effectively convey the message, including image, text, and related animation, between the learners is still a major issue to enhance the learning effect in cooperation AR environment. Moreover, If both partners are in remote AR environment, the virtual objects, which are produced by the trigger of each maker of their original AR environment, do not really exist. How then to make original content that does not exist, can be delivered to distant learners to share is the key success factor in the cooperative AR environment.

Therefore, based on the concept of reuse learning materials, easy on-line AR application for students, as well as effective learning in remote collaboration AR environment, the OMARIS is developed primarily to provide teachers and students to enhance their teaching and learning effect by using AR technology in educational environment.

3. System design of OMARIS

The OMARIS system is mainly divided into three parts, namely, maker and object database system, personal AR learning system, as well as multi-user cooperative AR learning system. The marker and object database system is to manage markers, objects, and the links between the markerS and objects relationship. The personal AR learning system is to provide instructors to set up learning scenarios, and students to explore individual AR learning activities. The last multi-user cooperative AR learning system is to provide students cooperative learning activities in AR environment. Detailed system design description, as described below.

3.1 Marker and object database system

In general AR system, the link between the marker and the virtual object are fixed, so that the materials of the AR system are difficult to reuse. Thereby, how to manage makers, objects, and re-setup the link relationship between them is the main idea of the system. Based on the idea, the marker and object database system includes three subsystems: marker database system, object database system and marker and object matching system. The first two material database systems basically manage the uploaded materials, including marker symbols and virtual objects by authorized users. The latter one application system is based on the needs of instructional designers or general users, to set up the link between marker symbols and virtual objects in the database systems and to output as a single XML learning script file for future instructional use. After the linking relationship processed by the system, it then will be provided as the necessary materials for the further AR learning system.

3.2 Personal AR learning system

Since the innovation development of AR technology in education, the AR application makes the learner more motivation and substance of learning, thus providing individualized and flexible AR learning system for the learners is a key factor of the system development. Based on the idea, the personal AR learning system is designed for the instructors and learners. The instructors can select the predefine AR learning scenario, defined from previously material database system, or can customize the current AR learning script file for specific instructional needs in the personal AR learning system. The learner then can choose related topic to explore the combinational effect of the reality scenes and virtual objects in personal AR learning system.

3.3 Multi-user cooperative AR learning system

This collaborative learning environment is especially to provide multiple users to be able to sharing mixed AR contents from their computer system, including reality scene and virtual objects. As the virtual objects are virtual feature in the client computer system, they can't be display directly through video devices to remote collaborative computers. Therefore, in this study, Flash Actionscript 3.0 with flartoolkit AR library and PaperVision three-dimensional display library, and the point to point transmission technology of Adobe stratus are used to solve the virtual display problem.

The principle of the design methodology is when a computer via a webcam captures the marker and the reality scene, and analyses the image data of the marker by the flartoolkit library to identify the number, location, size, tilt and rotation angle and other information of the virtual object, and then hands over those data to PaperVision library to calculate the corresponding three-dimensional model presentation, and finally merges the reality scene and virtual objects as a single image. (Figure 3.1 & Figure 3.2)

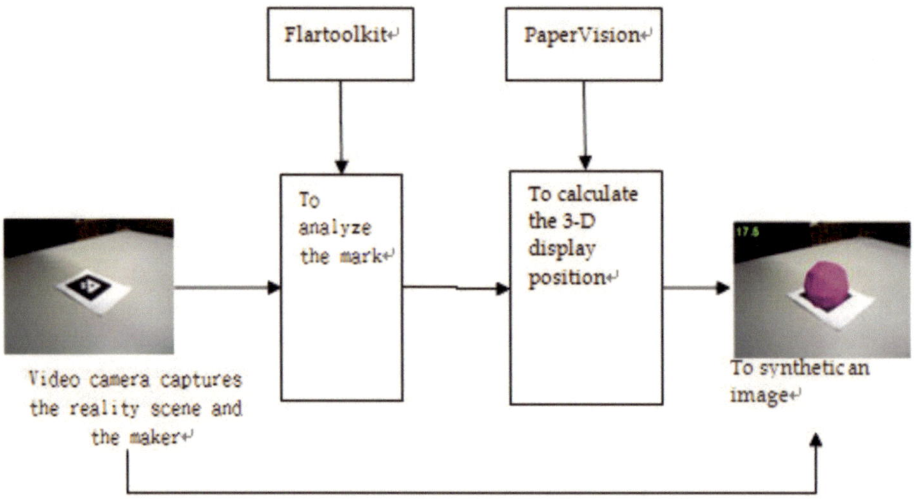

Fig. 3.1 The principle of reality scene and virtual object synthesis.

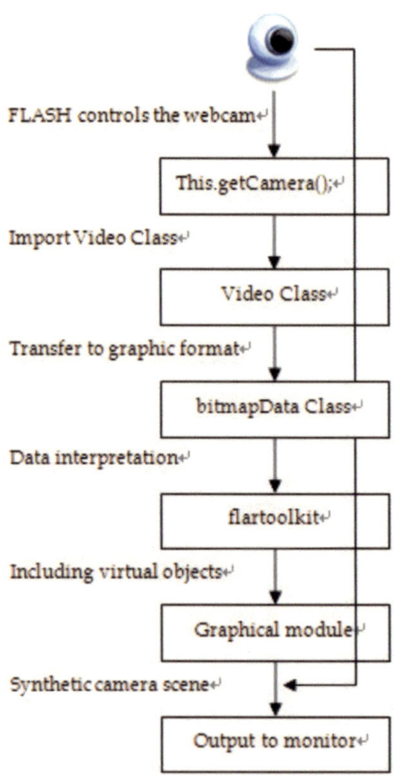

Fig. 3.2 The logic design of reality scene and virtual object synthetic process.

As both of individual computers have synthesized their reality scene and virtual objects image, they then can, through Adobe Status point to point technology, transfer those merged data to each other. (Figure 3.3 & Figure 3.4) Thus, the learners of OMARIS could process their cooperative learning activities to share ideas with each reality and virtual materials.

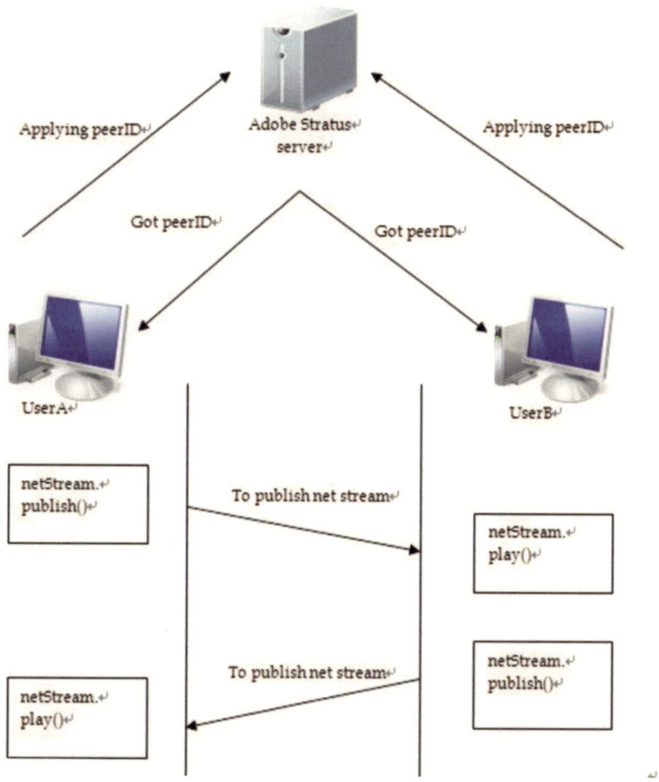

Fig. 3.3 The point to point transmission technology diagram.

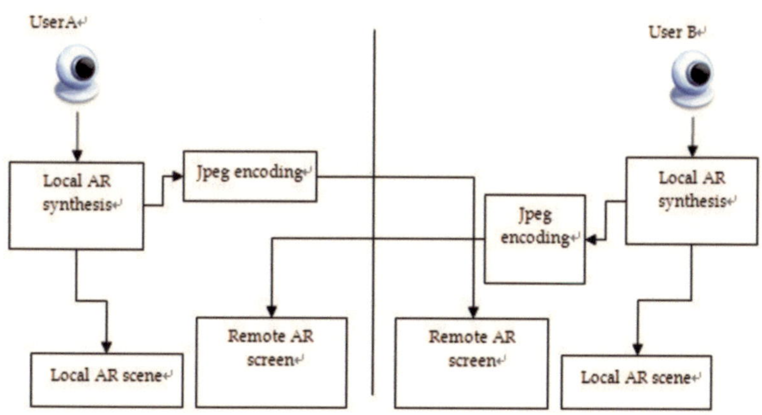

Fig. 3.4 The reality scene and virtual object encoding processing.

4. System implementation of the OMARIS

The OMARIS working processes can be divided into three main parts. These parts are AR instructional database building session, which is the basis of the OMARIS, second the personal instructional session, which is used for the single user AR learning system, and finally the collaborative learning session, which is used for the multiple users AR learning system. The working processes are discussed briefly as follows.

4.1 AR instructional database building session

First, the system users prepare their instructional materials which include marker pictures and responding learning materials, comprising static data and 2D or 3D animation. They then enter into the OMARIS system to build the AR instructional database. Every authorized user can view the whole items of the database and manage and match their own VR instructional materials for future instructional use as shown in Fig. 4.1 and Fig. 4.2

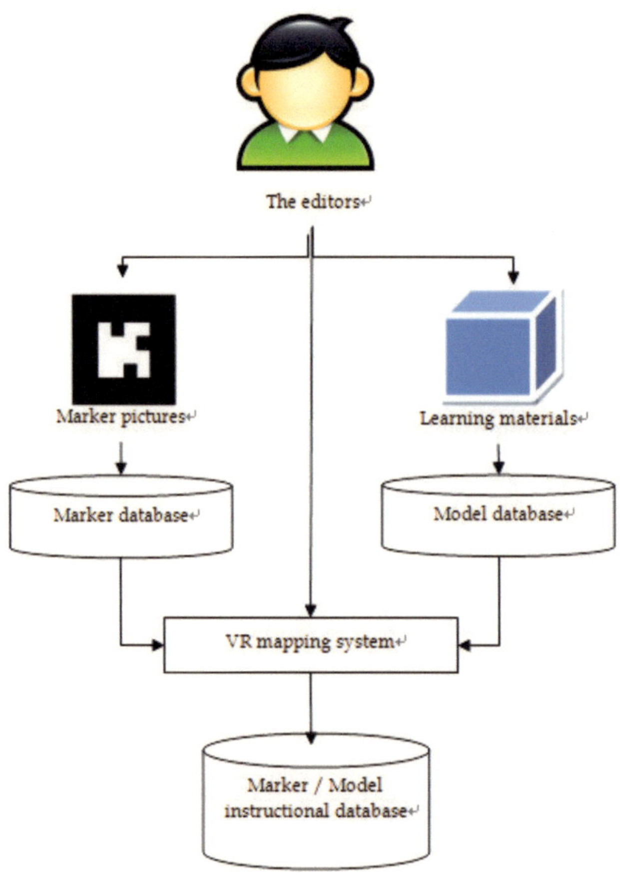

Fig. 4.1 AR instructional database diagram.

Fig. 4.2 Maker / model mapping interface.

4.2 The personal instructional session

During the personal instructional session, the instructor can first enter the OMARIS system to choose the predefine AR learning module, or to edit the additional learning materials for the specific learning purpose, then guides the students to login into the OMARIS system for AR-based learning activities.(Figure 4.3)

Fig. 4.3 Personal AR learning system.

4.3 The collaborative learning session

When learners enter the collaborative learning mode, each of them can choose same or different topic in their AR learning system. They then can send meesage to Adobe stratus to get their peerID for network connection. Once they take the individual's peerID, they can call each other peerID to synchronize video and audio for the cooperative activities. Through mutual learning and sharing activities, they can spread virtual objects with real-life situation in order to achieve the purpose of cooperative learning.(Figure 4.4)

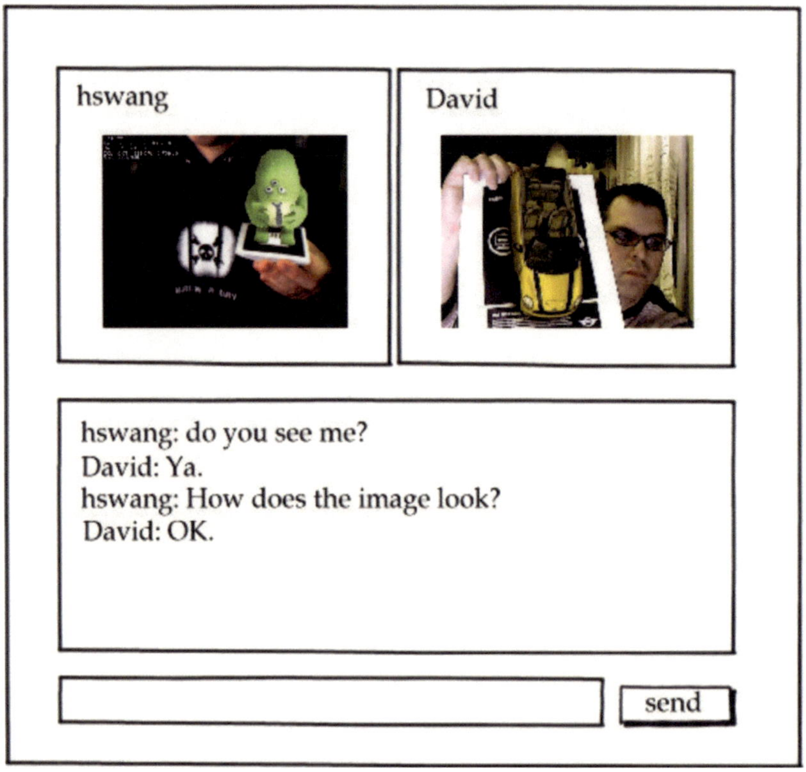

Fig. 4.4 Collaborative AR learning system.

5. Conculsion

As technology continues to progress and innovation, how to more effectively use in education to enhance students better productive learning is being constantly raised. Because of its creative feature of combining reality scene and virtual objects, AR technology has great attention in the use of education. Such AR based educational use, if the design of the applications considers the flexible material usability, facilitate use of equipment and the characteristics of cooperative learning, the effectiveness of the application will be more improved. The feature of the OMARIS is mainly from the educational view to use software engineering integrating technology components and learning materials to make an innovative combination in educational environment and to increase flexibly and value-added the AR learning system in the use of school setting. In particular, the system uses multi-user remote integrating technology to on-line combine and transfer each other's real scene and virtual learning objects, which originally do not exist in a client learning environment, to both cooperative learning sides. This is different with past collaborative AR learning systems which their cooperative learning environments are processing in multiuser real scenes but only a same virtual situation. Thus the OMARIS system tries to offer the instructional material system, personal AR learning system and collaborative AR learning system to be more flexible reuse AR materials, the better ease use of AR application and the more completely conveying and sharing integrated message of each other during cooperative learning. With the OMARIS model, how can the creation of innovative teaching strategies to achieve greater learning effectiveness, will be more in-depth issue of the future study.

6. References

Amaoka,T.; Laga,H.; Yoshie, M. & Nakajima, M.(2011). Personal space-based simulation of non-verbal communications. Entertainment Computing, Article in Press, Corrected Proof (Manuscript submitted for publication).

Angus Antley and Mel Slater.(2010). The Effect on Lower Spine Muscle Activation

Argelague, F.; Kulik A.; Kunert A.; Andujar, C. and Froehlich, B. See-through techniques for referential awareness in collaborative virtual reality. International Journal of Human-Computer Studies, 69, 6, 387-400.

Augmented Reality. Computers & Graphics, 35, 4, vii-viii.

Azuma, R.; Billinghurst, M.& Klinker, G.(2011). Special Section on Mobile

Beaney, D. & Namee, B. M.(2008). Forked! A Demonstration of Physics Realism in Augmented Reality. 2009 8th IEEE International Symposium on Mixed and Augmented Reality.171-172.

Bideau, B.; Kulpa, R.; Vignais, Nicolas.; Brault, S.; Multon, F. & Craig, C.(2010). Using Virtual Reality to Analyze Sports Performance. IEEE Computer Graphics and Applications, 30, 2, 14-21.

Billinghurst, M. , Belcher, D., Gupta, A., Kiyokawa K. (2003). Communication Behaviors in Colocated Collaborative AR Interfaces. Computer Interaction 16(3), pp.395-423.

Botella, C.; Bretón-López, J.; Quero, Soledad.; Baños, Rosa.; García-Palacios, A. (2010). Treating Cockroach Phobia With Augmented Reality. Behavior Therapy, 41 (2010), 401–413.

Cáceres, R. & Ebling, M. (2010). Gaming and Augmented Reality Come to Location- Based Services. Ieee Pervasive Computing (2010), 9, 1, 5-6.

Camera tracking and mapping in multiple regions. Computer Vision and Image

Castle, R.O. & Murray, D.W.(2011). Keyframe-based recognition and localization during video-rate parallel tracking and mapping. Image and Vision Computing, doi:10.1016/j.imavis.2011.05.002. (Manuscript submitted for publication)

Castle, R.O.; Klein, G. & Murray, D.W. (2011). Wide-area augmented reality using camera tracking and mapping in multiple regions. Computer Vision and Image Understanding, 115, 854–867.

Chastine, J. W.; Nagel, K.; Zhu, Y & Yearsovich, L. (2007). Understanding the Design Space of Referencing in Collaborative Augmented Reality Environments. Proceedings of Graphics Interface 2007 on GI 07, 2007, 207-214.

Chiang, H.; Chou, Y.; Chang, L.; Huang, H.; Kuo, F. & Chen, H. (2011). An Augmented Reality Learning Space for PC DIY. AH '11 Proceedings of the 2nd Augmented Human International Conference, 12.

Deng, C.; Xue, L. & Zhou, Z.(2009). Integration of Web2.0, Panorama Virtual Reality and Geological Information System. ICCIT '09 Proceedings of the 2009 Fourth International Conference on Computer Sciences and Convergence Information Technology. 1625-1628.

Dierker, Angelika; Pitsch, Karola; Hermann, Thomas.(2011). An augmented-reality-based scenario for the collaborative construction of an interactive museum. BiPrints Repository, urn:nbn:de:0070-bipr-49260.

Doru Talaba, Imre Horváth, Kwan H Lee.(2010).Special issue of Computer-Aided Design on virtual and augmented reality technologies in product design. Computer-Aided Design, 42, 5, 361-363, DOI: 10.1016/j.cad.2010.01.001.

Dougherty, M. A.; Mann, S. A.; Bronder, M. L.; Bertolami, J. & Craig, R. M.(2010) Patent application title: Augmented Reality Cloud Computing. Microsoft Corporation, 2010/0257252 A1.

Fernández, C.; Baiget, P.; Roca, F. X. & Gonzàlez, J.(2011). Augmenting video surveillance footage with virtual agents for incremental event evaluation. Pattern Recognition Letters, 32, 878–889.

GAO, X.; HU, H.; JIA, Q-X.; SUN, H-X. & SONG, J-Z.(2011). 3D augmented reality teleoperated robot system based on dual vision. The Journal of China Universities of Posts and Telecommunications, 18 , 1, 105-112.

Gee, A. P.; Webb, M.; Escamilla-Ambrosio, J.; Mayol-Cuevas, W. & Calway, A. (2011). A topometric system for wide area augmented reality. Computers & Graphics, 35, 854-868.

Godet-Bar, G.; Rieu, D. & Dupuy-Chessa, S.(2010). HCI and business practices in a collaborative method for augmented reality systems. Information and Software Technology (2010), 52, 492-505.

Grasset, R.; Dünser, A. & Billinghurst, M.(2008). Edutainment with a Mixed Reality Book: A visually augmented illustrative childrens' book. Proceedings of the 2008 International Conference on Advances in Computer Entertainment Technology (2008).292-295.

Guan1, T.; Duan, L.; Yu, J.; Chen, Y. and Zhang, X.(2010). Real Time Camera Pose Estimation for Wide Area Augmented Reality Applications. Computer Graphics and Applications, 31, 3, 56-68.

Hachet, M and Kruijff, E.(2010). Guest Editor's Introduction: Special Section on the ACM Symposium on Virtual Reality Software and Technology. IEEE TRANSACTIONS ON VISUALIZATION AND COMPUTER GRAPHICS, 16, 1, 2-3.

Hilsenrat, M. & Reiner, M.(2010). Hapto-visual Virtual Reality as a Tool in Psychophysical Research on Roughness Sensitivity. ACHI '10 Proceedings of the 2010 Third International Conference on Advances in Computer-Human Interactions, 139-142.

Holmes, N.(2010). The Varieties of Reality. *The varieties of reality.* Computer, 43,1,96,94-95.

Holz, T.; Campbell, A. G.; O'Hare, G.M.P.; Stafford, J. W.; Martin, A.; Dragone, M.(2011). MiRA—Mixed Reality Agents. J. Journal of Human-Computer Studies, 69 , 251-268.

Ishiguro, Y. & Rekimoto, J.(2011). Peripheral Vision Annotation: Noninterference Information Presentation Method for Mobile Augmented Reality. AH '11 Proceedings of the 2nd Augmented Human International Conference, 8.

Ismail, A. W. & Sunar, M. S.(2009). Collaborative Augmented Reality Approach For Multi-user Interaction in Urban Simulation. ICIMT '09 Proceedings of the 2009 International Conference on Information and Multimedia Technology. 19-23.

Ivetic, D.; Mihic, S.& Markoski, B.(2010). Augmented AVI video file for road surveying. Computers and Electrical Engineering, 36, 169-179.

Janssen, R .(2011).Augmented Reality -The Ethical Importance of a Shared Context.

Jeferson R. Silva, Thiago T. Santos, Carlos H. Morimoto.(2011). Automatic camera control in virtual environments augmented using multiple sparse videos. Computers & Graphics , 35 ,412–421.

Jiang, X.; Broelemann, K.; Wachenfeld, S. & Kruger, A.(2011). Graph-based markerless registration of city maps using geometric hashing. Computer Vision and Image Understanding , 115 , 1032-1043.

Jo, H.; Hwang, S.; Park, H. & Ryu, J-H.(2011). Aroundplot: Focus + context interface for off-screen objects in 3Denvironments. Computers & Graphics, 35 , 841–853.

Juan, M. C. & Pérez, D.(2010). Using augmented and virtual reality for the development of acrophobic scenarios. Comparison of the levels of presence and anxiety. Computers & Graphics, 34, 6, 756-766.

Kansaku, K.; Hata, N. & Takano, K.(2010). My thoughts through a robot's eyes: An augmented reality-brain–machine interface. Neuroscience Research, 66, 219-222.

Kato, H. and Billinghurst, M. (1999). Marker tracking and HMD calibration for a video-based augmented reality conferencing system. In IWAR '99, pp. 85-94.

Klein, G. and Murray, D. W.(2010). Simulating Low-Cost Cameras for Augmented Reality Compositing. IEEE TRANSACTIONS ON VISUALIZATION AND COMPUTER GRAPHICS,16, 3, 369-380.

Kroeker, K. L.(2010). Mainstreaming Augmented Reality. communications of the acm, 53 ,7, DOI: :10.1145/1785414.1785422

Langlotz, T.; Degendorfer, C.; Mulloni, A.; Schall, G.; Reitmayr, G.; Schmalstieg, D.(2011).Robust detection and tracking of annotations for outdoor augmented reality browsing , Computers & Graphics , 35 , 831–840.

Leblanc F, Senagore AJ, Ellis CN, Champagne BJ, Augestad KM, Neary PC, Delaney CP & Colorectal Surgery Training Group.(2010). Hand-assisted laparoscopic sigmoid colectomy skills acquisition: augmented reality simulator versus human cadaver training models. Journal Of Surgical Education (2010), 67, 4, 200-204.

Lee, H. S & Lee, J. W.(2008). Mathematical Education Game Based on Augmented Reality. Lecture Notes in Computer Science, 2008, Volume 5093/2008, 442-450, DOI: 10.1007/978-3-540-69736-7_48.

Lee, J, Han, S, Yang, J. (2011). Construction of a computer-simulated mixed reality environment for virtual factory layout planning. Computers in Industry , 62 , 86–98.

Li, S. & Xu, C. (2011). Efficient lookup table based camera pose estimation

Li, S.(2010). Research on Network Cooperative Learning System Based on Virtual Reality. IC4E '10 Proceedings of the 2010 International Conference on e-Education, e-Business, e-Management and e-Learning, 43-46.

Lievonen, M.; Rosenberg, D.; Dörner, R.; Kühn, G. & Walkowski, S.(2009). Augmented Reality as Means for Creating Shared Understanding. ECCE '09 European

Conference on Cognitive Ergonomics: Designing beyond the Product --- Understanding Activity and User Experience in Ubiquitous Environments, 17.

Livingston, M. A.; Azuma, R. T.; Bimber, O. & Saito, H.(2010). Guest Editors' Introduction: Special Section on The International Symposium on Mixed and Augmented Reality (ISMAR). IEEE TRANSACTIONS ON VISUALIZATION AND COMPUTER GRAPHICS, 16, 3, 353 - 354.

Martin, S.; Diaz, Gabriel; Sancristobal, E.; Gil, R.; Castro, M. & Peire, J.(2011). New technology trends in education: Seven years of forecasts and convergence. Computers & Education, 57, 1893–1906.

McCall, R.; Wetzel, R.; Lo¨schner, h.; Braun, A-K.(2011). Using presence to evaluate an augmented reality location aware game. Personal and Ubiquitous Computing, 15, 1, 25-35.

Morrison, A.; Mulloni, A.; Lemmelä, S.; Oulasvirta, A.; Jacucci, G.; Peltonen, P.; Schmalstieg, D. & Regenbrecht, H.(2011).Collaborative use of mobile augmented reality with paper maps. Computers & Graphics , 35 , 789–799.

Nilsson, S.; Johansson, B. & Jonsson, A.(2009). Using AR to support cross-organisational collaboration in dynamic tasks. ISMAR '09 Proceedings of the 2009 8th IEEE International Symposium on Mixed and Augmented Reality, 3-12.

Ong, S.K. & Wang, Z.B.(2011). Augmented assembly technologies based on 3D bare-hand interaction. CIRP Annals - Manufacturing Technology, 60 ,1-4.

Paelke, V. & Sester, Monika.(2010). Augmented paper maps: Exploring the design space of a mixed reality system. ISPRS Journal of Photogrammetry and Remote Sensing, 65, 256-265.

Pecchioli, L.; Carrozzino, M.; Mohamed, F.; Bergamasco, M & Kolbe, T. H.(2011).ISEE: Information access through the navigation of a 3D interactive environment. Journal of Cultural Heritage, 2011/02/25, doi:10.1016/j.culher.2010.11.001.

Peter Meier, CTO, metaio GmbH.(2010). Mobile Augmented Reality 2010. metaio AUGMENTED SOLUTIONS, 01/2010.

Phan, V. T. & Choo, S. Y.(2009). A Combination of Augmented Reality and Google Earth's facilities for urban planning in idea stage. International Journal of Computer Applications, 4, 3, 26-34.

Pintaric ,T. & Kaufmann, H.(2007). Affordable Infrared-Optical Pose-Tracking for Virtual and Augmented Reality. IEEE VR Workshop on Trends and Issues in Tracking for Virtual Environments. 2007/03/14 - 2007/03/17 ,44 - 51.

Polys, N. F.; Bowman, Doug A. & North, Chris.(2011). The role of Depth and Gestalt cues in information-rich virtual environments. Journal of Human-Computer Studies, 69 , 30–51.

Portalés, C.; Lerma , J. L. & Navarro, S.(2010). Augmented reality and photogrammetry: A synergy to visualize physical and virtual city environments. ISPRS Journal of Photogrammetry and Remote Sensing (2010) ,65, 1, 134-142.

Quy, PS.; Lee, J.; Kim, JH.; Kim, JI. & Kim, HS.(2009). Collaborative Experiment and Education based on Networked Virtual Reality. 2009 Fourth International Conference on Computer Sciences and Convergence Information Technology. ICCIT '09 Proceedings of the 2009 Fourth International Conference on Computer Sciences and Convergence Information Technology, 80- 85.

Rosenblum, L. & Julier, S. (2007). Action- and Workflow-Driven Augmented Reality for Computer-Aided Medical Procedures. IEEE Computer Society, September/October (2007), 10-14.

Samset, E.; Schmalstieg, D.; Vander Sloten, J.; Freudenthal, A.; Declerck, J.; Casciaro, S.; Rideng, O. & Gersak, B.(2008). Augmented Reality in Surgical Procedures. Human Vision and Electronic Imaging XIII.

Sayed, N. A.M. El.; Zayed, H. H.; Sharawy, M. I.(2011). ARSC: Augmented reality student card An augmented reality solution for the education field. Computers & Education, 56 ,1045–1061.

Sayed, N.A.M., El, Zayed, H. H., Sharawy, M.I.(2011). ARSC: Augmented reality student card An augmented reality solution for the education field. Computers & Education, 56, 1045–1061.

Shen, Y.; Ong, S. K. & Nee, A. Y. C.(2008). Augmented reality for collaborative product design and development. Design Studies (2010), 31, 2, 118-145.

Shen, Y.; Ong, S. K. & Nee, A. Y. C. (2011).Vision-Based Hand Interaction in Augmented Reality Environment. International Journal of Human-Computer Interaction, 27 ,6, 523-544.

Shin, D. H. & Dunston, P. S.(2010). Technology development needs for advancing Augmented Reality-based inspection. Automation in Construction, 19 (2010), 169–182.

Silva, R.; Giraldi, G. & Oliveira, Jauvane C.(2003). Introduction to augmented reality. Technical Report: 25/2003, LNCC, Brazil, 2003.

Taketomi, T.; Sato T. & Yokoya, N. (2011). Real-time and accurate extrinsic camera parameter estimation using feature landmark database for augmented reality. Computers & Graphics, 35, 768–777.

Uva, A.E.; Cristiano, S.; Fiorentino, M. & Monno, G.(2010). Distributed design review using tangible augmented technical drawings. Computer-Aided Design, 42, 364-372.

Walsh, J. A. & Thomas, B. H.(2011). Visualising Environmental Corrosion in Outdoor Augmented Reality School of Computer and Information Science University of South Australia.

Wang, H. S. (1999). The system design of on-line virtual reality courseware in computer assembly, Journal of Secondary Education, 6, 355-386

Wang, H. S. (2000). The study of using virtual reality software in art curriculum, Journal of Secondary Education, 7, 173-200

Wang, Y.; Shen, Y.; Liu, D.; Wei, S. & Zhu, C.(2010). Key Technique of Assembly System in an Augmented Reality Environment. ICCMS '10 Proceedings of the 2010 Second International Conference on Computer Modeling and Simulation, 1, 133-137.

Wither, J.; Tsai, Y-T. &Azuma, R. (2011). Indirect augmented reality. Computers & Graphics, 35, 810–822

Wrzesien, Maja.; Burkhardt,J-M.; Raya,M.A.& Botella, C.(2011). Mixing Psychology and HCI in Evaluation of Augmented Reality Mental Health Technology. CHI EA '11 Proceedings of the 2011 annual conference extended abstracts on Human factors in computing systems, 2119-2124, doi:10.1145/1979742.1979898.

Yabuki, N.; Miyashita, K. & Fukuda, T.(2011). An invisible height evaluation system for building height regulation to preserve good landscapes using augmented reality. Automation in Construction, 20, 228–235.

Yim, H. B. & Seong, P. H. (2010). Heuristic guidelines and experimental evaluation of effective augmented-reality based instructions for maintenance in nuclear power plants. Nuclear Engineering and Design, 240, 4096-4012.

Zhang, J.; Ong, S.K. & Nee, A.Y.C. (2011). System in an augmented reality environment. International Journal of Production Research, 49, 13, 3919-3938.

Zhang, J.; Ong, S.K. & Nee, A.Y.C.(2010). A multi-regional computation scheme in an AR-assisted in situ CNC simulation environment. Computer-Aided Design, 42, 1167-1177.

Ziaei, Z.; Hahto, A.; Mattila, J.; Siuko, M. & Semeraro, L.(2011). Real-time markerless Augmented Reality for Remote Handling system in bad viewing conditions. Fusion Engineering and Design, 18/02/2011, doi:10.1016/j.fusengdes.2010.12.082.

13

Physical Variable Analysis Involved in Head-Up Display Systems Applied to Automobiles

J. Alejandro Betancur
EAFIT University
Colombia

1. Introduction

The command dashboard of an automobile is the instrument where most of the information related to the current state of the vehicle is displayed, and visually it is the way the driver can have access to that information. Nowadays, it is a great risk not only for the driver, but also for the passengers that the driver has to focus his attention off the road to focus on the dashboard information; on situations like this, are when Head-Up Display (HUD) systems represent a significant breakthrough in terms of automotive safety.

The kind of HUDs here analyzed are the Optical See-through Augmented Reality systems, where the objects of an outer environment are combined with previously structured additional information, and the result is visualized by mean of a translucent display (combiner), which is generally the windshield of an automobile. On this type of system, what we want to accomplish is an interaction with the user through a series of visual stimuli and artificial scenes.

This chapter focuses on the approach of the functional design requirements that must include an HUD system applied to current automobiles, in which the fast acquisition of the vehicle's available functional information in its panel would imply a positive impact in terms of the vehicle's simplicity to be driven, security, handling information, communication, among others. The analysis of the functional aspects of this technology will be covered by the theoretical analysis and the instrumental implementation, so that we can understand the behavior of optic phenomena that are involved in these systems, in order to be able to determine which parameters are the most critical in the possible construction of an HUD. The appreciations and considerations expressed in this chapter are defined after several years of applied and exploratory research that gathers documental fields and laboratory aspects, using the characteristics from the scientific method as aid, determining what is transcendent and what is possible from the facts.

The general objective of this chapter is to evaluate the scientific and engineering phenomena from an HUD, in order to set main characteristics and crucial parameters in terms of physics, thus, determining what considerations are fundamental for the proper functioning of these types of augmented reality systems, and identifying the functional and physical characteristics from the basic optical elements of HUD's visualization systems adapted to automobiles.

This chapter is addressed in four phases: the first phase approaches the analysis of the conceptual information about what is currently structured like HUDs applied to automobiles; the second phase focuses on describing design alternatives for the conception of an HUD applied to an automobile; the third stage is where all the ideas presented in the previous stages (according to their real development potential) converge in a structured design proposal; finally, on the fourth phase we reach conclusions related to the most relevant data depicted in the chapter, reporting interpretations, relationships, reaches, and the structuring of a possible application.

Something very notorious in current HUD's applications is the degree of shyness in these systems in terms of images projected, since a level of sophistication has not been reached yet that allow to discard completely the tachometer and the different instruments clusters, by projected images on the windshield or on another type of element that works as a combiner; this situation proves that although significant goals have been achieved within the last few years, it is an understatement that more analysis and numerous resources are still needed with the intention of commercialize these type of devices to a higher level.

Finally, the HUDs technologies applied to automobile industries, should not only be considered as their exclusive field of application, since the use of augmented reality systems such as these are being incorporated into daily activities, i.e. answering the phone, studying, etc.

The study and the appropriation of concepts referred to this technology is appealing because it contributes to the design and redesign of several visual mobile technologies, and according to previous researches (Amezquita, 2010; Dawson et al., 2001; Betancur, 2010; Pinkus & Task, 1989), a tendency in most visualization devices to adopt the elements and the configurations that are present in HUD systems is noted.

2. Definition and justification of HUDs

Nowadays, we find a notable tendency in automobiles to offer a lot more information to the driver, which has its own direct repercussions in terms of driving, due to the lack of concentration that implies when having so many options, reason why, it is necessary to think in proposing a quick way to access the information that an automobile offers.

Starting from this point, we must think about a much more efficient communication interface between the user and the automobile that will not interfere with the user's driving; thus, augmented reality devices are born as facilitators and boosters that will give us application ideas to significantly reduce the time needed to be able to interact with the vehicle's diverse options (Brown et al., 1988).

Up until now, the best way to supply the need that we previously mentioned is with the augmented reality devices HUDs and HDDs (Head-Down Displays), which can be set up in a way that will provide to the driver the quick acquisition of information about vehicle's state, thus, obtaining a direct repercussion in the elimination of several risk situations.

In this chapter, we are looking to explain in a sequential way some coherent alternatives to link the driver to the systems and options offered by an automobile through the use of HUDs (being these systems our main subject of study) and HDDs. The operation context of these technologies can be seen in the Figure 1, where it is clear how the driver is influenced by the surroundings of an augmented reality through an image generated from an opto-electronical system.

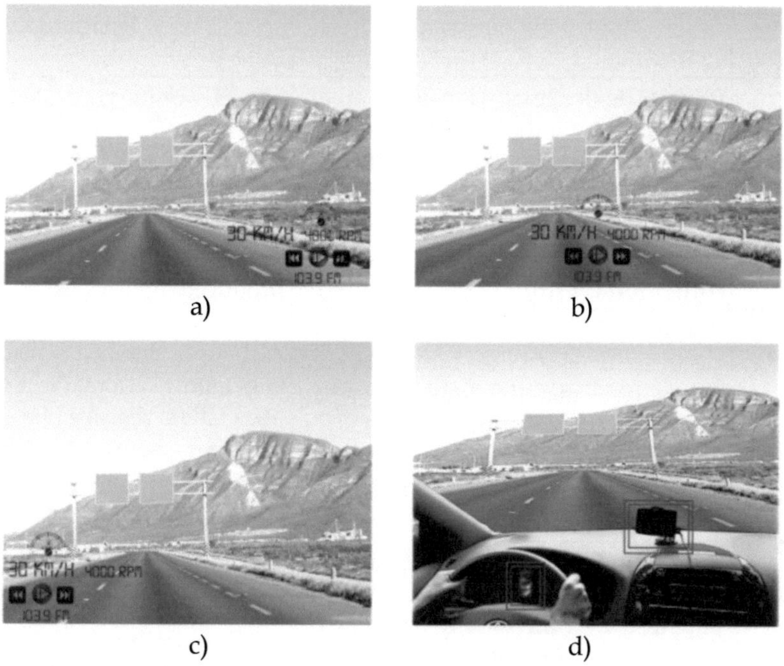

Fig. 1. (a) Right HUD; (b) Middle HUD; (c) Left HUD; (d) HDDs.

Although, there is still a lot more analysis to be done in these augmented reality systems with the intention of establishing regulation and utilization rules, it must be settled that the quantity of HUDs and HDDs applications found so far in automobiles are really efficient in terms of the driver's safety.

Next, Figure 2 represents the flow of information between the main sections of many augmented reality system; this, as a starting point to begin a discussion about the main considerations that must be taken into account in the configuration of the HUD system here proposed.

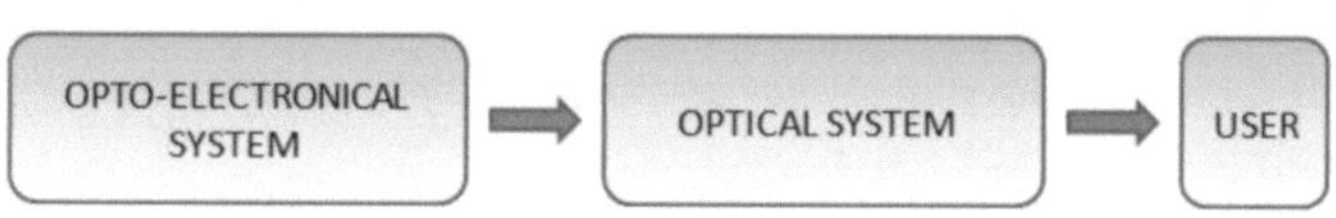

Fig. 2. Sections of the augmented reality system proposed.

3. Classification of physical components

The HUD system that is suggested here uses catadioptric elements as the main resource for the presentation of the information to the observer; according to Figure 2, it must be considered that independently from the principle of functioning of the HUD, three (3) essential sections are present in this kind of augmented reality system, which are detailed here below.

3.1 Opto-electronical system

Currently, a large quantity of options for emissive displays can be found, some of which will be mentioned on Table 1, where some essential relations and comparisons are included.

<table>
<tr><th>Emissive display</th><th>Functioning principle</th><th>Relations</th></tr>
<tr><td>SLM (Spatial Light Modulator)</td><td>It is a device that is based on the modulation of the intensity and/or phase of a light beam; this modulation depends on the position of incidence of the previously mentioned beam onto the recording mean of the SLM (Amezquita, 2010).</td><td rowspan="7">Only 1% of the generated light from LEDs (under daytime operating conditions) will get to the user.
Due to the energy loss by transmission on the windshield, less than 10% of the luminescence produced by a LCD will reach the user's eyes.
Although the LCDs usually have better poly-chromatic contrast than Mini CRTs, this last one usually has a higher mono-chromatic contrast than LCDs.
LCD panels tend to have a limited vision angle in relation to Mini CRT screens and plasma screens.
The organic layers of OLEDs are much more luminescent, malleable and thin than crystalline layers of a TFT-LCD, which results in saving space as well as energy consumption.
When emitting their own light, an OLED screen is much more visible under standard daytime lighting conditions than a LCD, in addition to offering a higher chromatic and contrast range.
"AMOLED screens are very thin and light with an enormous flexibility, with the possibility of "enrolling", even when being active, which is an interesting point of view when creating a display with self-distorted images" (Dawson, 1998).</td></tr>
<tr><td>Mini-CRT (Cathode Ray Tube)</td><td>It is a device that projects a beam of electrons over a phosphorus covered screen (this material lights up when impacted by electrons beams). The mini colored CRTs are made out of three (3) phosphorus layers: red, green and blue.</td></tr>
<tr><td>LED (Light Emitted Diode) array</td><td>It is a semi-conductive device that emits a reduced light spectrum when polarized in a direct way and electric current flows through it.</td></tr>
<tr><td>LCD (Liquid Cristal Display)</td><td>It is a screen made up of a number of color or mono chrome pixels placed in front of a light source. It is based on a layer of aligned molecules between two (2) transparent electrodes and two (2) polarization filters.</td></tr>
<tr><td>TFT-LCD (Thin-Film Transistors)</td><td>It is the result of a liquid crystal screen (LCD) with a better image quality than the later due to the use of thin-film transistors (TFT).</td></tr>
<tr><td>OLED (Organic Light Emitting Diode)</td><td>It is a diode that uses an organic component film that reacts to a specific electric stimulation, generating and emitting light by themselves (Dawson & Kane, 2001).</td></tr>
<tr><td>AMOLED (Active Matrix OLED)</td><td>It is a group of OLED pixels that are made up of an assembly of Thin-Film Transistors (TFT) in order to form a pixel matrix (Dawson & Kane, 2001).</td></tr>
</table>

Table 1. Types of opto-electronical devices.

It is important to mention that an inefficient system in terms of illumination could have a direct repercussion in a large quantity of consumed energy by the emissive display, and consequently, in the use of refrigeration systems due to the generation of heat, making the HUD systems more complex and expensive (Pinkus & Task, 1989).

3.2 Optical system

Next, on Table 2 a description of the potential general stages of an HUD optical system is made, with the purpose of examining and inquiring about the importance of some optical considerations to take into account in this type of augmented reality systems.

General stages of the optical system	Description
Determination of the position and the occupied space by the optical system.	It is necessary to determine the location of the HUD inside the vehicle, since 95% of the subsequent configurations depend on this initial parameter.
Positioning of the emissive display	The position of the emissive display in relation to the suggested optical system is critical in terms of the augmentation of the generated image, if it is real, virtual, straight or inverted.
Collimation of the image coming from the emissive display	The light generated by the emissive display that can be assumed as omni-directional in 180°, must become collimated light in order to be manipulated easier in further stages.
Introduction of aberrations to the projected images	- No matter the nature of the projected image, if it is collimated from mirrors, chromatic aberrations are not generated. - Some effects such as double refraction can be treated with the use of anti-refractive coatings. - A way to solve the astigmatism in this kind of systems is through Fresnel lenses (which are an excellent option in these systems due to their low volume) that can be configured to cancel the astigmatic aberration introduced by the windshield. - The projected images over an aspherical geometry like in a windshield, mainly are affected by distortion and astigmatism effects, so the option of introducing pre-distortion effects in projected images, is suggested through lenses, mirrors and systems of digital imaging pre-processing. - The use of cylindrical lenses is proposed in order to cancel the astigmatic effect introduced by the surface of the windshield; it must be clarified that the use of cylindrical lenses is appropriate depending on the windshield area that wants to be used to generate the virtual image visualized by the observer; such area has to be approximately spherical.
Compensation of the projected image	The aberrations introduced in the image through an optical system are compensated through the windshield, reason why a legible image would be appreciated.
Generation of the final image	The image generated by the HUD system must have some specified visual requirements that guarantee their own integrity and acceptance from the user, considering that independently from the quality of the image showed to the observer, we are looking to obtain a virtual, augmented, straight and collimated image.

Table 2. General optical stages in HUD systems.

3.2.1 Image forming optical system

The type of HUD system here described is an Optical see-through augmented reality, where the objects of an external environment are combined with additional information previously configured (avatars: overlapped objects on the scene), the result is visualized through a translucent screen or combiner; next, on Table 3, different types of configurations imposed to these HUD systems are analyzed in order to highlight the main elements that shapes these types of systems.

<table>
<tr><th colspan="2">Configuration 1</th></tr>
<tr><td>Elements</td><td rowspan="4">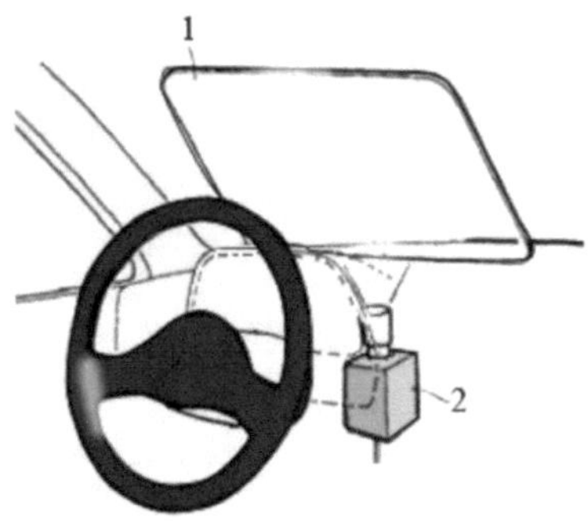

Fig. 3. Configuration 1 (Furukawa, 1991).</td></tr>
<tr><td>1. Flat combiner external to the windshield.
2. Emissive display.</td></tr>
<tr><td>Observations</td></tr>
<tr><td>In this type of configuration, astigmatism aberrations are not present, nor distortion, but a geometrical deformity is present, consequently, the projected image is visualized with a trapezoidal profile according to the incidence angle of the projected image over the combiner.</td></tr>
<tr><th colspan="2">Configuration 2</th></tr>
<tr><td>Elements</td><td rowspan="4">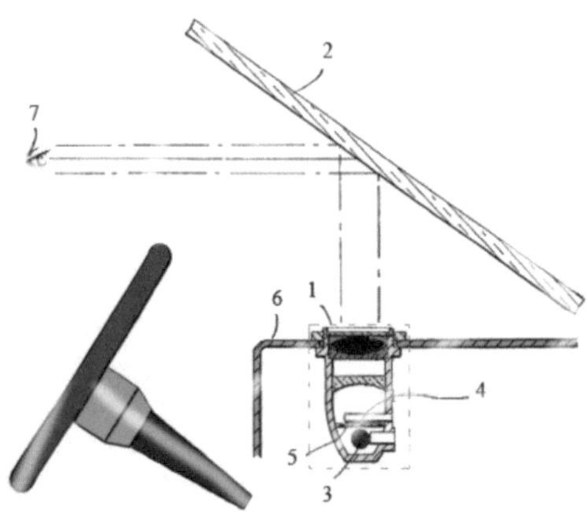

Fig. 4. Configuration 2 (Griffiths & Friedemann, 1975).</td></tr>
<tr><td>1. Optical system.
2. Windshield.
3. Incandescent lamp.
4. Diffusing screen.
5. Projected image.
6. Exit platform.
7. Observer.</td></tr>
<tr><td>Observations</td></tr>
<tr><td>It could be considered that certain region in the windshield might possess approximately spherical geometry (its central region), where the α angle formed between the chief ray of the projected image and the optical axis of the spherical region is considered, then, this angle defines the degree of astigmatism in the image presented to the observer.
Under this previous spherical consideration, we could think of cylindrical lenses to eliminate the astigmatic effect presented in the image projected to the user.</td></tr>
</table>

Configuration 3

Elements

1. Emissive display.
2. Combiner.
3. Mirror.
4. Back surface of the combiner.
5. Reflective coating (aspheric surface).
6. Frontal surface of the combiner.
7. Body of the combiner.
8. Observer.

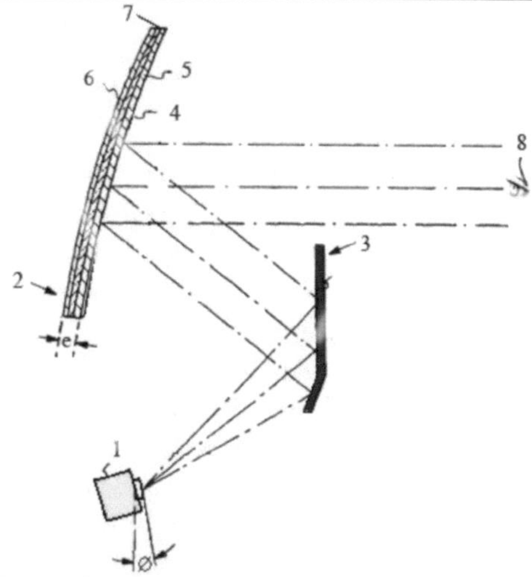

Fig. 5. Configuration 3 (Frithiof, 1972).

Observations

The surface of mirror (3) is covered with an aluminum semi-reflective coating (25%).
The surface (4) is a hyperboloid, and it is covered with an anti-reflective magnesium fluoride coating (5), its objective is to reflect a percentage of light that was reflected by the surface of mirror (3), and to additionally establish that a percentage from light of the outside is not transmitted towards the observer, thus, the outer light and the projected image by the combiner compete at an equal level.
The thickness of the combiner is defined as *e*, but sometimes that parameter cannot be assumed as a constant, since surfaces (4) and (6) that define the combiner are considered as none parallel, making the windshield behaves as a wedge.
The surfaces used to collimate the light from the emissive display are (3), (4) and (6), these surfaces are proposed to satisfy the requirement that an image is formed from combiner (2) with the same sagittal and southern magnification.
The angle ø is determined to correct the parallax errors on the image presented to the observer.

Configuration 4

Elements

1. Combiner.
2. Optical system.
3. User.
4. Distance of the virtual image.
5. Distance between the virtual image (showed by the combiner) and the observer.
6. Emissive display.
7. Distance between the combiner and the optical system.
8. Distance between the combiner and the observer.

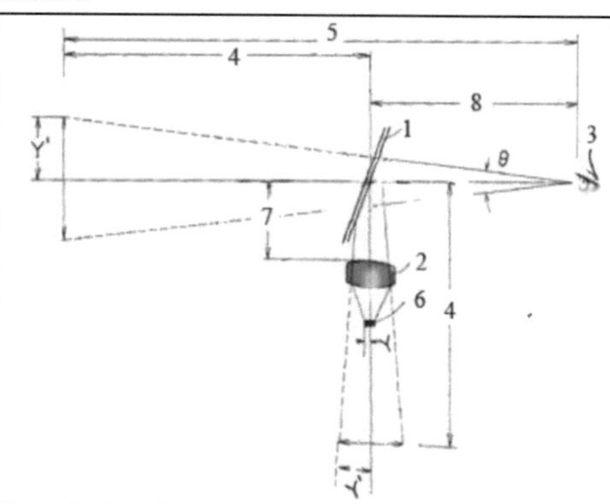

Fig. 6. Configuration 4 (Suzuki et al., 1988).

<table>
<tr><th colspan="2">Observations</th></tr>
<tr><td colspan="2">
It assumes that it wants to generate a virtual image Y´ over a flat combiner, which characteristics include being augmented, straight, collimated and without double refraction (or an acceptable parallax), so an optical system is configured (represented due to reasons of ease through a single lens).
There is also an attempt to reduce the parallax of the visualized image making sure the light beams of the projected image are as parallel as possible among them. We are looking to find, based on certain considerations of the geometrical optics, a way to get closer to the designing requirements: distance of the virtual image=infinite, L1/L2=0, and the minimum angle β, as it is observed on figures 6 and 7.
The binocular parallax is the horizontal and vertical dephase that the reflected image by the first interface of the windshield (air-glass) has in relation to the reflection of its second interface (glass-air); it can be corrected with a prism which works as a wedge, redirecting the light. As found on literature (Betancur, 2010), horizontal parallax is not corrected since it produces stereoscopic images that are tolerable by the user.
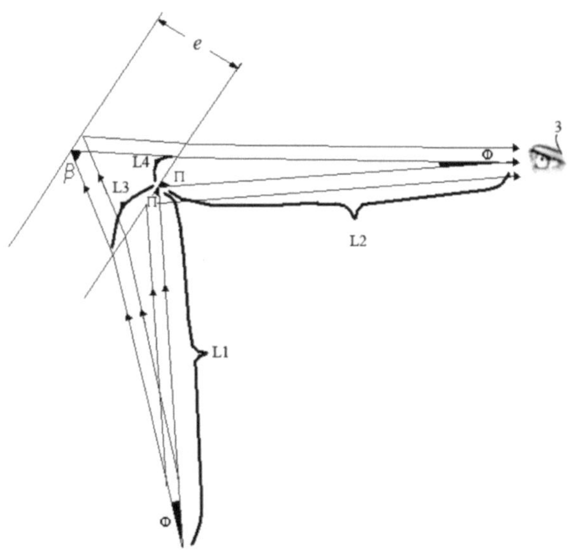

Fig. 7. Detail Figure 6 (Suzuki et al., 1988).
</td></tr>
<tr><th colspan="2">Configuration 5</th></tr>
<tr><th>Elements</th><td rowspan="2">
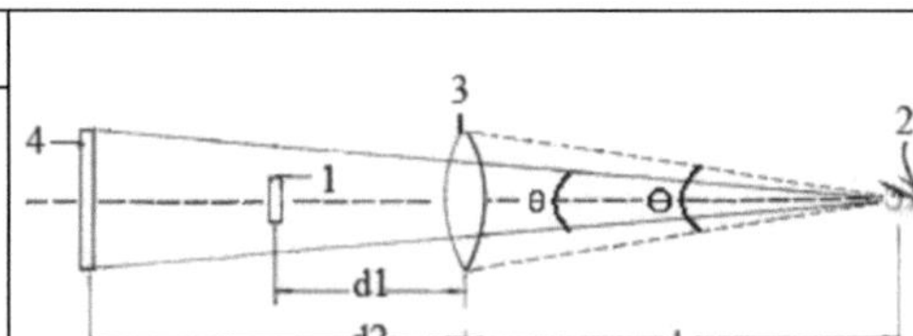

Fig. 8. Configuration 5 (Brown et al., 1988).
</td></tr>
<tr><td>1. Emissive display.
2. Observer.
3. Optical system.
4. Virtual image.
θ. Total Field Of View (TFOV).
Θ. Instant Field Of View (IFOV).</td></tr>
</table>

Observations

The position of emissive display (1) in relation to optical system (3) (a convergent lens for this type of configuration) defines the augmentation of the virtual image (augmentation = focal distance of the optical system / d1) that is visualized by the observer and the distance that it is going to be visualized from the optical system (d2).

The length of the lenses largely determines the exit-pupil of the optical system, for this application a squared formatted lens is used, to be able to generate a squared formatted exit-pupil that will adapt better to the head movements of the driver in the automobile.

Next, on Figure 9, the IFOV effect can be appreciated, since due to from its extension the eye-box also increases (defined as the volumetric space where the user can place his/her head and see the whole extension of the virtual image); it is noticeable on Figure 9 that with the IFOV's angle, the user may move and will continue seeing the whole virtual image generated, it also must be noted that the user will generally move his/her head in X and Y dimensions, reason why the eye-box must be rectangular, thus, rectangular lenses must be used. As a requirement, it is set out that the IFOV must be at least 1.5 times bigger than the TFOV.

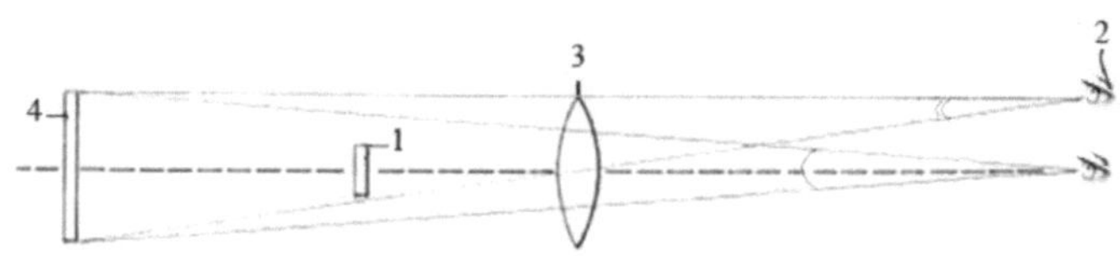

Fig. 9. Visual representation of the eye-box applied to configuration 5 (Brown et al., 1988).

The optical trajectory of this kind of HUD system might be fold through the use of mirrors as shown on Figure 10, which implies a reduction in the space needed to contain the elements of the optical system.

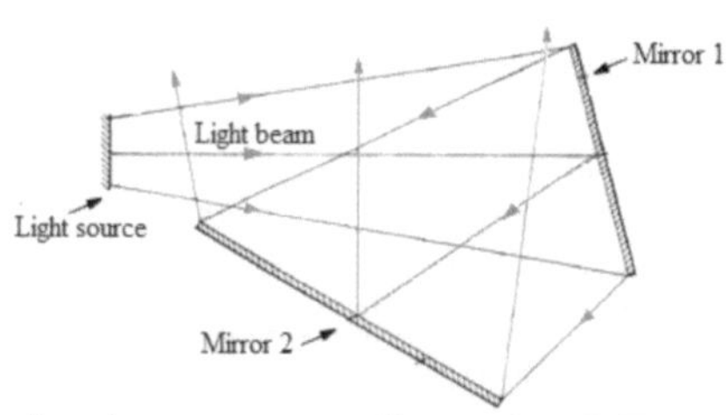

Fig. 10. Folding of the optical trajectory on configuration 5 (Brown et al., 1988).

Table 3. Types of configurations of an HUD.

3.3 User

In these devices, binocular vision is involved; this vision handles a horizontal FOV of 120° and vertical of 130° (being 60° upwards and 70° downwards).

The first requirement for good binocular vision is that the eyes converge to a single spot of the visual range, by using binocular vision inappropriately to see the outside scene and the generated image by the HUD device, may cause stress and vision difficulties such as diplophia (when the user sees two separate images at the same time).

On the other hand, with binocular vision if the luminance level is the same for both eyes, the scene that is being observed will be perceived brighter than what it really is, otherwise, if one of the eyes is subjected to more illumination than the other one, the visualized image might look less bright than what it is, thus, the importance of keeping constant illumination on the image that the HUD generates.

Additionally, the spectral sensibility of the eye must be considered in order to generate the maximum luminescence possible in HUD devices, that is, when the luminescence levels are higher than $3.18*10^{0.5}$ Cd/m^2 we talk about Photopic vision; on the other hand, for luminance levels under $3.18*10^{-3.5}$ Cd/m^2 we talk about Scotopic vision; when the eye is being used in one of these two regions its spectral sensibility changes, being higher for the Photopic region in 505nm and for the Scotopic region in 555nm, between the region that covers the spectrums of green and yellow respectively, that is why these colors tend to be used in HUD devices. If the wavelength emitted by the emissive display cannot be changed, it might be used a wavelength that is common on both levels of luminescence (525nm approximately).

Otherwise, retinal illumination is mentioned as the quantity of light that goes through the eye in relation to the scene's luminescence, this concept describes the Stiles and Crawford effect that talks about the visual sensation of the user, which is different for equal quantities of light in different places of the retina, being the rays that go through the center of the pupil (and which impact on the retina) more effective by a factor of 8 (Betancur, 2010).

In relation to visual sharpness (negatively affected by Scotopic vision and the little graphic details that the projected information by the emissive display has), we notice for the projected image that a user with low visual sharpness would not be able to differentiate the fine details that it possesses, therefore, this parameter should be considered when defining the type of image that the HUD device will generate.

Next, on Table 4 is detailed some of the most important visual requirements to be taken into account when an image is being presented in these HUD systems (Betancur, 2011; Díaz, 2005).

Requirements	Value	Description
Chromatic aberration	≈ 0	Considering that the projected image is polychromatic, the use of mirrors is necessary to avoid the chromatic aberration, or apochromatic doublets for the correction of such aberration (Velger, 1997).
Astigmatism aberration	≤ 0.25 Dpt	It is present by the toroidal geometry of the windshield and it is compensated commonly with cylindrical lenses. This aberration tends to null itself when the angle α (which defines the degree of astigmatism in the presented image to the observer) formed between the chief ray of the projected image and the optical axis of the projection region of the windshield (considered as spherical) tends to zero (Freeman, 1998).
Distortion aberration	≤ 1.5 %	This is especially noticeable when observing the image on the eye-box limit, where the visualized image is generated by the optical system's periphery, here the formation of the image is not as good as the center of itself.

Requirements	Value	Description
Vertical binocular parallax	≈ 0	Depending on the location of the display source in relation to the user, the horizontal binocular parallax produces stereoscopic images that can be acceptable, but the vertical binocular parallax produces fatigue on the user's sight, due to it is intended to be minimized by the use of prisms specially configured (Frithiof, 1972).
Double refraction	≈ 0	It must be minimized, looking to diminish the angle of incidence between the emissive display (with collimated light) and the combiner, and additionally using an anti-reflective coating over the inner surface of the combiner; on the other hand, this effect may be eliminated by including a wedge effect into the combiner, eliminating the parallelism between it inner and outer surface.
Accommodation	≤ ±0.25 Dpt	Depends on the visual capacity of the user (Hecht & Zajac, 2005).
Deformity	≈ 0	Related to the trapezoidal deformity effects on the image seen by the user.
Daylight luminescence	≤ 9000 ft-L	In relation to the literature (Velger, 1997; Brown et al., 1988), if we consider a system with a combiner reflectance of 30%, an optical system transmittance of 85%, and a contrast appropriate (1.3:1) for the view on a sunny day (10.000 ft-L), the image luminescence value (viewed by the user) may be calculated.
Night luminescence	≥ 3639 ft-L	Considering the night luminescence of 4000 ft-L, together with the optical and contrast parameters indicated in daylight luminescence, a value of night luminescence in the image viewed by the user may be proposed.

Table 4. Primordial visual requirements.

Also, here below, an analysis on perceptual factors must be done to those HUDs applied to automobiles:

3.3.1 Increase of visual time on the road

Most of the time that the driver spends on driving, his attention is directed to the road, however, there are short periods of time where the driver looks at the command board of the vehicle, which although very small, might mean the loss of a critical event; the use of an HUD while driving allows the reduction of observation time for the variables in the vehicle's panel from 0.25 to 1 second, that time can be crucial on a dangerous situation.

3.3.2 Reduction of re-accommodation time

The virtual image generated that is visualized by the user is typically located at a higher distance from the observer than the command dashboard and within the visual range of the user (looking towards the road), then, less accommodation is required when the driver switches to focus the virtual image of the HUD to the outside environment.

3.3.3 Distance of the virtual image

The distance of the virtual image must be between 2.5 and 4 meters from the eyes of the driver, in order to increase the time of recognition and accommodation.

3.3.4 Accommodation effect

When superimposed objects are located within the observer FOV, the object that has a shorter distance from the observer's focus, tends to dominate the accommodation answer, this situation is shown in HUD systems when using an external combiner instead of the windshield.

3.3.5 Intolerance to visual disorder

The results of case studies of drivers whose vehicles had an HUD system, showed that sometimes these system could be uncomfortable due to the quantity of information that is displayed toward the driver; although, this is currently discussed, because the analysis of this uncomfortable situation is highly related to the type of information being displayed, its organization and relevance to the driver.

3.3.6 Illumination interference

The overlapping of the symbology generated by the HUD over the driver's external scene, will tend to hide the outside objects via illumination interference, which results if the luminance of the symbology of the HUD is higher than the luminance of the outer objects of the vehicle, this can be a big problem according to the quantity of information shown by the HUD.

3.3.7 Cognitive capture

Under high working conditions there is a high level of temporary uncertainty for the unexpected appearance of outer objects, consequently, it is likely that a cognitive capture occurs by the HUD operation, that is, an attention deficiency to the surroundings due to the exposed symbology by the HUD, generating delays in the answers to outside events, which can result in the loss of external objectives.

3.3.8 Symbology of the display

The figures of the conformation symbology move with the elements of the outside world, this kind of symbology increases the acceptance of HUD systems among drivers.

3.3.9 Location

It is not appealing that the HUD simbology is located in the middle of the driver's visual range; many research documents suggest that the drivers prefer to locate this symbology below the line of the horizon, in a more peripheral position.

4. Implementations

Based on what was previously mentioned and as a starting point for this chapter proposal, an augmented reality system was set out based on phases, components and flows, as indicated on Figure 11.

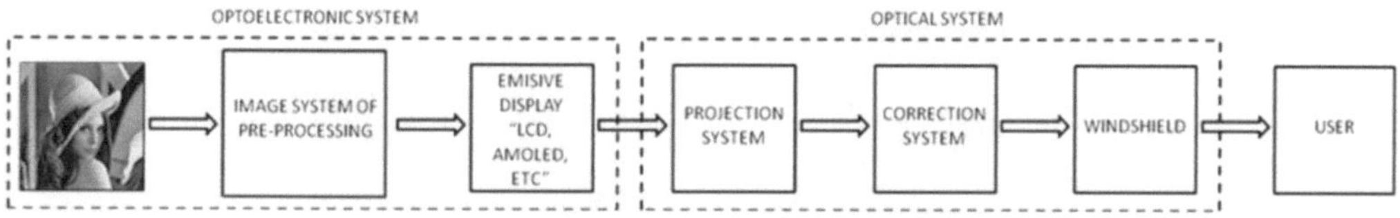

Fig. 11. Proposed augmented reality system.

As it can be appreciated, Figure 11 is a detailed view of Figure 2 previously described, being this last one the starting point for the design of any HUD. From the opto-electronical stage on Figure 11, the digital pre-processing stage of the projected image stands out, which is not very common in this type of augmented reality system, and its effect and reach is better appreciated next on Figure 12.

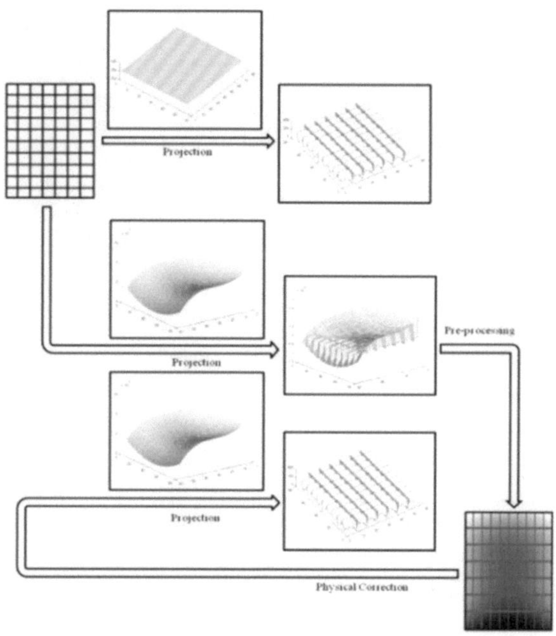

Fig. 12. Corrective pre-processing of images in the HUD system proposed (Betancur, 2011).

Now, based on the previously established considerations and in order to test other additional ones, the instrumental set up described on Figure 13 was developed.

From the instrumental set up described on Figure 13, these components are specially highlighted:

1. Windshield holder: this allows the rotation of the windshield in two of its axes.
2. Windshield: corresponding to the RENAULT LOGAN 2009 model reference G000463620_V02_01.
3. Projection system: as a result of the evaluation of the previously indicated alternatives on Table 3, an optical system proposal was established; whose designing requirements are detailed next on Table 5 and it is also represented schematically in figures 14 and 15.
4. User's position.

Fig. 13. Instrumental set up proposed.

Requirement	Description
Quantity of lenses in the optical system	It is proposed as a starting point, an optical system configured by two converging lenses.
Object distance of the system's first lens (S_{o1})	The main goal is that the object distance of the system's first lens to be as lower as possible (a maximum of 15 cm), so that this lens will collect as much light as possible and can consequently generate a brighter final image (S_{i2}).
Image distance of the system's first lens (S_{i1})	It is intended that this image distance be generated near the focal distance of the system's second lens.
Object distance of the system's second lens (S_{o2})	The definition for this system is: the distance (D) that separates the two lenses of the system minus the image distance of the first lens (S_{i1}).
Image distance of the system's second lens (S_{i2})	It is intended that this parameter, that is the distance from which the driver will see the final image due to its reflection in the combiner, will be minimally of 1.8 meters.
Longitudinal augmentation (M)	It is intended that the image is augmented by a maximum factor of 9, since, if the image's original dimensions are augmented, its resolution will be drastically decreased.

Requirement	Description
Distance between the system's lenses (D)	It is intended that the distance between the optical system's lenses is never higher than 40 cm.
Entrance pupil (En.P.)	The entrance pupil is where light enters to the optical system, in this configuration is located in the first lens.
Exit pupil (Ex.P.)	The exit pupil represents the produced image from the system's first lens (opening diaphragm) by the system's second lens, and additionally, according to its size, it limits the cone of rays of the virtual image that the user can observe.
Diaphragm of aperture (D.A.)	It is the element that limits the entrance of light from the object to the optical system, in this configuration is represented by the first lens of such system.
User distance (U.D.)	It is proposed in relation to previous conducted researches (Wood et al., 1990; Velger, 1997) that there is a distance of 0.8 meters from the user of the system's second lens.
The exit's pupil diameter (D1)	To know the size of the exit pupil, the distance between both lenses of the optical system (D) must be known, which (for the exit's pupil diameter calculation) will be recognized as the object distance of the second lens (S_{o2}), and it is also necessary to know the focal distance of the second lens (f_2); this way, by applying Gauss' equation for thin lenses we will be able to know the image's distance of the second lens (S_{i2}), then, through the longitudinal augmentation relation ($M=-S_{i2}/S_{o2}$) the augmentation can be known; finally, since the object and image distances are proportional to their heights, and knowing the opening diaphragm's diameter, it is possible to know the exit pupil's diameter (D1).
Image size generated by the optical system. (D2)	To know the size of the virtual image generated by the configuration of this particular optical system, it is necessary to multiply the generated augmentations for each of the lenses $M_t=M_1*M_2$ ($M_1=-S_{i1}/S_{o1}$, $M_2=-S_{i2}/S_{o2}$).
User distance from the exit pupil (U.D.1)	For the configuration of the optical system indicated a distance of 0.5 meter must be established.
User distance from the generated image (U.D.2)	According to previous research (Griffiths & Friedemann, 1975; Suzuki et al., 1988) and to preserve a good response from the user, it is established that this distance must not be lower than 2.5 meters.
Vertical visual range from the generated image (FOV-θ)	In relation to the optical system that was proposed, the FOV-θ is defined as the vision angle necessary that the user must have to visualize the vertical extension of the virtual image generated.
Vertical visual range generated by the exit pupil (FOV-α)	In relation to the optical system that is proposed here, the FOV-α is defined as the vision angle that the exit pupil allows the user to have of the vertical extension of the virtual image generated. In relation to Figure 15, it can be noticed that the higher the FOV-α is to the FOV-θ, then, the bigger will the system's eye-box be.

Table 5. Designing requirements of the optical system proposed.

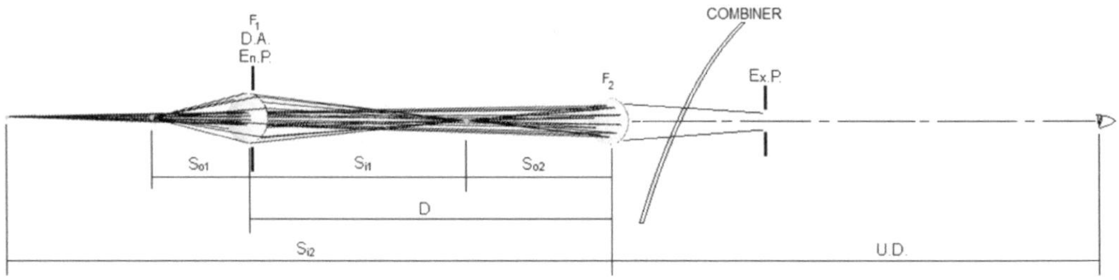

Fig. 14. Optical system proposal.

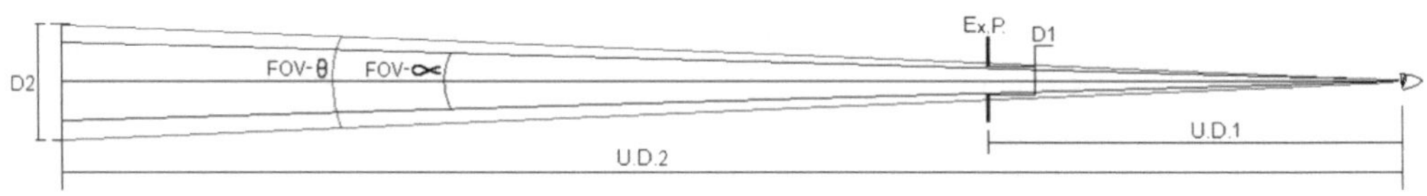

Fig. 15. FOV-θ in comparison to FOV-α.

The values used for the set up of the proposed optical system (figures 15 and 16), are indicated here below on Table 6.

Parameter	Value
S_{o1}	249 mm
f_1	135 mm
D	400 mm
f_2	110 mm
S_{i2}	2375.4 mm
M_t	8,7
Ex.P.	151 mm
D1	41,525 mm
D2	261 mm
U.D.	551 mm
U.D.1	551 mm
U.D.2	2926,4 mm
FOV-θ	2,35°
FOV-α	2,96°

Table 6. Values for the optical system proposed.

Next, on Figure 16, it can be seen the proposed optical system described on figures 14 and 15; Fresnel lenses were used due to their low bulkiness, with a squared format in order to accomplish a squared exit pupil that is more appropriate in relation to the user's movements.

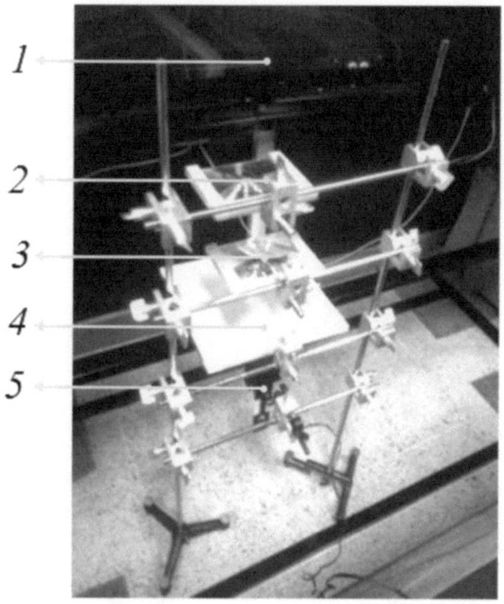

Fig. 16. Development of the optical system proposed.

1. Windshield.
2. Lens 1.
3. Lens 2.
4. Diffusing screen: that creates an image of the emissive display.
5. Emissive display: for this analysis a Pico-projector from MICROSYSTEMS ® was used, where the image of the projection is transferred from a computer that pre-processes the image according to the specific design parameters previously indicated.

Next, in order to show what the user would perceive from his/her driving position and under the implementations that were proposed previously; here below on Figure 17 a) and b) the proposed visualization of the HUD and the real visualization of the HUD are shown respectively.

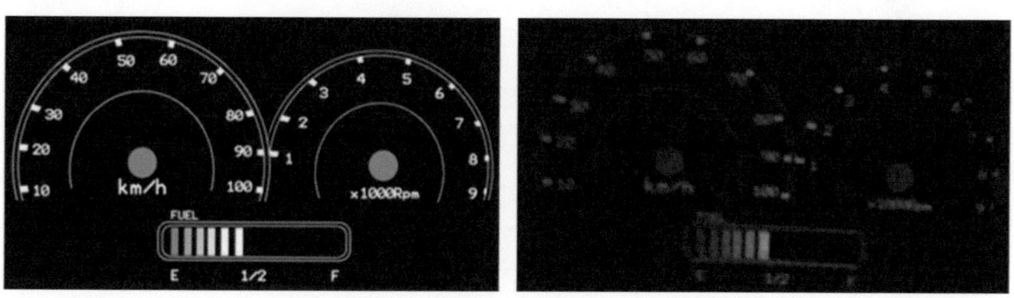

a) b)

Fig. 17. (a) Proposed image; (b) Visualization of the proposed image under previously described implementations (Betancur, 2011).

5. Applications

Next on Figure 18, a possible automotive configuration for this type of augmented reality systems is proposed.

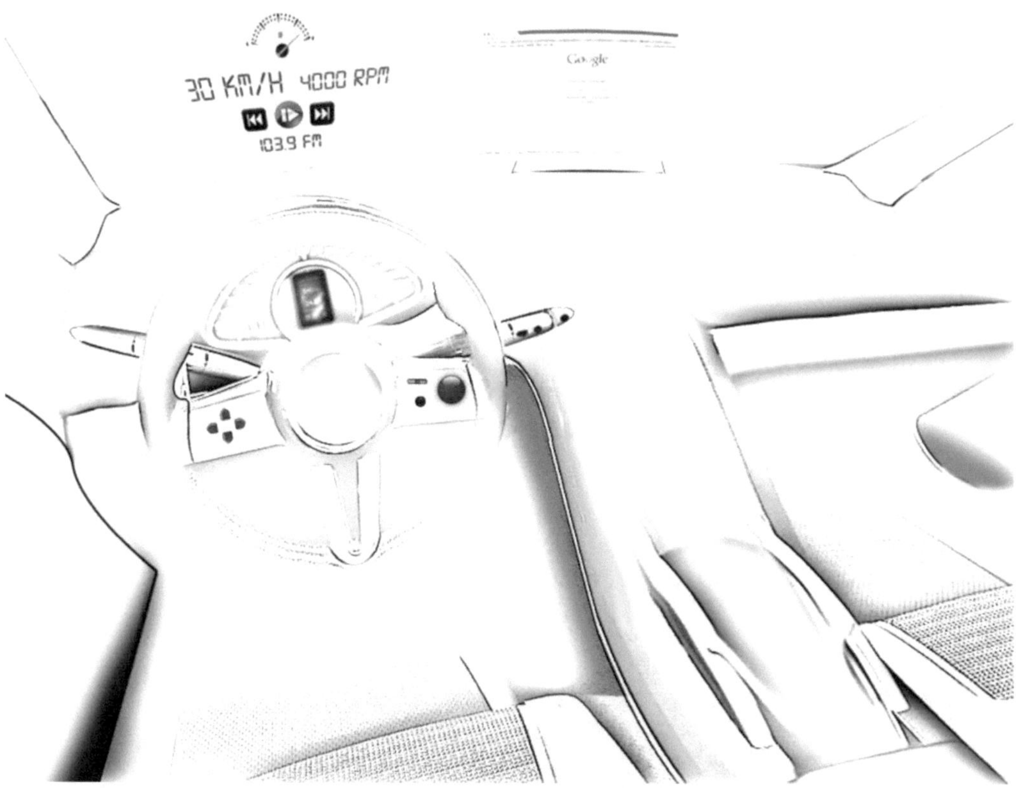

Fig. 18. General set up for the proposed HUD system.

Then, on Figure 19 we specify some of the main options that an augmented reality system should have under the configuration from Figure 18.

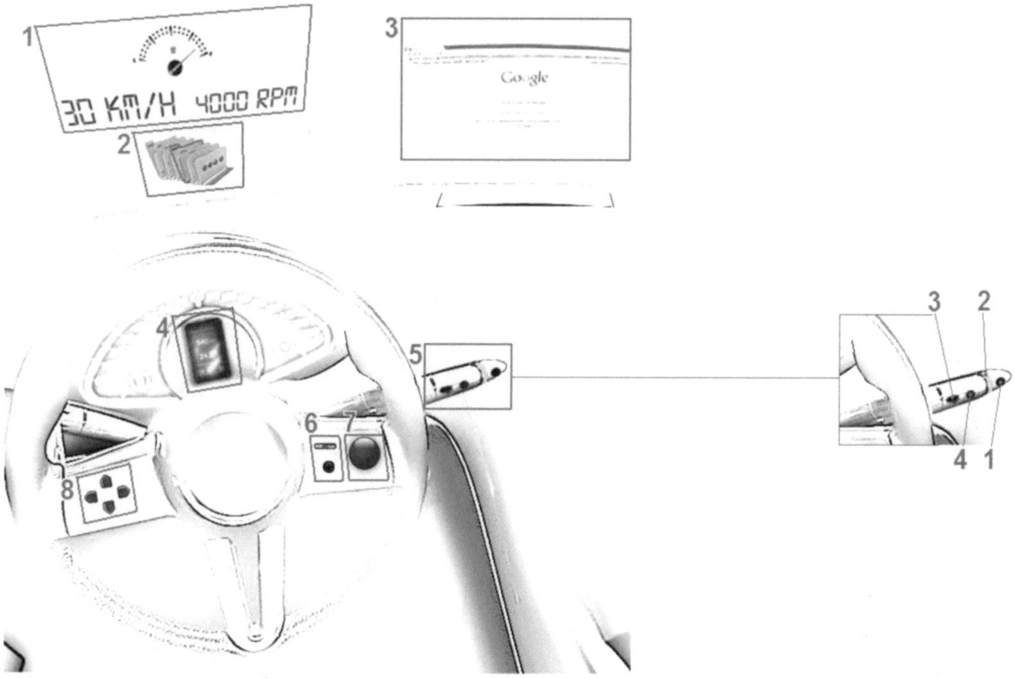

a) b)

Fig. 19. (a) Specific configuration for the HUD system proposed; (b) Detail of the operation mode from the HUD system proposed.

From Figure 19.a) the following items stand out:

1. HUD 1.
2. HUD 2.
3. HUD 3.
4. HDD 1.
5. Controls for HUD 1.
6. Controls for HUD 2.
7. Controls for HUD 3 (spherical scroll button -Mouse-).
8. Command buttons for the HDD 1.

From Figure 19.b) the following items stand out:

1. On/Off HUD 1.
2. Illumination of the presented image.
3. Proximity of the presented image.
4. Handling of the information from HUD 1 (Enter button).

Now, as a complement for Figure 19, it is proposed through Figure 20 to determine what other options should be taken into account specifically for this type of augmented reality system and under the interaction of a companion.

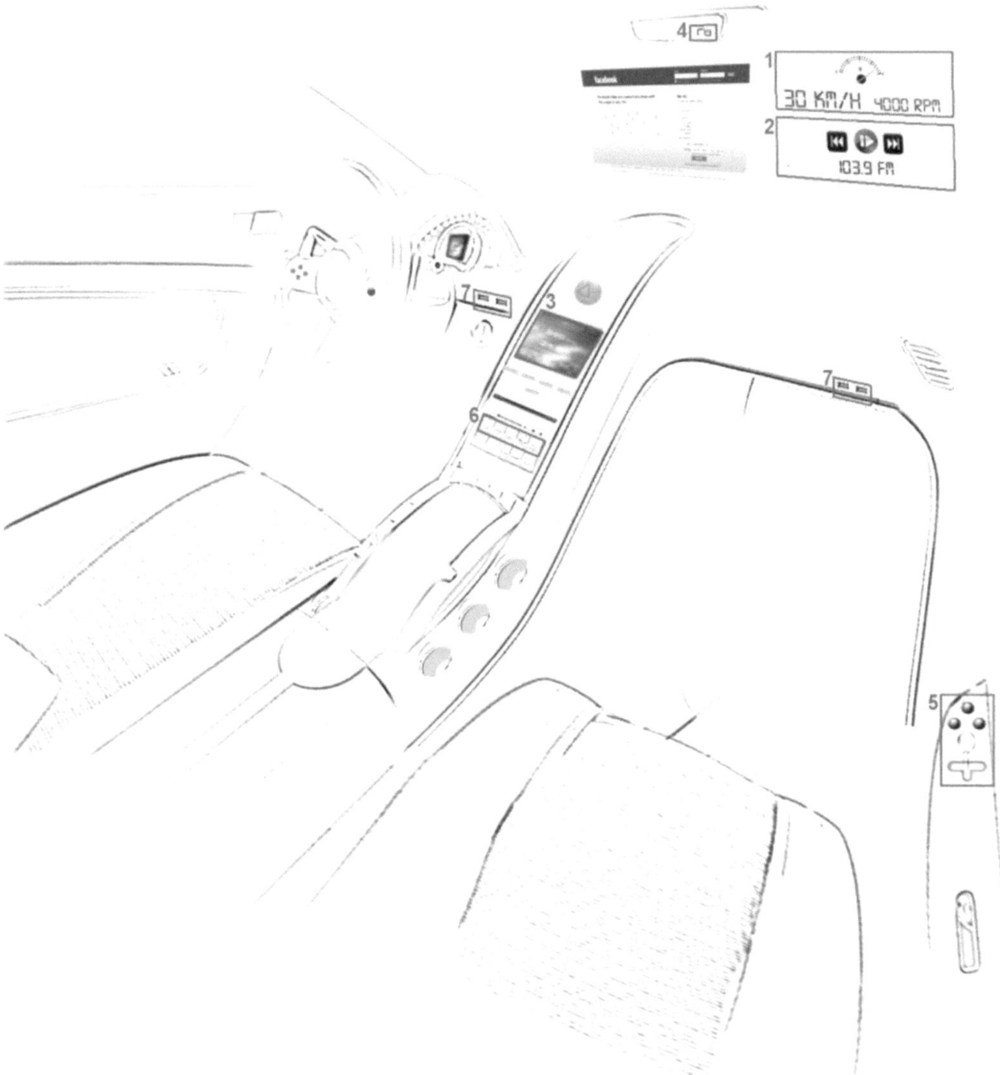

Fig. 20. Specific set up for the HUD system proposed.

From Figure 20 the following items stand out:

1. HUD 4 is the same HUD 1.
2. HUD 5 is the same HUD 2.
3. HUD 3 on the command panel is the HDD 2 (handled by touch screen).
4. Reticules projected onto the central driving mirror.
5. Control for the HUD 4 and HUD 5.
6. On/Off buttons for all the HUDs.
7. USB ports to connect a keyboard or any other device that helps the co-driver to manipulate the HUD 3 (this is not recommendable for the driver due to the big risk that could represent).

The projection configurations of the HUD 1 and 2 are indicated here below on Figure 21.

a)

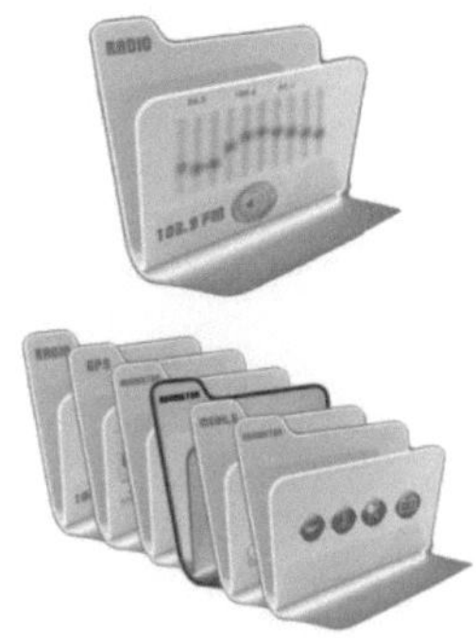

b)

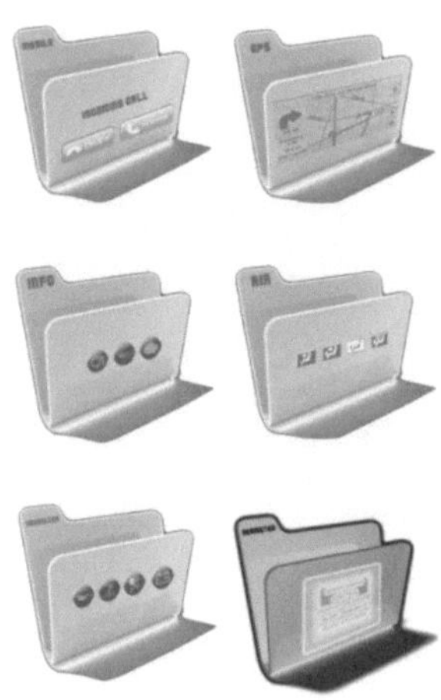

c)

Fig. 21. (a) Configuration of the projections of the HUD 1; (b) Configuration of the projections of the HUD 2; (c) Kind of projections in the HUD 2.

The considerations taken into account from figures 18 to 21 are imposed on Figure 22, which is considered as a good approximation to the functional design of the augmented reality system proposed in this chapter.

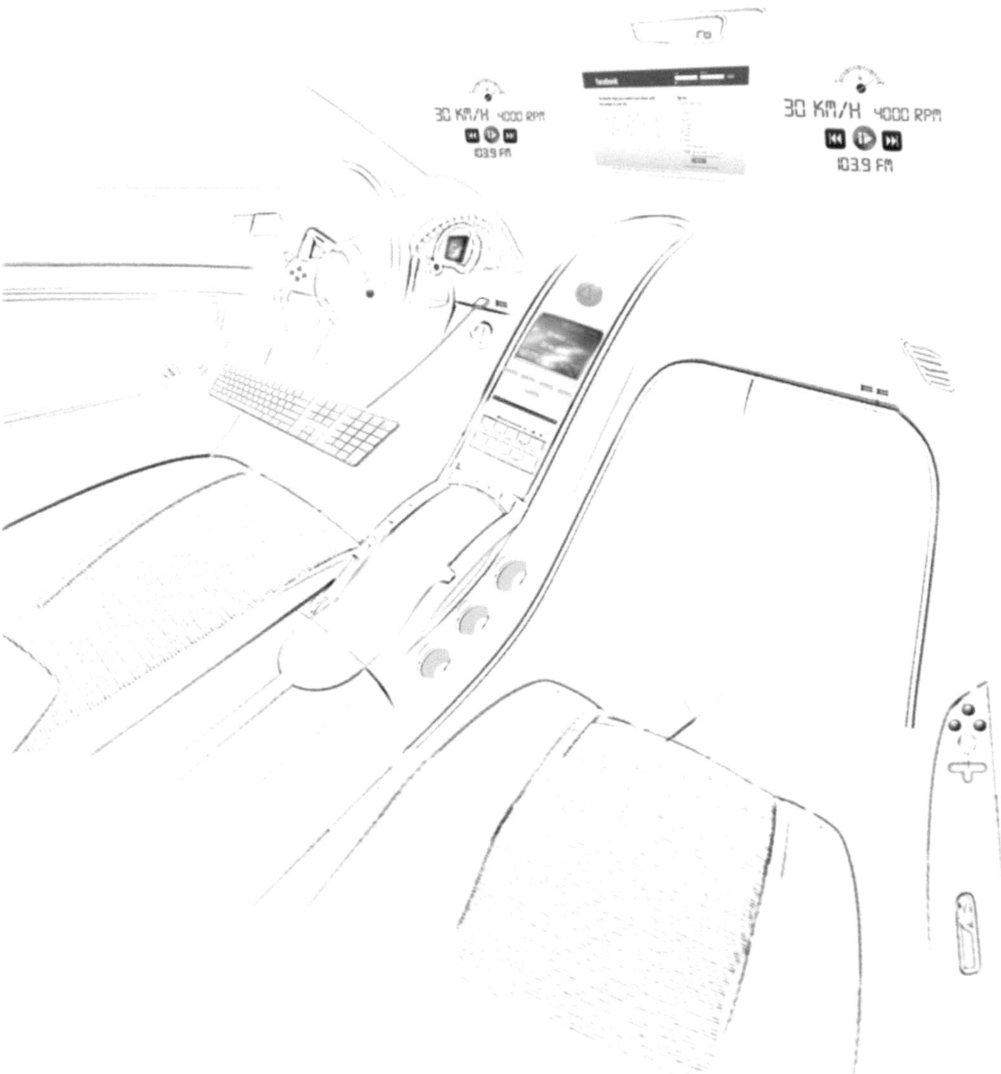

Fig. 22. Configuration of HUDs and HDDs in the augmented reality system proposed.

6. Conclusions

1. On the Figure 17 it is barely noticeable the aberrant component over the final image presented to the observer, in the same way, even if the virtual image presented is not perfectly coherent to the one initially proposed, it is adequately and without any major problem recognizable by the user; then, this image has not overcome the limits established as appropriate for the presentation of the information in HUD systems.

2. The optical qualities used to set up an HUD are diverse, being the needs required by the driver their main parameter of design; this way, the instrumental proposal here depicted, mainly focuses on presenting a virtual image to the user that is straight, augmented and

collimated, this group of qualities are the main requirements (demanded by the user) that these augmented reality systems must satisfy.

3. The approach of a two lens optical system is interesting when satisfying the established requirements between the longitudinal augmentation, the size and the exit pupil's position, the generated virtual image, the object location in relation to the optical system, among others; since, for a lens, to accomplish these requirements the same way the optical system proposed does, may be very complex and expensive; also, a three lens system for this type of application might be unnecessary, since, as it can be appreciated, a two lens system is enough to provide the basic requirements demanded.

4. The use of lenses with a squared format becomes necessary when trying to obtain a more appropriate eye-box in relation to the user's movements; in the same way, this format allows a presentation of images to the user, according to the square projection shapes from most of the emissive displays.

5. It is clear that the presence of optical aberrations (astigmatism, double refraction, chromatic, distortion, etc.) it is notorious in these kinds of systems, the way it corrects from analogical elements and through the stages of digital pre-processing are not yet completely generalized, so in consequence, being able to present a tolerable image in terms of such aberrations implies much more analysis and research.

7. References

Amezquita, Ricado. (2010). Aberration Compensation Using a Spatial Light Modulator LCD, In: *VII Reunión Iberoamericana de Óptica y X Encuentro Latinoamericano de Óptica, Láseres y Aplicaciones*

Betancur, J. A. (2010). HUD analysis using MAPLE, In: *Head- and Helmet-Mounted Displays XV: Design and Applications*, edited by Peter L. Marasco, Paul R. Havig, Proceedings of SPIE Vol. 7688 (SPIE, Bellingham, 76880J)

Betancur, J. A. & Osorio Gómez, G. (2011). General implications of HUD systems applied to automobile industries, In: *Display Technologies and Applications for Defense, Security, and Avionics V; and Enhanced and Synthetic Vision 2011*, edited by John Tudor Thomas, Daniel D. Desjardins, Proceedings of SPIE Vol. 8042 (SPIE, Bellingham, 80420E)

Brown, E.; Weaber, J.; Sargent, R.; Patterson, S. & Stephenson, M. (1988). Head-Up Display for an automobile, United States of America Patent, Number of patent: 4.740.780

Dawson, R. M. & Kane, M. G. (2001). Pursuit of active matrix organic light emitting diode displays, Dig. Tech. Papers, SID Int. Symp., pp.372 - 375

Díaz, L. (2005). Optical aberrations in Head-Up Displays, In: *Universidad Pontificia Comillas Madrid*

Freeman, E. (1998). Windshield for Head-Up Display system, United States of America Patent, Number of patent 5.812.332

Frithiof, J. (1972). Optical viewing system, United States of America Patent, Number of patent: 3.697.154

Furukawa, Y. (1991). Head-Up Display for a road vehicle, United States of America Patent, Number of patent: 5.051.735

Griffiths, D. & Friedemann, J. (1975). Speedometer optical projection system, United States of America Patent, Number of patent: 3.887.273

Hecht & Zajac (2005). *Optic*, Addison Wesley Publishing CO

Pinkus, A. & Task, H. (1989). Display system image quality, *Armstrong Aerospace Medical Research Laboratory. Human Engineering Division. Wright Air Force Base*, Ohio 45433-6573, United States of America

Suzuki, Y.; Ohtsuka, T.; Lino, T.; Kasahara, A. & Tomiyama, N. (1988). On vehicle Head-Up display with optical means for correcting parallax in a vertical direction, United States Patent, Number of patent: 4.787.711

Wood, R; Mark T.; & Desmond J. (1990). Automobile Head-Up Display system with reflective aspheric surface, United States of America Patent, Number of patent: 4.961.625

Velger, M. (1997). *Helmet-Mounted Displays and Sights*, Artech House, Boston-London